# DR. CHARLES M. MONELL
## CIVIL WAR
## HISTORY COLLECTION

Very Truly yours

W. S. N. Bryan

# A NARRATIVE

OF

# MILITARY SERVICE

BY

GENERAL W. B. HAZEN

BOSTON
TICKNOR AND COMPANY
1885

Reprinted by
BLUE ACORN PRESS
P.O. Box 2684
Huntington, W.Va. 25726


New material © 1993 Blue Acorn Press

ISBN 0-9628866-7-X

University Press:
John Wilson and Son, Cambridge.

TO

## THE SURVIVORS OF MY COMMAND,

AND TO

## THE MEMORY OF THE DEAD,

I Dedicate

THIS RECORD OF OUR SERVICE.

# INTRODUCTION.

*"I am always ready to cast stones at outrages."*

— William B. Hazen

Eighteen months after *A Narrative of Military Service* was published in 1885, its author died unexpectedly in bed — a victim of kidney poisoning and the results of a bullet fired into his body almost 30 years before. Many mourned his passing; others, however, were glad to see him gone.

William Babcock Hazen's death ended a brilliant, sometimes turbulent and often controversial military career that spanned four decades and marked him as a man greatly admired or deeply villified. Such variance of opinion among his military and political contemporaries began during the Civil War, which saw Hazen rise in rank from lieutenant and assistant instructor of infantry tactics at West Point in 1861 to major general and corps commander under General William T. Sherman in 1865. His actions in battle gained the respect and high regard of such leaders as Sherman, Don Carlos Buell, Emerson Opdycke and James A. Garfield (future U.S. President and boyhood chum with whom Hazen shared lifetime friendship). But other officers, notably David S. Stanley and Philip H. Sheridan, harbored animosity toward Hazen over wartime incidents at Shiloh and Missionary

Ridge, and this antipathy spilled over into their subsequent careers with profound overtones and bitter recriminations.

Nearly all of *A Narrative of Military Service* is devoted to the Civil War years. Hazen gives only brief treatment to his schooling at West Point from 1851 to 1855, and to the antebellum period of conspicuous conduct fighting Indians in the Pacific Northwest and Texas. Furthermore, he excludes all of his post-war career from the book (except for a brief resume taken from the 1884 Army Register), written at the height of controversy swirling around him. Today, these embroilments have faded into relative obscurity, as has his name itself. But from the late 1850s until his death on January 16, 1887, Hazen received widespread publicity in the press, and wrote on military subjects which received international attention. In November 1885, *The Nation* began its review of his book by stating: "Few officers of the army are more generally known than the author of this volume."[1]

William B. Hazen was born on September 27, 1830, at West Hartford, Vermont. Four years later he moved with his parents, Stillman and Ferona Fenno Hazen, to a farm outside the village of Hiram in Portage County, Ohio, where he attended school with James A. Garfield. Service in the army had been Hazen's goal throughout his childhood and teens, for in March 1851 he wrote to his congressman that "the desire to attend West Point has been the height of my ambition for years."[2] (One of his forebears, Moses Hazen, served with distinction as a junior officer in the French and Indian War, and later as colonel and brigadier general

---

[1] *The Nation,* November 5, 1885, Vol. XLI, 381.

[2] Hazen to Thomas Corwin, March 13, 1851, Records of the War Department, Adjutant General's Office, U.S. Military Academy File, National Archives, Washington, D.C., Record Group 94.

in Washington's army during the American Revolution).[3] His petition to enter the U.S. Military Academy (after another district nominee's disqualification) was made with urgency, for Hazen was six months shy of turning 21 — the cutoff age for admission. With one month of eligibility left, Hazen's nomination was recommended to the Secretary of War and his appointment confirmed on August 21, 1851.[4]

A serious student, Hazen's academic performance at West Point was nonetheless lackluster. In 1855 he graduated 28th in a class of 34, and immediately was assigned as a brevet second lieutenant to Company D, 4th U.S. Infantry, then operating in southwest Oregon. Escalating hostilities with local Indian tribes gave the novice officer his first taste of combat early in 1856 in what became known as the Rogue River wars. During this turbulent period, Hazen was selected to command a protective escort when several Indian bands were moved to Grande Ronde reservation near the northwest Oregon coast. The arduous mission was completed successfully, and Hazen laid out the site for a permanent post on the reserve which soon became known as Fort Yamhill. He remained there for the next 12 months, performing routine duty. With few diversions available at the isolated outpost, many soldiers availed themselves to liquor and frequent drunken brawls ensued, several ending in death. As a result, Hazen quickly developed a great aversion to alcohol and condemned its immoderate use for the rest of his life.[5]

In May 1857, Hazen left the Department of the Pacific with orders to join the 8th U.S. Infantry in Texas. His arrival there in February 1858 coincided with a vigorous effort to subjugate the

---

[3] *The National Cyclopaedia of American Biography*, (New York, 1893), Vol. I, 78.

[4] *The Register of Cadet Applicants, 1850-51*, Adjutant General's Office, Engineer Department, National Archives, RG 94.

[5] Glisan, Rodney, *Journal of Army Life*, (San Francisco, 1874), 376.

Indians of the southwestern plains. Brevet Major General David E. Twiggs, commanding some 1,500 troops in the Texas Military Department, ordered his men at several frontier posts to take the offensive after a sudden resurgence of Indian raiding. Hazen soon observed that in the Lone Star State, far more than in Oregon, public opinion overwhelmingly supported the view that "the only good Indian was a dead Indian," reservation inhabitants included.[6]

Over the next 21 months, Hazen led a grueling life on the sun-baked plains of southwest Texas, scouting and occasionally fighting Apache, Kickapoo and Comanche bands. One of his first forays was against a party of Mescalero Apaches that stole several dozen government mules near Fort Davis. He described some of the expedition's hardships in his after-action report:

> *Our route lay across a level sand prairie, which with a verticle*[sic] *sun soon became scorching hot, so much so as to heat the soles of the shoes to a painful degree. The metal of the guns became so heated that it could not be touched by the hand ... The little water that was in the canteens became too hot to be drunk. The slight breezes that would occasionally pass over the plains, were nothing less than siroccos, it was necessary to hold one's breath til they subsided. Several of the men drank their urine, which only increased their terrible thirst.*[7]

Two months later, Hazen was transferred from Fort Davis to Fort Inge, a small post located near Uvalde, Texas. In May 1859, he led another operation to the west fork of the Nueces River, where a small group of Kickapoo horse thieves was caught in a surprise attack. Killing or wounding all the Indians while his command of 10 soldiers, one scout and four citizen volunteers survived unscathed, Hazen was cited a second time in General Or-

---

[6] Kroeker, Marvin E., *Great Plains Command*, (Norman, Okla., 1976), 25.

[7] Hazen to Lieutenant William E. Dye (adjutant at Fort Davis, Texas), June 22, 1858, Adjutant General's Office, National Archives, RG 94.

ders from Headquarters of the Army "for gallant conduct."[8] He also was promoted to brevet first lieutenant.

By September of that year, the commander of Fort Inge considered Hazen his most successful Indian fighter. This growing reputation led to his selection the following month to pursue a small Comanche war party suspected of murdering two white settlers east of the fort. After four days of tracking, the Indians were discovered November 3, 1859, breaking camp near the headwaters of the Llano River. Hazen ordered a massed charge by his posse of 30 civilians and nine soldiers. Caught by surprise, the eight Comanches, armed with rifles, revolvers and bows, offered fierce resistance before all but one were killed or fatally wounded. During the five-minute, close-range battle, Hazen was shot through the hand, the bullet lodging in his right side between the sixth and seventh ribs. A week passed before he received medical attention at Fort Inge. Loss of blood and subsequent infection threatened his life for more than a month, but effective treatment by a specially assigned army surgeon saved his life. The bullet was never removed and Hazen carried it, sometimes in great pain, for the rest of his life. Twenty-eight years later, it ultimately contributed to his death.

A third citation in General Orders soon followed the incident, and Hazen was granted an extended leave in January 1860 to recover his health. After 12 months' convalescence he was appointed assistant instructor of infantry tactics at West Point, and assumed the position in February 1861 with promotion to first lieutenant in April. The assignment lasted until mid-summer, but the experience helped embue Hazen with a lasting and scholarly interest in military science. It also earned him the reputation of a strict disciplinarian. Cadet George A. Custer discovered that firsthand shortly before June graduation when Hazen, as officer of the

---

[8] General Orders Number 5, Headquarters of the Army, New York, November 10, 1859, Adjutant General's Office, National Archives, RG 94.

day, placed him under arrest in the aftermath of a fistfight. The
incident proved to be the genesis of ill feelings between them,
although years later Custer admitted that Hazen was a very meritorious officer who ''always rendered conspicuous services ever
since he has been in the service.''⁹

With the beginning of the Civil War, Hazen, further promoted
to captain on May 14, 1861, immediately sought active duty in
the field. Through the influence of James A. Garfield, an assignment was not long in coming. In September he was appointed
colonel of the newly-organized 41st Ohio Volunteer Infantry Regiment. Raised in and around Cleveland, the regiment's inexperi-
enced personnel quickly were transformed into a firmly disciplined body under Hazen's exacting instruction and drill. The in-
tensive training paid large dividends later in the war, and he always held the regiment in high regard.

As a brigade and division commander, Hazen led troops in
many important battles and campaigns fought in the western theater of operations: Shiloh, Stone River, Chickamauga, Missionary
Ridge, Resaca, Pickett's Mill, Jonesboro and Bentonville. In
1863, the earliest monument ever erected on a Civil War battlefield was placed to memorialize his brigade's conduct at Stone
River. A stone wall encloses the graves of 69 men of his command killed on December 31, 1862. The limestone monument
bears the epitaph, ''Their faces toward Heaven, their feet to the
foe.'' Two decades later, former opponent General Joseph E.
Johnston stated that, except for Hazen and his brigade, the Confederates would have emerged victorious at Stone River.¹⁰

His Fourth Corps brigade of Ohio, Kentucky and Indiana
troops performed brilliantly at Brown's Ferry in October 1863.
Their daring nighttime journey in pontoon boats down the Tennessee River to effect a bridgehead on Confederate-held ground con-

---

⁹ 44th Congress, 1st Session, *House Report No. 799*, VII, 164.

¹⁰ *The Washington Post*, March 16, 1885.

COLONEL WILLIAM BABCOCK HAZEN

Forty-First Ohio Volunteer Infantry,
recently promoted after six years' service in the Regular Army.

Brigadier General William B. Hazen, U.S. Volunteers.
Appointed in April 1863, he wears the regulation army coat.

In a rare, uncharacteristic portrait, Hazen poses
in a citizen's frock coat
and partially buttoned military vest.

A citizen's felt hat on his lap, Hazen looks the part
of a typical western–theater army officer.

C.C. Giers Portrait Gallery in Nashville, Tennessee, took this
informal portrait of Hazen wearing an officer's sack coat
with brigadier general's straps.

Cumberland Gallery Collection

In an 1865 portrait, Major General Hazen sat
for a Washington, D.C. photographer,
wearing the headquarters badge, Fifteenth Army Corps.

In 1866, Major General Hazen, USV,
was appointed colonel of the 38th U.S. Infantry.

Hazen poses in citizen's sack coat and military vest
about the time he left for Europe
to observe the Franco–Prussian War.

tributed greatly to raising the siege of Chattanooga. And late the following year, while commanding a division in the Fifteenth Corps, he was designated to spearhead the successful assault against Fort McAllister whose capture guaranteed the fall of Savannah, Georgia. It was the only wartime engagement commanded exclusively by Hazen, and the dramatic assault cemented a lasting, friendly relationship with his commanding general, William T. Sherman. It also earned Hazen promotion to major general of volunteers, personally presented by Secretary of War Edwin M. Stanton in Savannah.

Hazen was proud of his division's action at Fort McAllister, a feeling he could not express just four months earlier when he assumed its command in August 1864 during Atlanta's investment. With dogmatic adherence to strict discipline, organization and military regulation, he found a "deplorable" lack of all three throughout the Army of the Tennessee. Immediate orders were issued to bring his new command into line, which at first was met with derision by the veterans. One officer, Captain Henry S. Nourse of the 55th Illinois, later wrote:

> The division commander, a graduate from West Point and promoted from the Army of the Cumberland, exhibited a greater fondness for parade, and was more insistent upon the rules of military etiquette than our former generals. He summarily arrested Lieutenant-Colonel Mott of the Fifty-seventh Ohio, one day, because his men shouted "hard-tack" when they saw the general passing, they being at the time on short allowance of bread for some reason.[11]

But within two weeks, most of the same soldiers began to give "the outsider" a steady measure of respect, especially after experiencing his leadership in the battle of Jonesboro. This Federal victory, immediately preceding the fall of Atlanta, greatly en-

---

[11] *The Story of the Fifty-fifth Regiment Illinois Volunteer Infantry in the Civil War 1861-1865*, (Clinton, Mass., 1887), 372.

hanced Hazen's reputation in the Army of the Tennessee and he, in return, paid respect to his new command. "Nothing could have been more admirable than the marching and fighting of the Second Division," he wrote. "The whole Army of the Tennessee recognized it, and warmed toward me; and I found myself, from Jonesboro on, standing solidly in my shoes."[12]

Throughout his wartime service Hazen also acquired a number of adversaries among the Federal high command. Major General David S. Stanley bore a deep-rooted grudge against him for years, and after the war accused Hazen of cowardice, deserting his men under fire, and deliberately distorting his role in the battle of Shiloh. Official battle reports from superior officers do not bear this out; on the contrary, Army of the Ohio commander Major General Don Carlos Buell praised Hazen's conduct and recommended his promotion to brigadier general.

Another controversy developed in 1863 shortly after the Federal victory on Missionary Ridge, pitting Hazen against division commander Major General Philip H. Sheridan. Both claimed to reach the crest first on November 25, and Sheridan's report alleged that "General Hazen and his brigade employed themselves in collecting the artillery from which my men had driven the enemy, and have claimed it their capture." Sheridan charged that 11 cannons were "gleaned" by Hazen's men in rear of his advance, and rightfully belonged to his division.[13]

With an elaborate array of evidence, Hazen refuted the charges and refused to give up any captured guns to Sheridan, whom he first met back in 1856 at Grande Ronde, Oregon, when both were lieutenants. This controversy, raised again years later, so incensed Hazen that he devoted more than 50 pages of *A Narrative of Mil-*

---

[12] Hazen, *A Narrative of Military Service*, 298, 299.

[13] *War of the Rebellion: A Compilation of the Official Records of the Union and Confederate Armies*, Series 1, Vol. XXXI, Part 2, 191-192.

*itary Service* to official reports and correspondence supporting his argument — which a *National Tribune* reviewer in 1885 called "an amount of space wholly disproportionate to [the incident's] importance."[14] Nonetheless, veterans from Hazen's brigade and Sheridan's division carried on the debate for years in the pages of the *Tribune*. The episode fueled animosity which each man carried to his grave.

With the capitulation of the Confederate armies in early spring of 1865, Hazen's division and the Army of the Tennessee left North Carolina where they saw their last fighting. The destination was Washington, D.C., site of a two-day grand review of the victorious Union armies. En route on May 19, Hazen was elevated to corps command, and five days later at the age of 35, he rode down Pennsylvania Avenue at the head of the Fifteenth Corps — Sherman's old command at Vicksburg. His veteran troops mustered out in July, but Hazen's Regular Army career continued.

After a 30-day furlough, he assumed command of the District of Middle Tennessee and held that post until the following summer. In July 1866 he returned to the West, as acting assistant inspector general of the vast Department of the Platte, encompassing Iowa and Minnesota and the territories of Nebraska, Wyoming, Montana, and portions of Dakota. For three months he roved through the department's Mountain District, assessing Indian temperment and the efficacy of military forces and posts. Although his exhaustive inspection resulted in no immediate action, it did provide his superiors and the government with valuable information concerning conditions in the Northern Plains and Rocky Mountains. He also bluntly recommended a policy toward the region's Indians: Allot each tribe its prescribed territory or reservation, give them food and clothing but definitely no weapons, and make "vigorous, unceasing war on all that do not obey

---

[14] "Gen. Hazen's Book," *The National Tribune,* November 5, 1885.

and remain upon their grounds.''[15]

Hazen was in Utah Territory in October 1866 when he learned of his promotion to colonel in the reorganized Regular Army, commanding the 38th U.S. Infantry, a new black regiment stationed in New Mexico Territory. Before beginning this assignment, he received permission to spend the winter in Europe and joined the regiment in March 1867. The 38th Infantry was part of the Division of the Missouri, whose commander, General Sherman, soon found other, more important duties for him.

During late summer of 1868, Sherman selected Hazen, whose views on Indian affairs coincided with his own, as one of two special agents assigned to moving the division's Indians onto their reservations and started toward the path of "civilization." Hazen's Southern Indian Military District comprised an area "bounded on the east by the state of Arkansas, south by Texas, north by Kansas and west by the 100th meridian." He was charged with "the supervision and control of all issues and disbursement to the Cheyennes, Arapahoes, Kiowas and Comanches, and such other bands as are now or may hereafter be therein located by proper authority." The order made Hazen responsible only to Sherman except in matters "affecting the troops stationed in said district," when he would then be subject to the commander of the Department of the Missouri — his old nemesis Phil Sheridan.[16]

As special agent, Hazen's first task was to assist in separating peaceful tribes from declared hostile ones. Frustrating difficulties ensued as many of the Indians were wary of the white man's assurances and intent. Past promises of food, shelter and fair treatment had been broken many times. Hazen also believed that Sheridan might attack friendly bands before they could assemble

---

[15] *High Plains Command,* 67.

[16] General Orders Number 4, August 10, 1868, Headquarters, Division of the Missouri.

at his new post, Fort Cobb, Indian Territory (Oklahoma). His fears were realized on November 27, 1868, when Lieutenant Colonel George Custer and the 7th U.S. Cavalry attacked and killed Chief Black Kettle and many of his Cheyenne band along the Washita River. Seven days earlier, Black Kettle, although belonging to a hostile tribe, had conferred personally with Hazen about suing for peace.

Three weeks after the battle, Hazen defended a group of Kiowa Indians and narrowly prevented an attack on its village by Custer and Sheridan, who resented his interference.[17] Strained relations continued as Hazen next devoted his energies to adjusting friendly Indians to a sedentary life. His services as Sherman's special agent ended in June 1869, when he left Fort Cobb for Fort Gibson and command of the 6th U.S. Infantry. Upon arrival, he also found he was to assume "the duties appertaining to the Office of Superintendent of Indian Affairs for the Southern Superintendency."[18]

These duties, lasting 12 months, were performed with competency and fairness. Historian Marvin E. Kroeker characterized this important, albeit unglamorous period of Hazen's career in the following manner:

*Although Hazen believed in severe punishment of hostile Indians for their depredations, he felt just as firmly that the peaceful should be treated honorably and with justice. It was in this context that as a temporary superintendent of Indian affairs he initiated a successful movement to secure farming lands for the dispossessed Wichita Indians. Also during his*

---

[17] Shortly after publication of Custer's *My Life on the Plains* in 1875, Hazen published a rebuttal entitled "Some Corrections to My Life on the PLains," (St. Paul, Minn., 1875) which was reprinted in *Chronicles of Oklahoma*, Vol. III, December 1925. Custer accused Hazen of allowing himself to be victimized by the Kiowas and preventing their "merited chastisement."

[18] Special Order Number 157, June 30, 1869, Headquarters of the Army, Adjutant General's Office, National Archives, RG 75.

*superintendency, a thorough and honest determination was made of the claims of Loyal or Union Creeks for losses sustained during the Civil War. The Hazen-Field investigations laid the basis for what could have been a reasonable and equitable settlement; unfortunately legal technicalities and congressional opposition dealt the Indians still another defeat. They were forced to settle for only a small fraction of the sum Hazen established as a just reward.*[19]

Hazen's dual role as military commander and superintendent ended in August 1870 when he was granted an indefinite leave by President Ulysses S. Grant to observe the Franco-Prussian War. During a three-month visit to France he viewed several battles, including the investment of Paris, and personally interviewed Otto von Bismarck and General Helmut von Moltke. The resulting observations and research convinced Hazen that the U.S. Army was sadly mismanaged, and lacking in up-to-date tactical and logistical organization. With a cumbersome administration, the Army could never successfully wage war with a foreign power. Government and military officials, he said, could profit greatly from a study of the successful German military system. His stinging criticism of the military establishment, coupled with suggestions for reform, were published in 1872 as *The School and the Army in Germany and France.* The *New York Times* stated that the book established the author as "one of the best military critics in the country," while the *Army and Navy Journal* praised him for "the moral courage to speak his whole mind without regard to personal consequences."[20] But most of Hazen's colleagues regarded the book with opposition or complete indifference.

Before returning to 6th Infantry command, Hazen married Mildred McLean, the 21-year-old daughter of prominent *Cincinnati Enquirer* owner Washington McLean. The marriage provided

---

[19] *High Plains Command,* 168-169.

[20] *New York Tribune,*July 3, 1877. *Army and Navy Journal,* July 20, 1872.

Hazen with important social and political connections, as the McLean family had considerable influence in Ohio Democratic circles. A son, John, was born to the couple in 1876, but died at the age of 22 in 1898. Twelve years after Hazen's death (and only one year after the death of her son), Mildred married Admiral George Dewey, the hero of Manila Bay of Spanish-American War fame.

Back on the western frontier, Hazen gloomily faced the prospect of long-term garrison duty at Fort Hays in Kansas. Indian troubles seemed to be waning, and with them chances for military honors and promotion. Through correspondence he maintained close ties with Garfield, an influential Ohio congressman. He also continued a friendly relationship with Sherman, who became commander of the army in 1869. Sherman's replacement as head of the Division of the Missouri was none other than Phil Sheridan, whom Hazen in 1871 called "a selfish, weak, unscrupulous man," and most responsible for stunting his career.[21]

Another roadblock in Hazen's eyes was Secretary of War William W. Belknap, a former regimental and brigade commander in the Army of the Tennessee. Beginning in 1872, Hazen brought evidence to Garfield's attention that Belknap was involved in influence peddling through army post traderships, specifically at Fort Sill. Persistent rumors of graft and corruption in the War Department, some fueled by Hazen, continued to fly over the next four years. Meanwhile, Hazen and his regiment transferred to Fort Buford, an isolated post near the Yellowstone River in northwest Dakota Territory — a Sheridan directive which Hazen bitterly regarded as banishment. His spirits further flagged when the Comanche bullet in his side shifted and caused temporary partial paralysis in his legs.

From his quarters at Fort Buford, Hazen immersed himself in

---

[21] Hazen to Garfield, July 23, 1871, James A. Garfield Papers, Library of Congress, Washington, D.C.

further controversy. Between 1872 and 1875 he took on railroad
and land speculators who, as Hazen viewed it, were attempting to
develop the Northern Plains into an agricultural empire through
"wicked deception."[22] An acrimonious debate flared in the press
over land that Northern Pacific Railroad agents vigorously promoted, with Hazen squarely opposing an array of critical rebuttals
— perhaps the most influential coming from Lieutenant Colonel
George Custer, who denounced Hazen's characterization of the
country as "misrepresentations."[23]

The irascible Hazen fired back with a detailed barrage of facts,
statistics and personal observations defending his belief that the
"great middle region" was worthless for agricultural expansion.
In a national magazine article, he echoed earlier charges against
special interests, especially those representing the Northern Pacific Railroad, whose promotions to prospective bond purchasers
were riddled with "flagrant falsehoods." He cautioned that settlement beyond the 98th meridian should proceed "naturally" with
"eyes open," and not be stampeded by land speculators.[24]

Soon after the article appeared, Hazen published *Our Barren
Lands,* a detailed and scientific description of the public lands between the 100th meridian and the Sierra Nevada mountains. Intended as a defense of his views and reputation, the treatise also
sought to repudiate the "myth of the great fruitful garden." In
assessing this work, Marvin E. Kroeker claimed the author "went
too far in the opposite direction, dismissing most of the high
plains as incapable of sustaining substantial settlement. Nevertheless, he correctly predicted that undependable rainfall would pose
an insoluble problem for a generation or longer ... Not until new

---

[22] *New York Tribune,* February 7, 1874.

[23] *Minneapolis Tribune,* April 17, 1874.

[24] Hazen, "The Great Middle Region of the United States, and its Limited Space of
Arable Land," *North American Review,* Vol. CXX, January 1875.

seeds and new techniques of farming were introduced was agriculture feasible on the Great Plains.[25]

"Hazen's statements of caution to would-be settlers were at least partially justified by events in the decades following his publications, during which time hundreds of emigrants were wrecked in hopes and fortune by venturing across the 100th meridian into the inhospitable limits of the arid lands."[26]

Early in 1876, Hazen's feud with Secretary of War Belknap reached a climax. A congressional committee's investigation (which included testimony from Custer less than three months before his death at the Little Big Horn) uncovered "uncontradicted evidence" of malfeasance in office by Belknap arising from management of army post traderships. The committee's report revealed that Belknap received about $20,000 in kickbacks between 1870 and 1875 from the Fort Sill trader's contract.[27] Confronted with this evidence, the secretary immediately resigned. An impeachment trial began in April and lasted until August. Called twice to testify, Hazen was painted by the defense as the vindictive cause of Belknap's downfall. In the end, Belknap was acquitted — not because two-thirds of the Senate considered him innocent of the articles of impeachment, but because 23 members insisted the Senate lacked jurisdiction over the case.[28] Still, Hazen was pleased. "I have waited patiently four years," he wrote, "never doubting but I should be finally vindicated, although at times feeling very heavily the weight of the displeasure of those

---

[25] *High Plains Command,* 170.

[26] *Ibid.,* 142.

[27] *Congressional Record,* 44th Congress, 1st Session, *Proceedings of the Senate, Trial of William W. Belknap,* 1876.

[28] *Ibid.*

high in power for daring to tell the truth.''[29]

He returned to Fort Buford after the trial and remained idle during the campaign to crush Chief Sitting Bull and the Sioux. But in June 1877, through the influence of Garfield and father-in-law Washington McLean, Hazen was appointed military attache to the U.S. legation in Vienna, Austria. Before he reached Washington, D.C., however, David S. Stanley, colonel of the 22nd U.S. Infantry and a Belknap confidant, preferred charges of perjury against Hazen's testimony. Stanley also castigated Hazen's Civil War record, accusing him of ''disgraceful conduct'' at Shiloh and impugning his actions at Stone River, Missionary Ridge and Pickett's Mill. The allegations were dismissed by President Rutherford B. Hayes and Hazen sailed for Europe. While there he observed fighting on the Danube-Balkan front during the Russo-Turkish War.

Trouble with Stanley was far from over, as Hazen soon discovered upon his return in November 1878. Failing to press his charges the previous year, Stanley attacked Hazen in the press with the same allegations. Hazen now retaliated with a formal request that Stanley be arraigned for libel. The resulting trial has been described as ''one of the most remarkable court-martial cases in American military history.''[30]

As commander of the army, General Sherman tried unsuccessfully for several years to mediate an end of hostilities between the two officers. Wishing to remain neutral in the controversy, Sherman reluctantly recommended on March 19, 1879, that Stanley and Hazen be tried *jointly* by the same court-martial.

During the trial, Hazen, along with many fellow Union officers, was forced to fight much of the Civil War over again. Stan-

---

[29] Hazen to Hiester Clymer (chairman of the House Military Affairs Committee), March 15, 1876, in the *New York Tribune*, March 30, 1876.

[30] *High Plains Command*, 155.

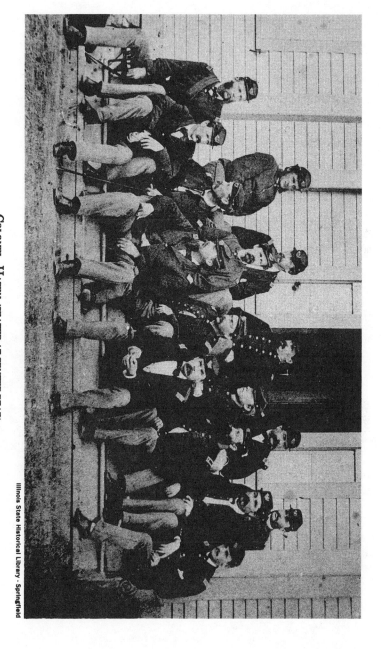

COLONEL HAZEN (SEATED AT CENTER REAR)
WITH OFFICERS OF THE SIXTH AND SEVENTH U.S. INFANTRY, CIRCA 1872

GENERAL HAZEN

Circa 1885, when he was chief signal officer of the Army.

ley's star witness regarding Missionary Ridge was General Sheridan, who read from his 1864 official report that his division reached the crest before Hazen's brigade, and that Hazen appropriated guns captured by his troops. Hearing this claim again must have rankled the combatative Hazen, and certainly provided reason for the detailed attention paid to the episode in *A Narrative of Military Service.*

The trial lasted two months and was marked by personal denunciations and vicious invective. Fourteen years after the war's conclusion a large can of worms was opened and long-harbored ill will spilled out, leaving officers in both camps with unhealing scars. Stanley was found "guilty of conduct to the prejudice of good order and military discipline" and sentenced to "be admonished in General Orders by the General of the Army" — the lightest sentence possible under regulations.[31] The two-year military statute of limitations had long since expired, so the case against Hazen was dropped. As a result, his side of the story was not granted a thorough review and newspaper coverage of the trial only served to widen circulation of Stanley's accusations. Convinced that he would be unable to ever state his case effectively in court, Hazen began working on the first draft of this book.

Following the verdict, Hazen resumed command of the 6th Infantry at Fort Buford. He imagined he was destined to finish out his career in the dreary desolation of Dakota. Events back East, however, soon buoyed his low spirits.

In 1880, James A. Garfield was elected President, and through his old friend and confidant's continuing influence, Hazen was promoted to brigadier general and appointed chief signal officer of the Army.[32] This Washington staff position compensated him

---

[31] General Court-Martial, Order Number 35, Headquarters of the Army, June 18, 1879, Adjutant General's Office, National Archives, RG 94.

[32] The announcement actually was made on December 6, 1880, by outgoing President Rutherford B. Hayes. Hazen's appointment was confirmed on December 17.

for any loss of prestige he suffered in the public squabble with Stanley. Prominent editor Whitelaw Reid, writing in the *New York Tribune,* considered Hazen an excellent choice for the post, stating:

> *Among the colonels in active service it would be impossible to designate one better fitted by mental powers, scholarly habits and scientific tastes to fill the service. There is opportunity enough to make it more thorough and accurate, which a vigorous man, not fond of running in old ruts, will early see ... [Hazen is] a representative of the element in the Army which studies hard and works hard, believes that an officer has something to do in time of peace besides drinking whiskey and playing cards, and does not think the old saying need ever be verified that a full colonelcy and complete imbecility come to a man at the same time.*[33]

Reid's assessment proved uncannily prophetic, for one of Hazen's lasting legacies in this new role was propelling the development of meteorologic science. In managing the Weather Bureau, he employed expert physicists, meteorologists and electricians to conduct careful investigations, "emphasizing especially the necessity of the study of instruments and methods of observing and investigation of the laws of changes going on in the atmosphere."[34]
He elevated the personnel of the signal corps by employing college graduates, established regular courses of instruction, and increased the practical application of the service to commerce and agriculture. "I like my work," he wrote Garfield, "and the field opens larger every day."[35] But even in this capacity, it was not long before another controversy began swirling at Hazen's feet.

In May 1880, Lady Franklin Bay in the Arctic Circle was cho-

---

[33] *New York Tribune,* December 17, 1880.

[34] Hazen quoted in *The National Cyclopaedia of American Biography,* Vol. III, 408.

[35] Hazen to Garfield, December 25, 1880, Garfield Papers, Library of Congress.

sen as the site for a signal service polar station. After Hazen became chief signal officer, he took a personal interest in the project and the initial two-year expedition was sent in 1881 under command of Regular Army First Lieutenant Augustus W. Greely, a Civil War veteran from Massachusetts who was wounded at.Antietam.[36] Greely and his 25-member party expected to see relief expeditions, but the first failed in 1882. A second attempt was disrupted by ice. In September 1883 Secretary of War Robert Todd Lincoln decided it was too late in the year to send another relief. Greely's party was left to spend a third winter in the Arctic. In June 1884, rescuers finally reached the station and found only Greely and seven others alive. The rest froze or starved to death. One man was executed on Greely's orders for repeatedly stealing food.[37]

Hazen never forgave Lincoln for his inaction, and in 1884 Lincoln censured Hazen for his criticism. Hazen replied to Lincoln by letter, which was returned with a warning to keep the matter private. Instead, Hazen went to the press and stated in a published account that he wrote such a letter.[38] He immediately found himself ordered before another court-martial, which resulted in a reprimand by President Chester A. Arthur for "unwarranted and captious criticism" of Lincoln.[39] This latest imbroglio temporarily interrupted his duties in the signal office, and Hazen found consolation among colleagues, including Greely, who supported his position.

---

[36] Powell, William H., *Records of Living Officers of the United States Army*, (Philadelphia, 1890), 246. Greely served as a private, corporal and orderly sergeant in the 19th Massachusetts Volunteer Infantry. He finished the war as a captain and brevet major in the 81st U.S. Colored Infantry. After Hazen's death, Greely replaced him as chief signal officer in March 1887.

[37] Greely, A.W., *Three Years of Arctic Service*, (New York, 1894), 699-700.

[38] *Washington Evening Star*, March 2, 1885.

[39] *New York Herald*, April 18, 1885.

Health problems slowed his work habits in 1886, but near the end of the year diabetes, a kidney ailment and recurring pain from his Texas wound forced Hazen to obtain a 12-month leave of absence. On January 13, 1887, he attended a White House reception where he caught a cold. Confining himself to bed (his wife Mildred and 10-year-old son were in Europe), his condition improved then quickly deteriorated over the next three days.[40] Lapsing into unconsciousness, Hazen died at 8 p.m. on January 16. He was 56 years old.

Richard A. Baumgartner
Huntington, West Virginia
March 1993

---

[40] *New York Times,* January 17, 1887.

# ACKNOWLEDGMENTS.

Many individuals and institutions provided photographs used in this edition of *A Narrative of Military Service.* Their contributions are noted where each image appears throughout the text. Charles Hale of Kenova, West Virginia, graciously assisted with photographic reproductions.

Larry M. Strayer, Dayton, Ohio, a longtime student of Hazen's Civil War career, first suggested publishing the reprint, provided a rare, original copy of the book, edited the Introduction and selected most of the enhancing photographic additions. Some of the original edition's engravings were replaced with the exact photographs from which the engravings were copied.

Richard A. Baumgartner adapted the full-page, foldout battle maps from the 1885 edition. The original maps, cluttered and difficult to read, were redrawn and typeset for clarity with retention of keys and important features relevant to Hazen's narrative.

# PREFACE.

THOSE who make history do not write it, for they stand too near the event. It is their province to furnish the theme and supply the material for the shaping hand of the future historian. Ever since the war I have felt it a duty which I owed to my men, and, in some sort, to myself, to tell the story of our common service. The materials for this work have been derived mainly from three sources: first, my own recollection; secondly, the official record; and, thirdly, private letters from actors in the struggle, to the writers of which I here, once for all, make my acknowledgment.

This narrative contains, with much that will be familiar, some things that are new. It touches on, and may set at rest, a few disputed questions of fact, and it crosses the lines of certain personal controversies about which the public are supposed to know little. Every great war engenders an ignoble swarm of jealousies and calumnies which buzz and sting for long years after kindly Nature has repaired the battlefields. I have had my share of these annoyances, and may feel bound, at some future time, to prepare for the official and pro-

fessional eye a formal presentation of my own case, to
the end that testimony may be perpetuated and the
record purged of error.  But from these pages I have
excluded controverted matter, except so far as the telling of a plain tale for the general reader necessarily
involves it.

I send out this book as my contribution toward the
history of our heroic age.  It may awaken proud recollections in the breast of an old comrade; it may make
a son's heart exult at the sight of his father's name;
above all, it may help to reveal, to establish, and to
confirm the truth, which it is the part of every one
to tell, and from which neither the brave men whom
I led, nor their leader, have as soldiers anything to
fear.

WM. B. HAZEN.

WASHINGTON, D. C., Jan. 1, 1885.

# CONTENTS.

## APPENDIX.

# ILLUSTRATIONS AND MAPS.

# A NARRATIVE

OF

# MILITARY SERVICE.

---

## CHAPTER I.

### THE FORTY-FIRST OHIO.

IN February, 1861, I gave up the unexpired portion of a long leave of absence granted on account of wounds received in Indian warfare,[1] which were yet unhealed, and with my hand in a sling asked for duty, and was assigned as assistant instructor of Infantry Tactics at West Point. When the war began, I did what I could to take the field at once. My first offer of volunteer service was from General J. D. Cox, as inspector-general upon his staff in West Virginia. Leave of absence to accept this position was denied. I lost, in the same way, two field positions in volunteer regiments. I had a three days' leave to engage in some capacity at the battle of Bull Run, but arrived in time only to be caught in the retreat and carried back with it. It is difficult for one who did not actually face that rush to realize its character. It was a physical impossibility to stem it; and I can bear full testimony to

[1] An account of this episode of my early service, when hard knocks were less plenty than they afterward became, will be found in the Appendix.

1

the accuracy of Dr. Russell's description, printed in the
" London Times."

Finally in September, 1861, a committee of gentlemen
from Cleveland, Ohio, near my home, visited the President
and applied for my services as colonel of the Forty-first
Ohio, a regiment about to be organized at Cleveland, with
J. A. Garfield as lieutenant-colonel. Mr. Lincoln approved
this, and gave the necessary orders. Before I joined, Garfield had been made colonel of the Forty-second Ohio.

The action of the Government at this time in placing
obstacles in the way of the acceptance by regular officers of
volunteer positions has never been satisfactorily explained.
The theory of the Military Academy from its foundation
has been to keep alive ready, practical acquaintance with
military subjects, to be imparted in emergencies to volunteer armies, the country's only real military defence. Yet
quite the opposite was done ; officers were given volunteer
duty, only upon the strong appeal of personal friends.
Perhaps that most remarkable saying of General Scott,
who favored this restriction, that " the regular army must
be kept intact to fall back upon, if the volunteers fail,"
may give the key; but it seems incredible that such an
utter want of appreciation of the situation, and of the vital
needs of the country, could have existed. There can be
hardly a doubt, that if the regular army had ceased to
exist as a field organization, and all its officers, non-
commissioned officers, and good soldiers been scattered
among the volunteer armies, its usefulness would have
been greatly increased.

The Forty-first Ohio, when I joined it, was recruiting
rapidly. It had its inception in Geauga County, under the
immediate care and patronage of the Hon. Peter Hitchcock,
of Burton, a widely and most honorably known citizen.
Three young men, Elias A. Ford (nephew of the late
Governor Seabury Ford), Henry W. Johnson, and Lester F.

Patchin, were the nucleus. They went from village to village, and from neighborhood to neighborhood, with the old flag flying, to the step of fife and drum, and the first company was soon enrolled, as the result of their good work. Patchin was killed in one of the early battles. Ford was shot at Stone River, but recovered, and is a well-known railroad man in Pittsburg. Johnson was my efficient quartermaster in the war. He afterward declined a commission in the regular army, and is now a manufacturer at Michigan City. I joined my regiment, then about half filled, on the 16th of September; and the following orders, published then and soon after, indicate how the work of making soldiers out of citizens was begun. It was by the rigid enforcement and observance of these and of others that will be given, that the regiment was enabled to perform most remarkable service throughout the war, — a service which, so far as my observation enabled me to determine, no regiment, either volunteer or regular, surpassed : —

HEADQUARTERS FORTY-FIRST OHIO VOL. INF'T'Y,
CAMP WOOD, OHIO, Sept. 16, 1861.

*Regimental Orders, No.* 1.

I. Colonel William B. Hazen, Forty-first Regiment Ohio Volunteer Infantry, hereby assumes command of the camp and regiment. In entering upon the duties of organizing and disciplining the regiment, he trusts that every individual of the command fully appreciates the importance of the first principle of the soldier, — obedience to commands. Without it there can be no efficiency; and he feels confident that every officer and soldier has determined to carry out this principle cheerfully.

II. Cleanliness is next in importance, and captains of companies are especially charged with attention to this. The colonel will frequently cause inspections to be made of the men, with bare feet and with shirts unbuttoned.

III. The hair is to be kept short. This applies to all members of the regiment.

IV. Officers are required to appear at all times in uniform, unless on leave of absence for a longer period than three days.

V. No member of the regiment will be permitted to leave camp, except on duty, without authority, which in case of enlisted men must be in writing, setting forth the necessity, signed by their company commander, and countersigned by the colonel; and with officers, verbal authority for time less than twelve hours, when they must register their names at the adjutant's office in a book kept for that purpose, where gone, and time of return. For longer periods, the Army Regulations will be strictly followed.

VI. The attention of the regiment is called to such portions of the Articles of War as will be read to it from day to day on parade, and particularly those portions relating to profanity and drunkenness, the observance of the Sabbath and attendance at divine service; and officers are required to repress all irregularities.

By order of
<br>Colonel W. B. HAZEN.
<br>J. R. SANFORD, *Adjutant.*

CAMP WOOD, OHIO, Sept. 17, 1861.

I. Hereafter the non-commissioned officers will be formed by first sergeants of companies and marched to the adjutant's quarters at calls for recitation and officers' drill.

II. The recitation of officers will hereafter be at two P.M., and that of non-commissioned officers will be held by captains of companies at three P. M. Recitation will be held one hour. Commissioned officers will assemble at the adjutant's quarters under charge of their captain, who will report to the adjutant.

CAMP WOOD, OHIO, Sept. 18, 1861.

I. Hereafter captains of companies will inspect details for guard, and no one will appear at guard-mounting except in uniform, coats buttoned, and bearing a neat and cleanly appearance. The adjutant is directed to send to their companies all who fail to appear as prescribed.

II. No one has authority to excuse men from drill except the colonel and surgeon of the regiment.

III. Hereafter there will be two beats of the drum at roll-calls, the first to be sounded five minutes before the time for the call, when all the men will repair immediately to their company parade-grounds. At the second call all the men will be in the ranks by the time the drum ceases to beat, when they will be called to attention by their first sergeants.

IV. The field-officers will attend punctually all drills.

V. There will be no more noise in camp between taps and reveille. The officer of the guard will frequently patrol camp between these hours and promptly suppress all violations of this order.

VI. Hereafter reveille will be sounded at daylight.

CAMP WOOD, OHIO, Sept. 20, 1861.

I. Hereafter, in addition to the drills already established, there will be a squad drill of men by non-commissioned officers between the hours of two and three P. M.

II. There will be no drills Saturday afternoon, but the time will be devoted to policing the camp and tents and cleaning the soldiers' clothing.

III. For squad drills the battalion will be formed on the general parade-ground, and squads told off and assigned only to such drill-masters as have already received instructions in this camp.

CAMP WOOD, OHIO, Sept. 21, 1861.

．　．　．　．　．　．　．　．　．　．

II. Captains will hereafter cause the new men of companies, and awkward men, to take their places on the left of companies, for drill in separate squads.

CAMP WOOD, OHIO, Sept. 25, 1861.

．　．　．　．　．　．　．　．　．

II. There will be a drill from three to four P. M. of officers and non-commissioned officers, and squad drill from half-past four to half-past five.

CAMP WOOD, OHIO, Oct. 10, 1861.

I. The attention of officers is called to the necessity of cleanliness and neatness of person and dress. Little in this way can be expected of the men, unless a proper example is set by their officers.

II. The adjutant will hereafter attend in person the three stated roll-calls, — reveille, parade, and tattoo, — and will assure himself of the whereabouts of every member of the regiment and report the result to the commanding officer.

.    .    .    .    .    .    .    .    .    .

V. Hereafter the officer of the day will pass along the line at all drill roll-calls and receive from the commandant of each company the report of present and absent, and will immediately turn out and send to drill all absentees.

VI. The field-music, unless employed at practice, will attend all drills with their companies.

VII. There will be a drill of officers at the bayonet exercise hereafter between the hours of three and four P. M.

CAMP DENNISON, OHIO, Nov. 11, 1861.

I. The officers of the regiment are arranged for instruction for the present as follows : —

*First Section.* — Lieutenant-Colonel Wizeman, squad-marcher ; Major Mygatt ; Lieutenant and Adjutant Sanford ; Lieutenant and Quartermaster Chamberlain ; Captain Tolles ; Lieutenant Munn ; Lieutenant Johnson ; Lieutenant Opdycke ; Lieutenant McCleery ; Captain Wiley ; Lieutenant Kimberly, — Colonel Hazen, instructor, — will recite daily, Sundays excepted, from one to three P. M.

*Second Section.* — Captain Cole, squad-marcher ; Lieutenant Pancoast ; Lieutenant Hardy ; Lieutenant Proctor ; Captain Stone ; Lieutenant Morgan ; Lieutenant Jones ; Captain Leslie ; Lieutenant Holloway ; Lieutenant Kirkendall ; Captain Hamblin, — Captain Wiley, instructor, — will recite daily from half-past one to half-past two P. M., Sundays excepted.

*Third Section.* — Captain Pease, squad-marcher ; Lieutenant Sisson ; Lieutenant Kyle ; Lieutenant McRoberts ; Captain

Williston; Lieutenant Rymers; Lieutenant Beebe; Captain Goodsell; Lieutenant Horner; Lieutenant Gaylord; Lieutenant Steele, — Lieutenant Kimberly, instructor, — will recite daily, Sundays excepted, from half-past one to half-past two P. M.

II. Squad-marchers will be held responsible for the presence of their squads. Instructors will keep a record of the result of each recitation, and no officer should question the instructor as to the mark he may have received. Transfers will be made from one section to another according to proficiency.

. . . . . . . . . .

IV. Squad drills by non-commissioned officers during recitation are discontinued. There will hereafter be a drill of the whole regiment at bayonet exercise from half-past two to half-past three P. M.

CAMP JENKINS, Dec. 2, 1861.

The first section of non-commissioned officers, composed of the non-commissioned staff and such non-commissioned officers of Companies A and B as have been selected by the colonel upon examination, will commence recitations to-morrow. . . .

CAMP WICKLIFFE, Feb. 12, 1862.

. . . . . . . . .

II. First sergeants will appear in accurate costume when marching their details on guard. Non-commissioned officers of the guard will also appear in proper military dress. First sergeants will enforce the same observance with privates that march on guard. Failure in any of these particulars will jeopardize the position of any non-commissioned officer so offending. . . .

These extracts show the rules by which we worked, and their rigid enforcement made the regiment one of the best ever in any service. In addition to school studies, it was directed in courses of military reading, many hundred dollars being expended in the purchase of books for this purpose.

The regiment was fully organized on the 2d of November,

and so reported. The mustering officer, Lieutenant Neill of the Eighteenth Infantry, was sent for, the regiment paraded, and as he read the oath all the members simultaneously repeated it in a distinct voice. This ceremony was at once impressive and inspiring; and I believe every man in the regiment resolved at that moment, as I know the colonel did, to perform every duty to the best of his ability.

The regiment was composed of excellent men from northern Ohio. The Seventh Ohio Infantry, Colonel E. B. Tyler, and Second Ohio Cavalry (known from its patrons as the "Wade and Hutchins Regiment"), Colonel Doubleday, had drawn to their ranks the largest part of the young men from the schools; but I could not wish for better material than came to the Forty-first. Individual exceptions must be made; but most of the officers proved themselves competent, and from the enlisted men excellent officers soon came to take the places of the inefficient. The amount of effort devoted to the study of the military profession, not only at our first camp but in all our camps, until the close of the war, would be considered very unusual in a regular regiment. There was no idle time. Officers' drill (which included non-commissioned officers) was conducted by the colonel; while drills of the men in squads, companies, and battalion, with policing, recitations, bayonet exercise, and other camp duties, occupied all the day. I never saw such a rapid progress, nor such interest in rudimentary military instruction, as I observed in this organization.

Officers not suited to their places, either from want of industry, character, or other causes, soon made their unfitness evident in many ways; and when there was no more hope, they either voluntarily resigned or were informed in a kind way that they were not likely to be useful, and quietly went home. It is remarkable now, in looking over the first roster, to notice that, as a rule, fitness was found to exist inversely with rank. Thus, of the captains, only four ever went into battle or were suited for the office they held; and but one, Aquila Wiley, of Wooster, Ohio, arrived at special distinction. Of the first lieutenants, all but the two regimental staff-officers continued in the war with credit, Emerson Opdycke reached distinction, and Holloway became colonel of the regiment. Of the second lieutenants, all made their mark. McCleery gained the brevet of brigadier-general, and afterwards was elected to Congress; Kimberly became colonel of another regiment, and Beebe lieutenant-colonel.

The schools were a prominent feature. Recitations were marked and recorded, and this record became an unerring indication of the future of these officers. My table of class-standing then, gave the true relative place held at the end of the war by each officer who continued in the service. No part of the regiment ever faltered or failed in the least particular in the performance of every duty assigned it. The thoroughness of its instruction, the accuracy of its drill, its soldierly habit, promptness, and correctness in the performance of duty, steadiness and gallantry under fire, and general efficiency, were at all times marked. It was conspicuous in most of the great battles of the West, — at Shiloh, Murfreesboro', Chickamauga, Chattanooga, Mission Ridge, East Tennessee, Rocky-faced Ridge, Resaca, Pickett's Mills, Atlanta, Jonesboro', Franklin, and Nashville; and it lost by the bullet nearly two hundred per cent of its average strength. It was never surprised nor assailed at a disadvantage, nor failed to repay fully any punishment received. It was as easily manœuvred as a platoon, and its steady volley-firing on the field was heard above the din of battle. If any regiment at any time has had a better record, I do not know it.

Long before the war closed, the wisdom of what to many appeared harsh and unnecessary (I mean uncompromising rigor of discipline and instruction) was so fully justified and admitted as to bring to me that confidence and respect which is a soldier's best reward.

Our first field of duty was at Gallipolis, Ohio, where my regiment was sent by boat from Cincinnati just after the burning of Guyandotte, which was attributed to Jenkins, called the "Guerilla." Jenkins's place was situated on the Ohio, and in passing we stopped, believing it our duty, and seized a large lot of supplies, consisting of corn, horses, and hogs. Mrs. Jenkins, a very accomplished lady, was at home. My duties at Gallipolis necessarily involved service on both sides of the river; and no one in my camp thought that the south side of the stream was in a separate department, commanded by some other officer, or that any one would object to my taking the troops there. On arriving I reported as follows : —

> HEADQUARTERS FORTY-FIRST OHIO VOL. INF'T'Y,
> GALLIPOLIS, OHIO, Nov. 16, 1861.

General S. M. WADE, Volunteer Service, Cincinnati, Ohio :

I arrived here safely this evening. I find the people here, and for a considerable distance in the interior, very much frightened, and more so than there is cause for. Ceredo has not been captured, nor have there been any Rebel troops within thirty miles of it for a long time. I stopped there, and found about two hundred effective men in command of Colonel Zeigler. The people across the river are firmly of the opinion that Floyd has a force over there. I shall move into that region of country soon, and ascertain everything about it.

> Very respectfully, your obedient servant,
> W. B. HAZEN,
> *Colonel Forty-first Ohio Vol's.*

Jenkins's place happened to be in General Rosecrans' department, who in a day or two, hearing of my landing and seizures at Jenkins's, sent me the following despatch, which led to further correspondence : —

By Telegraph from Camp Gauley,
West Virginia, Nov. 21, 1861.

To Commander of Ohio Regiment, at Gallipolis, Ohio.

Do you consider yourself under orders from this department? If so, you are ordered up to Red House, on the Kanawha.

Joseph Darr, Jr.,
*Major and A. A. Adjutant-General.*

Headquarters Forty-first Ohio Vol. Inf't'y,
Gallipolis, Ohio, Nov. 21, 1861.

Act'g-Assist. Adjutant-General, U. S. Army, Camp Gauley, Virginia :

I do not consider myself under orders from your headquarters. The regiment was sent here for a special purpose, with an especial promise that it should not go up the Kanawha.

W. B. Hazen.

Headquarters Forty-first Ohio Vol. Inf't'y,
Gallipolis, Ohio, Nov. 21, 1861.

Assist. Adjutant-General U. S. Army, Cincinnati, Ohio :

Sir, — I require to be informed how far it is expected that I seize the property of persons in arms against the United States. I have already taken from the farm of the notorious Jenkins about ten thousand bushels of shelled corn, one hundred and fifty hogs, and ten horses. . . .

Very respectfully, your obedient servant,
W. B. Hazen.

By Telegraph from Headquarters Dep't of
Western Virginia, Nov. 23, 1861.

Colonel Forty-first Ohio Volunteer Infantry :

The commanding general of this department desires me to say, that while he is very glad of your presence at Gallipolis, and has no desire of bringing you under his control, yet when you undertake to operate in his department and participate in the critical matter of capturing property, he desires at least to be consulted ; and you should know that no troops should be marched into a department, either for duty or other reasons for coming in, without the consent of the commander of the department.

JOSEPH DARR, JR.,

*Major and A. A. Adjutant-General.*

HEADQUARTERS FORTY-FIRST OHIO VOL. INF'T'Y,

GALLIPOLIS, OHIO, Nov. 23, 1861.

Act'g-Assist. Adjutant-General, Department of Western Virginia :

All that I did was contemplated in my verbal instructions. I am confident, however, that they were given without thinking that they were encroaching upon General Rosecrans' department. Such was the case with myself. I have now respectfully to request that Colonel Zeigler's companies be returned to him, and that I, with my regiment and his, be permitted to make an expedition to Logan Court House.

W. B. HAZEN.

BY TELEGRAPH FROM HEADQUARTERS DEP'T OF

WESTERN VIRGINIA, Nov. 24, 1861.

Colonel Forty-first Ohio Volunteer Infantry:

Your despatch received. The idea strikes the commanding general favorably. He would prefer to hear the details of your plan for the excursion to Logan Court House, as he is well acquainted with that country, and may be able to so co-operate as to effectually quiet it for some time. Jenkins, with some of his men, has been reported within three days, at Raleigh. What will you do for transportation ? Have your troops india-rubber coats and satchel knapsacks ? Please communicate freely and fully. Zeigler's company can be returned.

JOSEPH DARR, Jr.,

*Major and A. A. Adjutant-General.*

HEADQUARTERS FORTY-FIRST OHIO VOL'S,

GALLIPOLIS, OHIO, Nov. 25, 1861.

Act'g-Assist. Adjutant-General West Virginia :

I propose landing my regiment and section of artillery at Ceredo at evening, march to Trout's Hill and Wayne Court

House before day, where there is one company of Jenkins's men; then by a forced march reach Logan Court House the second day, and return in two days to Guyandotte *via* Barbourville. I will take no train, but four days' rations of hard bread in haversacks, and procure beef in the country. We have no india-rubber coats nor satchel knapsacks. I can have a few hundred horses sent up from Cincinnati.

W. B. HAZEN.

HEADQUARTERS FORTY-FIRST OHIO VOL. INF'T'Y,
GALLIPOLIS, OHIO, Nov. 25, 1861.

Act'g-Assist. Adjutant-General, Camp Gauley, Virginia:

I have just received orders to remove my command to Louisville, Kentucky, so the contemplated move to Logan Court House cannot be made. I am not a little surprised at the tenor of your last despatch. Experience on the Indian frontier teaches that these expeditions, such as I propose, without trains, almost invariably succeed, and are the only ones against irregular mounted men that will succeed.

Very respectfully, your obedient servant,

W. B. HAZEN.

We were transferred to Louisville by the splendid steamer " Telegraph No. 2," that had taken us up the river and remained with us. The Army of the Ohio was then under its third commander, General Buell, and the regiment was assigned to the division of General William Nelson, which soon started out in the direction of Bowling Green, and went into what was known as Camp Wickliffe, about thirty miles from Louisville, where we remained till the 14th of February, when we moved on to Nashville. Our experience at Camp Wickliffe was perhaps the most dispiriting of the war. All the diseases to which new troops are most subject here afflicted us. Diarrhœa, fevers, measles, and pneumonia attacked a large part of the regiment, and the fatality was very great.

Whenever possible I sent the sick at once to their homes, and in so doing, while violating the orders of the camp, I saved many lives; and now, when I go home, some one almost invariably relates how his life was saved by removal from Camp Wickliffe in the night, when no one knew it.

# CHAPTER II.

## THE NINETEENTH BRIGADE.

O N the 7th of January, 1862, I was assigned to the command of the Nineteenth Brigade of Buell's Army of the Ohio, consisting of the Forty-first Ohio, Forty-sixth and Forty-seventh Indiana, and the Sixth Kentucky Infantry. This was a new brigade, organized with reference to my commanding it, and was assigned to Nelson's division.

The new regiments were composed of admirable material, but their instruction had been very imperfect. The Forty-sixth and Forty-seventh Indiana were commanded respectively by Colonels Slack and Fitch, both men of high character. Fitch had been United States Senator, and Slack was a well-known and highly esteemed gentleman of Indiana. Colonel Whitaker, of the Sixth Kentucky, had been a member of the legislature of his State, and was perhaps as well known as any gentleman in it.

The following orders and extracts are a part of those, the observance of which brought the brigade to a high standard, and enabled it to perform most distinguished and valuable service : —

CAMP WICKLIFFE, KENTUCKY, Jan. 7, 1862.

I. The commanding officers of the Forty-sixth and Forty-seventh Indiana and the Sixth Kentucky Volunteers will at once take the proper steps to prevent their commands from wandering away from their regimental grounds.

II. They will send their adjutant, or some proper person, to these headquarters, to take copies of all division orders, which will be read in front of the regiments this evening.

III. All persons in this brigade are reminded that official communications to higher authority, in order to secure recognition, must pass through the proper military channels.

CAMP WICKLIFFE, KENTUCKY, Jan. 8, 1862.

II. Schools of instruction are hereby established for the three new regiments, and the following assignment of instructors is made. Captain Aquila Wiley to the Forty-sixth Indiana Volunteer Infantry ; Captain Emerson Opdycke to the Forty-seventh Indiana Volunteer Infantry ; and Lieutenant James McCleery to the Sixth Kentucky Volunteer Infantry. They will be obeyed and respected in the particular functions herein assigned them, accordingly. They will at once enter upon these duties, and be excused from all others. Commencing with the School of the Soldier, they will exercise in drill all the commissioned line officers from eight to nine A. M. each day, Sundays excepted, as per division orders, and render such other assistance in instructing the regiments as may be in their power. They will form the officers of each regiment into two sections for study and recitation, who will recite one hour each day, Sundays excepted, commencing with the School of the Soldier ("Revised Tactics"). It is enjoined upon every officer to provide himself at once with this book. No officer will absent himself from either of the above duties as prescribed, unless excused by the colonel commanding the brigade or by the surgeon. Instructors will keep a record in writing of each recitation, reporting to the colonel commanding the brigade at the end of each week. They will also report from day to day the absentees, if any, who did not appear to have been absent by proper authority. . . .

CAMP WICKLIFFE, KENTUCKY, Jan. 17, 1862.

II. The chaplain of each regiment, with the regimental officer of the day and one of the medical officers of the regiment, will inspect all the messes of the enlisted men once each day, between the hours of eleven A. M. and twelve M., and see by actual observation if the cooking is properly done. The officer of the day will visit the camp after taps and see by personal inspection if the tents are properly ventilated, and will report in writing to these headquarters, to be handed in with the morning report of regiments, stating that these duties have been performed, and making such suggestions as his observation may dictate.

.    .    .    .    .    .    .    .    .    .

VIII. ... The coat should be buttoned, the hair kept short, and the belts should receive more attention in their adjustment. Citizens' clothing is hereby prohibited. The condition of the arms of some of the companies that have reported to these headquarters for duty as pickets has been scandalous, evincing no care or attention on the part of the officers with regard to the efficiency of their men.

IX. The books of regiments and companies will be regularly and neatly kept, in ink, and all reports will be signed by the proper person at the time they are made. Weekly inspections will be made, to see that these requirements have been observed. A file of all orders will be neatly kept by each company and regiment.

X. Battalions will be marched to and from drill in columns of platoons or sections.

XI. All orders will be read in the presence of the battalion at the next dress-parade following their receipt.

CAMP WICKLIFFE, KENTUCKY, Jan. 20, 1862.

Recitations in Evolutions of the Line (vol. iii. of Scott's " Infantry Tactics ") will commence this evening ; the first lesson commencing at the beginning of the book and extending to the bottom of page 31. The second lesson will extend to page 50, and each lesson after that will be twenty-five pages, — recitations to be held from six to seven P. M., at the quarters of the colonel commanding the brigade. The field-officers and their instructors are required to attend.

The non-commissioned officers of the entire command were also formed in sections for study and recitation; and recitations were held daily, Sundays excepted, beginning with the School of the Soldier (" Infantry Tactics "). The instructors reported in person to the regimental instructors for lessons, and at the end of each week they reported in writing, in such manner as to indicate progress for the week to their regimental instructors.

CAMP WICKLIFFE, KENTUCKY, Feb. 6, 1862.

I. Colonels of regiments will at once see that all officers in their commands, field and staff, sutlers and retainers about camp, are fully instructed in the division and brigade orders pertaining to the police and discipline of the camp. . . .

The foregoing faintly shadows the system of discipline and instruction applied to the various regiments that were assigned at different times to my command.

After passing some three months at Camp Wickliffe, beset with camp diseases, especially diarrhœa and measles, — the latter singularly fatal, — we marched to the mouth of Salt River, and there took boat down the Ohio, to join the campaign against Fort Donelson, but before arriving at Paducah learned of the capitulation.

We here found General W. T. Sherman in command. I met him for the first time. He detached Fitch's and Slack's regiments from my brigade, — by what authority I never knew, — and I never saw them again.

We met here a portion of the prisoners captured at Fort Donelson, and among them General Buckner and his staff. They were the first men I had seen in Confederate uniform. General Sherman and I went on board the steamer to see Buckner, and found him with his officers sitting upon the floor of the cabin, against the side of the boat. I had known him in the army very well. He was a man of many fine qualities, and I confess I was touched at seeing him our prisoner. As I met him, he exclaimed, "Well, Hazen, have you come, too, to subjugate us?"

The meeting was destitute of any element of cordiality, — a few cold words only passing between Sherman and Buckner, — the latter taking Sherman to task for opposing peaceable secession, who replied that the Southern people had no right to seize the public property, and that they must not expect submission. I was not agreeably impressed by the meeting, and a regretful feeling was left upon my mind, which always recurs whenever I think of it.

We went up the Cumberland to Nashville, arriving at and taking possession of the city early one Sunday morning. The Rebel army had retreated, but the people showed great bitterness. As I rode through the city, a little distance in front of the brigade, and had just turned a corner, a lady in handsome toilet stamped vigorously upon the sidewalk and cheered for Jeff Davis. At that moment the command, which she had not before seen, filed around the corner, with its splendidly cadenced step and glistening arms, when she betook herself at double-quick to the nearest house. I halted at the St. Cloud Hotel, and was met by the hospitable and well-remembered host, Mr. Carter, who invited me and my staff, his first Union guests, to his scanty bar. He tasted everything first himself, in order, as he said, to assure us. Upon his register was a single name of our men, who had preceded us. It was that of William Babcock, of Illinois, a cousin I had not seen since a child of three years, and never since. We found in the hotel, fast asleep and very drunk, one Rebel soldier, the largest man I ever saw in uniform. As I sent him away with a single guard, he looked like a veritable giant guarded by a pygmy; and we all wondered if he was a sample of the men we were about to encounter.

I was at this time just past thirty years of age. I was strong, and my heart was in the work, both from patriotism and professional zeal. I never tasted liquors, and gave the work my utmost powers. It is now a matter of surprise that the officers of the command, with so very few exceptions, gave such loyal and absolute support to what was so necessary, — although it must have seemed arbitrary, — the rigor employed in bringing the command to the high state of discipline and efficiency it attained. It is certain that the American citizen, properly commanded and instructed, makes the best soldier in the world. This is due mainly to his intelligence, perfect amenability to the highest discipline, and to his full appreciation of its necessity.

The Sixth Ohio was now ordered to the brigade, and military duty in all its rigor was resumed, as will be seen by the following orders : —

CAMP ANDREW JACKSON, TENNESSEE, Feb. 27, 1862.

I. There will be bayonet exercise in all regiments of the brigade hereafter from nine to ten A. M., and battalion drill from eleven to twelve.

II. There will be police-call sounded at four P. M., when the entire brigade will assemble and the regimental grounds be thoroughly policed under direction of the officer of the day.

III. The officers of the Sixth Ohio Volunteers will be drilled by the lieutenant-colonel of the regiment, those of the Sixth Kentucky Volunteers by the major, and those of the Forty-first Ohio Volunteers by Captain Cole. Officers' drill, until further orders, will be that of skirmishers, and during such time the non-commissioned officers will also be assembled with them. None are excused from the above duties, unless by the surgeon or by reason of other duty. Sergeants will be detailed from the Forty-first Ohio Volunteers, to instruct in the bayonet exercise, on application of the commanders of other regiments. . . .

While at Nashville, we were very busily engaged with drills and in preparation for moving forward. It was here that the Ninth Indiana was assigned to the brigade. It was commanded by Colonel Gideon C. Moody, a most gallant officer. He was a captain in the regular army, and until very recently was United States District Judge at Deadwood, Dakota. The regiment had for its first colonel, General Milroy, a graduate of Captain Patridge's Military School at Norwich, Vermont, and I naturally expected more of it in the way of accurate soldiership than from the other regiments. On the contrary, it was not only far behind the others, but seemed fixed in many vicious habits, acquired while in the three months' service in Western Virginia. To correct this, some severity was indispensable; and in exercising it, while most of the officers gave ready support, a very few took umbrage, which they still entertain.

The following is about the first salutation the new regiment received: —

CAMP ANDREW JACKSON, TENNESSEE, March 6, 1862.

Colonel Ninth Indiana Volunteers (newly assigned):

The colonel commanding the Ninth Indiana Volunteers will take the orders of his division and brigade, and the Army Regulations and Tactics, as his invariable guides in the performance of all military duties. In order to facilitate his success in the duties of a regimental commander, he will convene all the officers of his regiment each evening and read to them these orders, the Articles of War, and the Regulations of the Army, until they are properly understood by all. In order that the drill may be taught successfully and correctly, he will notify his regiment what portion of the Tactics will be employed on drill from day to day, and caution the officers to study such parts. His attention is called to the "Manual of the Sword, or Sabre, for Officers," on page 190 of "Revised Tactics," and will see that his officers are made conversant with it. His attention is also called to the subject of "Color Guard," page 10 of "Revised Tactics," and he will immediately establish his guard in conformity with these instructions, placing the colors in ranks where prescribed.

He will also cause his regimental officer of the day to instruct
the sentinels of the police-guard in their duties, strictly in conformity with the Regulations, their first duty being to walk
their post, which few of them are in the habit of doing. He
will also take measures to prevent any further shouting, such as
was faintly heard on the return of the regiment from the execution yesterday. He is also reminded that marching of regiments
by flank, unless to pass defiles, is prohibited.

CAMP NEAR SPRING HILL, TENNESSEE, March 24, 1862.

Squad drills will be resumed to-morrow. The Forty-first Ohio
Volunteers from 8 to 9 A. M., the Ninth Indiana Volunteers from
9 to 10.30, and the Sixth Kentucky Volunteers from 10.30
to 12 M. The entire regiments will be formed at the hours specified, by the acting-assistant adjutant-general, without arms,
and told off in squads. The field-officers will superintend these
drills, and will not leave the grounds while their regiments
are drilling.

CAMP NEAR SPRING HILL, TENNESSEE, March 28, 1862.

. . . . . . . . . . .

V. Hereafter Captains Wiley and Opdycke, Forty-first Ohio
Volunteers, at squad drills will not take squads, but will move
rapidly among the squads and see that the letter of the Tactics is
rigidly observed.

From here we marched to Pittsburg Landing, where,
with the exception of the Ninth Indiana, already veteran,
we were to receive our "baptism of fire." Arriving at
Duck River, we halted five days for the leading division,
McCook's, to build a bridge; but at the end of that time,
becoming impatient, General Nelson asked permission to
cross by fording, and in doing so took the advance of the
army, which we kept through the entire march.

The men were new to war, and I confess to have had
some anxiety as to what their conduct would be in battle;
but that was soon dispelled. They knew nothing of taking

cover, and at Shiloh they went into the fight with an impetuousness I never saw equalled afterward. The splendid part we took in the action will be described in the chapter specially devoted to it. The brigade opened the battle the second day, or what may be more properly called Buell's battle, and made the most obstinate and persistent attack and charge of that day, losing more men in fair fight than any other brigade. This charge was the first really serious blow at the turning of the battle, and was the beginning of victory. History will not fail to give the army commanded by General Buell the full measure of praise for its vital part in that battle. No discussion upon that point is necessary, nor can it change the facts and final verdict.

# CHAPTER III.

## SHILOH.

TWO days before reaching Savannah, a small town on the Tennessee River, ten miles below Pittsburg Landing, on our march from Nashville to join the Army of the Tennessee, we met the construction party of the telegraph line, and received at the same time a despatch from General Grant, directed to the " Officer in Command of the Advance of General Buell's Army," stating: "There is no need of haste; come on by easy marches." This despatch was handed me and read, and then sent to General Nelson, who commanded the division. We arrived within a mile of Savannah about noon, on the 5th of April; and at about seven A. M. of the 6th, after moving down to the town, were startled by the sound of battle. Our first orders were to advance at once; but afterward we were directed to take rations for three days, and wait till further orders. These orders were not received till one P. M. We then moved rapidly on the east side of the river to a point opposite Pittsburg Landing, and arrived there between four and five P. M. At that time shot, both large and small, were passing over our heads from the battlefield on the opposite side. Crossing began at once, Ammen's brigade leading, followed by Bruce's. There appeared to be no well-organized line of our troops opposing the enemy here, and the men of our division were put in line on the left of the Army of the Tennessee, touching Hurlbut's left, as fast as they reached the western bank. Exactly at twenty minutes past five our troops that were in line began firing, and they continued till a few minutes past seven, when the conflict ceased for the day.

My brigade, being the last of the three to cross, did not get over till after dark. We were posted on the right of the division, about three hundred or four hundred yards from the landing. On our arrival, and until dark, a great number of dispersed men of the Army of the Tennessee were congregated about the landing, occupying a cleared space of twenty or thirty acres; while a continuous stream of men, a rod or more in breadth, was pressing rapidly down that bank of the river and under its shelter. The boats returning to our side seemed to bring back as many of these men as they carried over of our own. At about eight P. M. General Buell called together the principal officers of our division, and in a few admirably chosen words briefly sketched the condition of the battle, and his plan of attack in the morning. His ideas were most forcibly expressed, and carried with them confidence in our work next day. I have always ascribed to them much of our great success; nothing in the war impressed me more. We stood at our arms all through the night, which was rainy, and in the midst of the debris of unkempt and unpoliced camps, while the wails of the wounded, but a short distance away in our front, were constantly heard. I passed the night by the side of an oak-tree, holding my horse, and tormented by the disgusting smells of old camps moistened by the rains.

At the break of day we moved forward, being on the right of the division. We had not gone a hundred yards before we came to the corpses of the killed of the day before; and I particularly remember that among the first I saw was the dead body of Lieutenant-Colonel Kirkpatrick, of the Chicago Artillery. After advancing from one to two miles, the skirmishers of the Sixth Kentucky, of my brigade, engaged those of the enemy. This was the beginning of this day's battle. Those of the Ninth Indiana were very quickly engaged also; but we pushed on, the pickets of the enemy retiring for about a half-mile, when our skirmishers drew the fire of a regiment and then halted, the main line moving up to near the same position. The enemy had already opened upon us with artillery, with slight effect. Soon after, perhaps at half-past seven o'clock, the Ninth Indiana was thrown forward to a clump of log houses and against a fence, to engage a battery on the far edge of the field, we being at its eastern side. They soon became sharply engaged with the enemy's infantry. The fight continued an hour or more, and the regiment lost heavily. The enemy then retired out of infantry range; but his artillery kept active, and he was evidently trying to get on our right flank. The Sixth Kentucky was sent to check him, and other parts of the brigade went to support Bartlett's and Mendenhall's batteries on our right and front. This movement caused something more than a half-face to the right of my entire command. Desultory fighting continued till nearly noon, when the enemy in continuous lines could be plainly seen, about a thousand yards in my new front, preparing for a formal attack. My brigade was at once put in readiness to meet him, changing its direction still more to the right. It was not ready too soon, for at the moment the movement was completed the enemy were seen and heard advancing with shrill yells. Generals Buell and Nelson were both just in the rear of my brigade, and the preparations for attack occupied their attention. General Buell himself gave the command to advance, which I at once repeated, and the brigade all moved off with determination, except four companies of the Sixth Kentucky, which did not advance, but became confused and broken. Its colonel failed to get them started; when Major Wright, of

LIEUTENANT CHRISTOPHER C. PECK

(Sixth Ohio.)

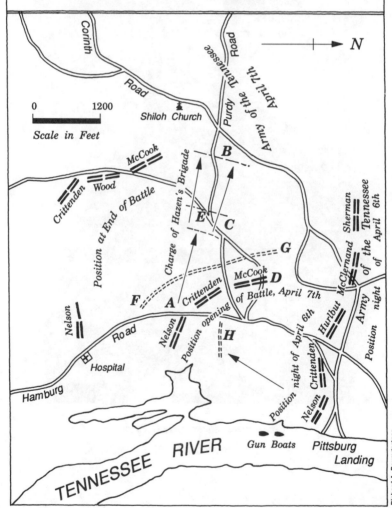

# POSITION OF BUELL'S TROOPS
## *at*
# SHILOH.

**A** *Beginning of Charge, 19th Brigade (Hazen).*
**B** *Ending of Charge.*
**C** *Field with high Fence.*
**D** *King's Brigade.*
**E** *Cemetery of Forty-first Ohio Volunteers.*
**F & G** *Confederate line at beginning of Charge.*
**H** *Confederate Pickets, morning of April 7th.*

Corinth Road

Tennessee Road

Purdy Road

Army of the April 7th

N

0      1200
Scale in Feet

Shiloh Church

McCook

Crittenden    Wood

Position at End of Battle

Charge of Hazen's Brigade

B

E    C

G

Sherman

Army of the Tennessee
of April 6th

Nelson

Road

Position opening of Battle, April 7th

Crittenden    McCook    D

F    A

H

Hospital

Hamburg

McClernand

Hurlbut

Army of the Tennessee
Position night of April 6th

Nelson    Crittenden

Gun Boats    Pittsburg
Landing

TENNESSEE RIVER

Richard A. Baumgartner

General Buell's staff, and myself, both spurred our horses in front of them, and shouted to them to follow. They did so, and very quickly regained their proper place in line. I still continued in front, and led my brigade until the line became broken up by the thick undergrowth ; and in all the rest of the charge — at least one half-mile — I was with the foremost men.

The firing began in earnest after we had advanced a few hundred yards, and the battle was terrific, and continued so through the woods and over the country, for about a mile in all, till we could go no farther. We had met the enemy fairly, and had run over such of them as were not shot down or had not escaped. Captain Soulé, of the Louisiana Infantry, directly in my path, had been slightly wounded, but showed fight ; and one of my men was in the act of running him through with his bayonet, when, seizing his shoulder, I drew the soldier back. The captain whose life had been saved promised to report to the rear. In the same manner we left a great number of prisoners whom I never heard of afterward ; but I presume they were gathered up by the troops behind us. We had kept on, stopping for nothing, till we pushed up to and captured a battery, and still beyond, where we came upon a new line of the enemy. We here received an enfilading fire of shrapnel from our left, and more than a third of the brigade were disabled. Others went back to aid the wounded, so that there was the merest scattering of men at the front. The officers I remember seeing there were Colonel Whitaker, Sixth Kentucky ; Captain Opdycke, Forty-first Ohio ; and Lieutenants Beebe and Gaylord, of my staff. My adjutant-general, Kimberly, had been previously wounded, and left behind. There were, of course, many officers present, but the line of three regiments extended far beyond sight ; besides, in the charge the troops had opened out considerably to the right and left.

On reaching the new line of the enemy the advance stopped, and what remained of the command went back as fast as it could go, and without the semblance of formation. My staff and myself did all we could to rally the men, and they were perfectly willing to stop; but as fast as one group was left, while attention was given to others the first would move to the rear, and so everything went back in utter disorder. On coming to a large field, directly in our line of retreat, I could see our men swarming across it. Many went round it, as I did myself, fearing that my horse could not leap the fence. This field was surrounded on all sides by a dense undergrowth; and in moving on, as I supposed, in the right direction, I lost my course, and did not see the main body of my brigade till late in the afternoon.

I will describe very carefully everything connected with this circumstance, for it has been made the occasion of a ridiculous misrepresentation of the facts, and the basis of a charge that I was unjustifiably absent from my command.

Colonel Bruce, commanding the brigade on my left, was ordered to support that flank. He describes in his report what he did, as follows. He did not continue far with me in the charge, but it will be seen that he changed front to the right to conform to my direction. He says: —

" After the engagement became general, the colonel commanding the brigade was ordered to assist the Nineteenth Brigade (Colonel Hazen). He ordered the First Kentucky Regiment to change direction to the right, and advance to the support of Colonel Hazen's left. The regiment sustained a galling fire of grape and canister while carrying out these orders. The Twentieth Kentucky was ordered up to support the First Kentucky in this movement, which it did under a very severe fire. Both these regiments deserve the highest commendations for the manner in which they executed their orders."

Colonel William Sooey Smith's brigade, of Crittenden's division, was on my right, and was ordered forward also ; but he did not change front to conform to my direction, and, moving more slowly than I did, passed entirely across my track and in rear of my brigade, and caused for a time great consternation by firing into the rear of our line. I sent two members of my staff successively to request him to cease firing till we had passed beyond his front. The following passage is taken from his report : —

"The brigade, after having bivouacked during the night of the 6th instant on the hill near Pittsburg Landing, was put in motion at six A. M. on the 7th, and marched to the front, and placed in position in prolongation of the line of General Nelson's division, then hotly engaged. . . . The enemy's skirmishers retired, and all was quiet in front of our line for nearly one nour, when our skirmishers again engaged those of the enemy, and this was soon followed by a serious attack upon our whole front. The right recoiled, while the left and centre stood firm. The Twenty-sixth Kentucky was then sent forward to support our right, and a heavy cross-fire to our front was opened from Bartlett's battery, which was in position on our right. The enemy soon yielded, when a running fight commenced, which extended for about one mile to our front, where we captured a battery and shot the horses and many of the cannoneers. Owing to the obstructed nature of the ground, the enthusiastic courage of the majority of our men, the laggard discharge of their duty by many, and the disgraceful cowardice of some, our line had been transformed into a column of attack, representing the various grades of courage, from reckless daring to ignominious fear.

"At the head of this column stood a few heroic men, not adequately supported, when the enemy returned to the attack with three fresh regiments in good order. We were driven back by these nearly to the first position occupied by our line."

The distance gained by Colonel Smith compares very accurately with my estimate of that gained by us, and he

was evidently confronted and driven back by part of the
same line, and far to the left of it. But the conflict bore
slight comparison with that which my men engaged in,
since he, with four regiments, lost in the entire battle but
188 men, while my losses, in three regiments, were 399
men. That part of the battlefield, as is well known, excepting the farm, was a dense thicket, through which had
been cut a great number of roads, all leading out from the
landing to the various camps, diverging like the spokes of
a wheel; but there were no cross-roads  We were a great
distance in front of our line, and the firing had temporarily
ceased along the centre, but was heavy on both flanks; and
I mistook the direction of the left flank, where I intended
to go, for that of the right flank, where I did go.  Captain
Opdycke, afterward Brevet Major-General Opdycke, and
well known to the country for his services at Franklin,
and myself kept together.  There were a great number of
our men scattered through the woods going in the same
direction.  We continued on as it seemed a long time, and
came upon a road which we were told by a teamster led in
the direction of Crump's Landing.  This was the first clew
to our position.  We then turned directly to the right,
and soon came near a line of mounted troops still upon
our right hand, who fired upon us, and proved to be the
enemy.  We then proceeded in a direction away from
the enemy, and very soon came to troops massed and at
rest.  They proved to be some battalions of regulars under
Major John H. King, — now General King, retired, —
belonging to Rousseau's brigade, of McCook's division.
After a short conversation with King, and getting our
proper direction as well as he could give it, we again
set out to find our own troops, by seeking a road which
King said was near, that would take us where they probably were.  But the great number of roads all alike left
us in as much uncertainty as before.  Supposing we

GENERAL EMERSON OPDYCKE

(Lieutenant and Captain, Forty-first Ohio;
Colonel One Hundred Twenty-fifth Ohio.)

GENERAL WALTER C. WHITAKER

(Colonel Sixth Kentucky.)

were very near the landing, I determined to go there, and
then take the course we went over in the morning, to make
certain of no more mistakes ; but the landing proved to be
some three miles away ; and being mounted, while Opdycke
was on foot, I hurried on and saw no more of him till
I joined the brigade.  On this road I met successively
Dr. Murray, Medical Director of the Army, now Surgeon-
General, Captain Bush, of General Buell's staff, and, near
the landing, General Garfield, at the head of his brigade.
By the time I arrived at the landing the battle was virtually over.  I met there the servants of my command, who
were at their meals, and ate with them, — having eaten
nothing since the morning of the day before, — and here
dismounted for the first time since the battle opened.
Troops were disembarking who proved to be a brigade of
Wood's division, and with them were General Wood and
Captain Gillem.  I then mounted and rode out on the
Hamburg road, the one near which we had marched in
the morning.  In going out I met Lieutenant Peck, of the
Sixth Ohio, acting commissary to the division, until lately
living at Maple Creek, Nebraska ; and farther on, Colonel
Fry, afterward Provost-Marshal-General, now General Fry,
retired.  He was then Buell's chief-of-staff.  Upon a little
rough map he pointed out where my brigade was re-
forming, and I at once joined it and made dispositions
for the night.  The men continued to come in all that
evening and night and the next day.

The accompanying map is accurately reduced from the
official map of the battlefield made from surveys under
direction of an engineer officer of the army, and may be
assumed to be correct.  All that is added is the charge of
my brigade and the approximate position of the enemy
at the moment of that charge.  But of the accuracy of the
representation of the ground passed over in the charge there
is no doubt.  The large field at B, the first we crossed in the

charge, where our slaughter of the enemy was frightful, and where our own loss chiefly occurred, is at once recognizable, as is the one at *C*, along which the new line of the enemy formed, which checked and terminated our forward movement. The three houses at *E* were the best-known and most distinctively marked feature of the battlefield, and it was there the dead of my regiment (the Forty-first Ohio) were buried. The spot has since been visited by many of the friends of the dead, and is a point in our advance thoroughly well known. The distance passed over, as shown here, agrees accurately with my official estimate of it (one mile), and as nearly as would be reasonable to expect with that of the very many others who have stated it, — that it was from three fourths of a mile to a mile. In closely studying this field, and the official records of the battle, I find that I have always been in error as to the point where Opdycke and myself came upon our line in falling back. I always believed it was between Crittenden and McCook; but in drawing this map I see it was quite to the right of McCook, and between him and the Army of the Tennessee. This will readily be seen from the map. In the retreat we came to the large field and fence somewhere near *B*, where we with many others passed to our left and into the dense woods toward *G*. Our own troops at *D*, which is the position of King's brigade, were the nearest, and were the troops we first came to. I had supposed that Crittenden's whole division moved forward when we did, because Smith's brigade, joining mine to the right, did so, and that it held the ground gained. But General Crittenden says in his report: " The enemy being driven from before us, our troops quietly and in order came back to their original position. I did not deem it right to advance my lines without an order from General Buell, lest I might expose the right of General Nelson, now pressed with a terrible conflict on my left." I learn from other reports that only Smith's brigade moved any considerable distance to the front at this time; and Smith's movement, as the direction of his front indicates on the map, was quite across the rear of my command. And it appears that he fell back also, probably bringing the prisoners we had left behind.

It will be seen that in moving forward we passed in a diagonal direction quite across Crittenden's front, and far in advance of McCook. It was about two P. M. when I reached the landing, and the battle was then over. General Beauregard says in his report, "About two o'clock P. M. the lines in advance which had repulsed the enemy received orders to retire." When my command had completed its charge, it was three fourths of a mile in advance of any troops on either flank, excepting Smith's brigade far to the left. The effect of that charge on the final result of the battle was very important. Colonel Whitaker, of my command, says in his report : —

To Colonel HAZEN, Commanding Nineteenth Brigade, General Nelson's Division.

At the battle of Pittsburg Landing the Sixth Kentucky, on the right, was put in advance on the night of the 6th of April, the Ninth Indiana on the left, and the Forty-first Ohio in reserve. At five o'clock on the morning of the 7th, line of battle was formed, and the fight began at half-past five, between the skirmishers of the Sixth Kentucky and the Ninth Indiana and the pickets of the enemy. The enemy's pickets were driven back, and at about six the action began between the enemy and the Ninth Indiana, which was gallantly sustained by them. At ten o'clock Mendenhall's battery, which had rendered efficient service, was assailed by a large force of the enemy. It was supported by three companies of the Sixth Kentucky, under command of Lieutenant-Colonel Cotton. They were severely pressed, and a charge was made by the remainder of the Sixth Regiment at the point of the bayonet, headed by Colonel

Whitaker and Adjutant Shackleford. The acting brigadier-general, Colonel Hazen, most gallantly accompanied them in the charge. The enemy were routed from their cover behind logs and trees with terrific slaughter. The pursuit and fight was continued by Colonel Hazen's brigade (Ninth Indiana and Forty-first Ohio Volunteers) until the enemy were driven beyond their batteries. The action was most hotly and vigorously contested by the Sixth Regiment. Captains Johnston, McLeod, Stein, and Hedden, and Lieutenant McGraw were wounded at the head of their companies.

I can personally bear testimony to the efficient service of your brigade (the Nineteenth) and General Nelson's division throughout the terrific fight.

W. C. WHITAKER,

*Colonel Sixth Kentucky Vol's.*

General Nelson says : —

HEADQUARTERS OF FOURTH DIVISION,

CAMP ON THE FIELD OF BATTLE, April 10, 1862.

. . . At four A. M. I roused up the men quietly by riding along the line, and when the line of battle was dressed and the skirmishers well out and the reserves in position, I sent an aide to notify the General that I was ready to commence the action, whereupon the Fourth Division of the Army of the Ohio, in perfect order as if on drill, moved toward the enemy. At 5.20 I found them, and the action commenced with vigor. My division drove them with ease, and followed them up rapidly, when at six A. M. I was halted by commands from General Buell, as I had gone farther forward than I should have done, and my right flank was exposed. . . . Colonel Hazen, commanding the right brigade of this division, carried it into action and maintained it there most gallantly. The heavy loss of his brigade attests the fierceness of the conflict at this point. He drove the enemy and captured the battery which so distressed us, but was forced back on his reserves. . . .

To Colonel Hazen, commanding the Nineteenth Brigade, I beg to invite the General's attention. The gallantry with which he led his troops to the attack was most conspicuous, and he

handled them ably. During the long and bloody action the fortitude of the Fourth Division was sorely tried, — pressed as it was
by such superior numbers, — but maintained itself gloriously.
I refer the General to the reports of the brigade commanders
for the part each regiment took in the action, reserving to myself only to mention that during the action I rode up and
thanked the Ninth Indiana Regiment for its gallantry. . . .
The loss of this division, I regret to inform you, is heavy. It
went into action 4,541 strong, of whom 6 officers and 84
enlisted men were killed, 33 officers and 558 enlisted men
wounded, and 58 enlisted men missing; making a total loss of
739, more than half of which occurred in Hazen's brigade. . . .

W. NELSON,<br>
Brig.-Gen. Commanding Fourth Div.

General Buell says : —

HEADQUARTERS ARMY OF THE OHIO,<br>
FIELD OF SHILOH, April 15, 1862.

. . . Soon after five o'clock on the morning of the 7th General Nelson's and General Crittenden's divisions, the only ones
yet arrived on the ground, moved promptly forward to meet the
enemy. Nelson's division, marching in line of battle, soon came
upon his pickets, drove them in, and about six o'clock received
the fire of his artillery. . . .

In front of Nelson's division was an open field, partially
screened towards his right by a skirt of woods, which extended
beyond the enemy's line, with a thick undergrowth in front of
the left brigade of Crittenden's division ; then, an open field in
front of Crittenden's right and McCook's left ; and in front of
McCook's right, woods again, with a dense undergrowth. . . .

The obliquity of our line, the left being thrown forward,
brought Nelson's division first into action, and it became very
hotly engaged at an early hour. A charge of the Nineteenth
Brigade from Nelson's right, led by its commander, Colonel
Hazen, reached the enemy's second battery ; but the brigade sustained a heavy loss from the fire of the enemy's batteries, and
was unable to maintain its advantage against the heavy infantry force that came forward to oppose it. The enemy recovered

the battery and followed up his momentary advantage by throwing a heavy force of infantry into the woods in front of Crittenden's left. . . .

In the mean time the division of General McCook on the
right, which became engaged somewhat later in the morning
than the divisions on the left, had made steady progress until
it drove the enemy's left from the hotly contested field. The
action was commenced in this division by General Rousseau's
brigade, which drove the enemy in front of it from his first
position and captured a battery. The line of attack of this
division caused a considerable widening of the space between it
and Crittenden's right.        6 7 H

The brigades of General Wood's division arrived just at the
close of the battle, but only one of them (Colonel Wagner's) in
time to participate actively in the pursuit, which it continued
for about a mile, and until halted by my order. . . . The loss
of the forces under my command is 263 killed, 1,816 wounded,
88 missing; total, 2,167. . . .

For the many other officers who won honorable distinction,
I refer to the reports of the division, brigade, and regimental
commanders, transmitted herewith, as also for more detailed
information of the services of the different corps. I join cor-
dially in the commendations bestowed by those officers on those
under their command. . . .

D. C. BUELL, *Maj.-Gen. Commanding.*

There was no fighting by my command after I was separated from it, nor was the brigade in a condition to fight.
It had lost 399 men in killed and wounded. My brigade
suffered one fifth part of the entire loss in Buell's army,
forty-nine more casualties than occurred in Crittenden's
entire division, and twice the average of Buell's troops.
As many more had gone away with their wounded comrades, and the remainder were scattered.

When my conduct at Shiloh was called in question, the
soldiers of my command from every quarter of the land
spoke in unmistakable terms.

These letters were peculiarly touching, and a few of them will be given. They came from my own and other commands that fought at Shiloh, from officers and men of all grades, — from the paymaster who paid us, and the sanitary agent who carried home our dead and wounded, who had lived with us on the battlefield and in camp, and knew all that was done and heard all that was said. Their evidence is all alike sincere and truthful. Such unanimity, indignation, and cause for it I have never seen, for there was not the remotest cause for the accusation. I will first give General Opdycke's statement. Opdycke, it will be remembered, was with me all the time that day till I neared the river. He says : —

I was captain in the Forty-first Ohio Infantry, and acted as major of it at the battle of Shiloh, 1862. The regiment then formed a part of Hazen's brigade. This brigade met the enemy about sunrise, April 7th, was heavily engaged at short musket-range for several hours, and then made an effective assault, drove the enemy in disorder, and captured several pieces of artillery. The ground over which this charge was made was in the main covered by a dense growth of timber. From this cause, and from heavy losses in the fighting previous to the charge, the continuity of our line was necessarily broken. Unfortunately, no troops came to support us, and we were forced to yield to the advance of the enemy's second and solid line of battle. Not having anything with which to spike the captured guns, we rendered them useless during the remainder of the battle by ramming them with mud. I saw Hazen on horseback riding along his line encouraging his men by words and example during the whole of the fight and charge, and while retiring we were together in constant endeavor to rally the remnants of his command. E. OPDYCKE,
*Late Brevet Major-General Vol's.*

To show the estimates of General Opdycke by those who knew him best, I will add the following. An official

recommendation to promotion, indorsed by General George
H. Thomas, testifies : —

"At the battle of Franklin, Opdycke (formerly colonel of the
One Hundred and Twenty-fifth Ohio) displayed the very highest
qualities as a commander.   It is not saying too much to declare
that, but for the skilful dispositions made by General Opdycke
(all of which was done entirely on his own judgment), the
promptness and readiness with which he brought his command
into action at the critical and decisive moment, and the signal
personal gallantry he displayed in a counter-assault on the
enemy, when he had broken our lines, disaster instead of victory
would have fallen on us at Franklin."

ONEONTA, NEW YORK, April 17.

MY DEAR COLONEL, — . . . I know you were with the brigade
at Shiloh, when we charged the enemy's right, about one P. M.,
April 7th.   During all the time we were in reserve you sat on
your horse, at the right of the Forty-first, and were mounted
when your horse was struck.   Yourself, Nelson, and Buell were
all present when your brigade charged.   I saw you and spoke
with you as the remnants of the brigade fell back.   The brigade
was cut in pieces, and in retreat through the brush became scattered, so that the Forty-first, which held well together, had only
eighty-four men present when they halted and rallied ; and no
man of them ran away, but they did get lost for a time.

J. B. CLEVELAND,
Late Lieutenant Forty-first Ohio Vol's.

NEWPORT, KENTUCKY, April 19, 1879.
General W. B. HAZEN, New York City :

DEAR SIR, — . . . I can most positively swear that I saw you
in the charge, of which I have before spoken to you, between half-
past eleven and one o'clock.   This charge, you will remember,
was immediately preceded by a very severe action in which my
regiment (the Ninth Indiana) suffered its greatest loss.   I am
almost certain that you and Colonel Blake were the only
mounted officers with us at the time.   I know I saw no others ;

and when the concealed battery opened on us you were not over three rods in rear of my company. . . .

Truly yours,

FRANK P. GROSS,

*Late Captain Ninth Indiana Infantry,*

*now U. S. Army, Retired.*

NORTHFIELD, SUMMIT CO., OHIO, April 28, 1879.

General W. B. HAZEN, New York City:

DEAR SIR, — In regard to the battle of Shiloh, one incident may be overlooked, which might be of importance. You will probably recollect that you rode to the extreme front, after the brigade came to a stand. Companies E and K of the Forty-first were in the advance. I was a sergeant of Company K, Fred McKay a sergeant of Company E; there were no commissioned officers with us. The enemy had commenced firing on us from the steel-gun battery to the left and in front, and had just opened from another battery in front. You came up and passed a rod or two in front of us and observed the situation. As you returned I asked you if you had given the order to halt, as the rest of the regiment did not appear to come up. You replied, that the rear never could halt unless we halted first in front. I was near by and heard the directions you gave to the captain of the battery for dislodging the Rebels from the log house before the charge was made. Also saw you out on picket that evening.

I was discharged for disability, at Columbus, in December, 1862.        Yours respectfully,

A. L. BLISS.

WOOSTER, OHIO, April 12, 1879.

DEAR CAPTAIN, — Yours of the 31st ult. came duly to hand. I have had a press of matters on hand since, and have delayed answering longer than I should have done. I desired to refresh my memory by a reference to any available memoranda before answering your inquiries, but have not had time to do so. I will give you my off hand recollection of the events to which you refer. At the battle of Pittsburg Landing our brigade consisted

of the Ninth Indiana, Sixth Kentucky, and Forty-first Ohio
regiments. Shortly after daylight on Monday morning it was
formed for battle within about four hundred to six hundred
yards of the steamboat landing, and southwest of it. The order
of battle was the Ninth Indiana and Sixth Kentucky in the first
line, the Forty-first in the second line, and two hundred or
three hundred yards in rear of the Ninth and the Sixth Kentucky, in double column. We moved in a southerly direction in
the above order through open woods with some underbrush, but
not very dense, and over ground undulating but not very
unequal, for a distance of eight hundred or one thousand yards.
During this advance the skirmishers of the Ninth Indiana met
with some resistance, and at the distance above indicated, the
Ninth halted at a rail-fence at the edge of a wood with open
ground in their front, their skirmishers rallying on the regiment.
They seemed to have developed the enemy in some strength in
front, and they continued for about an hour and a half, say till
about nine or half-past nine o'clock, tolerably briskly engaged.
During this time the Forty-first Ohio lay about two hundred
yards in rear of the Ninth in line of battle, and the Sixth Kentucky about the same distance in rear of the Forty-first, and in
double column. About this time a Rebel battery opened on our
right flank, and kept up a desultory firing for some time, say
half an hour, but overshooting us ; then a scattering infantry-
fire reached us from the same direction. At this time Lieutenant-
Colonel Mygatt received an order from Hazen to change the
front of the Forty-first in that direction. Mygatt told me to
make the change, and I gave the command, "Change front to
rear on the left company," and it was executed. This brought
the Forty-first in line facing west, as I think, and at right angles
with and in rear of the left of the Ninth Indiana. I am not
certain whether we rested in that position, or advanced till we
came in rear of and at right angles with the right of the Ninth,
and then halted and rested. My impression is that we then
waited for twenty or thirty minutes expecting an attack. General Hazen gave an order for the Forty-first to advance. It
moved to the front in line of battle, and, as I think, in a westerly

direction, through open woods with some underbrush, but not very dense, and over tolerably unequal ground, for a distance of six hundred or eight hundred yards, under a very heavy and effective fire, when I ordered it to halt and fire by file. This was, I think, about ten or half-past ten o'clock. I think at this time the Sixth Kentucky had changed direction also, and had been deployed in line of battle and was supporting us about two hundred or three hundred yards in our rear. When the Forty-first halted, it was receiving an exceedingly destructive fire from a line of infantry then not more than one hundred and fifty to two hundred yards in our front, in a slight depression of the ground, and in a wooded country. After returning their fire vigorously for twenty or thirty minutes, I gave the command for the regiment to cease firing and to advance, which it did. At that time I noticed Captain Opdycke in advance of Company C, with the colors in his hands, leading the advance. I went to the front and took them from him and was leading in person, when I was shot down. We had not then advanced more than fifty yards from the position where the Forty-first had halted to deliver its fire. After I fell, which I think must have been about eleven o'clock, the Forty-first continued to advance, followed by the Sixth Kentucky. Having at the beginning of the advance, after the change of front above described, moved off at right angles from the Ninth Indiana, I did not again see it in the fight. Shortly after the Sixth Kentucky had passed me after halting, I was carried to the rear, and I saw no more of the brigade.

During all the morning up to the time I was hit, General Hazen directed all movements of the troops, except the halt my regiment made to open fire, which I myself ordered, as the fire we were receiving was so destructive that I feared we could not continue the advance. During the time we lay in rear of the Ninth Indiana I saw him up at the front line reconnoitring the front, while the Ninth was engaged. He afterwards gave the order for the change of front of the Forty-first, when the artillery-fire indicated the probability of an attack from that direction. He gave the order to advance after the change of front, and followed it in person on horseback, attended by his staff.  I remember him as riding back and forth all the morning, from one part of the command to another, with a little switch [rattan] in his hand, that I think did more to inspire his command with coolness and firmness than the most imposing weapon would have done.  It was my first engagement, and I did n't feel any too solid myself, and I remember distinctly that the sight of that switch steadied me. . . .

Yours truly,

AQUILA WILEY,<br>
Late Colonel Forty-first Ohio Infantry,<br>
and Brev. Brig. Gen.

Captain BEEBE.

No. 53 K STREET N. E., WASHINGTON CITY, D. C.,<br>
April 20, 1879.

General W. B. HAZEN :

DEAR GENERAL, —. . . As to your conduct at Shiloh, I remember you as we were moving into position, from the fact of an unexploded shell knocking one of my men down.  It was picked up and shown to you, when you told the man to throw it away.  I think I saw you when Patton (Adjutant of Ninth Indiana) was killed.  You were always, whenever I saw you, either at Shiloh or elsewhere, perfectly calm and seemingly without fear; and it was a subject of remark in our regiment that whilst the men did not like you in camp on account of your strictness of discipline, they always had the utmost confidence in you in battle. . . .

Most respectfully and truly your friend,

W. P. LASSELLE,<br>
Late Lieut.-Colonel Ninth Indiana.

CLEVELAND, OHIO, Aug. 22, 1880.

DEAR GENERAL, — During the long period since the war — that era from which all time is reckoned in my calendar — I can recall but one casual meeting with you.  I have often thought of sending to you a brief statement of the battle of Shiloh as I saw it and can recall it.  A recent meeting with some of the surviving members of the old brigade confirmed this purpose.

To my young children the great war is a far-away tragedy ; to all of us it remains a more or less confused but intensely pathetic reminiscence ; to me personally it is the one colossal and over-shadowing episode in my obscure and otherwise uneventful life. To be garrulous is a privilege conceded to the "broken soldier" from immemorial time. So I shall write freely to my old com-mander.

At the time of the trial in New York I went so far as to draft a letter to you, detailing what little I knew touching the matters under consideration ; but as the reports seemed to indicate that the main reliance was on the testimony of officers of some rank, and as it seemed probable that there would be available abundant testimony concerning the only matters on which I could throw any light, I delayed forwarding it. After mature consideration, at this late date I have decided to send it, and only regret that I cannot speak from a recollection less misty and uncertain.

You may have forgotten me entirely ; indeed, this is quite probable, when we consider the length of time that has elapsed since the war, and the inconspicuous position held by me in your command. To refresh your memory, I will state that I was a private soldier in Company A, Forty-first Ohio Volunteer Infantry, until after Stone River, when I was commissioned. In Colonel Wiley's official report of the battle of Chickamauga I was honored with a special mention for meritorious service (see his official report appended to yours, Putnam's Rebellion Record, vol. vii. p. 239). I was selected as one of the officers, and was wounded in the affair at Brown's Ferry. This may suffice to establish my identity in your mind.

At Shiloh I was in the ranks. My recollections of the inci-dents of the battle are necessarily confused. Concerning points of the compass, time of day, and other such matters, my conclu-sions would be wholly untrustworthy, — in fact, the merest guesswork ; and, from the nature of things, my observations were confined to a limited field. But you well know how, in times of extraordinary excitement and tumult, particular inci-dents arrest the attention and become fixed in memory. Where

and under what circumstances I saw you at Shiloh I will try
to explain to you. It would not surprise me in the least to
learn that the particular circumstances that impressed me so
powerfully had faded wholly from your mind. It is but a few
weeks since a member of my company wrote to me about a
pension matter, stating that I was within three feet of him when
he was wounded ; but to my serious annoyance, I could not recall
the faintest reminiscence of the case. Thus, in the tumult of
the moment, a matter of supreme importance in his personal experience appears to have left no lasting impression upon me.
Why we sometimes have a vivid recollection of trivial matters,
while occurrences obviously more noteworthy are wholly forgotten, is something not easily explained ; we only know that it is so.

While the first line of our brigade was engaged (the Ninth
Indiana Regiment was in our front, I think), a body of Confederate troops appeared, advancing through the thicket upon our
right flank. The regiment changed front to rear upon the left
company, to meet the attack. The movement was barely completed when firing began, and the brigade moved forward
to the charge. The enemy gave ground rapidly. How far we
advanced, or in what direction, I cannot tell. It was a wild
pursuit, for a long distance, over a rough country. We loaded
and fired as we ran. All semblance of organization was lost in
the grand rush. Probably a change of direction took place early
in the advance which tended to complicate matters still more
and complete the disorder in the ranks. The flying enemy must
have suffered severely in crossing an open field in full view.
We followed on ; how far, I cannot form any correct idea. It
must have been quite a distance, for I know that I was completely exhausted. It was my first battle, and I can now recall the wild exultation of the moment, when it seemed to me
that the whole Southern Confederacy was racing through the
thicket before us. I remember emerging upon a commanding
piece of ground and seeing the plain below covered with fugitives
rallying behind a line of battle, in front of a row of tents. Officers were riding up and down the line, waving swords and shouting. I cannot say whether their main line was advancing, or

had stopped to rally the fugitives. I turned and looked about me, and found myself almost alone. The onward movement had spent its force, and the inevitable reaction had come. The scattered command drifted back, under a terrible fire of grape-shot. At the top of the hill I saw you sitting on your horse, looking at the enemy's line, as I have described it. Whether you were alone, or accompanied by staff-officers, I do not know. It is my impression that you were nearly alone. I remember raising my musket and giving a faint hurrah, or something of the kind, and you said, "Fall back, men, to a new line!" You turned and rode back, and I continued my retreat, without the remotest idea where I should find my command, which seemed to have wholly disappeared. Our command was not again engaged. It was re-formed near the point at which the charge commenced, if I am not mistaken, and in the evening went on outpost duty.

Summing up my recollections of the battle, I conclude that, utterly carried away by the unwonted excitement, I advanced beyond almost any of the command; and I distinctly saw you, and personally saluted or addressed you, at the extreme front when our part in the battle ended, and on the very spot where the head of the disordered column rolled back after the long charge. On this point I am not mistaken. The whole scene is as vivid before my mind as an occurrence of yesterday. Deprived of the inspiration of the presence of numbers and the magnetic touch of the elbow, I can recall with what a painful feeling of isolation and despair I commenced my flight. Nearly or quite one half of my company engaged had been killed or wounded.

In this sketch I could only bring out what I wished to communicate to you by entering into little personal details trivial in themselves; but this you will readily understand. Perhaps you will find nothing in it to interest you specially, or to throw light upon the story of the battle; but such as it is I submit it for your consideration, in the sincere hope that you may find it of some use.

I remain, General, with high regard, your obedient servant,

CHARLES W. HILLS,

*Late Second Lieutenant Forty-first Ohio Vol's.*

The following statement is by Captain James McMahon, of Cleveland : —

"We were halted on the roadside, and three days' rations were issued to us. We were every moment expecting an order to fall in for the scene of action; but for some cause unknown to me (although our division seemed ready) none was received until about one o'clock, when we fell in and marched, arriving on the bank of the Tennessee River, opposite the battle-ground, about six P. M. After some preliminaries, a little side-wheel steamboat came across and ferried us over. When we landed on the other side the bank seemed steep and high, but in terraces where whole companies could lie under cover from the firing above. The men were so thick we had to pass single file up through, they using such expressions as, — 'You'll catch it on the hill;' 'I am the only one left of my company;' 'This little squad is all that is left of our regiment;' and many similar remarks. We got on the hill, and by nine or ten o'clock at night General Nelson's division was in line to attack the enemy at daylight, we lying on our arms all night, a heavy rain pouring down on us. But we lay there till daylight, when the enemy was attacked. This battlefield was so filled with heavy timber and under-scrub oak that in some places a man could not see all of his own regiment. Our regiment lay in reserve till about two o'clock, when we heard the Rebels coming toward us, yelling, 'Bull Run! Bull Run!' About ten or fifteen minutes before this, General Hazen and staff rode to our regiment, and stood there for some time talking to the officers. . . . About this time, or very soon after, we heard the yelling mentioned; and I can't say now which general (Hazen or Nelson) gave the order to charge, but my impression is it was Hazen. At all events, we charged with four hundred and fifty men of our regiment, and made the Bull Run the other way; but it cost us one hundred and forty of said number killed and wounded. The enemy was then or soon after retreating. I did not see the general again till about five or six P. M., when he came along leading his brigade, and marched us out on a clearing, where we camped for the night. It again rained very heavily all night. We were without tents or blankets. Our brigade was complimented by other troops for our good fighting. I never heard of Hazen losing his brigade or being away from it during the fight of the 7th of April, 1862."

This story of misconduct, one utterly without truth, was never heard of till ten years after the war. But since that time, whenever I have had an adversary he always repeats the falsehood.

The battle of Shiloh will be a fruitful theme for criticism as long as the events of our Civil War remain of interest to mankind. There are a few facts connected with it that will form the leading topics of this criticism. The first and chief will be that a co-operating army arrived at the point of concentration in front of an enterprising enemy with which it was expected to fight, and remained there waiting the arrival of the other army for some days, with a broad and deep river running parallel to the line. The questions will naturally arise, why that army did not take advantage of the river as an obstacle, instead of going into camp on the enemy's side; why the different divisions of this isolated force were not posted with some relation to mutual defence; why there were no works erected in its front; why there were no roads cut, in rear of and parallel to the line, through the thick undergrowth, for easy inter-communication and support; and especially, why the front of that army was not thoroughly reconnoitred.

The question whether our men were surprised seems scarcely to merit attention. The facts covering this point are well known, and all that remains is to define the military meaning of "a surprise." This ought not to be difficult, for it simply means so sudden and unexpected an appearance of an enemy as to compel a force to act under disadvantages such as might have been averted by timely knowledge of his presence; as, for instance, to surrender, to retreat precipitately with loss of material, or to accept

battle without having made every preparation and to
have secured the greatest chances of success. What
would constitute a surprise to a force depends much upon
its size and functions. A picket must see the enemy the
first moment he can be seen, so that he can fire his piece,
warn the picket reserve, or do whatever his special instructions require of him.

For a detachment, time is necessary to call in the patrols, and prepare for such resistance as is expected of it;
and for an army, time to call in its detachments, to adjust
its lines, prepare its front for battle, send its trains and
sutlers to the rear, and all non-combatants and unnecessary property away from the front, and to learn from
scouts, deserters, and reconnoissances the enemy's position
and intentions. To do this, an army must actually control
and occupy, by patrols and other light troops, a considerable territory in its front; so that when the enemy approaches there will be sufficient time to communicate
from the front to the main army, and to permit all these
preparations before the enemy can pass over the same
distance.

In short, if a hostile force secretly places itself where
it can force a battle before all this can be done, and the
troops can in all respects make themselves ready, then a
surprise is effected.

At Shiloh, officers' horses were captured at the picket
line, their blankets were taken by the enemy, and the
sutlers' supplies played an important part by tempting
the enemy.

# CHAPTER IV.

## AFTER SHILOH.

AFTER the smoke of battle cleared away, and the dead were buried, drills were resumed, and every preparation made to move in the direction of the enemy. Pope's army was joined to our own, and Halleck assumed command of all. The routine of our work can be best understood by means of the orders that directed it.

BATTLEFIELD OF SHILOH, April 17, 1862.

.    .    .    .    .    .    .    .

II. The officers of the Twenty-seventh Kentucky Volunteers (newly assigned) will be exercised the first hour of drill daily by Lieutenant Cobb, of the Forty-first Ohio Volunteers.

III. The brigade officer of the day is charged especially with the duty of seeing that all drills are promptly attended, and will himself be present at the roll-calls to see personally that all are present.

FIELD OF SHILOH, April 18, 1862.

.    .    .    .    .    .    .    .

II. The hours of drill of officers of the Twenty-seventh Kentucky Volunteers will be from eight to nine A.M.

III. There will be a drill of drill-masters of other regiments at the same hour. They will be formed and marched to headquarters.

FIELD OF SHILOH, April 21, 1862.

Paragraph Number 734, page 106, of Army Regulations, will be read at each evening parade for the next four days; and any one hereafter on the field violating this paragraph will be reported and punished as a skulker.

In Camp, April 30, 1862.

I. It having come to the notice of the colonel commanding the brigade that a portion of the ceremony of guard-mounting is omitted by all the regiments, in positive disobedience to general orders from the headquarters of the army, and it appearing that the regimental adjutants and officers of the day are either ignorant of their duties or wilfully negligent in this particular, the commanding officers of regiments will hereafter attend guard-mounting, and personally see that it is properly conducted.

. . . . . . . . . .

III. Ten men, the most distinguished for bravery and valor, will be named by the colonel in each regiment, who will always, on forming for attack, without further command, take their places ten paces in rear of their regiments, with bayonets fixed. These men will be particularly instructed by the colonel in their duties.

In Camp, May 16, 1862.

. . . . . . . .

II. Hereafter, at all formations to meet the enemy, all orderlies, clerks, cooks, and convalescents will take their places in ranks. The attention of colonels is particularly called to this paragraph.

On the 29th of April the army moved from Shiloh in the direction of Corinth. The march was uneventful till we neared that place, when the army was regularly deployed and works thrown up. I was attacked with malarial fever here, and sent home, and did not join the army again until the 5th of July, near Athens, Alabama, the command of the brigade falling to the senior colonel, Whitaker, of the Sixth Kentucky. The following orders were soon issued : —

CAMP HOUGHTON, ALABAMA, July 8, 1862.

. . . . . . . . .

III. All the commissioned officers of the brigade will assemble at these headquarters for instruction from eight to nine o'clock, P. M., daily, until further orders.

CAMP AT ATHENS, ALABAMA, July 15, 1862.

To the Governor of Ohio.

The following officers of Ohio volunteers having served under my command, and having arrived at a high state of efficiency as officers, and having shown themselves at all times men of high moral character, and upon the field of battle of unqualified courage and gallantry, I take the opportunity of recommending them to your notice as worthy of the command of regiments; namely, Major Aquila Wiley, Forty-first Ohio Volunteers; Captain Emerson Opdycke, Forty-first Ohio Volunteers; Captain J. M. Kendrick, Assistant Adjutant-General, U. S. Volunteers; and First Lieutenant James McCleery, Forty-first Ohio Volunteers.

I am very respectfully your obedient servant,

W. B. HAZEN.

CAMP NEAR ATHENS, ALABAMA, July 29, 1862.

To the Governor of Ohio.

The following members of the Forty-first Ohio Volunteers having become thoroughly proficient in the duties of regimental officers, being gentlemen of rare intelligence and high character, and having highly distinguished themselves in battle, I would respectfully call your attention to their claims for promotion in the forces now being raised in the State; namely, Captain John W. Steele, Forty-first Ohio Volunteers, and Captain R. L. Kimberly, Forty-first Ohio Volunteers.

After remaining a few weeks at Athens, and passing a month in repairing the Nashville Southern Railroad, the brigade took post at Murfreesboro', where it remained till the retrograde movement was made to Louisville. Nelson had gone to take his new command, afterward so disastrously defeated at Richmond, Kentucky, and General Jacob Ammen was placed in command of the division. But he, with the other brigades, was not present, and my command became in a measure independent, and a large number of troops—some ten regiments—were temporarily added to it. Drills were at once resumed, under provisions of the following order: —

MURFREESBORO', TENN., Aug. 14, 1862.

I. The officers and non-commissioned officers of each regiment of this brigade will be formed into classes by their colonels, and will be assigned lessons, and recite, at least one hour each day, to such instructors as may be appointed. . . .

On the 21st of September our retrograde movement began, under the following order: —

IN CAMP, Sept. 20, 1862.

I. On the march to-morrow no straggling will be allowed. Colonels will attend to this; they can prevent it if they will. Halts will be made for filling canteens as often as practicable.

II. All clerks, orderlies, servants, and cooks will take arms and go in ranks. In case there is not a sufficient supply of arms on hand, they will nevertheless go in ranks, depending on the battlefield to supply the deficiency.

III. Ten men, the most distinguished for bravery and good conduct in each regiment, will be placed ten paces in rear of the regiments in action, with special instructions regarding men falling to the rear unnecessarily. The wounded will receive attention after the fight is over, excepting only such as can be given by the surgeons' corps.

IV. No officer will use a gun in action, but will perform the higher duty for which he was commissioned, of keeping his men in their places, and seeing that they perform their duties correctly.

V. Each commandant of a regiment will take with him a drummer in action, to sound the roll to cease firing, and will be careful to see that his men do not waste their ammunition.

VI. Colonels will be particular to see that every officer is publicly disgraced who leaves his post unnecessarily in action, or fails to exert every effort to execute his duty efficiently.

VII. Colonels will call together the officers of their commands, and impress upon them the fact that everything depends upon the proper performance of their duties, and that they must exercise absolute power over their men, who are always ready to do their duty.

We saw at Murfreesboro' much of the Southern people. Here was the home of the estimable family of the Hon. Joseph Ready, a former Member of Congress, and a pleasanter family is seldom met. On our leaving Murfreesboro' every servant they had followed us, and the condition of the family was pitiable. We moved back to Nashville, camping on the place of Andrew Ewing, where we had first camped on our arrival the preceding February, then a spot of rare beauty. After occupying it a month I had left it in its full perfection. But what a change! Not a fence, nor a spear of grass on the beautiful lawn; and the park-like spread of great oaks was an open, mud-tramped common, covered with stumps and scraggy parts of prostrate trees, the branches having been used for fuel. The flower-garden, which I had taken such pleasure in preserving, was destroyed; the negro tenements were nearly all carried off. The residence was empty, and without windows or doors; and the negroes, who had served us so faithfully, and with a gentleness that spoke so well for the people they had served, receiving from us the same protection and reward they would at any other time, were huddled into one little cabin, where they all lived, their dress and whole appearance showing plainly how they had fared. This was the roughest picture of war outside of battle I had seen, and I left it next morning with a saddened heart.

We continued our march to Louisville, while Bragg, moving in the same direction, was on our right and about a day's march away, with his advance somewhat ahead of us. We arrived at Louisville the 23d of September, and remained in camp, organizing for the new struggle, till the 28th of September. In the mean time General Ammen gave up his division, being physically unable to bear the strain, and General William Sooey Smith, who as a colonel commanded the brigade on my right at Shiloh, was

assigned to it. On the 27th of September General Nelson
gave a dinner-party; and this dinner has a history. One
evening, while on the march with the army from Shiloh to
Corinth, General Nelson, Colonel James Jackson, of Kentucky, and myself were together. Nelson remarked that
on his next birthday he would be glad to have us dine with
him at the Galt House, in Louisville. Jackson asked him
when that would be. He replied, " The 27th day of September." Jackson remarked that it was very strange, but
that was his birthday also; and, very much stranger still, it
was also mine. So remarkable a coincidence, which by the
law of chances would occur but once in one hundred and
forty thousand such meetings, led to the engagement for the
dinner, wherever we might be. But to continue the strange
part of this story, our next birthday found us at the very
spot Nelson had first proposed, — at the Galt House, in
Louisville. This remarkable chain of coincidences did not
stop even here, as the tragic sequel will show. The dinner,
which was attended by nearly all the officers of high rank
in the city, and by the Hon. J. J. Crittenden and other
notable citizens, was very elaborate and elegant. General
Buell, although invited, was not present. He had fallen
under very great criticism because Bragg had appeared in
Kentucky,—an event for which he was not responsible,—
and the clamor ran high for his removal. McCook was
mentioned by his friends for the succession, and his name
was often heard in the halls of the Galt House, where he
had his quarters, as the incoming man. At the dinner,
Mr. Crittenden proposed and drank the health of " General
McCook, the coming leader of the Army of the Ohio."
This act, which, if not prearranged, at least met with considerable favor, and at a table made up largely of General
Buell's officers, where Buell had been invited, impressed
me unpleasantly, and I have always associated it with our
failure at Perryville. It was the last time I ever saw

GENERAL WILLIAM SOOY SMITH

GENERAL JAMES S. JACKSON

either Nelson or Jackson. The dinner appointed that rainy, dismal night in front of Corinth to celebrate our common birthday was to be our last meeting. The next day Davis shot Nelson, and on the 8th of October, eleven days after, Jim Jackson was killed in battle at Perryville. I was in the hotel office when Nelson was shot. Hurrying towards the stairs where the firing took place, I met Davis, whom I had never seen before. He was in his shirt-sleeves, without a hat, and greatly agitated. I at once seized him. He told me who he was, and I released him. The army moved on to Perryville almost immediately after, many of the officers of rank delaying part of a day to attend the funeral obsequies of Nelson.

Of Nelson, excepting his quarter-deck manner (he had been a lieutenant in the navy), which in all its rigor he could never lay aside, and which he practised toward almost everybody, everything was in his favor. To an extraordinarily large stature were added a perfect figure, robust health, and a commanding presence. By diligent reading and much travel he had acquired an ample fund of that kind of knowledge and anecdote which, with a memory that seemed never to fail him, and great readiness of description, formed the most attractive social qualities. I knew him only as a kind and genial gentleman. As a soldier he was vigilant and painstaking to the last degree. In quick perception and industry, so necessary for a commander in the field, he was unsurpassed. No man could be braver, more just to those he thought meritorious, or more severe with every manner of dereliction; but at times he was very harsh and petulant. This latter quality led to a storm that very early endangered his career, and finally cut it short. Except for this unhappy and, as it proved, fatal characteristic, he might have attained to the very pinnacle of the army. His loss to the country at that time was very serious.

Nelson, for some reason, had taken a violent dislike to Indiana, Davis's State, and to all the people who came from it. Excepting Governor Morton, of whom he always spoke in the highest praise, I never heard him say a kind word of any person from that State, and the mere mention of it was like shaking the red rag at a bull. I have often heard him describe the origin of its colonization as coming from the "poor trash" of the mountains of Kentucky, Tennessee, and North Carolina; and he would refer to his brother Tom, Minister to Mexico, of whom he was fond, as having lost his good manners by living in Indiana, and cite his habit of sitting with his feet resting on the mantel-piece. Buell, who can speak as authoritatively of Nelson as any living man, says:—

"You can hardly say too much in commendation of him as a soldier. He was watchful about the well-being and efficient condition of his troops, exacting about the duty of his inferiors, habitually alert to the extreme of prudence, and yet bold and impetuous in action. He never hesitated about obeying orders, and he threw into his obedience the force of a conspicuously strong physical and mental organization. In view of his known character for energy and zeal, the attempt that has been made in certain quarters to impute tardiness to him on the march from Savannah to Pittsburg Landing, at the battle of Shiloh, is as puerile as it is groundless. It is unnecessary to speculate as to what he might have accomplished in the highest military command, though with his energy in action was combined cultivated talent of a high order. But in regard to the chief subordinate positions nothing remained in uncertainty; and with a complement of officers such as he proved himself to be, it would be difficult to limit the achievements of an army short of the utmost bounds of possibility. While holding up for deserved admiration his high qualities as a soldier, and his fine general attainments, you will not be able to acquit him of a sometimes harsh and imperious temper in command,—a blemish

GENERAL WILLIAM NELSON

GENERAL JEFFERSON C. DAVIS

that unfortunately is not rare in the composition of a strong character. Perhaps in his case it was increased by the exacting nature of his naval training. But he had a manly disposition to make atonement for injustice, and often his conduct toward his subordinates was marked by a gentleness and consideration that belong to the most delicate susceptibilities. He had withal a keen perception, and a thorough contempt for sham in the motives and conduct of men. In his patriotism there was no selfishness or false pretence. It was like his character, direct, positive, comprehensive. He never hesitated or faltered; but thrusting aside disdainfully all local considerations, all the schemes of ambitious partisans, and all the envenomed prejudices of both sections, he threw the whole weight of his strong nature into the broad cause of Union and Nationality. Such a man ought not to have perished at such a time, and in such a manner." [1]

The following narrative by General Stanley Matthews, of Cincinnati, now of the Supreme Court, gives a more correct impression of Nelson's real character than any description can possibly do. Its prophetic warning adds to its interest.

"It was in the winter of 1861, I think, that we were at Camp Wickliffe, near New Haven, Kentucky. The late General Nelson's division, as it then existed, was there, and was part of Buell's army. I was the colonel commanding the Fifty-first Ohio Regiment, which formed a part of the brigade under the command of Colonel Jacob Ammen. General Hazen was Colonel of the Forty-first Ohio Regiment. At that time the brigade commanders were Colonels Ammen and Hascall. There were only two brigades at that time; a third was afterward created, and given to Colonel Hazen.

"I had made the acquaintance of General Nelson sometime before I had been assigned to his command. Indeed, I had met him in Cincinnati, when he was engaged in the preliminary work of organizing the Union sentiment, and getting arms in the

[1] Published by permission, from a letter to Mr. A. N. Ellis.

hands of the Union men in Kentucky, — a sort of secret service, to which he was assigned by President Lincoln, and which he was very successful in executing. After I became attached to his command, without any knowledge on my part of how it came to happen, I found myself in some relation of intimacy and confidence with him; so much so, that, although ordinarily a man of great self-reliance, and not disposed to enter into consultation and take opinions from others, nevertheless he did on several occasions ask advice from me in regard to matters in which he thought I could be of service to him. There was in the command a surgeon, Dr. Bradford, of Augusta, Kentucky, who was, I think, a brigade surgeon. He was an old and intimate friend of General Nelson, and a strong and mutual confidence and attachment existed between them. General Nelson was very fond of him, and was very anxious that he should become the division surgeon; in which, however, he was disappointed by the appointment of Dr. Mussey, of Cincinnati, to that position.

" On the occasion of the incident I will now relate, General Nelson and Dr. Bradford had been together, as I think, driving or riding from the town of New Haven, which was the depot for our supplies, and on their return to camp I happened to meet Dr. Bradford, and found him in a state of great agitation. He told me that there had occurred a very unpleasant passage between himself and General Nelson, which had disturbed him very much, and in which General Nelson had been guilty of doing him a great wrong, and had very grossly insulted him, as he thought. Dr. Bradford narrated the circumstances in detail. My memory of the particulars has now grown faded and vague. The quarrel, however, was concerning a negro man, who was a favorite servant of Dr. Bradford. This servant was in company with them when the occurrence took place. If I recollect aright, the difficulty sprung up in consequence of General Nelson accusing this servant-man, upon suspicion and without just foundation as Dr. Bradford thought, with having done something wrong. Dr. Bradford interposed in the negro man's defence, when General Nelson, irritated at the interposition,

turned rather savagely upon Dr. Bradford and exploded his
wrath upon him, which Dr. Bradford resented immediately and
strongly, and they parted with a good deal of bitterness and
resentment. Sometime after, but on the same day, I received a
message from General Nelson, asking me to come over to his
quarters, which I immediately proceeded to do. I found him
alone, in a state of great indignation and wrath, pacing the floor
very impatiently. He told me that he had sent for me to tell me
the circumstances of an unpleasant controversy he had gotten into
with Dr. Bradford, and how badly he thought Dr. Bradford had
treated him. He then proceeded to give me his version of the
occurrence, and wanted my judgment upon it as to whether he
was not in the right. I told him that Dr. Bradford had given
me his side of the affair, and I said to him (Nelson), 'This is an
unpleasant matter between friends, in which I have no disposition to intermeddle, and do not want to be called upon to
express an opinion.' He insisted, however, on talking the
matter over, and extorting from me some judgment on it, when
I said to him, 'General, do you really wish me to express an
impartial judgment in respect to this matter?' He replied,
'Certainly.' I said, 'Are you willing to accept it; to receive it,
even though it may be adverse to you?' He said, 'Certainly;
I want your opinion, I want your advice.' 'Well,' I said, 'if
you will give me your word of honor that you will receive any
opinion from me that I may be willing to give, in the spirit in
which I offer it, and will not treat it as an interference because
it may not be agreeable, I am willing to tell what I think.' Said
he, 'I want to know just what you honestly and sincerely think
about it.' I then proceeded to inquire of him, on the basis of
the statement of Dr. Bradford, in regard to the occurrence, so as
to make sure that I had the facts correctly. I then said to him,
'General, I am compelled to say that I think in this matter you
have done your friend a grievous wrong.' He turned on me with
surprise and astonishment, and asked if I really thought that, and
what was the ground of my opinion. I stated to him the grounds
on which I had formed my judgment. He said, 'What do you
think I ought to do?' I replied, 'There is but one thing for a

gentleman under such circumstances, and a man in your position, to do ; and that is, to immediately communicate with Dr. Bradford, and tell him that on reflection you are satisfied that you have done him a wrong, and offer an apology for it, expressing your regret.'

"The advice seemed at first to be unpalatable; but after a, few minutes' further conversation he seemed to brighten, and said, 'I will go right down to Dr. Bradford's quarters and make the best amend that I can offer.' I then said : 'General, do not let us part without giving me an opportunity of saying one final word. You are two different men, according as you are looked at from the outside or as you are known from the inside. The outside man is rough, overbearing, inconsiderate, and tyrannical, easily giving offence, and not overlooking offence given by others; but the inside man is generous, open, frank, fearless, magnanimous. You forget that the inside man is known only to a few intimate friends, and that the world at large sees only the outside man. Some of these days you will come in contact with some person, in some offensive way, who not appreciating more than he can see from the outside will, in resenting your offensive manner, shoot the outside man, and in doing so kill the inside man.'"

I have always felt that the country never understood the loss it sustained in Nelson's death, and that it little appreciated his real value and character. His men, and those persons who clamored against him, knew him little more than if he had never lived. That there was no serious attempt to punish this crime, will be held by future generations as a deep stain upon our administration of affairs at that time.

OCT- 62'

In reorganizing at Louisville, a great number of new and perfectly raw troops were added to the army, and the weakness of our military system was in this example more plainly shown than in any other instance that came under my notice. The One Hundred and Tenth Illinois, an "Egyptian "[1] regiment under Colonel Thomas S. Casey, a most admirable gentleman, and a son of one of the former governors of his State, was added to my brigade. It was 1,100 strong. The men were of large stature, and their appearance in ranks excellent; but they were without instruction, and unused to camps and marches. They with the other raw troops were given, and set out on their first march with the full allowance of equipments, — blankets, overcoats, and in fact all that mysterious and curiously contrived gearing which for so long a time we gave to foot-soldiers, and which no old soldier would, and no new one could, wear. The poor fellows struggled under these loads as long as possible; but in spite of every exertion on my part, and that of regimental officers, the number of men that fell by the way each day on our march to Perryville was frightful, and they could muster at that battle, after a march of ten days, but about seven hundred men. The tone of the regiment seemed to fade away; and at Nashville, where we arrived about the 20th of November, five weeks later, before the battle of Murfreesboro', more than forty men died of nostalgia, without any real assignable disease, and while the other regiments were ordinarily well. At Stone River, their first battle, where they fought excellently, they mustered about five hundred; and soon after, General Palmer, the division commander, broke up the regimental organization, making of the remnant of some one hundred and eighty men a battalion for his headquarters guard. In three months, before arriving at Stone River, and without having been in battle, the regiment lost some six hundred men, largely owing to being overweighted with an absurd equipment.

We arrived near Perryville on the 8th of October, overtaking Bragg's army. Our own could not be made fully ready for battle till the 9th, and every preparation was ordered

[1] From Southern Illinois.

by General Buell to assail it on that day; but McCook, who at Louisville was put at the head of a corps, advanced incautiously so far as to draw the attack. This grew into an engagement of the entire corps, which was badly cut up and beaten. Buell was not apprised of the real situation in time to render the necessary aid, and during the night Bragg retreated and escaped. Although the corps under Crittenden, to which my brigade belonged, was formed in line on the right about midday, and not more than two or three miles from the battle, it was not engaged. Our failure at Perryville was a great misfortune to our arms; for had the battle been fought as contemplated, there can scarcely be a doubt of an overwhelming victory for us.

The position of the Union commander at that battle was most anomalous and unfortunate. Before we left Louisville General Thomas had orders from Washington to supersede him, but declined; and his next prospective successors were his corps commanders, McCook and Crittenden, who possessed the ambition of all good soldiers.

These facts have given occasion to much discussion upon the management of the battle, and, justly or not, the questions involved must remain unsettled. Our own acts, though mistaken, may not be wilful, but the world may hold us responsible for them. These acts may arise from influences which the actor cannot control, and for which he is not at fault. The fact will always remain, that from some cause the battle was fought the day before Buell ordered it or was prepared for it; that he was not notified in time to prevent a disaster,[1] which confirmed the previously formed

---

[1] General Fry, Buell's chief of staff, says of this in his able review of Buell's command, "It is a remarkable fact that from the beginning to the end of the action McCook did not report to Buell that he was engaged even ;" and Buell, in referring to this action, says, "I ascribe it [meaning want of greater success] to too great confidence of the general commanding the left corps [Major-General McCook], which made him believe he could manage the difficulty without the aid or control of his commander."

decision to remove him; and that the nature of the battle was such that, had it been successful, the credit would not have been his, nor would the ill fate that overtook him have been averted by it.

Except a little skirmishing by the picket line, my brigade was not engaged at Perryville; and I closed my report of the day's operations by saying, "It is but just to express the keen disappointment of the entire brigade at not having the opportunity to engage the enemy."

On the 11th of October the brigade, reinforced by Colonel Woodford's Kentucky regiment of cavalry, made a forced reconnoissance through the town of Danville. We found the enemy drawn up a mile in front of the town, and moved on him at once, driving him through it and two miles beyond. The Hon. J. J. Crittenden entered the town with us, and there met a part of his family. This was the home of the late Rev. Dr. Breckinridge and a great number of stanch Union people like him, and we met here the only real gala-day patriotic reception, with banners and bumpers, I ever saw given our troops in the South. With the loss of three men, we killed several of the enemy, captured thirty, and a large hospital of about five hundred sick.

The remainder of this sketch, till the close of the pursuit of Bragg eight days afterward, on all but one of which my brigade was in the advance, will be given by extracts from my official report. Speaking of the conduct of the troops at Danville, it says: —

"I must mention the universal good behavior of all the troops of the command. . . . On the 12th the division was moved forward near Camp Dick Robinson, returning to the Harrodsburg pike, three miles from Danville, where it bivouacked until the morning of the 14th, when it took up its march on the Stanford road, bivouacking near that place until twelve o'clock at night, when it was again put in motion in the direction of

Crab Orchard, reaching that place about midday of the 15th and passing to within two miles of Mt. Vernon. On the morning of the 16th the brigade was put in motion at daybreak at the head of the division, which had the advance of the Twenty-first Army Corps. On passing about two miles beyond that place, the rear of the enemy was seen drawn up in line of battle. The Sixth Kentucky was advanced rapidly as skirmishers, which, with a few shots from Cockerill's battery, soon dispersed them. On moving forward some four miles farther, the enemy was found strongly posted, with his cavalry dismounted and acting as infantry supports to artillery. A brisk fire was opened by them upon a company of the Second Indiana Cavalry, which was reconnoitring on foot. They met the fire gallantly, and were immediately relieved by the Sixth Kentucky, which moved forward splendidly, and after a brisk skirmish of thirty minutes the enemy retired precipitately. In this skirmish the Sixth Kentucky lost one killed and two slightly wounded. The enemy lost eleven killed and several wounded. The Ninth Indiana now relieved the Sixth Kentucky as skirmishers, and pushing forward about two miles, found the enemy again posted with dismounted cavalry and artillery in their favorite position, being on the hillside opposite an open valley. One wing of the Ninth Indiana, under Lieutenant-Colonel Suman, by a rapid movement succeeded in flanking the enemy, and came near capturing his artillery, which we failed to do only by the rapidity of its retreat. A sharp skirmish was kept up during this movement, resulting in the killing and wounding of several of the enemy and the capture of several more, including a captain. In moving forward the remainder of the day an almost uninterrupted skirmish was kept up, the enemy impeding our progress by felling timber. The brigade bivouacked at Big-Rock-Castle Creek. The prisoners of this day amounted to between thirty and forty. On the 17th the command moved only to Camp Wild Cat, a distance of four miles, the Nineteenth Brigade being in the rear of the division.

"On the 18th, it being reported that the enemy were posted in strong force a few miles in our front, I was ordered forward to drive him from his position. This was effected after a sharp skirmish in which the Ninth Indiana and Forty-first Ohio took part, the enemy losing several officers and men, without casualty to our arms. In obedience to orders, the command was marched back to Camp Wild Cat and bivouacked for the night. On the 19th I received orders to march to Pitman's Cross Roads, but not beyond it without orders. The Forty-first Ohio was deployed as skirmishers, and the command moved forward without coming upon the enemy until within five miles of Pitman's. The roads had been blocked with fallen timber almost continuously; but by the hard labor of the pioneers we were enabled to reach within one half-mile of Pitman's by nightfall, a sharp skirmish taking place about sundown, in which Lieutenant Hardy, Adjutant of the Forty-first Ohio Volunteers, had his horse shot, and one man of the same regiment was slightly wounded. The enemy posted himself with artillery at the cross-roads, throwing shot and shell over my lines, but doing no damage. The Forty-first Ohio was pushed forward under cover of the darkness to examine their position ; the people of the country reporting that a strong force of all arms was strongly posted there for an engagement. The women and children of the neighborhood had been sent away, which gave color to the report. The reconnoissance was pushed within fifty yards of the artillery, when the regiment was withdrawn some four hundred yards and posted for the night behind a spur of the hill. Disposition was then made for an attack at dawn. At ten o'clock P. M. the artillery of the enemy took up its march, followed by his other troops, the rear getting under way at four o'clock A. M. On the morning of the 20th a patrol was sent through the town of London, and on returning they brought some twenty-five prisoners, reporting the enemy six miles from that place. On the 22d the command, in obedience to orders, marched back to Camp Wild Cat, carrying with it seventy-five prisoners.

" In summing up the advance, it appears that in eight days the brigade engaged in six skirmishes, killing twenty of the enemy, wounding many more, and capturing, including the sick,

between five hundred and six hundred prisoners. Our own loss
was one killed and five or six wounded.

"The conduct of the entire brigade could not have been better.
Lieutenant-Colonel Suman, of the Ninth Indiana, deserves the
warm thanks of his commander. I was an eye-witness to all
that occurred on the entire march. The course of the road over
which we passed after leaving Mt. Vernon was through narrow
gorges, occasionally debouching into narrow valleys, and of such
a character as to render our movements necessarily cautious, and
affording opportunities for an energetic foe to have stopped our
progress at almost any point. It is doubtful if the rear of the
army proper was ever reached, but merely a light force of from
1,500 to 3,000 held back against our advances to feel our
progress. It always yielded when closely pressed.

"It is proper to add that during the entire campaign, although
we were destitute of many of the comforts usual in campaigns,
without tents, often with insufficient food, through inclemencies
of weather and marches of almost unprecedented length, I have
never heard a murmur, and have now to report a condition of
health better than ever before known in the brigade, and a state
of thorough discipline in the highest degree satisfactory."

The brigade now moved to Nashville *via* Somerset, Columbia, and Glasgow, and there joined its division, having been separated from it in the pursuit and for some
weeks afterward. In the mean time General Buell had
been superseded by General Rosecrans, the organization
into army corps was confirmed, and the designation of the
army changed to the Army of the Cumberland. Soon after,
General William Sooey Smith was superseded as division
commander by General John M. Palmer, an officer who
had not previously served with that army. The change
of army commanders I have always believed unfortunate.
Without in the least detracting from those generals whose
good fortune permitted them to serve to the close of the
war, and who now enjoy the full honors gained by doing

GENERAL WILLIAM S. ROSECRANS

GENERAL DON CARLOS BUELL

so, I have at all times said and believed that General Buell was the best general the war produced. He was a victim to the demand for success; and the confidence of the country, so necessary for a commander, was in his case greatly impaired by the necessary falling back to the Ohio, and the partial success only at Perryville, the real causes for which the people did not discriminatingly understand.

Probably his removal could not have been avoided, but that army was never again as good tactically as while under Buell. As soldiers, the two commanders, Buell and Rosecrans, hardly admit of fair comparison, they differ so widely.

While waiting at Nashville, before the great battle of Murfreesboro', we were fully occupied in changing arms, drilling, and getting ready for the anticipated onset. Foraging upon the country became necessary, and the following fairly illustrates the method of doing it: —

HEADQUARTERS NINETEENTH BRIGADE,<br>IN CAMP NEAR NASHVILLE, Dec. 13, 1862.

Act'g-Assist. Adjutant-General Fourth Division :

SIR, — I have the honor to make the following report of the operations of this brigade yesterday on foraging duty : —

The order to proceed with my entire brigade was received the evening before. On inquiring where forage could be found, I was informed that the command which went out that day under Colonel Stanley Matthews, consisting of two brigades, had skirmished all day and returned with half their wagons empty, and that the chances for procuring forage were very poor, but very good for a fight. My command was in motion at daylight, with one hundred and seventy wagons, and troops disposed with every military precaution. We found forage in sufficient quantity to fill all our wagons in the vicinity of Stone River. We saw no enemy; and if any were in our vicinity, the position of the troops was always such that nothing less than an open fight with superior forces could have availed them anything. We were compelled to ford Stone River twice, causing considerable delay, night coming on when we were five miles from camp. The command reached camp at nine P. M., the wagons all filled. There was not a case of straggling during the day, except three mounted orderlies sent out from the headquarters of the Twenty-second Brigade. As these men were not reported to me, and were straggling the entire day, I have to report them as being out in violation of General Orders, No. 30.

I have also to report Captain Fee, quartermaster, in charge of the division train, who, as night came on, rode ahead of the column to camp, taking with him his assistants; in fact, abandoning his charge, leaving the colonel commanding the brigade in the darkness to act as wagon-master over an almost impassable part of the road. I am, Sir, very respectfully,

Your obedient servant,

W. B. HAZEN.

The army broke camp and moved towards Murfreesboro' December 26; but I was detained in Nashville as a witness in the Buell investigation, and the brigade moved out under command of Colonel Whitaker. On arriving near Lavergne, in taking position, a portion of it was moved forward without properly advanced skirmishers, and unnecessarily exposed, suffering a small loss. I arrived after it had taken up a position for the night, and next day was sent forward, supported by two additional brigades, on the Jefferson pike, to secure the bridge over Stewart's Creek, which was admirably done in a breakneck chase by a detachment of Michigan cavalry under an intrepid officer, Captain Maxey, and my mounted staff and orderlies. General Crittenden says of it: "The seizure of two bridges, one by General Hascall and the other by Colonel Hazen, . . . is worthy of notice."

My own report describes it as follows : —

"Being summoned before the commission then sitting for the investigation of the official course of Major-General Buell, I did not until evening join the brigade, which had marched to within two miles of Lavergne. Just before my arrival two regiments of my brigade had been thrown forward to the right of the road, into a dense cedar brake ; and as the temporary commander did not think it necessary to send skirmishers in advance, the flank was marched upon a force of the enemy, who, firing from cover upon the head of the column, killed one of the Ninth Indiana, wounded another, and wounded two of the Sixth Kentucky. At twelve M., December 27, I was ordered to proceed on the Jefferson pike to Stewart's Creek, and save, if possible, the bridge crossing it. Ninety men of the Fourth Michigan Cavalry under Captain Maxey were sent to me, which I placed under charge of my Assistant-Inspector-General, Captain James McCleery, Forty-first Ohio, with directions to keep me thoroughly informed of all that transpired in front, and as soon as the advance of the enemy was started, to put spurs to his horses and not slacken rein until the bridge was crossed. The distance did not exceed five miles ; and by disposing flankers for perfect security and urging the infantry and artillery to their fullest speed, I was enabled to keep within supporting distance all the time. The enemy was met three miles from the bridge, and by closely following my directions the whole affair was turned into a steeple-chase. The enemy formed upon the opposite side of the bridge, but were soon dispersed by a few discharges from our artillery.

" In this affair we lost one cavalry-man, wounded and taken by the enemy. We took ten prisoners, one of them an officer, and killed one officer and several men. Too much credit cannot be given to Captain McCleery, of my staff, and Captain Maxey, of the Fourth Michigan Cavalry, for spirit and daring in this affair. On reaching the bridge my little party was upon the heels of the fugitives; and had they been armed with sabres instead of rifles, by slashing upon their rear the rout must have been pushed to a panic."

The two brigades, Colonel Sam Beatty's and Colonel Fyffe's sent to support me, remained under my command for two days ; but there was no more fighting here. In fact, it was one of the most quiet spots I ever camped upon. Many of the people from the little town of La-vergne, which was nearly destroyed the day before, came here for safety. One of these refugees, I distinctly re-member, was a very handsome and interesting young lady, known as the " Belle of Lavergne." She was very bitter in her denunciations of the Yankees, — excepting one, Colonel Ben Harrison, commanding the Seventieth Indiana, and who has since become well known, who for some kind act seemed to have won her entire admiration. At the close of the war, when nearing Louisville, as we stopped at a station on the railroad there came from a neat little cottage to see us a young matron, with her husband and two flaxen-haired little ones; and who should it be but the maid of Lavergne, with one of the same Yankee offi-cers she had abused, as her husband.

And now we come to the battle of Stone River, or Mur-freesboro', where my command had so interesting and important a part, proving, as I had anticipated, in the most convincing manner the immense value of persistent instruction in schools and drills.

## CHAPTER V.

### STONE RIVER.

THE best service rendered by my command in the war was at the battle of Stone River. As the battle reached the left, we seized a little eminence, not more than three feet higher than the ground around it, just to the left of the Murfreesboro' pike and in front of a little clump of timber known as the Round Forest. This ground had been held by the troops of General Thomas J. Wood, but had just been given up by them, as they had all been withdrawn to help the right, excepting two regiments of Wagner's brigade which held a ford a half-mile away. We successfully defended it against the repeated assaults of the enemy through the entire day. It was the only part of the original line of battle that was held, and it proved to be the pivotal point and key of the Federal position. My brigade sustained the first assault alone, but later we were aided by other troops. My account of this battle will consist chiefly of official statements made at the time by the participants in it. I will begin with my own official report : —

HEADQUARTERS NINETEENTH BRIGADE, ARMY OF THE CUMBERLAND,
SECOND BRIGADE, SECOND DIVISION, LEFT WING,
CAMP NEAR MURFREESBORO', TENN., Jan. 5, 1863.

. . . On the 29th of December I was ordered across to the Nashville and Murfreesboro' pike, and joining the division, proceeded to within three miles of Murfreesboro'. On the night of the 30th the brigade was ordered to the front line to relieve the

Tenth Brigade. This position we held at the commencement of the general action of the 31st, and it deserves special notice. It was in a cotton-field, two and a half miles from Murfreesboro', on the place of Mr. Cowan, whose house was burned during the battle, the line being at right angles with the Nashville and Murfreesboro' pike, the left resting on the pike at a point about five hundred yards towards Nashville from the intersection of the pike with the Nashville and Chattanooga Railroad. The railroad and pike, at this point, cross at a sharp angle. The position was utterly untenable, as it was commanded by ground in all directions with covers of wood, embankment, and palisading at good musket-range in front, right, and left. My brigade was formed in two lines, the right resting against a skirt of woods, which, widening and extending to the right, gave concealment to the Twenty-second Brigade, which adjoined mine, and farther on to the entire divison of Negley. On the left of the pike was Wagner's brigade, of Wood's division. The Sixth Kentucky and Forty-first Ohio were in the front of my line; the Sixth being on the right and the Forty-first on the left. The Ninth Indiana and One Hundred and Tenth Illinois were in the second line; the Ninth being on the right and the One Hundred and Tenth on the left. A fierce fight had begun at daylight on the right of the army, and progressed with ominous changes of position until about half-past eight, when it could no longer be doubted that our entire right was being driven around in rear of our position and nearly at right angles to its proper line. At this moment authority was given me to move forward to seize the commanding positions in front, and the house of Mr. Cowan. The line advanced about twenty yards, when orders were given (by the division commander) to face to the rear. The necessity of this order was but too apparent, the enemy having by this time pushed around quite to our rear. At the same moment he broke cover over the crest in front, at double-quick, in two lines. I faced my two right regiments to the rear, and then moving them into the skirt of woods on my right, began to engage in that direction. My two left regiments were retired some fifty yards and moved to the left of the pike to take

GENERAL THOMAS J. WOOD

COLONEL McKEE

Colonel Samuel McKee belonged to a most patriotic and gallant family.
He was born near Lancaster, Garrard County, Kentucky, Nov. 10, 1832,
and was the third son of James and Mary C. McKee. His uncle, William
R. McKee, was killed at the storming of Buena Vista; his cousin,
Lieutenant McKee of the Navy, at the fight with the Coreans; and
nearly all his relatives were killed in the war of the Rebellion.

cover of a slight crest [the position the monument now occupies] and engaged to the front; the regiment of Wagner's brigade which had occupied that ground (the Fortieth Indiana, Colonel Blake) having withdrawn much to the rear of it. The enemy had by this time taken position about the Cowan house, and the action became terrific at my position. The efforts of the enemy to force back my front and cross the cotton-field, out of which my troops had moved, were persistent, and were prevented only by the most unflinching determination upon the part of the Forty-first Ohio Volunteers to hold their ground. All the troops of General Wood, posted on our left, except two regiments guarding a ford some distance away, had been withdrawn to repel the assault upon the right, so that the Nineteenth Brigade was the extreme left of the army. Upon this point, as a pivot, the entire army oscillated from front to rear during the whole day. The ammunition of the Forty-first Ohio Volunteers was by this time nearly exhausted, and my efforts to replenish were fruitless. I despatched word to the rear that assistance must be given, or we must be sacrificed, as the position I held could not be given up, and gave orders to Lieutenant-Colonel Wiley to fix his bayonets, and to Colonel Casey (without bayonets) to club his guns and hold the ground at all hazards, as it was the key of the whole position. The responses satisfied me that my orders would be obeyed so long as any part of those regiments was left to obey them. I now brought over the Ninth Indiana from the right, and immediately posted it to relieve the Forty-first Ohio Volunteers. In advancing to this position under a galling fire, a cannon-shot passed through the ranks of the Ninth Indiana, but the ranks were closed without checking a step. The Forty-first Ohio retired with its thinned ranks in perfect order, as if on parade. A few discharges from the fresh regiments sufficed to check the enemy, who drew out of our range, and at half-past nine a lull occurred in the battle. At about ten A. M. another furious assault, in several lines, was made upon our front by the enemy, who succeeded in pushing a strong column past the Cowan house, covered by the palisading, to the wood occupied by the Twenty-second Brigade and the Sixth Kentucky. All of the

Federal troops occupying these woods now fell back, exposing my right flank, and threatening an assault from this point that would sweep away our entire left. General Palmer, seeing this danger and knowing the importance of this position, sent the Twenty-fourth Ohio Volunteers (Colonel Jones), the Third Kentucky (Colonel McKee), and other regiments whose designations I do not know, and a fragment of the Thirty-sixth Indiana under Captain Woodruff, to my support. I posted these, and the Forty-first Ohio Volunteers, with the left of the line resting upon the Ninth Indiana, and extending to the right and rear so as to face the advancing column. It was a place of great danger, and our losses here were heavy, including the gallant Colonels McKee of the Third Kentucky, and Jones of the Twenty-fourth Ohio Volunteers; but with the timely assistance of Parsons's battery the enemy was checked, and the left again preserved from what appeared certain annihilation.

The enemy now took cover in the wood, keeping up so destructive a fire as to make it necessary to retire behind the embankments of the railroad, which only necessitated the swinging to the rear of my right, the left having been posted on it when the action commenced in the morning. A sharp fight was kept up from this position till about two P. M., when another assault in regular lines and in great force, supported by artillery, was made upon this position. This assault was resisted much more easily than the previous ones, there being now a large force of our artillery bearing upon the enemy from this point. The enemy also extended his lines much farther to the left, causing something of a diversion of our troops in that direction. General Rosecrans sent me the One Hundredth Illinois (Colonel Bartleson), which I posted with the One Hundred and Tenth Illinois and Ninth Indiana in line of the original front, with the right of these three regiments resting on the railroad. Here, with a German regiment (I think the Second Missouri), these forces fought the remainder of the day. Some troops not known to me temporarily occupied this position, and retired on the last approach of the enemy. A period of about one hour now ensued, with but little infantry firing; but a

*Fred. C. Jones*

(Colonel Twenty-fourth Ohio.)

" My country is my home, her people my friends, her enemies
mine; if I fall in this strife, and it needs the poor offering of my
life, I will die like a soldier and a patriot. "

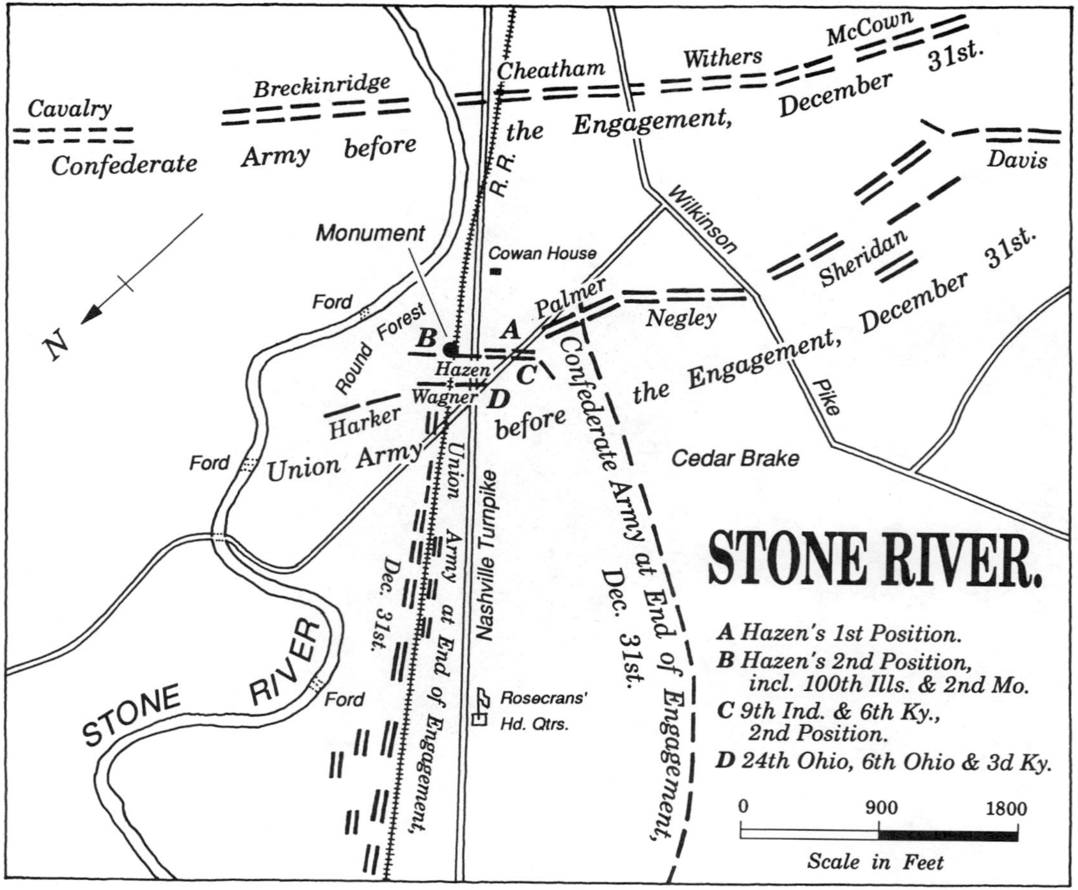

# STONE RIVER.

A Hazen's 1st Position.
B Hazen's 2nd Position,
   incl. 100th Ills. & 2nd Mo.
C 9th Ind. & 6th Ky.,
   2nd Position.
D 24th Ohio, 6th Ohio & 3d Ky.

Scale in Feet

0    900    1800

Richard A. Baumgartner

Confederate Army at End of Engagement, Dec. 31st.

Union Army at End of Engagement, Dec. 31st.

Nashville Turnpike

Rosecrans' Hd. Qtrs.

Cedar Brake

Pike

Wilkinson

Negley

Palmer

Cowan House

Hazen

Wagner

Harker

Round Forest

Monument

Ford

Ford

Ford

Ford

STONE RIVER

Cheatham   Withers   McCown
the Engagement,   December   31st.
Davis
Sheridan   December   31st.

Breckinridge

Confederate Army before

Cavalry

Confederate

N

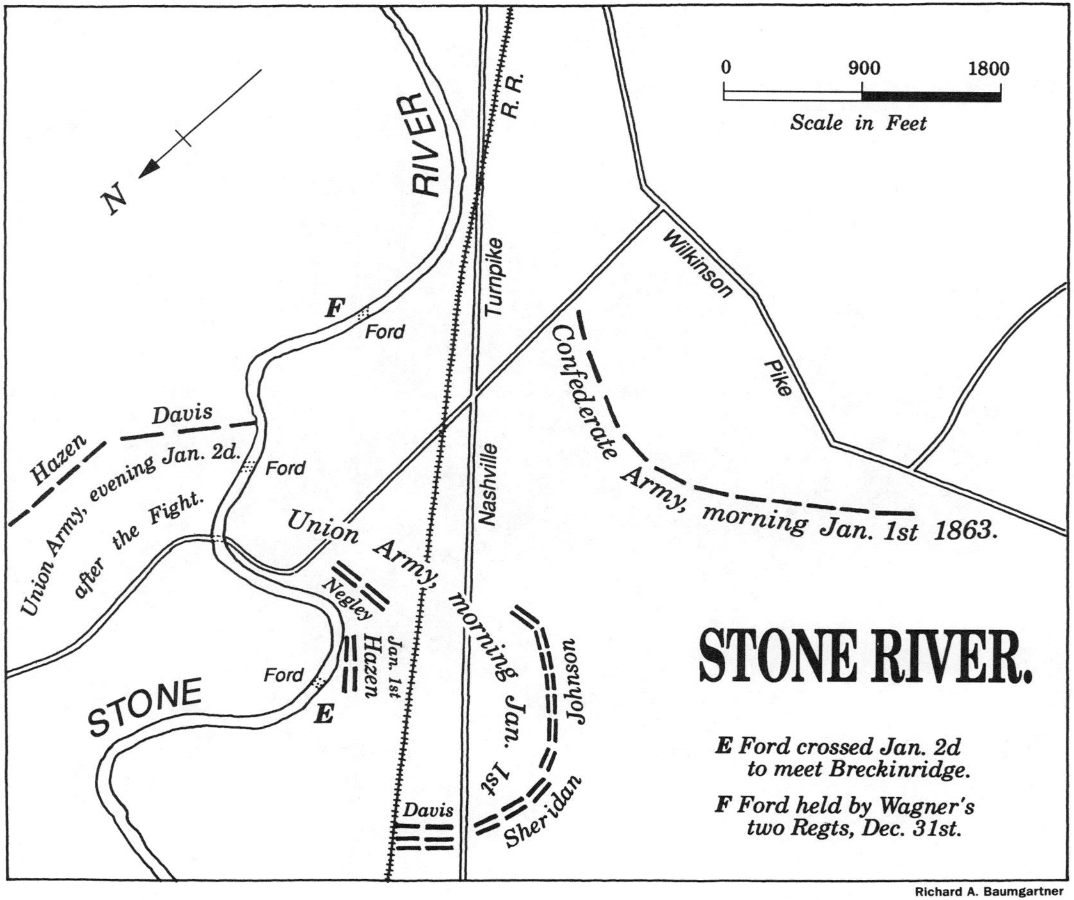

STONE RIVER.

E Ford crossed Jan. 2d
to meet Breckinridge.

F Ford held by Wagner's
two Regts, Dec. 31st.

Richard A. Baumgartner

Scale in Feet

0    900    1800

Confederate Army, morning Jan. 1st 1863.

Wilkinson    Pike

R.R.    Turnpike    Nashville

Union Army, morning Jan. 1st

Johnson

Sheridan

Davis

Jan. 1st    Hazen
Negley

E

STONE

Ford

Ford    F    Ford

RIVER

Davis

Hazen    Union Army, evening Jan. 2d.
after the Fight.

N

LIEUTENANT COLONEL GEORGE T. COTTON

(Sixth Kentucky.)

murderous and concentrated shower of shot and shell was rained from several directions by the enemy's artillery upon this position, which was covered by a thick growth of timber. A portion of Wood's division, now commanded by General Hascall, was also posted in these woods in rear of my troops. At about four P. M. the enemy again advanced upon my front in two lines. The battle had hushed; and the dreadful splendor of this advance can only be conceived, as no description can properly portray it. His right was even with my left, and his left was beyond my vision. He advanced steadily and, as it seemed, certainly to victory. I sent back all of my remaining staff successively to ask for support, and braced up my own lines as perfectly as possible. The Sixth Kentucky had joined me from the other side sometime before, and was posted just behind the embankment of the railroad. They were strengthened by such fragments of troops as I could pick up, until a good line was formed along the track. Some men of Sheridan's division, after retiring from their original position, were also but a few hundred yards in rear replenishing their boxes, and some of General Hascall's troops were on the right of the railroad. The fire of the troops was held until the enemy's right flank came in close range, when a single volley was sufficient to disperse this portion of his lines, his left passing far around to our right. This virtually ended the fight of the day. My brigade rested where it had fought, till withdrawn at dawn next day, — not a stone's-throw from where it was posted in the morning.

The Sixth Kentucky was not under my immediate observation from the first assault till late in the day, but during the time it was with me (and I have reason to believe, at all other times) it fought unflinchingly, and is deserving of all praise. It repelled three assaults of a Rebel brigade from the Cowan house, endeavoring to reach the wood, and retired only when its ammunition was exhausted. Among its killed are Lieutenant-Colonel Cotton and Captain Todd, who possessed in the highest degree the esteem and confidence of their men, and will be deeply lamented by a large circle of friends. The One Hundred and Tenth Illinois, a new regiment never before under fire, displayed that fearless courage one admires in veterans. Its losses from artillery were heavy. The Ninth Indiana and Forty-first Ohio maintained fully their well-known reputation of perfect discipline, dauntless courage, and general fighting qualities. Their steadiness under fire was incredible. The latter regiment was taken by its commander, while resting, without orders, to repel an assault of the enemy's cavalry upon our train, which object it effected, and returned to its position. . . .

I am under many obligations to the commanders of troops (not of my own brigade, — many of their names I do not know) for their implicit obedience to my orders ; but particularly to Colonel Bartleson, of the One Hundredth Illinois, for valuable services.

To the officers commanding regiments of this brigade too much consideration cannot be given either by their commanding generals or the country. Besides the actual service rendered this day, such heroic and daring valor justly entitles these men to the profound respect of our people. To them the commander of the brigade feels that he owes everything, as there were times when faltering upon their part would have been destruction to the left of the army. He owes the success of this day not only to proper conduct on the field, but also to strict obedience to orders, and a manly co-operation in bringing the brigade to its present high state of efficiency and discipline, through constant care, labor, and study, for a period of over twelve months. These have insured this proud result. To Lieutenant-Colonel Suman also, of the Ninth Indiana, twice wounded, great credit is due for gallantry. Captain Cockerill, Battery F, First Ohio Volunteer Artillery, showed, as he always has, great proficiency as an artillery officer. He also was severely wounded. Lieutenant Osborne, of the same battery, who was at the rear to fill his caissons when the train was menaced, turned his pieces upon the enemy, and greatly assisted in dispersing them. Lieutenant Parsons, of the Fourth United States Artillery, was in the thickest of the fight near my position all day, and is deserving of the warmest consideration of the Government for the efficient manner in which his battery was manœuvred. . . .

Illinois State Historical Library - Springfield

COLONEL BARTLESON

Colonel Frederick A. Bartleson, born at Cincinnati, Ohio, was the first man to enlist in his
county. He was Captain and Major in the Twentieth Illinois, and first Colonel of the One
Hundredth. He lost an arm at Shiloh, was captured at Chickamauga, was a prisoner in Libby
Prison, and was finally killed at Kenesaw, June 23, 1864, in his thirty-first year.

There was no more prompt or gallant officer in the war.

GENERAL JOHN M. PALMER

I am under many obligations to the general commanding the division for his confidence in resting with me the management of so important a portion of the field.  By seizing the little crest occupied by my troops early in the morning, when the Fortieth Indiana withdrew from it, — an elevation not more than two feet high, — and later the railroad embankment, hundreds of lives were saved, the strength of my brigade doubled, and the position successfully held.  Close observation of the conduct and character of our troops for the past few days, when compared with those I have so carefully taught for more than twelve months, has confirmed me in a long-settled belief that our army is borne down by a lamentable weight of official incapacity in regimental organizations.  The reasonable expectations of the country can, in my opinion, never be realized until this incubus is summarily removed, and young men of known military ability and faculty for command, without regard to previous seniority, are put in commission.  I saw upon the field company officers of over a year's standing who neither had the power nor the knowledge to form their men in two ranks.  Our casualties at Stone River were four hundred and twenty-nine.

The foregoing extract gives an account of the battle, without any attempt at general description, sufficiently detailed to make the conduct of my command at Stone River thoroughly known.  But I will add what others thought of it.  The most critical period of the defence of that point was before General Hascall came to my support, and in this no troops but my own participated. Here my personal orderly and my horse were killed, and I was twice struck.  It was here that General Palmer spoke of the necessity of falling back, and my regimental commanders reported their want of ammunition.  The orders I gave them are reported by themselves.  My division commander, General Palmer, says : —

" Orders were sent to Colonel Hazen to fall back from the open cotton-field into which he had moved.  He fell back a short distance ; and a regiment of Wood's division (Fortieth Indiana), which had occupied the crest of a low-wooded hill between the pike and the railroad, having been removed, he took possession of that, and there resisted the enemy. . . . I could see that Grose was losing a great many men ; but the importance of Hazen's position determined me, if necessary to do so, to expend my last man in holding it. As soon as Colonel Grose was relieved, he came up on the left and co-operated with Colonel Hazen.

"Colonel Hazen proved himself a brave and able soldier by the courage and skill exhibited in forming and sheltering his troops, and in organizing and fighting all the material around him for the maintenance of his important position. I recognized during the battle the Forty-first Ohio (Hazen's), which fought until it expended its last cartridge, and then was relieved by the Ninth Indiana, which came into line under a heavy fire, with a shout that inspired all with confidence."

Of this position General Crittenden says : "It was evident to me that it was vital to us that this position should be held." The following extract from the report of General Polk, the opposing Confederate corps commander, is a graphic account of the character of the defence of this point : —

'"When the attack reached our right, Palmer's division constituted the left of the Federal army, and it was now ten o'clock. The slaughter was terrific at every point on both sides in this assault, which resulted in driving the enemy from every point except his extreme left. This point, which was the key of the enemy's position, was called the Round Forest."

After describing the morning's assault, where regiments withdrew leaving two thirds of their men on the field, he says : —

"The enemy was now driven from every point, his extreme left alone holding its position. This occupied a position well chosen and defended. The brigades of Adams, Jackson, Preston, and Palmer had pointed out to them the object to be accomplished, — to drive the enemy's left, and especially to dislodge him from his position in the Round Forest. This point carried, and his left driven back on his right, would have completed his confusion and insured an utter rout. It was, however, otherwise."

General Bragg, in his report, after describing the battle, says of it : —

" We succeeded in driving the enemy from every position except his strong one on his extreme left. Later, General Polk was directed, with his reinforcements (two brigades), to throw all his force against the enemy's extreme left, which had until now resisted us so successfully. . . . The three brigades of Adams, Preston, and Palmer were successively reported for the work. How gallantly they moved to the task their losses will show. After two unsuccessful efforts, the attempt to carry it with infantry was abandoned. We then assembled our heavy artillery and rifled guns of long range, which were concentrated upon this point. . . . At daylight, January 1, the enemy had abandoned this point."

General Joseph E. Johnston, in his narrative, says of this defence : —

" The attack was taken up by the brigades of Polk's corps successively from left to right, but they encountered a more determined resistance. . . . When the right brigade of Polk's corps became fully engaged, the Federal right and centre, except the left brigade, had been driven back. . . . They rallied on a new line perpendicular to the original one, their left joining the right of the brigade that still held its original position. The Confederate troops could make no impression on the new and stronger line, and the contest ceased except where the new and old line met. The brigade there, with the aid of several batteries and an excellent commander,[1] repelled the successive

[1] General Hazen.

attack of two detachments of two brigades, each drawn from the Confederate right.  The fight was not resumed."

Of our part a writer unknown to me, in " Battles of America," says : —

" It is no disparagement to any of the other division or brigade commanders, or to the men whom they led, to say that to Hazen and his brigade must be freely accorded the honor of having saved the day."

I add some private communications which come to me unsought.  The first of these is from Mr. Lowdermilk, who was my acting ordnance-officer that day, and was at the date of his letter proprietor of " The Civilian," a paper published at Cumberland, Md.  The second is from Lieutenant Crebbin, late of the Ninth Indiana, who built the monument to my brigade.

"THE CIVILIAN," CUMBERLAND, MD., June 10, 1879.
General W. B. HAZEN :

MY DEAR GENERAL, — . . . I can see Wiley now, as with wild excitement he begged me for a few more rounds of ammunition, and can hear his nervous voice as he repeated to his men the order I took him from you to " rely on the bayonet. "   He was then with the Forty-first, right on the spot now occupied by the monument.  Do you not remember that Palmer came to you there when you were holding the key against odds and said to you, " Hazen, you 'll have to fall back !" and your classic but rather discouraging reply, " I 'd like to know where in h—l I 'll fall back to " ? . . .

Yours faithfully,
WILL H. LOWDERMILK.

NATIONAL MILITARY HOME, DAYTON, OHIO, April 21, 1879.
To the Editor of the " Cincinnati Gazette."

. . . It has been stated by General Wood [on the witness stand, under oath] that none of General Hazen's men fell where the monument is standing.  In justice to the fallen brave I must say and do assert, that on and around the spot where the monument was erected, eleven men of my own company were killed and wounded, and to the best of my recollection one hundred and thirteen men of our regiment (Ninth Indiana) were killed and wounded there. I was an officer in General Hazen's brigade, and was at that battle from beginning to ending, and afterward commanded the detachment of General Hazen's brigade which erected the monument, and am and have been acquainted with every foot of ground on which the battle of Stone River was fought. I have been over that ground a great many times since the war. I stayed in that neighborhood after the war up to 1873. . . . I know that the Ninth Indiana belonged to Hazen's brigade, and that on the morning of the 31st of December we relieved the Forty-first Ohio (which had expended all their ammunition), and held that position between the railroad and turnpike all day, and toward night the right of our regiment fell back behind the railroad embankment. The left held their position where the monument was erected, except toward night they fell back about twelve feet; and it was during the day of the 31st that the Ninth Indiana boys fell, General Stanley and General Wood to the contrary, notwithstanding. The words on that monument record facts. General Hazen's men did fall there, and where the monument was erected.

### HAZEN'S BRIGADE.

To the memory of its soldiers who fell at Stone River, Dec. 31, 1862. Their faces toward heaven, their feet to the foe.

That inscription is true in every word, and it is to be hoped the monument will ever remain standing as a memorial of the gallant and patriotic men of General Hazen's brigade who fell on that day in defence of the Union and liberty.

E. K. CREBBIN,
*Late First Lieutenant Ninth Indiana Vet. Vol's.*

OFFICE OF E. S. HOLLOWAY, ATTORNEY AT LAW,
COLUMBIANA, OHIO, April 28, 1879.

General W. B. HAZEN, New York City:

MY DEAR GENERAL, — . . . To you and your brigade belonged the credit in a great measure of turning what at one time seemed

an inevitable rout of the entire army into a victory in the battle
of Stone River.  In our judgment, the stubborn manner in which
you maintained your position, on the left of Palmer's division,
with left resting on the railroad, on the very spot where the
monument was afterward erected, saved the army from a complete rout. . . .

E. S. Holloway,
*Late Colonel Forty-first Ohio.*

Chicago, March 28, 1879.

Dear General, — . . . I saw your roan charger shot from
under you at Stone River and one of your escort killed while
removing the saddle.  I was an orderly at your headquarters
in that battle, and if you will look in Greeley's " History of the
Rebellion," you will find where it says, " Hazen's brigade was
the only one on the line that held its position.". . .

Your old comrade,
Finley A. McDonald,
*Corner Fourth Ave. and Twelfth St., Chicago, Ill.*

The facts as shown by these accounts are all clearly and
specifically stated by the Comte de Paris, the most careful
and impartial annalist who has written upon our war, in
his " History of the Civil War in America."  They have
been disputed by some of the command that occupied this
position before being withdrawn, particularly by General
Wood, who commanded that division.  None of his division, except Colonel Bartleson's regiment after he reported
to me, again reached this front line after they were withdrawn to help the right.  A portion of it under General
Hascall and Colonel Buell returned after the repulse of
the enemy by my command the second time, and on the
new line, facing across the pike, fought admirably all day.
But excepting Wagner's two regiments at the Ford,
and Bartleson, none ever returned to the old line facing
Murfreesboro'.

The following is in continuation of the narrative of what

can be called Stone River, although the great battle closed
on the evening of the 31st of December.

Just before dark all the troops on this portion of the
field except my own were withdrawn about one mile, and
there established a new and short line ; but we remained,
momentarily expecting orders to follow, till four o'clock
next morning. Great numbers of boxes of small-arm ammunition had been left near my position on the field, and
I sent back for wagons and secured them. It was a bitter
cold night, and we had no blankets. A Rebel came over to
our position, wrapped in a blanket, which he gave me. It
was stiff and glazed with blood and long use, but it proved
the most comfortable blanket I ever saw. Just before day
we were withdrawn to the new line, and posted in a little
patch of wood at a ford on Stone River, just back of the
high ground on which had been admirably posted a large
number of field-pieces, by which Breckinridge's assault
afterward was so successfully met. At daybreak I took
position near this artillery, watching for the advance of
the enemy, and was afterward joined by General Crittenden, and later by other general officers. The drifting
mists at break of day had a most remarkable likeness to
advancing troops in gray, and it was difficult to control
the imagination, so deceiving was this appearance. Until
Breckinridge's assault, however, late in the afternoon the
next day, the field was quiet. My part in checking that
last assault is described in my report : —

. . . On the 2d instant my brigade was ordered across the river
to support Colonel Grose, commanding the Tenth Brigade, then
in reserve to General Van Cleve, whose division (the only one
on that side of the river) had been vigorously attacked by the
enemy. I reached the field about four P. M., and found his entire
division put to rout. The enemy had been checked by Colonel
Grose and a portion of Negley's division, and the several batteries from the point occupied by General Cruft's brigade. It was

difficult to say which was at this moment running away the more rapidly, — the division of Van Cleve to the rear, or the enemy in the opposite direction. I found myself in command of all the troops on that side of the river. Leaving three of my regiments in position as a reserve, I pushed forward with the portion of Colonel Grose's brigade already in motion, and the Forty-first Ohio Volunteers, and pursued the enemy beyond all the ground occupied by our forces before the fight. I here formed the best line circumstances would admit, the Forty-first Ohio Volunteers being the only regiment wholly in hand. The others were badly broken, the only idea of their officers seeming to be to push on pell-mell, — which, if carried beyond the point then occupied, might have resulted disastrously.

I succeeded in checking the straggling to the front with the aid of Colonel Grider, of the Ninth Kentucky, who came forward and performed this valuable service after his regiment, which belonged to Van Cleve's division, had gone to the rear. I was relieved by the fresh division of Jeff. C. Davis, who arrived just at dark. When far advanced in the pursuit, a portion of General Negley's batteries, far in the rear, were firing on my line, and continued to do so, without damage, until an aide-de-camp was sent over the long distance to ask that it be discontinued. After forming my advanced line, a battery of the enemy, about four hundred yards in front, continued to fire upon us with great rapidity. I ordered the Forty-first Ohio to fire a volley upon it. No more firing took place on either side, and the weakness of my line prevented my going farther. The next day three caissons and several dead horses and men were found at this point. It was in this fight that the famous Rebel, General Roger Hanson, was killed and General Adams wounded. . . .

I am, very respectfully, your obedient servant,

W. B. HAZEN,
*Commanding Nineteenth Brig., Second Div., Left Wing.*

General Davis says of this : —

"After relieving the troops of General Palmer and Colonel Beatty, and particularly the brigade of Colonel Hazen, which

COLONEL WILLIAM GROSE

(Former commander Thirty-sixth Indiana.)

GENERAL HORATIO P. VAN CLEVE

had so nobly vindicated its courage in this the closing conflict, I ordered a heavy line of skirmishers thrown out. . . . Night again brought a cessation of hostilities."

The following are extracts from the reports of commanders in Cruft's and Grose's brigades, of General Palmer's division, to which my brigade belonged.

Captain Parsons, of Parsons's battery, says : —

"On the morning of the 31st I thought it in accordance with my instructions to remain where I then was. . . . At eight A. M. our infantry commenced falling back. . . . He [the enemy] reappeared shortly after to our left; but, on receiving our fire, soon fell back. I then took up a position near the pike, to check the advance on General Rosecrans' position, . . . after which both batteries changed front and opened fire on the brick house, to co-operate with General Hazen's brigade."

Captain A. M. T. Cockerill, commanding Twenty-fourth Ohio, says : —

"We had rested but a few minutes from this terrible encounter (the morning of the 31st), when an orderly of the gallant General Palmer delivered orders to move double-quick to support the Nineteenth Brigade (Colonel Hazen), which was at the time gallantly resisting a furious charge in an open cotton-field on our left. We almost instantly formed on their right, Parsons's battery being on our left. We remained in this position about an hour and a half, amidst a most terrible shower of ball and shell. Colonel Jones was mortally wounded, and carried from the field. The command now devolved on Major Terry, who during his brief period of command displayed great coolness and bravery. Major Terry was struck in the head by a fragment of a shell and mortally wounded."

Colonel William Grose, commanding the brigade to which the foregoing troops belonged, reports : —

"After this, between eleven and twelve o'clock (the 31st of December), the front of the brigade was again changed, so as to assist Colonel Hazen in the direction as formed in the morning. The Twenty-fourth Ohio and Thirty-sixth Indiana were thrown forward, and had a terrible conflict. Here Colonel Jones and Major Terry were both carried from the field in a dying condition."

Lieutenant Osborne, of Battery F, First Ohio Artillery, says : —

"December 31 we were ordered forward with the Nineteenth Brigade (Hazen's) to take up a position near the burnt brick house (Cowan's) ; but before getting into position, the right being turned, it was deemed imprudent to advance farther. We received orders from Colonel Hazen to fall back, and we took up a position between the railroad and the pike. [This is the exact position on which the monument stands, and which was originally occupied by Cox's battery, behind which was Blake's Fortieth Indiana.] The enemy opened a destructive fire with shot and shell before we got into position. We opened our battery and maintained our position, supported by the gallant Nineteenth Brigade (Hazen's), which suffered terribly. One caisson was blown up here."

Colonel Whitaker, Sixth Kentucky, says : —

HEADQUARTERS SIXTH KENTUCKY INFANTRY,
BATTLEFIELD OF STONE RIVER, Jan. 5, 1863.

. . . Shortly after sunrise on the morning of the 31st the pickets were attacked by the enemy, but maintained their position. Heavy firing was soon heard on the right of our army, and gave indications of the rapid advance of the enemy. The enemy soon made a most furious attack upon our left ; the pickets of the Sixth were driven in by a large force, who, protected by the palisade and outbuildings of Mr. Cowan's house and the high ground, opened a galling fire on the Sixth, who were in the open ground. They gradually advanced under cover, with the intention of flanking the Sixth on the right. Changing position by the right flank, the regiment was formed in line of battle in the skirt of timber south of the cotton-field, — an advantageous position, — under cover of the timber. Here we were assaulted by a large body of the enemy ; from their numbers I estimated them as a brigade. Three times they advanced, and as often were they driven back with great slaughter. Some of the enemy's skirmishers having after two hours' hard fighting gained position in the edge of the wood, the Sixth was thrown forward to drive them from their cover. While in the act of advancing, the enemy, who had driven in General Negley's force on the right, opened a fire on the right flank of the Sixth, by which my lieutenant-colonel (Cotton) was killed. After some hard fighting the enemy were driven from their cover. Then changing front, the right wing defending one flank and the left wing the other, the Sixth fought the advancing foe until their ammunition was exhausted. Changing position in good order, they took another position in rear of the railroad, where, having replenished their ammunition, they formed in line of battle on the north side of and under cover of the embankment of the railroad ; the Ninth Indiana being on their left and the Forty-first Ohio and One Hundred and Tenth Illinois being in reserve.

The battle had been furiously raging from eight in the morning until noon. About two o'clock P. M., the right of the army having been driven back, the enemy appeared in heavy force on the crest of the ridge east of Mr. Cowan's burnt dwelling. Massing their forces, they intended, if possible, to crush the Nineteenth Brigade (Hazen's), which had maintained its position during the day against overwhelming numbers. Onward they came ; the colors of five or six regiments advancing abreast in line of battle were visible on the crest of the ridge. A further view of this line was intercepted by intervening inequalities of ground and woods. Firmly they advanced until within good range of the guns of the Sixth and Ninth. A most destructive fire was opened upon them by these regiments, by Captain Cockerill's and Captain Parsons's batteries, and by the Fortieth Indiana regiment, commanded by Colonel John W. Blake. They broke in confusion, but rallying, advanced again. Three or four times they rallied and advanced to the attack ; each time they

were driven back with great loss, the last time in such confusion
that it became a rout.  The day was ours.  We camped that
night on the position that had been so ably and successfully
defended.  The Sixth has to regret the loss of two of her
bravest and most gallant officers.  Lieutenant-Colonel George
T. Cotton was killed, nobly encouraging the men on the right ;
Captain Charles S. Todd, commander of Company C, the color
company, fell, pressing his men on to victory.  Scion of illus-
trious patriots, a braver spirit has not been offered up on the
altar of his country ! . . .

WALTER C. WHITAKER,
Colonel Commanding Sixth Kentucky Infantry.

Colonel Casey, of the One Hundred and Tenth Illinois,
says : —

HEADQUARTERS ONE HUNDRED AND TENTH ILLINOIS VOL'S,
CAMP NEAR MURFREESBORO', TENN., Jan. 8, 1863.

. . . On the morning of December 31 the regiment which
was in double column in reserve was advanced to take position
in the second line of battle, its left resting on the right of and
near the Murfreesboro' and Nashville pike.  About eight A. M.
the regiment began its advance on Murfreesboro'.  Just then the
firing, which had been heard at an early hour on our right, appeared to be rapidly nearing our right and rear ; and the regiment had advanced scarce its front, when the "right about" was
ordered, and it was moved to its former position, faced to the
front, and almost immediately after moved by the left flank to
a slight elevation [this is the exact position of the cemetery and
monument] on the right of the railroad, the highest point of
which joins the railroad embankment, and there faced to the
front, its left extending across the railroad, its entire right wing
about twenty paces in rear of and parallel to the left wing of the
Forty-first Ohio Volunteers, which was then engaged with the
enemy, who had advanced upon the front of our brigade.  This
position was maintained for a considerable time.  I advanced
the left wing of the regiment to the crest of the hill, where
they became immediately engaged with the enemy, who had

broken cover at the burnt brick house. Twice the enemy came forward as if intending to charge, when Colonel Hazen directed me to have my command "fix bayonets." I replied that we had no bayonets, and received the answer that we should "club muskets" if attacked. But the enemy did not charge our position. The whole right of the army having apparently given way, I was ordered to cross the railroad. Having crossed the road, we took a position perpendicular to it and in front of the wood facing the enemy, the One Hundredth (Bartleson's) Illinois Volunteers being on our right. This position had scarcely been taken before the enemy appeared in force beyond the fence and across the cotton-field, directly in our front. The firing began at once. Here the fire of small arms was incessant and terrific. My command suffered mostly from the Rebel batteries to the left and rear of the burnt brick house. Here the enemy appeared twice on our front in column, but failed to cross the fence. Night ended the conflict. My command slept on the ground we fought on, in the extreme advance, until the early dawn of the 1st instant, when we, with the rest of the brigade, took a position on the bank of Stone River. . . .

THOMAS S. CASEY,
*Colonel One Hundred and Tenth Illinois.*

Colonel W. H. Blake,[1] Ninth Indiana Infantry, says : —

HEADQUARTERS NINTH INDIANA INFANTRY,
IN CAMP NEAR MURFREESBORO', TENN., Jan. 6, 1863.

I have the honor to submit the following report of the part taken by the Ninth Indiana Infantry in the battle of Stone River, Dec. 31, 1862 : —

Bivouacking in the dense cedars on the right of the Nashville pike the night preceding the engagement, I moved at dawn in double column to the front, relieving the Thirty-sixth Indiana Infantry, of the Third Brigade. As there was no indication of an immediate advance, I stacked arms and permitted my men to build fires. At half-past six A. M. heavy cannonading and

---

[1] This officer must not be confounded with his brother, Colonel John W. Blake, commanding the Fortieth Indiana.

continued discharges of musketry were heard on our extreme right, which gradually approached our position, and were borne rapidly to our rear, until the sound of conflict was immediately in our rear on the Nashville pike. At seven A. M. I received an order to advance in line of battle, supporting the Sixth Kentucky Infantry; moving forward but a short distance, received orders to face by the right-about and march to the rear. At this time the enemy's artillery in our rear had opened fire on our columns. We halted, and moved by the left flank in the direction of the pike and railroad. I here received orders to move rapidly to the support of Colonel Grose's brigade, then hotly engaged with the enemy's infantry, but a few paces to my right and rear. While forming on the left of the Third Brigade I lost two men killed and several wounded by an enfilading fire from the enemy's artillery on my former front. The Third Brigade was closely engaged firing obliquely to their right. The enemy did not appear in my front, and by orders I changed front to the rear on first company and ordered my men to lie down. The enemy had advanced in our front, occupying the burnt house and grounds with a force of infantry and a battery of artillery. Remaining in this position but a short time, I was ordered to relieve the Forty-first Ohio Infantry, whose ammunition was exhausted. I marched by the left flank at double-quick time, passing under the enemy's fire; five men of Company H were knocked down by a single shell, two of whom were mortally wounded. Forming on the left of the pike with my right resting near it, my left on the railroad, I moved forward in line of battle to the low crest [this is the spot the monument is on], and relieved the Forty-first Ohio Volunteers.

The Rebels then occupied the burnt house with one battery, and their infantry were partly covered by the outhouse and a stockade fence, extending to the pike. I at once opened fire on them, and but a short time intervened until their artillery limbered up and retired in confusion to the rifle-pits on the ridge, where they went into battery and opened fire. After three quarters of an hour the fire from the infantry in our front slackened, and many of them ran to the rear in disorder. At this time a brigade of

the enemy's infantry advanced from their rifle-pits and marched
obliquely in the direction of my position; although at long
range, I at once opened fire on them, which thinned their ranks
as they continued to approach. As they drew nearer, one of the
regiments moved to the front and advanced at the charge-step
upon my position. My men poured upon them a galling and
deliberate fire that halted them within seventy-five yards of our
line, where they lay down, covered somewhat by the cotton-
furrows, and opened fire on us, from which we suffered. Their
colors had been struck down three times during their advance,
and every field-officer of the regiment was killed. (The regiment
was the Sixteenth Louisiana, Colonel Fish, of General Chalmer's
brigade, composed of the Ninth and Tenth Mississippi and Sixteenth Louisiana. These facts were obtained from prisoners
and burial parties that evening, and I presume are reliable.) I
received orders to "fix bayonets" and hold the position until
details could be sent to the rear for cartridges; my sixty rounds
were almost entirely exhausted. At this period of the engagement Lieutenant-Colonel Suman received a wound in the arm
and side; Lieutenant Kesler was mortally wounded; Captain
Pettit was severely wounded in the thigh and borne from the
field; Lieutenant Brinton and Lieutenant Creswell were both
severely wounded; also Sergeant-Major Armstrong severely
wounded in the leg; and many enlisted men killed and
wounded.

The One Hundred and Tenth Illinois Infantry, Colonel Casey,
were in reserve directly in my rear, quietly awaiting an opportunity to render me support, which was not needed. Captain
Cockerill advanced one section of his battery to my support,
and opened on the enemy with marked effect, and continued his
fire until his ammunition was exhausted; he had his horse shot
under him while directing the fire of his guns, and displayed the
utmost coolness and courage.

At eleven o'clock A. M. our forces were being driven from the
cedar grove on the right of the field. The enemy began to cross
troops from the burnt house to the timber. Being well within
range, I opened fire on them as they marched by the flank.

The whole line was subjected to a severe fire as it passed successively the open space. At half-past eleven A. M. the enemy's fire in my front had grown feeble; many had retired in disorder; many were killed or wounded (as the ground where they fought clearly attested at the close of the day. I picketed the ground near their line that night). The enemy occupying the heavy timber on my right, and the whole line on my right having retired, I received orders to withdraw my right and open fire on the forces in the timber, who were then opening fire on us. In performing this movement my brave color-bearer, Charles Zoellars, was killed. My left and centre still engaged the enemy in front. I was compelled again to withdraw my right from the severe flanking fire from the timber, which brought me to the railroad, where I received orders to cross and open fire upon the enemy obliquely to my left (then my right), detaching at the same time Companies K, G, and B, in charge of Major Lasselle, to occupy the elevation on the right of the railroad [the position of the monument], that had just been held by my left. At this time Lieutenant Braden fell, severely if not mortally wounded; he was an officer brave and without reproach. The One Hundred and Tenth Illinois Infantry were ordered up to my support, and formed on my right. At half-past one P. M. General Rosecrans appeared in person on this part of the field and ordered the Second Missouri and Seventy-third Illinois Infantry to assist in holding the position. The Second Missouri came into action gallantly, both forming on the railroad; the colonel of the Second Missouri was killed at this point. At half-past two P. M. these regiments were withdrawn, and the Sixth Kentucky Infantry forming on my right, I was ordered to open fire over the railroad track upon heavy bodies of the enemy then occupying the timber opposite, and directly in our front. I maintained this fire until the enemy, reinforced, again appeared on my left and rear; I again faced by the rear rank and opened obliquely to my left.

During the time my regiment occupied the position on the left of the railroad we were subjected to a cross-fire from two of the enemy's batteries on their right and centre, but owing to the nature of the position did not suffer severely. At four P. M. the fire of the enemy's musketry ceased, while that of their batteries continued until the close of the day. Before twilight I sent details to collect and bury my dead upon the ground where they fell; a mutual truce was granted, in which the soldiers of both sides, without arms, gathered their fallen comrades without interruption. The fierce and deadly strife had given place to the mutual expressions of kindness and regard. While thus engaged, one gun of Captain Cockerill's battery having been abandoned well to the front by the explosion of a caisson, I had it removed to the rear; the movement drew a fire from one of the enemy's batteries, but without effect.

For the brave men who stood by their colors from seven A. M. until four P. M. continually under fire, no word of mine could do justice to their unfaltering courage. The officers of the Ninth Indiana Infantry I regard as among the bravest of the brave. Many of the captains and commandants of companies exhibited the highest courage and capacity under a severe and long-continued fire. But where perhaps none failed in doing their duty, it would be an invidious distinction to name any one for marked honor. Lieutenant-Colonel Suman stood gallantly at the post of duty until wounded, when he retired from the field. Major Lasselle exhibited great courage, coolness, and efficiency throughout the day; Adjutant Willard repeated his heroism of Shiloh; Sergeant-Major Armstrong was wounded severely while executing an order. A sergeant, ten enlisted men, and one corporal deserted their colors during the action; I will take prompt measures to publish the infamy of their conduct and bring them to punishment. . . .

W. H. BLAKE, Colonel Commanding.

Lieutenant-Colonel A. Wiley, Forty-first Ohio, reports as follows: —

HEADQUARTERS FORTY-FIRST REGIMENT OHIO VOLUNTEERS,
CAMP NEAR MURFREESBORO', TENN., Jan. 6, 1863.

. . . A little before daylight on the morning of the 31st, Companies D and I were deployed as skirmishers and relieved Companies A and F, which were then assembled, and took their position in line. About eight o'clock the signal "Forward!" was sounded, and the regiment began to advance toward Murfreesboro'. At this time the firing, which had commenced at an early hour on our right, appeared to be nearing the pike to our right and rear, and the regiment had not advanced more than about one hundred paces, when the command "Right about!" was given, and it returned to its former position and again faced to the front. At this time the enemy appeared advancing in line across the open country directly in our front. The regiment was then moved by the left flank across the turnpike, its left resting on a slight elevation [the position of the monument] to the right of and near the railroad. The enemy, then moving by his left flank to gain cover of a wood on our right, made an oblique change of front to rear on the left company. The skirmishers, who during this time under the command of Captain J. H. Williston, acting major, had been engaged with the enemy with slight loss, were now rallied and put in position on the right of the regiment. In this position the regiment opened fire, and continued firing until its ammunition was about exhausted, when it was relieved by the Ninth Indiana, and retired a short distance and replenished its boxes. It then took up position on the right of the brigade, extended obliquely across the turnpike, and again opened fire. It here continued firing until a battery of the enemy opened upon our right flank, when it retired across the railroad, and took up position on the left of the brigade, the right resting near and perpendicular to the railroad, the rest of the brigade having taken position behind and parallel with the railroad. . . .

AQUILA WILEY,
*Lieut.-Col. Forty-first Ohio Vol's,*
*Commanding Regiment.*

The facts made plain in this account are confirmed by the official reports of General Wood's commanders.

MONUMENT TO HAZEN'S BRIGADE AT STONE RIVER.

## CHAPTER VI.

### READYVILLE.

IN posting the army for its long halt after the battle of Murfreesboro', my brigade was placed at Readyville, on the extreme left flank of the army, ten miles from Murfreesboro', and four miles from Cripple Creek, where Cruft's brigade, the nearest detachment, was posted.

It was the best school of practical soldiering we could have had. The isolation, and proximity to the Rebel right, demanded the utmost vigilance; while the four companies of cavalry, given me for patrolling, during a large part of the time skirmished with the enemy nearly every day; many of their dashes being highly successful and creditable. Readyville was a hamlet of little more than a dozen houses, and was the old homestead of the Ready family, where the well-known Congressman and father of Mrs. John Morgan was born.

After getting established in our new camp, instruction was resumed under the following order: —

READYVILLE, TENN., March 4, 1863.

A general school for instruction will be opened in this brigade as follows : —

Lieutenant-Colonel Wiley, Forty-first Ohio Volunteers, instructor. The entire brigade, including staff and headquarters, to be instructed and consolidated as the instructor may decide. Theoretical instruction will commence immediately, with Hardee's " Tactics." All commissioned officers are to recite daily from 10 to 11.30 A. M. A complete report of recitations will be submitted daily.   Practical instruction will also begin immediately.   The brigade is to be consolidated in one battalion, and divided by the instructor in subdivisions for exercise in all the drills as he may direct, including bayonet exercise at such hours before noon each day, Sundays excepted, as he may designate; and for exercise in one or more battalions, for battalion and brigade drill, in the afternoon of the same days.   The Forty-first Ohio Volunteers will be carried through the course already prescribed as rapidly as possible ; then beginning with Jomini's "Art of War," and reading in Napier's "Peninsular War."   The officers of this regiment are informed that it is expected that they will keep up the course of study and reading that they have entered upon, as long as they remain in the service.

The foregoing school is in view of an examination by a board of officers, before which it is purposed to bring every officer of the command.

The main operation of interest during our station at this point is described in the following report.   Although the expedition was not as successful as was desirable, it thoroughly broke up the menace to our advanced posts and foraging parties.

READYVILLE, TENN., April 4, 1863.

Assist. Adjutant-General, Second Division :

I have the honor to make the following report of the expedition made on the 2d instant, under my command to Woodbury.   The expedition was to have consisted of Cruft's brigade —which should report to me at this post by ten P.M. of the 1st— and my own.   That would enable me to put two columns in motion at eleven P. M., for the purpose of flanking and getting in the rear of Woodbury by daylight.   The brigade of Cruft did not report until something after midnight, enabling me to start one column, composed of the Forty-first Ohio and Sixth Kentucky, under Lieutenant-Colonel Wiley of the former regiment, at one A. M., which went to the right of Woodbury; and a column, composed of the Ninth Indiana and First Kentucky,

COLONEL ISAAC C. B. SUMAN

(Ninth Indiana.)

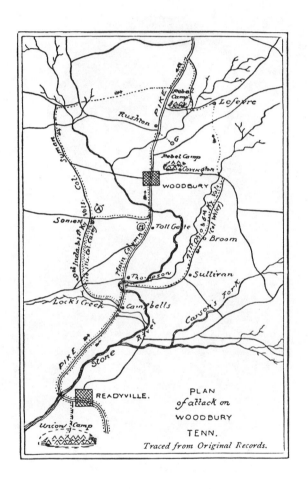

PLAN
of attack on
WOODBURY
TENN.
Traced from Original Records.

under command of Lieutenant-Colonel Suman of the former regiment, at 1.30 A. M., to proceed to the left of Woodbury. The One Hundred and Tenth Illinois, under Colonel Casey, accompanied as far as the point on the map marked *A*, whence they were to turn to the right, and proceeding cautiously to the Woodbury pike, in rear of the picket post of the enemy, marked *B*, where sixty men were on picket, remain concealed until the main column — composed of the Second Kentucky and an Ohio regiment, with Standart's battery and the battalion of Third Ohio Cavalry, commanded by Colonel Enyart, First Kentucky, which started at three A. M. — should drive the picket-guard into the ambuscade. The delay of two hours by Cruft's brigade made it nearly two hours after day before the different columns arrived at the points intended. The One Hundred and Tenth Illinois, in consequence, did not reach the pike in time to be of service. I, however, directed the cavalry to charge this post, which they did in fine style, sabring and capturing a dozen of the picket. We pushed on through the town, and came upon the main body of the enemy at six A M., one regiment (Smith's cavalry of about six hundred) drawn up to receive us about one mile beyond. Keeping my main column concealed, I permitted my advance to parry with him for about an hour, giving more time for the columns to get in position. I then pressed him forward, about four miles beyond the town, upon Wiley's column. On seeing our troops at this point, they at once scattered among the hills in all directions. The columns all gained their position promptly, correctly, and unknown to the enemy, marching about fourteen miles to do so. Had I not been delayed two hours, the results of the day would probably have been much more satisfactory, as then my original plan, which was to capture entire their main picket, and regulate the speed of all the columns so as to have gathered upon the camp at dawn, would probably have succeeded perfectly. As it is, I have to report three of the enemy killed (wounded unknown), twenty-five prisoners, fifty horses, four wagons, eight mules, with all their baggage and provisions. Colonel Suman captured one picket post almost

entire, as did also Colonel Casey.    I have to speak in the
highest terms of the battalion of the Third Ohio Cavalry, commanded by Major Seidel.    A brigade of such cavalry, well
mounted, armed with revolvers and sabres, would be invaluable.
Colonel Suman reports to me that the First Kentucky, in command of the major, straggled in going out so as at one time
to be a mile long, and detained him nearly one hour.    We
returned to our camp at twelve o'clock.

Our service at Readyville, with all our exposure and
constant vigilance, drilling and lessons, was a continued
picnic.    The season and climate were perfection.    We set
up a market at the forepost, with a pavilion and dan-
cing-floor, and established market-days twice each week.
The country people were invited to bring in their stores
and hear the music.    Our band was excellent, and the
girls from all the country round came regularly, some to
sell their marketing, others to dance; and the men off
duty, with their arms stacked, ready for use, were expected
to be present.    Two days in the week were thus spent in
amusements, while our tables by this means were bountifully supplied with all the luxuries of the country.

The bugle-call that sent us away from Readyville sent
grief and wailing to many hearts; and our good fortune
never again brought to us such service, so busy and so
happy.

# CHAPTER VII.

## MANCHESTER.

OUR march from Readyville was taken up the 26th day of June, after a halt of nearly six months, and until the 8th day of July it rained almost incessantly. The Tullahoma Campaign, or more properly the first stage of the movement on Chattanooga, ending with the battle of Chickamauga, encountered opposition only on the centre and right, the left not coming in conflict with the enemy. After he retreated from that point there was a halt at Manchester, Tenn., for about one month. It was alleged that this was to repair the railroads necessary for our further march. Instruction was at once resumed, as will best be understood by the orders given at the time.

MANCHESTER, TENN., July 14, 1863.

Drills will be resumed as soon as the grounds will permit, as follows : —

Company drills from 6 to 7.30 A. M. The first call will be sounded ten minutes before six. For this exercise colonels will organize a suitable number of companies with a full complement of officers and men, enough to make the companies of respectable size. For this purpose the regiments will be formed on the regimental parade-ground. At the option of regimental commanders every third drill may be that of skirmishers, provided the Tactics are implicitly followed.

One field-officer from each regiment will attend and have charge of morning drills. The brigade officer of the day will also attend, with a bugler, and indicate rests of ten minutes every half-hour. The troops will not be rested at any other time. These exercises will commence at the beginning of company drills, and the same order as indicated in the Tactics will be observed. Particular attention will be given to " Marching to the front," and that the ranks keep closed to thirteen inches.

There will also be battalion or brigade drills from 4.30 to 6 P. M.

If it is desired that there be brigade drill, an aide-de-camp will so inform the regimental commanders on marching to the grounds. Companies at morning drill will not be taken away from the plain in front of the camp.

MANCHESTER, TENN., July 21, 1863.

*Instructions for Corporals.* — As soon as your relief is formed, face it to the right, take No. 1, and relieve the sentinel over the arms, leave him behind, and take your place on the left side of the right file of the relief, and command, " Relief, support arms ! Forward, march !" When you arrive at six paces from No. 2, command, " Relief, halt !" See that your relief comes to a shoulder promptly, and that the sentinel to be relieved comes to a shoulder and faces the relief; then command, " No. 2, arms port !" See that both the relieving and the one to be relieved execute this movement. If not done properly, have it repeated until it is. Have the instructions turned over under your correction. When the sentinel is relieved, see that he marches in quick time to his place in the rear of the relief, and so on until the whole are relieved. Never post a sentinel without seeing that he thoroughly understands the instructions.

*Instructions for Sentinels over arms, at Guard Quarters.* — Take charge of this post ; permit no one to meddle with or remove any of the arms from the stack, without permission from an officer or non-commissioned officer of your guard. Present arms to all general and field officers, and to the officer of the day. Carry, or shoulder, arms to all captains and lieutenants. Turn out the guard for the officer of the day and for all general officers, giving the command; that is, " Turn out the guard ! The commander of the brigade," — division, corps, or department, as the case may be. If a general officer approaches, and you do not know what his command is, call, "Turn out the guard! A general officer." Always when you call "Turn out the guard!" for any officer, call loud enough to be distinctly heard by him, that he may know why the guard is turned out.

*Instructions for Sentinels.* —Take charge of this post; salute all officers according to rank; present arms to all general officers, field-officers, and to the officer of the day; carry, or shoulder arms, to all captains and lieutenants. In. saluting, face always outward from camp. Permit no enlisted man or citizen to pass your post, going to or from camp, without an order to do so from an officer or non-commissioned officer of the guard. Hold no conversation with any one not necessary for the proper discharge of your duty. Never sit down, stand still, or bring your piece to an order, but walk your post briskly. If you wish to be relieved for any necessary purpose, call, " Corporal of the guard!" adding the number of your post. Commit these instructions to memory and turn them over to your successor.

*Night Instructions for Sentinels.* — In addition to the day instructions, challenge all persons approaching your post. If answered, "Friends with the countersign," command, "Halt, friend," or "friends," and call, "Corporal of the guard!" adding the number of your post. Never allow any one to approach nearer than the point of your bayonet until you have received the countersign, or he has been examined by an officer or non-commissioned officer of the guard; and never let any more than one approach you until you satisfy yourself that the party is what is represented.

The officer of the guard will, before breaking ranks after guard-mounting, read to the non-commissioned officers the first part of these instructions, and all that part of the regulations of the army pertaining to the duties of sentinels, on pages 61, 62, 64, and 65, Revised Army Regulations. He will also see that each sentinel is made familiar with his duties as specified in this paper. For that purpose, after the relief is posted, a non-commissioned officer will teach each sentinel these instructions pertaining to his duties, until he can repeat them. Each relief, after the first, will be marched past these headquarters before it is posted. These instructions will be turned over by each officer of the guard, and when worn out a new copy will be furnished from these headquarters.

MANCHESTER, TENN., July 29, 1863.

I. In future the troops of the brigade will drill on Saturday mornings.

II. There will be company drills, conducted as at present, from six to seven A. M. on Mondays, Wednesdays, and Fridays.

III. There will be squad drills (the first four drills without arms) until Aug. 20, 1863, and afterwards skirmish drills from six to seven A. M. on Tuesdays, Thursdays, and Saturdays.

IV. Guard-mounting will be at 7.30 A. M.

V. There will be target practice from 8 to 9.30 A. M., on Mondays, Wednesdays, and Fridays. This exercise can be prolonged at the discretion of the colonels.

VI. There will be bayonet exercise from 8 to 9.30 A. M. on Tuesdays, Thursdays, and Saturdays.

VII. There will be brigade drills daily (Saturdays and Sundays excepted) from five to seven P. M.

VIII. In all these exercises the book will be scrupulously followed. One field-officer from each regiment will superintend the morning exercises, and a regimental commander, to be detailed from these headquarters, will also attend, whose duty it will be to see that all the requirements of this order are observed.

IX. Colonels, under the direction of the brigade commander, will select a sufficient number of drill-masters, most distinguished for soldierly bearing and efficiency, without regard to rank, to drill the squads. No more than eight men will be put in the same squad.

It is hoped the effort will be continued to make of the command soldiers who are worthy to be called so.

## CHAPTER VIII.

### IN FRONT OF CHATTANOOGA.

ABOUT the middle of August the movement to the Tennessee River, with Chattanooga as our objective point, was resumed. We were still on the left, and after crossing a very poor and hilly country, — the Cumberland Mountains, — we came into the Sequatchie valley, which is separated from the river by Waldon's Ridge. The valley, although not extensive, is one of the finest in the State, both in soil and in the beauty of its surroundings. Here my brigade was detached to cross Waldon's Ridge to the river at Poe's Tavern, ten miles above Chattanooga; and I was placed in command of all the troops opposite and above that place, consisting of two brigades of infantry, my own and Wagner's, and two of cavalry, Wilder's and Minty's, with two batteries of artillery. In the mean time the army went below Chattanooga, to cross at Bridgeport. Our object was to watch the fords, and to demonstrate as if the whole army was seeking to cross there.

We picketed the river and watched every possible point of crossing for fifty miles, gained much valuable information, gathered a great quantity of forage and food, and were hospitably entertained by a rather primitive and strongly Union people. In my command, systematic foraging was here introduced. The Tennessee valley, on the north side, is from half a mile to three miles wide, being shut in by the almost vertical face of Waldon's Ridge, with but few practicable ascents, which we very soon found and thoroughly understood, and as they were easily defensible, our position was excellent; for if hard pressed, we had only to take possession of the ridge and defend these few passes. The season and weather were again perfection, with an enemy full of enterprise and alarm just across the river; so that with so large a command and responsibility my headquarters became a centre of activity both day and night.

The records shall again give the story of our work there: —

POE'S TAVERN, TENN., Aug. 22, 1863.

Colonel FUNKHAUSER, Commanding Cavalry at Harrison's Landing:

General Palmer has gone to Dunlap. I can see no harm in opening moderately upon the enemy this morning. I would not waste a great amount of ammunition, as you cannot expect to effect much with artillery, with a broad stream between you and the enemy that will prevent you from taking advantage of what you might otherwise gain.

POE'S TAVERN, TENN., Aug. 26, 1863.

Colonels of Regiments:

In future, one pass will be approved at these headquarters from each regiment, permitting two men from a company to go out for the purpose of purchasing provisions. The colonel of each regiment will detail a competent officer to take charge of the squad while absent. This officer will be responsible for any depredations the men may commit. Before leaving camp, the officer will take the names of the men, and see that each has his gun and a proper amount of ammunition. Upon returning to camp he will report with his men to the commander of his regiment.

POE'S TAVERN, TENN., Aug. 26, 1863.

J. R. MUHLEMAN, Captain and Assist. Adjutant-General Second Division, Twenty-first Army Corps:

Colonel Funkhauser met thirty of the enemy at Harrison's Landing this morning, this side of the river, attacked them, killing three — one of them a lieutenant — and capturing two. The prisoners say that the "Chattanooga Rebel" of this morning reports the fall of Charleston. They say further that it reports the defeat of Lee by Meade. I give these as prisoners' reports. May God grant their truth! They report further what, if true, is important to us, — that the enemy opposed to us are moving towards Atlanta. This morning I sent a forage-train to Thatcher's Landing, and with the escort, — a section of artillery, — a few shots were fired across at the enemy's works, when a general stampede took place. All the fords and crossings are occupied by a few regiments of the enemy with a few guns, with light works. They have for several nights past sent small parties across to capture some of our men, to gain information. They are reported to be poorly informed of our purposes and force. A very reliable report reached me this evening, that yesterday the advance of Burnside's forces reached Kingston, and after a short engagement thrashed Forrest.

I am now making two thousand pounds of flour per day. The condition of the command was never better.

Poe's Tavern, Tenn., Aug. 26, 1863.

Until further orders there will be two drills daily, Saturday afternoons and Sundays excepted.

Company drills from six to seven A. M. Regiments will be divided into equal companies and fully officered for this drill; battalion or brigade drill from five to six o'clock P. M.

At police-call in the morning the entire command will be turned out and camps thoroughly policed.

Poe's Tavern, Tenn., Aug. 29, 1863.

Colonel FUNKHAUSER, Commanding Cavalry:

To save trouble, whenever any property is taken, no matter from whom, duplicate vouchers will be given, and if the parties are disloyal or doubtful, state it on the vouchers. This is as much for the protection of government as of the individual; for if none are given, some officer some day will be induced to give good vouchers to disloyal people on false pretences. All people are equally entitled to vouchers, with their *status* declared.

I am a good deal annoyed by persons presenting memoranda. There is ample time for making complete papers.

POE'S TAVERN, TENN., Sept. 1, 1863.

Colonel WILDER, Commanding Cavalry :

Colonel Funkhauser has been compelled to give memorandum receipts for all his supplies in this neighborhood, having no proper quartermaster. The people are more loyal than many of those of Ohio and Indiana, and often the corn and hay belongs to women whose husbands are in our army, and who with their own hands have actually made the crop. These women are not able to visit your headquarters to get their pay or proper vouchers. Can you not send over your quartermaster or a clerk to settle these claims ? It will be an act of simple justice, and save these poor people a world of trouble, and not a little to ourselves, as we may move soon. Please reply.

POE'S TAVERN, TENN., Sept. 4, 1863.

Colonel MINTY, Commanding Cavalry :

The courier will carry the order placing the forces of this flank under my command. Be pleased to keep me advised of everything that transpires. Contract your left as much as the presence of Burnside's forces there will make it practicable to do. Post at least one company at Thatcher's, relieving one of Wilder's now there. Inform me at once, if you have not already done so, about the supplies at Pikeville. Have you any reason for believing that Burnside will need them ?

POE'S TAVERN, TENN., Sept. 4, 1863, nine P. M.

Lieut.-Colonel GODDARD, Headquarters Dep't of the Cumberland :

A Tennessee conscript has just been brought to me, having deserted from the Forty-fifth Tennessee and swam the river to-day. He says the troops across the river are moving down, each garrison relieving the one below it each day ; also that the troops on the upper Tennessee are concentrated at Charleston, having burned the Loudon bridge.

He is an intelligent man, and, I believe, truthful.

Colonel Robert H.G. Minty

(Fourth Michigan Cavalry.)

COLONEL JOHN T. WILDER

(Former commander Seventeenth Indiana.)

Poe's Tavern, Tenn., Sept. 5, 1863.

Colonel Minty, Commanding Cavalry :

I have just received from the department headquarters directions for you to communicate with General Burnside, which I believe you have already done. Keep thoroughly acquainted with what takes place above you, and, as circumstances permit, contract your left, moving down the river. Make all your reports as before being placed under my command, besides those you make to me.

Poe's Tavern, Tenn., Sept. 5, 1863, eight A. M.

Lieutenant-Colonel Goddard, Assist. Adjutant-General :

Clouds of dust and the general movements observed from lookouts upon the hills on this side of the river all day yesterday strongly indicated a general movement of the enemy in the direction of Tyner's Station. All possible vigilance and means of obtaining information are used ; the whole line of the river from General Burnside's forces is carefully picketed. I am withdrawing Minty's left as rapidly as circumstances will permit, and am preparing boats that will be ready as soon as needed. Movements intended to deceive the enemy have been made, I think successfully. I can conceive of nothing that has been left undone, contemplated by instructions or made necessary by circumstances. All further developments will be carefully noticed and promptly acted upon.

Poe's Tavern, Tenn., Sept. 5, 1863, five P. M.

General Wagner, Commanding Brigade :

Colonel Wilder, opposite Chattanooga, reports that the enemy has put the pontoon bridge in readiness to swing around, as if to cross over. Learn all you can about it ; and if they threaten to cross, move your artillery, and direct Wilder to move his, where you can command the crossing, and contest any such attempt.

P. S. If you move, take infantry enough to support your artillery.

Poe's Tavern, Tenn., Sept. 6, 1863.

Colonel Minty, Commanding Cavalry, First Brig., Second Div.:

Forrest's force is opposite here at Igo's, Harrison's, and at all the fords, threatening to cross. A pontoon bridge has been constructed at Chattanooga by the enemy, as if to cross there also. I believe this to be only a feint while the army retreats. If, however, he should cross his army, you will proceed to take up a position on the mountain toward Pikeville, where you can effectually check any attempt at crossing there, having first sent out all your property.

You will receive orders this morning to come down to Sole Creek. Be able to report to me from there this evening. Look well to the river as far as Igo's.

Poe's Tavern, Tenn., Sept. 6, 1863, six A. M.

Colonel Wilder, Commanding Brigade :

In case the enemy should cross, it will be of the utmost importance that he be prevented from reaching the Sequatchie valley by any route below you. Be pleased to let me know fully what you can do in that quarter. Show this to Wagner, and say that should any crossing be made I shall expect him and you to hold all passes below the Chickamauga.

Poe's Tavern, Tenn., Sept. 6, 1863, six A. M.

Lieut.-Colonel C. Goddard, Assist. Adjutant-General, etc.:

The enemy at Chattanooga laid pontoons yesterday as if to cross.

Forrest's force suddenly appeared last evening at Igo's, Harrison's, and the other crossings, making displays of artillery and otherwise threatening to cross at all points. A deserter, who came across at Chattanooga, reported that Jackson's brigade was ready to cross on the pontoon. I believe this to be only a feint while the army retreats. The garrisons have been regularly relieved above, coming down the river, withdrawing their pickets, so there is nothing now above Thatcher's. Minty had a man across at Blythe's yesterday, and found nothing. For perfect security, however, I have sent all heavy property on the hill, and have traced every path by which a deer can climb the mountains this side of Pikeville, and can successfully prevent any crossing of the enemy this side, or at that place. I have to report the most valuable and efficient co-operation upon the part of the cavalry (Minty's and Wilder's).

POE'S TAVERN, TENN., Sept. 6, 1863, ten A. M.

Lieut.-Colonel GODDARD, Assistant Adjutant-General :

The officer on picket at Igo's reports sharp firing across the river, supposed to be Burnside's advance with the rear of the enemy.  Forrest's command garrisons the river for several miles up and down.  From the clouds of dust yesterday it would seem that he has in charge the enemy's trains, which seem to be pointing toward Tyner's.  The great amount of pounding across the river last night led everybody to believe they were making boats to cross, and the impression prevailed at Wilder's camp, and with the citizens, that they were crossing.  Wagner went down opposite Chattanooga with a battery and two regiments of infantry.  The effort there proved to be a feint, nothing like crossing going on, and the great noise opposite here was probably from repairs of trains.  It is possible that Forrest may contemplate a crossing to raid in our rear.  I have made such dispositions that, in case he does, if I fail to destroy him he will have to go far around Pikeville, and this will give ample time for troops in the rear to prepare for him.  I do not think it probable, however, that any crossing will be attempted here.

POE'S TAVERN, TENN., Sept. 6, 1863.

Colonel MINTY, Commanding First Brig., Second Cav. Div.:

I am directed by General Hazen to say that present indications point to an expedition under Forrest to cross the Tennessee at two or more points above Harrison's Ferry.  In case this occurs, the General desires you, as already directed, to attempt to hold the passes across the mountains.  You will, of course, be prepared to obstruct such roads as will admit of it, in case of failure to hold them without.  The several roads leading from Pikeville to McMinnville can probably be obstructed at the mountain, so as to cause a delay of a day or so, or a detour toward Sparta, which would amount to the same thing.  Robinson's road, leaving the Sequatchie valley several miles below Pikeville, is understood to be the only practicable road across the mountain toward McMinnville, between Pikeville and Dunlap.  These roads the General desires you to be prepared to obstruct in advance of your arrival in the Sequatchie, should you be forced across the mountain and ordered down the Sequatchie valley.

R. L. KIMBERLY,
*Lieut.-Colonel and Act'g-Assist. Adj.-Gen.*

POE'S TAVERN, TENN., Sept. 7, 1863, six A. M.
Lieut.-Colonel C. GODDARD, Assist. Adjutant-General, etc.:

Very large clouds of dust were seen all day yesterday across the river, up and down, for considerable distances. The clouds seemed to point down the river and back towards Tyner's. The last twenty-four hours have been remarkably quiet along the immediate line of the river. Minty still reports the enemy falling back from the river. General Buckner has ordered that all able-bodied negroes be sent to Macon, Georgia, to work on fortifications. I would sooner believe they were to organize into an army. My acting-assistant adjutant-general, Lieutenant-Colonel Kimberly, Forty-first Ohio Volunteers, has established communication, by signals, with the aid of plain flags, black and white, and a simple code, between these headquarters and all the crossings up and down the river for sixteen miles.

POE'S TAVERN, TENN., Sept. 7, 1863, eight P. M.
Colonel MINTY, Commanding First Brig., Second Cav. Div.:

The river is clear of the enemy to-day as far down as below Harrison's. I think there is nothing at all behind. Be pleased to move early in the morning to Sole Creek Ford (said to be the shallowest between Chattanooga and Kingston), and if possible make a crossing there with your entire command, after leaving a sufficient guard for your train, and move cautiously down, always keeping the country so thoroughly patrolled in your front and flank opposite the river as to avoid all danger. On arriving at Harrison's, communicate with me. If at any time in moving down you have sufficient reason therefor, recross the river. I am of the opinion that there are several fords between Sole Creek and Harrison's practicable for cavalry.

If you find no practicable ford, move down on this side to

Loudon Creek and report, keeping your train with you. If you cross, direct your train to move down to the Chickamauga Creek. Keep me advised of all you do.

P. S. Your note of three P. M. is just received. You will now be guided by this letter, together with the information you have received. If your information is reliable, it would not be advisable to come down just now. Whatever you do, let me know.

POE'S TAVERN, TENN., Sept. 8, 1863, six A. M.

Colonel MINTY, Commanding Cavalry :

Two deserters, just in from Forrest's command, report that he has gone to Rome, Georgia. They say that Pegram is at Blythe's, with about two brigades. That the question of raiding on our rear is certainly strongly thought of, I have no doubt. Their pickets all along here were withdrawn night before last. Funkhauser will endeavor to cross at Harrison's, and Wilder at Chickamauga, to-day. I am now anxious that you should cross as directed in my modified letter of instruction, if later intelligence warrants it.

POE'S TAVERN, TENN., Sept. 8, 1863, eight A. M.

Colonel WILDER :

Yours of last night is received. Funkhauser went down to Dallas at daylight, with orders to cross if possible. I sent orders to Minty last night to cross at Sole Creek this morning and move down to Harrison's, but a subsequent report of Rebels above him may prevent his doing so. The pickets opposite here were withdrawn night before last. My boats will be done to-night, and I should like to cross my entire brigade early to-morrow morning. Learn all you can, and let me know. I have a regiment of infantry and a section of artillery at Fryer's Island. Try and learn if infantry and wagons cannot ford after ferrying to the island.

POE'S TAVERN, TENN., Sept. 8, 1863, ten A. M.

Colonel MINTY, Commanding Cavalry :

From information just received, it is pretty certain that Pegram is opposite you with two brigades. I find also that the fords between you and Harrison's are too uncertain to be relied upon without actual trial upon your part. So for the present do not cross more than reconnoitring parties, and do not move lower down until you know more of the force between you and the Hiawassee.

POE'S TAVERN, TENN., Sept. 8, 1863, four P. M.

General WAGNER:

I herewith enclose papers this moment received from Colonel Minty. It would seem from these papers that a crossing is attempted; whether as a feint or a reality, I have no means of knowing. I have directed him to move up his artillery to cover the crossing, with what force he can spare, and repel any attempt that may be made.

These reports make it quite uncertain where Forrest is. It has been reported to me by prisoners and citizens that he has gone below. Four deserters from Buckner are just in. They left him last night at Ettawah. Everything was packed to march, and the sick placed on the cars. He has two divisions of two brigades each.

POE'S TAVERN, TENN., Sept. 8, 1863, five P. M.

Colonel MINTY:

Your enclosures have just been received. If you are of the opinion that a crossing is to be attempted, move up your artillery and what force you can, and prevent it. It has been a part of their tactics to always raid upon our rear, and they probably intend to do so now, in the way you state. If the case really demands it, some infantry could be sent off from here. I presume you have received my note to postpone any crossing other than a reconnoissance. Let me know speedily of any further developments.

POE'S TAVERN, TENN., Sept. 8, 1863, eleven P. M.

Colonel Wilder, Commanding Mounted Infantry:

Your note is just received. I will send the eight companies you desire. You can say to the Forty-first Ohio to remain where they are until after you make your demonstration. There is a regiment of Georgia cavalry to-night at Harrison's. This morning Buckner's corps was at Ettawah with much of Bragg's army at or near Tyner's. If you cross, move very cautiously, learning all you can, letting me know early, and I will cross my brigade if the enemy have given a chance.

You must make certain of their position and intentions, so we may not be led into the error of crossing to be destroyed. Let me hear from you early.

POE'S TAVERN, TENN., Sept. 9, 1863, six A. M.

Brigadier-General WAGNER :

Your note of ten P. M. yesterday is just received. I am of the opinion the Rebels will cross if they are permitted. It has been their tactics always to do so, and I know they have intended to do so now, and as Minty fears. They can be prevented if they attempt it. I will go up myself to learn all I can about it. They are not crossing yet. I consider his information as very inconclusive.

If we are to cross, we can hardly spare all of Wilder's command, as it will be too dangerous to cross infantry and artillery in boats until the country is thoroughly reconnoitred. The Fifth Georgia Cavalry was at Harrison's yesterday with other cavalry in the neighborhood, and Buckner's corps at Ettawah, and a portion of Bragg's army at or near Tyner's. It will not do for us to place ourselves between the river and much of a force, until we are pretty sure that they are beyond striking distance, unless we have cavalry to feel well in our front. I am all ready to cross.

POE'S TAVERN, TENN., Sept. 9, 1863, six A. M.

Lieut.-Colonel C. GODDARD, Assist. Adjutant-General, etc.:

The Fifth Georgia Cavalry was at Harrison's yesterday and last night. For nearly a day previous there were no troops at all on the river-bank, the infantry being all withdrawn. Pegram's brigade, to which this regiment belongs, appeared along the river yesterday, and it is probable that Scott's is near also.

We have two boats at the mouth of the Chickamauga completed, and everything is ready to cross as soon as it will be reasonable to do so. A note was received from General Wood a day or two since, urging that a crossing be made at the earliest possible moment. This will certainly be done. Yesterday, however, Buckner's corps was at Ettawah, and much of Bragg's command at or near Tyner's, with a force of cavalry in direct communication with them and the river.

Everybody is active, and ready for any service. Citizens from above still report that the able-bodied negroes have been ordered to Macon. Buckner has two divisions of two brigades each. He was packed yesterday morning ready to march. Minty receives reports that the enemy's cavalry will attempt to cross, to raid in our rear, and boats, or a bridge made of them, is now up the Hiawassee.

I shall go up there to-day in person and endeavor to learn all the facts about it. I have already directed Colonel Minty to hold his artillery and a sufficient force of other troops ready to move to any threatened point, and will endeavor to take such steps as will prevent the crossing should it be contemplated.

POE'S TAVERN, TENN., Sept. 9, 1863, seven A. M.

Colonel WILDER :

I am going up to see Minty and learn what reason there is for the alarm manifested about a crossing of the enemy there. The fords and crossings along here are strongly picketed by the enemy this morning. It is not expected of us to cross the river to fight a battle. We have a specific purpose here, and to cross the river with uncertainties in our front is not part of it. We should do no more than to make thorough cavalry reconnoissances at first, and until we make sure, by actual observation, that we will not be compromised by crossing. If we had a bridge in place of boats, the thing would be quite different. Show this to Wagner. We cannot depend upon appearances, or reports of prisoners, for the movement of our infantry and artillery.

In addition to the very active duties above mentioned, we had performed a good deal of " dumb but noisy show " in stationing the bands and field-music, divided into many detachments, in different parts of the valley, and causing

GENERAL SIMON B. BUCKNER, C.S.A.

GENERAL GEORGE D. WAGNER

them to play as for parades, tattoo, and reveille, as if there were at least one army corps present, with more troops constantly arriving.

The purpose for which we were sent to the Tennessee valley was fully executed; our army had crossed at Bridgeport and below undisturbed, and the Confederates were falling back toward Lafayette. I had built some large boats in the North Chickamauga, and on the 10th of August crossed over at Harrison's Landing. We found that the troops, by following a very circuitous course, could easily wade the river, the boats being used with mule-teams for ferrying the baggage. The day was beautiful, and the river at this point broad and exceedingly picturesque; while Waldon's Ridge, colored with the bright tints of autumn, rose high behind us, and the opposite side of the river was invested with the interest which always attaches to what is unknown.

The brigade, with colors flying, crossed in the early morning, and the windings of the ford made the line appear to double upon itself very curiously. The bright morning, the glistening of the arms, the orderly movement of the column crossing with buoyant spirits, while the bands, already across, played the national airs, made of this one of the most wonderfully interesting spectacles I ever beheld. This, like the attack on Mission Ridge, was unsurpassably grand and interesting,— a panorama which few may ever hope to see.

Just before crossing over, a communication was received from department headquarters, placing General Wagner, the commander of the other infantry brigade, in command over me. Wagner had raised the question of our relative rank. Our commissions bore the same date, and he was the elder colonel. Our rank, however, had been fixed in orders from the War Department. I was his senior by some twenty files, and the question he raised had no bearing upon the case. I at once accepted the situation however, appealed, and was sustained. The following is some of the correspondence : —

POE'S TAVERN, TENN., Sept. 6, 1863.

Brigadier-General WAGNER, Commanding Second Brigade, First Division, Twenty-first Army Corps :

DEAR GENERAL, — I forward a despatch, or rather communication, directing you to assume command under the belief that I am junior in rank. This paper was handed me open, and I at once forward it.

I am of the opinion that the grounds on which you ask that the rank be decided are not those which govern the question. The rule you quote (paragraph 5, Army Regulations) applies only to different regiments, and officers within them. The rule that has always applied to general officers is the order of appointment as arranged by the War Department. I have enclosed a correct copy of the list as so arranged. You will see that the names whose dates differ are arranged as they date, and that those of the same date are arranged according to order of appointment. . . .

I had no knowledge until quite recently that there was any question whatever of the nature you have raised. I am very certain that there is none at all in fact ; and this will only lead to unnecessary changes of command, as the authority of the appointing power to arrange the order of rank of its appointees has never been questioned. Be pleased to let me hear from you.

P. S. This question of rank frequently leads to jealousies and bickerings in the army. Do not let it be so in our case.

POE'S TAVERN, TENN., Sept. 6, 1863.

Brigadier-General GARFIELD :

I have the honor to call your attention to the fact that the order placing me in command of the forces composing the left flank of the army, dated, " Headquarters Department of the Cumberland, Stevenson, Ala., Sept. 3, 1863," has been abrogated by indorsement upon Brigadier-General Wagner's letter to you of Sept. 4, 1863, which directs General Wagner to assume command.

I respectfully represent that the ground upon which General Wagner bases his claim to superior rank (namely, that he was the ranking colonel when we received appointments as brigadiers) does not appear to be well taken ; and that in my opinion the question of previous rank does not at all affect the question.  Paragraph 5, Army Regulations, prescribes that between officers of the regiment or corps rank is to be decided by the "order of appointment," date of commissions being the same. . . . In the order of appointment I stand at least twenty files above General Wagner.  The privilege of regulating the rank of his appointees by this "order of appointment" has always been exercised by the President ; and his right to do so has never, I believe, been questioned.

I respectfully invite your attention to this matter, believing that action has been taken hastily.

I have the honor to report that I shall immediately turn over my command to General Wagner, in obedience to your order indorsed upon his communication, pending action of the War Department.

I thought this a hardship, as the decision was plainly wrong, and given without due consideration.  But it proved one of those blessings in disguise which seem mysteriously guided by unknown power.

By the old military custom, Wagner, being in command of the troops to first occupy Chattanooga, was made the commandant of that place, and was not at Chickamauga ; while I went on, after all the work on our flank had been done, joined my proper division at Graysville, and had my full share in the battle.  But my position as to our rank was sustained at Washington.

The following is my official report of the occupation of the Tennessee valley : —

CHATTANOOGA, TENN., Oct. 8, 1863.

Lieutenant-Colonel C. GODDARD, Assist. Adjutant-General, Headquarters
Department of the Cumberland :

In obedience to orders received at Poe's Tavern, Tenn.,
Sept. 3, 1863, from headquarters of the department, I assumed
command of all the troops in the Tennessee valley, embracing
Wagner's and my own brigade of infantry, Minty's brigade of
cavalry, and Wilder's brigade of mounted infantry, — in all
between six and seven thousand men; with orders to keep
these forces well in hand, closely watch the movements of the
enemy at all the crossings of the Tennessee River, make such
dispositions of the force as should lead the enemy to believe
that the valley was occupied by a large force, and cross and
occupy Chattanooga at the earliest opportunity.

The forces were scattered from Kingston to William's Island,
— a distance of seventy miles, — watching the entire line of the
river for this distance, and guarding at least twenty-five ferries
and fords. I at once visited the length of the line in person,
making such dispositions as I thought best for carrying out the
design of the command, withdrawing as much as possible the
left of the line, and giving orders for the construction of boats
in the North Chickamauga to be floated down and used for
crossing when needed at the mouth of the stream. Troops were
made to appear simultaneously at three or four different crossings; and by ingeniously arranging camp-fires and beating calls,
and by the dexterous use of artillery, they contrived to represent
a division of troops at each place.

The object desired was fully attained. I also placed all
heavy stores on Waldon's Ridge; and as the enemy threatened
to cross his cavalry in heavy force, made preparations to receive
him, and in case of failure to destroy him, to drive him up
the valley beyond Pikeville, where he could be met by General
Burnside. A battery and two regiments of infantry were placed
opposite Chattanooga, and the enemy at that point was annoyed
and two of his boats disabled. I also established communication
by signal between all crossings near me and my headquarters.
On the 2d the enemy burned Loudon Bridge, and Buckner's

corps began moving slowly down the river, making strong demonstrations upon the banks at several places, as if to cross.
They moved on Tyner's Station, reaching that point on the 6th
and 7th, followed by a heavy cavalry force that took the place
of the infantry on the river as they were relieved; and from
their numbers Colonel Minty reported that indications made it
pretty certain that a crossing was about to be attempted. At
the same time the pontoon bridge of the enemy was moved to
Chattanooga, as if to cross over troops at that point. All the
crossings were closely watched, and the troops held in readiness
for any movement. On the 8th the river was cleared of all
Rebel troops above Chickamauga; and I directed Minty to cross
over at the mouth of Sole Creek, reconnoitring the country well
in his front, and move cautiously down to Harrison's, always controlling one of the fords near him, so as to cross back if it should
be necessary. Before this order could be obeyed, a heavy cavalry
force confronted him on the opposite side of the river, and the
crossing was not attempted. That night, however, they all
retired from above Fryer's Island, and at eleven A. M. on the
9th, from their works opposite that island. The city of Chattanooga was also evacuated the same morning, and the troops of
General Wagner crossed over and occupied it. A portion of
Wilder's force crossed at Fryer's Island, reconnoitring thoroughly
the country opposite and towards Chattanooga. Colonel Minty
was at once ordered down to cross and report to Colonel Wilder;
while all the troops not already over were on the night of
the 9th concentrated at Fryer's Island, and on the morning of
the 10th crossed by fording, which was accomplished within the
space of six hours, without loss of life or material. The boats,
although completed, were not required except for towing baggage. I found in the Tennessee valley abundance of subsistence
for my troops, and brought out of it seventy beeves for the
army. The casualties in all these operations were two killed,
one drowned, and five or six wounded. Several hundred
prisoners and deserters were sent to the rear.

I have earnestly to commend to the attention of the Government the services of Colonels Wilder and Minty, commanding
cavalry brigades.

## CHAPTER IX.

### CHICKAMAUGA.

TO the question, Was the battle of Chickamauga necessary to the holding of Chattanooga ? no answer satisfactory to all has yet been given.  It is perhaps the most
serious question of all those raised by the war, and will in
the future claim careful study of the military critic.

It was very clear, soon after taking up our march into
Georgia, that we were not following a retreating army, but
one falling back for strategic purposes.  There was no track
of pillage, no destruction of property, and no straggling.
We moved slowly, passing through Ringgold and Gordon's
Mills, and on the 12th made a reconnoissance nearly to
Lafayette, where we met and skirmished with the enemy,
and came within plain sight of his encampments.  We
then moved to Gower's Ford, on the west of Chickamauga,
where, on the morning of the 17th, my pickets were most
vigorously attacked by a mounted enemy.  I, with a single
aid, was on the Lafayette road at the picket post.  The
attack was so sudden that the horsemen were upon us,
and some passed us and were captured before they could
check their horses.  The pickets instantly took cover, while
I sought the friendly shelter of a field of high corn.  The
affair was over almost in an instant, with a repulse and a
loss to the enemy of one captain and several men.

In studying this battle of Chickamauga one is mainly
impressed with the lack of steady and systematic direction
in placing and manœuvring the different parts of the army.

That there were grave errors from some cause, both by the commander-in-chief and by subordinates whose high rank gave them in action the broadest discretion, seems almost beyond question. My part is told in the following official report : —

CHATTANOOGA, TENN., Sept. 28, 1863.

Captain D. W. NORTON, A. A. Adjutant-General Second Division:

. . . September 12th we marched to within two miles of Craw-fish Springs, and during the night of the 18th to a position one mile north of Gordon's Mills, where we formed in line of battle on the left of General Cruft and near the Lafayette and Ross-ville road. Here we remained, with an occasional shot in our front, until about eleven o'clock A. M. of the 19th, when I received orders to move in the direction of the firing, then growing quite severe, about one mile and a half to the left, in front of General Thomas's position. On reaching the field, on the east side of the Lafayette and Rossville road and one half-mile south of Kelley's, the brigades of the division were formed in two lines, facing the east, the second line being doubled by regiments on the centre. My brigade was on the left of the division, General Cruft being on my immediate right. The line was then moved forward in echelon by brigades, my brigade commencing the movement. The enemy was struck after advancing about three fourths of a mile, when a terrific contest was here added to the already severe battle on our left. The enemy gave ground freely, and the troops to the left of us at this juncture making an advance, all the ground desired there was carried, extending to the right as far as the echelons of the Second Division extended. I was at this time relieved by General Turchin, and ordered by my division commander back to the road to fill my boxes with ammunition, already twice exhausted (I had carried a six-mule wagon-load of ammunition with me), and to take charge of some batteries left there without supports. This I had just accomplished, when a vigorous attack was made upon that part of our line immediately to the right of the ground fought over by the right echelon of our division. I at once moved my brigade to the right, and forming it so as to face the sound of battle, moved it forward and placed it in position as a support to some troops of General Reynolds, my left resting on the Lafayette and Chattanooga road, near the field before referred to, where we first formed line, the right being thrown forward, forming an angle of about forty-five degrees to the road. The battle neared my position rapidly. At this moment I met General Van Cleve, whose division the enemy had engaged still farther to the right. He told me that his men had given way, and that he could no longer control them. The enemy continued to advance steadily, and the line in my front gave way. My own men then advanced to the top of the crest and withstood the shock until they were completely flanked on the left, then obliqued well to the right and took position upon a high elevation of ground, confronting the left flank of that portion of the enemy which had broken our centre. The advance of the enemy was now steady to the northward, nearly in the direction of the Lafayette and Rossville road, while another line of the enemy to the east of and parallel to that road was advancing to cross it. I found myself the only general officer upon that part of the field, and to check the farther advance of the enemy was of the utmost importance. I hastily gathered and placed in position, pointing down that road, all the artillery then in reach, being the batteries I had been sent to guard, including a portion of Standart's, Cockerill's, Cushing's, and Russell's, — in all about twenty pieces, — and with the aid of all the mounted officers and soldiers I could find, succeeded in checking and rallying a sufficient number of straggling infantry to form a fair line in support of the artillery. My brigade could not be brought into position in time, as there were but about two minutes to make these dispositions before the blow came, when the simultaneous opening of all the artillery with grape checked and put to rout the confronting columns of the enemy.

It is due Lieutenants Baldwin, First Ohio Artillery, commanding Standart's battery, Cockerill of the same regiment, commanding battery, Cushing and Russell, Fourth United States Artillery, commanding batteries, to state that for accuracy in manoeuvring and firing their guns in the immediate presence of

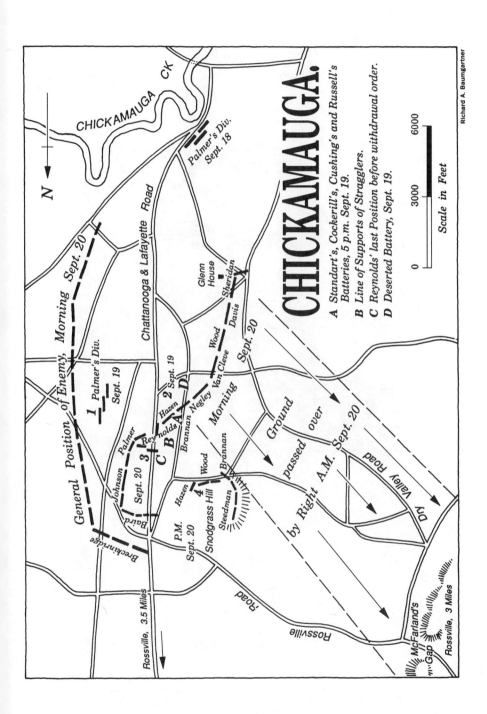

N

CHICKAMAUGA CK

CHICKAMAUGA.

A  Standart's, Cockerill's, Cushing's and Russell's
   Batteries, 5 p.m. Sept. 19.
B  Line of Supports of Stragglers.
C  Reynolds' last Position before withdrawal order.
D  Deserted Battery, Sept. 19.

Scale in Feet

0        3000        6000

Richard A. Baumgärtner

Palmer's Div.
Sept. 18

Chattanooga & Lafayette Road

Glenn
House
Sheridan

Davis

Wood

Van Cleve

Sept. 20

Morning

Ground

passed over

by Right A.M. Sept. 20

Dry Valley Road

General Position of Enemy, Morning Sept. 20

Palmer's Div.
Sept. 19

1

2 Sept. 19

Hazen

Reynolds

Brannan Negley

D

C B A

3

Johnson

Palmer

Sept. 20

Baird

Breckinridge

P.M.
Sept. 20

Hazen

Wood

Brannan

4

Snodgrass Hill

Steedman

Rossville, 3.5 Miles

Rossville Road

McFarland's
Gap

Rossville, 3 Miles

GENERAL GEORGE H. THOMAS

the enemy, on the occasion above referred to, the army and country are placed under lasting obligations.

Major-General Reynolds, whose division had been driven back, came to this position soon afterward and made further dispositions of troops; but, excepting a fierce attack made at dusk upon General Johnson, the fight was closed for the day. Soon after the above repulse General Thomas came to this place and took command of all the troops in this part of the field.

It would appear that all the troops except General Johnson's division had been withdrawn from the portion of the field he (Johnson) occupied, leaving him well advanced and entirely unsupported. When the attack was made upon him my brigade was sent with the others of the Second Division to his support; but the firing ceased when we had marched some four hundred yards east of the Lafayette and Rossville road, opposite Kelley's house, and we were here placed in position for the night, and the fight of Sunday found us in the same spot.

Although my losses this day had been great, including Colonels Payne and Shackleford severely wounded, and Lieutenant-Colonel Rockingham killed, besides the loss of four hundred and thirty-nine officers and men, the brigade, with the exception of the Sixth Kentucky, was in good condition and with few absentees. The latter regiment, from the great mortality among its officers, was very much broken, and its fragments were attached to the other regiments of the brigade.

On the morning of the 20th the men were roused at three o'clock and directed to make coffee in case they had water in their canteens, and at daybreak a breastwork of logs and rails was begun, which was taken up and carried through our entire division and that of Reynolds on our right and Johnson and Baird on our left. Wherever this work was made, the line resisted with firmness all attacks from the front the entire day, and with little loss. At about eight o'clock the attack was commenced upon the left of this line, and swept along toward the right, arriving at my position about fifteen minutes afterward, passing on, but producing no effect until it had passed General

Reynolds. This assault was kept up without interruption until about eleven o'clock A. M. with a fury exceeding that upon the field of Shiloh or Stone River. The repulse was equally terrific and finally complete. A few light attacks were made on this front up to one o'clock P. M., after which everything, up to the withdrawal from the field, was comparatively quiet. The value of this simple breastwork will be understood, from the fact that my loss this day was only about thirteen men during a period of more stubborn fighting than at Shiloh and Stone River, or even the preceding day, when the same brigade, at each place, lost over four hundred men. Our left flank was twice turned and partially driven out of its works, but the enemy was easily checked, and our lines speedily restored. At about ten o'clock A. M. our couriers for ammunition, previously prompt to return, did not come back, and it came to be believed that our trains had been captured. I at once cautioned my colonels, who fired only by volleys, not to waste a single round of ammunition, and my battery was similarly cautioned. During the quiet that afterward settled upon us several officers were struck by sharpshooters from distant trees. Ascertaining the proper direction, I caused volleys to be fired into the tops of the trees, and thus brought several of the enemy's sharpshooters from their hiding-places, checking for a time this species of warfare. Skirmishers sent out along the front reported the execution of our arms during the engagement to have been terrible beyond anything before seen in the war, as I believe the fight from eight to eleven o'clock to have been.

The stillness that now hung over the battlefield was ominous. We had four divisions in line that, although they had withstood one of the most terrific assaults on record, had hardly felt the battle. There were two more divisions on our right, with General Thomas, as fresh as we were. But the feeling that our ammunition was gone was like a leaden weight. The men, however, were confident of success. It afterward appeared that the breaking up of the troops on our right had swept away our ammunition and much else, along with their fragments, to Chattanooga.

No new dispositions of troops on our part of the line were

made, nor attempted, except that General Reynolds's right was somewhat withdrawn to cover that flank. General Wood, General Brannan, and one division of the reserve corps (two brigades of each of these divisions) were formed in a line at right angles with and directly in rear of the right of the positions before described; the left of this line being about one half-mile from Reynolds's right. At about three o'clock P. M. a fearful onslaught was made upon this new line. The battle raged for an hour with apparently varying fortunes, when several general officers at our position expressed the opinion that it was necessary for a brigade to move over and, as they said, strike the deciding blow. No one appeared to have any ammunition. I found upon examination, that, thanks to my care in controlling the fire of my men, I still had about forty rounds per man, and with the approval of my division commander I immediately moved my men over at double-quick, with a front of two regiments, skirmishing all the way. Arriving near the scene of action, I caused a partial change of direction to the left, and was quickly pouring in volleys, my second line alternating with my first. The action lasted but a few minutes, when the enemy retired. There was no more fighting, and at dusk I received orders from General Thomas to retire on Rossville, which I did quietly and in perfect order, the pickets of the enemy following mine closely as they were withdrawn, and confronting an officer sent to see that the withdrawal was thoroughly done.

There are several lessons to be learned from this fight, and to me none more plainly than that the iron hand which is just but always firm can alone make soldiers that can be relied upon in the hour of trial. The effect in my command of firing by volleys upon the enemy has invariably been to check and break him. It further gives a careful colonel complete control of his fire. The effect of sending in fractions to fight against an entire army is to waste our own strength without perceptibly weakening his.

My entire brigade has my warmest thanks for its services. Colonel O. H. Payne, One Hundred and Twenty-fourth Ohio, and Colonel George T. Shackleford, Sixth Kentucky, both of whom fell early in the fight of Saturday, carried in their commands bravely and at the opportune moment. The One Hundred and Twenty-fourth Ohio, although in its maiden engagement, bore itself gallantly and efficiently. Major Hampson, who commanded this regiment after the fall of its colonel, bore his part with ability and success. Colonel Wiley, Forty-first Ohio Volunteers, and Colonel Suman, Ninth Indiana Volunteers, with their regiments, are veterans so often tried that it is unnecessary to praise them. The country cannot too highly cherish these men. Colonel Wiley had his horse shot under him. The services of Lieutenant-Colonels Kimberly, Forty-first Ohio, and Lasselle, Ninth Indiana, were conspicuous and valuable, and Lieutenant-Colonel Kimberly had two horses killed under him. Of the noble dead there are Lieutenant-Colonel Rockingham, Captains McGraw, Johnston, and Marker, Lieutenants Lachmann and Enbanks, all of the Sixth Kentucky; Lieutenants Criswell, Nickerson, and Parks, of the Ninth Indiana Volunteers; with a long list of others, as brave and true, but bearing no title. Many tears will be shed in their memory.

My staff were efficient, performing every duty assigned them with promptness and accuracy. Captain H. W. Johnson, Forty-first Ohio Volunteers, acting-assistant quartermaster, was with me the entire day on Saturday, and at night brought upon the battlefield such portions of his train as were needed for the comfort of the command, taking them away before daylight. . . . Of my orderlies, Shepherd Scott was particularly distinguished for bravery and good conduct. He on two occasions brought brigades to my assistance when greatly needed. His horse was shot and he killed or captured. Should he be restored, I recommend that he be appointed a second lieutenant.[1] Quite a number of horses were killed and disabled in the service of my staff. The commander of the brigade was twice struck, but not injured. The casualties of the brigade were four hundred and ninety-five. . . .     W. B. Hazen, *Brigadier-General.*

As the division was marching from its position, a mile north of Gordon's Mills, it made a detour to the left from

---

[1] Scott was captured, and died at Andersonville.

the Lafayette road, as the enemy was said to hold it, passing Glenn's, where General Rosecrans had taken up his headquarters. He hailed me, and gave me minute directions for going into action, which afterward were repeated to the division commander.

We soon arrived at a point on the main road which appeared to be opposite the extreme right of our troops, already seriously engaged, at a little field on the east side of the road about one half-mile south of Kelley's, and the division was faced by the right flank. By General Palmer's direction I began the movement. I was on the left. After advancing a half-mile, the enemy could be plainly seen across an open space, and very soon, after a severe engagement, he retreated precipitately. The brigades on my right halted as soon as mine, still maintaining the echelon distances, which served as a check on my advance, — except the One Hundred and Twenty-fourth Ohio on the left of my front line. This holding back of the two right brigades seriously impaired the effect of our attack. The One Hundred and Twenty-fourth Ohio continued on far to the front, where Payne, its colonel, fell. We kept up the fight till the ammunition in the boxes and in the two wagons I brought into action was exhausted, when General Turchin's brigade, just in the rear, by direction of General Palmer relieved mine. I then by order of my division commander fell back to a point on the road about midway between the field where we first formed and Kelley's; when again, after filling the boxes, we had another most desperate conflict with a strong force (as mentioned in my report), which had driven Van Cleve and one brigade of Reynolds, so far as I could see, quite off the field. As I hastened forward to learn the condition of affairs, I met General Van Cleve, a division commander of Crittenden's corps, riding wildly up the road, with tears running down his cheeks, who asked if I had any troops, as they were wanted badly "just down there," — pointing in the direction I was going, — saying he had not a man he could control. He was accompanied by a single officer, his adjutant-general, Captain Otis. He was an elderly, gray-haired man, a West Point graduate, and since the war has been the Adjutant-General of Minnesota. His distress was not feigned. I rode forward with all possible speed, and there found in the field just south of and opposite the one we had formed in, a battery without horses, gunners, limber, or caissons, standing on a little eminence just to the west of the road. Everybody in that vicinity had fled, except two or three mounted men, who rode out, as I did, to see what was coming next. There was not a moment to spare, and my brigade, except the One Hundred and Twenty-fourth Ohio, not then re-formed from the last desperate fight, was put in on the west of the road, its right thrown forward, and was then generally engaged. It was here that the Sixth Kentucky lost so fearfully, and with the Ninth Indiana, both fighting most gallantly, became too much broken to be at once available for further use. The part taken by the Forty-first Ohio at this juncture was most praiseworthy. This regiment, although intact, had moved so far to the right as to be, for momentary use, beyond reach; and at this instant I was, so far as concerned my own command, in the same condition Van Cleve reported himself in a few minutes before. But there was not a moment for inactivity. This line of the enemy was checked; but another line in great force was heard advancing from the same direction, and in two minutes would be crossing the Lafayette road. There were four batteries, Standart's, Cockerill's, Cushing's, and Russell's, which I had been charged to look after, just in the little skirt of timber to the west of the road between Kelley's and the field in which the abandoned battery stood. To get these in position to take the enemy's line in flank when it should uncover from the wood was scarcely the work of a minute. Almost as quickly we had gathered from the multitude of stragglers both mounted and on foot what appeared a fair line of support. At the proper time these guns opened with such effect as to completely check and disperse the enemy's advance. For two or three minutes all the guns fired at point-blank as rapidly as possible. When the smoke cleared away, several rider-less horses came galloping up the road, but there were no troops there. Passing quickly to the open field to the right, two Rebel regiments that had crossed the road on their extreme left before the batteries opened, were in plain view at quite the far side of the field beyond what was known as the Tanyard, still going on to the westward in perfect step. I called to an officer standing near, to get troops from somewhere and meet them. He replied that he had two regiments in hand, and started instantly to the work. This officer, whom I had never before seen, proved to be General B. D. Fearing, of Marietta, Ohio, now deceased. General Reynolds came upon the ground at this moment, and very soon afterward assumed direction, and in a few minutes was followed by General Thomas. My brigade now being assembled, he took us to the aid of Johnson, just then violently assailed, but soon posted us for the night on the spot where we fought next day, just opposite and on the eastern skirt of the field in which Kelley's house is situated.

During the night our quartermaster, Captain Johnson, of the Forty-first Ohio, brought to the brigade in wagons ammunition, food, and such comforts as he could command, which were most welcome. At daybreak Colonel Suman, of the Ninth Indiana, came to me and suggested a breastwork along our front, which no one before seemed to have thought of. I at once gave orders that one rank work at this while the other stood to their arms, and went to urge the commanders on my left to do likewise.  General R. W. Johnson at first objected that noise would attract the attention of the enemy; but in a very few minutes the whole line, including his division, were at work, and long before the attack at eight A. M. the cover was ample against musketry.  This was our first really useful improvised cover for infantry.  The line on our flank consisted of the divisions of Baird on the extreme left, then Johnson, Palmer, and Reynolds, belonging to the three corps of Thomas, McCook, and Crittenden.  All to the right of that was either withdrawn or driven out of the line by the enemy.  The attack came, and was the most fierce and persistent that one can conceive.  It came obliquely from the left, and swept along our front, continuing from one to two hours; and while the repulse was complete and crushing, our line scarcely felt the shock, my brigade losing but thirteen men against over four hundred the previous day.  This is a good example of the advantage of the defensive behind shelter.  About ten A. M. the attack of Breckinridge was made on our left flank; this succeeded in turning all the troops to the left of my brigade out of their works; but the attack was driven back and our line at once restored.  This repulse of Breckinridge was the only occasion in the war on which I saw two opposing lines deliberately advance to close quarters and fire in each other's faces.  My brigade engaged in the same manner at Shiloh, but a screen of bushes separated us.  The combat with Breckinridge was in the northern portion of the open field in which the Kelley house was situated, along the eastern skirt of which our line was posted.  The shot of the enemy for a few moments came from an angle of at least twenty-five degrees from our rear and left, and except for this successful repulse, which General Thomas directed in person, the battle must have ended then.  The troops who rendered

GENERAL THOMAS L. CRITTENDEN

GENERAL ALEXANDER McD. McCOOK

this timely and most valuable service were Van Derveer's brigade of Brannan's division, and Grose's of Palmer's division. It was the most anxious moment of my life. About the same time, Reynolds's right being turned, it was refused, and his entire division formed nearly a right angle to the rest of the line.

It was about this time also that the disaster took place on our right. After this we could no longer hear from our ammunition wagons, and General Thomas went over to the right, where the short line of Brannan and Wood was maintained. He could not be communicated with, as the space which separated us was occupied by the enemy's light troops; and until the order to withdraw was received, between five and six o'clock, no tidings were had from him. After eleven A. M. it was quiet on our front, and quite a number of general officers were congregated, discussing the condition of the fight, among them two major-generals, Reynolds and Palmer; and it was urged that it was necessary to have a general commander of our four divisions. Reynolds, the senior, declined positively to assume it, remarking that it would be only assuming a disaster which was certainly impending. I have always believed that by assuming general charge he would have prevented much of the loss and confusion that took place when the withdrawal, each division by itself, without unity of action, was finally made.

The command of the whole really rested on him as definitely as that of his own division, and his refusal to exercise it was, in my opinion, an inexcusable and most serious neglect of duty. The break in the centre and right was never repaired, and it had left Brannan and Wood, with two brigades each, in line facing nearly due south, and about on the prolongation of Reynolds's last position, but with a gap between them of half a mile. Our forces remained in this separated condition for the rest of the

day, Thomas being with this isolated and smaller portion.
When the serious assaults were made there, our own front
had been quiet for several hours; and feeling that the
gauge of battle rested with the right, I asked authority of
General Palmer to go over and aid them. My brigade
was replaced in the line by Grose's brigade of our own
division.

This movement caused a partial advance of the enemy,
and I was halted in the middle of the field, just behind
our line, to await the result, but soon had orders to go on.
I found the forest on the west side of the Lafayette and
Chattanooga road, through which we had to pass, filled
with the enemy's stragglers and pickets, requiring a sharp
skirmish all the way. This explained why none of our
messengers had returned for the past five hours. My advance brought me directly on the left flank of our force
there, which was Opdycke's One Hundred and Twenty-
fifth Ohio Regiment of Wood's division. I found him
firing by volley with great rapidity, — a species of tactics
he had been taught when a captain in the Forty-first Ohio
Regiment. The position was admirable, being a little
crest at the south side of the field at the Snodgrass house.
The men, alternating by companies, would advance up to
this crest to deliver their fire, and then fall back a few
yards for shelter and to reload. I at once formed upon
Opdycke's left, and began volley-firing also. The position
was in a cornfield, and the bullets rattled through the dry
corn in a very uncanny way. General Brannan asked for
a regiment to take post on his right, and I sent the Ninth
Indiana, then in reserve, and it remained with him until
withdrawn at twilight. The battle had ceased, and the
great volume of cheers of the enemy on the left, just after
the withdrawal of that portion of our line, was almost
appalling. The cheers would start up again at different
points for an hour afterward. I now received an order

from General Thomas in person to withdraw to Rossville, following Brannan. It was then sundown, and it seemed a long time before Wood and Brannan were on the road; and the stars were shining brightly when my troops moved off. In withdrawing, my skirmish line was thrown well out to the front and left, and the officer in command confronted the Confederate officer posting his pickets, but there was no conflict. Neither seemed anxious for one. As I marched northward in the middle of the field where the Snodgrass house is situated, and reached the lane which divided it from east to west, Reynolds, at the head of his division, came up it and sung out, " Hold on, Hazen; it's my turn now!" So again I halted in the same field till his whole division filed past, and it seemed a very long time; and then it was full night. The Ninth Indiana held its position also till Brannan had withdrawn, and in the twilight a singular episode occurred there. A Confederate officer, supposing all our troops had withdrawn, moved his regiment up quietly to occupy the high ground, and the two commanding officers were close to each other before the mistake was discovered. The Confederate demanded Suman's surrender, who, always brave, collected, and ready, replied, " Oh, I have surrendered already!" The officer, being satisfied, turned to make further dispositions, when one of Suman's men, seeing the whole affair, shot and killed the officer, bringing in his sword, pistols, and other equipments, and Suman quietly led his regiment away and joined the brigade, before the enemy knew what had happened. This is Suman's version of the affair. We then marched to Rossville, where we arrived precisely at eleven P. M. There were no troops behind us, and the bivouac at Rossville was wrapped in sleep. The night was now intensely dark, and we found a place to lie down. There was a little clump of houses near, alongside of which I spread my blanket and slept till morning, when we found ourselves in an old cattle-corral. The house near by was the headquarters of General Steadman, and in the little town of Rossville.

The battle of Chickamauga may be described as an attempt, on the 18th, by the Rebel commander to interpose his army between us and Chattanooga. On the same day, while General Rosecrans was endeavoring to reach the fords of the Chickamauga, to either take up that line or hold the fords, he became engaged by detachments with superior forces, already across the stream, and was in the main beaten and driven west of the Lafayette road; but the enemy held no ground there, unless it was far to his left. On the morning of the 19th the Confederates began an offensive battle by attacking our line from the east, swinging upon his left flank as a pivot, in which he was repulsed with crushing severity along the front of the five divisions on our left, when the sixth division, Wood's, by an order sent at this inopportune moment by General Rosecrans, who was not present, and obeyed without due discretion, caused an opening through which the enemy passed, and succeeded, by an attack in flank and rear, in driving our four right divisions — Jeff. C. Davis, Sheridan, Negley, and Van Cleve — from the field; so that they did not participate in the battle again that day, but carried with them in the rush the commander-in-chief, two corps commanders, — McCook and Crittenden, — and two commanders of division, — Negley and Van Cleve.

The enemy then endeavored, with Breckinridge's division, to turn our left flank, but was repulsed. He then attempted with great force to crush our new right flank, a crotchet of four brigades, but was repulsed with the opportune aid of two brigades at that point. This timely force was Steadman's, — a reserve which came in at its own motion, — and with it came the corps commander, General Gordon Granger. That might have closed the battle of the day; but General Rosecrans, then in Chattanooga, ten miles away, ordered a withdrawal to Rossville. The four divisions of Baird, Johnson, Palmer, and Reynolds, on the left, were intact and confident. The same may be said of the six brigades of Brannan, Wood, and Steadman, on the right. The greater portion of Sheridan's and Jeff. C. Davis's divisions were already near the field, returning with their commanders, and with the most of Van Cleve's and Negley's divisions, so near that they could have been brought up and the whole army posted most advantageously that night.

Our army, fighting on the defensive that day, had suffered in killed and wounded comparatively little. The order for the withdrawal on the left was communicated to division commanders separately, — there being no recognized commander of the whole on the left, — and executed by them without co-operation, the enemy at once assaulting; and our losses and disgrace in consequence were heavy.

The causes of our disaster, where there ought to have been a decided victory, may be simply stated. The line of battle, on the night of the 18th, should have been compactly and completely posted for the battle, under the eye of the commander-in-chief, and nothing should have prevented this. During the progress of the battle no troops in the front line should have been ordered out of it by any one not actually present, and acting upon actual knowledge, and especially not from a point ten miles away. With the line properly posted on the night of the 19th, and with Negley in position, as Thomas says he was promised early the previous evening that he should be, our success would have been nearly certain. If the army had been re-posted instead of withdrawn on the night of the 20th, as was clearly practicable, there can hardly be a question that we should have been successful on the next day.

The troops from the right that remained upon the field were withdrawn in perfect order, as the left also might have been if the movement had been judiciously executed, the several divisions co-operating.

As a result of this battle, Rosecrans, Crittenden, McCook, Negley, and Van Cleve were deprived of their commands, and virtually passed out of the war.

Of the six divisions that remained intact on the field on September 19th, Brannan, Baird, and Reynolds belonged to Thomas's corps, Palmer and Wood to Crittenden's, and Johnson to McCook's. Of the four swept to the rear and out of the fight, Sheridan and Jeff. C. Davis belonged to McCook, Negley to Thomas, and Van Cleve to Crittenden.

In carefully studying this battle, one cannot fail to be impressed with the most worthy and heroic service of two division commanders who stand out conspicuously from all the rest, — Brannan and Baird. They both went back to comparatively obscure places in the regular army, where Baird is now serving, and Brannan has been retired.

For carrying my brigade across to help the right on the 20th, General Thomas, who at the time was not aware of it, afterward recommended me for promotion to a major-generalship, — a fact unknown to me until after the close of the war.

The following extract is from General Palmer's report:

CHATTANOOGA, TENN., Sept. 30, 1863.

. . . I have the honor to report that on the 1st day of September Hazen's brigade, with Cockerill's battery, was at Poe's Tavern, in the Tennessee valley, and not then subject to my orders. . . . At Graysville Hazen's brigade joined the division, and the whole moved to Ringgold and bivouacked that night. . . . About noon on the 18th I received orders to move up my whole division to the assistance of our troops then engaged. After marching quickly for perhaps a mile and a half, guided by the sounds of the firing, and forming lines to the right of the road, I ordered Hazen, who was on the left, to march in the direction of the firing, Cruft to keep well close up to him on his right, with Grose in reserve, reinforcing the right, and to engage as soon as possible. At this moment I received a note from the general commanding the army, which led to a slight, but it turned out a most advantageous, change of formation. He suggested an advance in echelon by brigades, refusing the right, keeping well closed on Thomas. This suggestion was adopted; the brigades, at intervals of about one hundred paces, pushed forward, and engaged the enemy almost simultaneously. At once the fight became fierce and obstinate. . . .

Hazen had been relieved by General Turchin, who had formed on Cruft's left, and he (Hazen) had retired to fill his boxes, and protect some artillery which was threatened from the rear. I then committed the error of directing Grose to move to the right, to engage in a severe fight going on in that direction. I only for the moment saw that our troops were hard pressed, and that mine were idle, but did not observe that one brigade was not enough to relieve them. While riding towards Cruft's brigade to order him to move to the right to support Grose, a heavy force came upon him and Turchin. For ten minutes or more our men stood up under this fire, and then the enemy charged them and bore them back. Cruft, Turchin, and all their officers exerted themselves with distinguished courage to arrest the retreat, and I gave them what assistance I could. It seemed as if nothing would prevent a rout; but, as if by magic, the line straightened up, the men turning upon their pursuers with bayonet, who, as they quickly turned and fled, were in turn pursued. Many prisoners were brought to me at this point by soldiers for orders. I told them to break their muskets and let them go, and then go back to their places in the ranks. By this time the enemy had passed to our rear (around the right), and I felt much apprehension for Hazen. I rode in the direction of heavy firing, near the Rossville road, and found him, with a part of his own brigade and a large conscription of stragglers and several pieces of artillery, resisting an attempt of the enemy to cross an open field in his front. His fire was too hot, and they abandoned the attempt. Very soon other troops of Reynolds's division came up. . . .

About dark the enemy made a furious attack upon General Johnson's command, which I then learned was upon my left. I at once ordered Cruft and Hazen to proceed rapidly to his support. They moved off with great alacrity, but did not reach the scene in time to participate in the affair. . . . Early on the 20th I was directed by Major-General Thomas to form along a ridge running from northeast to southwest, and terminating near the Rossville road, closing on the left on Johnson's division. Intending to avoid what seemed to me the common error of the day before (too extended line), Hazen and Cruft were put in position in two lines, and Grose in double column in reserve. The men hastily constructed barricades of logs, rails, and other materials, and awaited the attack. The engagement commenced by a furious assault upon the position of Baird on the extreme left, and soon extended along the whole front. This was repulsed with great slaughter. Then a new persistent attack was made, the chief weight of which fell upon the extreme left. Some troops posted there fell back. By direction of General Thomas my reserve brigade moved in that direction and took part in the obstinate contest there. . . .

At two o'clock unusually heavy firing was heard on the right of our position, which seemed like a determined effort on the part of the enemy to force the centre of our line. Hazen was ordered by me in that direction. He moved off rapidly, in obedience to the order. I heard his volleys when he went in, and saw him no more that day; that his command did its duty I have no doubt. I refer to his report for the details. The remains of Grose's brigade had by this time returned, and now took Hazen's position in the line; but no formidable attempt was made upon us afterward. . . .

I can only say, in conclusion, that I am satisfied with the conduct of Brigadier-Generals Cruft and Hazen and Colonel William Grose, commanding brigades. They have earned a real title to my respect and confidence; while subordinates of all grades maintained the character for hardy courage and endurance which had been won by good service upon many fields.

Referring to the time the Rebels drove the right, General Brannan says : —

"Wood, being taken while marching by the flank, broke and fled in confusion ; and my line, actually attacked from the rear, was obliged to swing back on the right, which it accomplished with wonderful regularity under such circumstances (with, however, the exception of a portion of the First Brigade, which, being much exposed, broke with considerable disorder). The line being now broken, and severely pressed at this point, and great confusion prevailing in the support, — composed of Wood's and Van Cleve's divisions, — I formed the remnant of my command, and such stragglers from other commands as I could rally and bring into position, in line to resist, if possible, the pressure of the now advancing Rebels. In this manner I succeeded in holding the enemy in check for a considerable time, until I found that the Rebels were moving on my right to gain command of the valley, by which the right (McCook) was retreating. . . .

"I remained in this position, heavily engaged, until sunset, reinforced at intervals by the Ninth Regiment Indiana Volunteers, sent me at my request by General Hazen, and the Sixty-eighth and One Hundred and First Regiments Indiana Volunteers, sent by order of General Thomas."

General Negley also says : —

"Finding it impossible to organize any of the passing troops, and unable to communicate with General Thomas, and being informed by a staff-officer that Generals Rosecrans, McCook, and Crittenden had left the field, I deemed it vitally important to secure the safety of the artillery, which appeared to be threatened with immediate capture by a large force of the enemy, who was pressing forward on my front and right. I immediately took the Seventy-eighth Pennsylvania Volunteers and marched to the mouth of the gap (McFarland's), two miles from Rossville, the first open ground where the troops could be collected and reorganized.

"I found Colonel Parkhurst here with the Ninth Michigan

Volunteers, energetically checking the stragglers. He informed me that General Crittenden had passed some hours before, and had ordered him, with all the troops, to fall back to Chattanooga. . . .

"As soon as I had cleared the gap of the artillery and transportation, which extended back some distance, and was in great confusion, and had formed the scattered troops in battalions, I learned that General Sheridan was close at hand with some fifteen hundred men. I rode forward, and respectfully suggested to General Sheridan to move to the support of General Thomas, stating that I would join him with all the troops I had collected. He stated that his object was to march to Rossville. I then rode forward to communicate with General Thomas, but found the enemy's cavalry in possession of the road between us, which prevented my further passage. I then returned, and held a consultation with Generals Davis and Sheridan and Colonel Ducat.

"It was decided to be advisable to proceed to Rossville to prevent the enemy from obtaining possession of the cross roads; and that from there General Sheridan should move to the support of General Thomas, *via* the Lafayette road. The column reached Rossville at dark, and the scattered troops were organized as rapidly as possible. Provisions and ammunition, of which the troops were destitute, were telegraphed for and received from Chattanooga.

"At this moment I learned that General Granger had gone to the assistance of General Thomas, that he was safe, and that the troops were retiring to Rossville; also that General Sheridan had halted three miles from Rossville. I therefore continued the organization and preparation of the troops, to hold our position against a force of the enemy, who were reported to be advancing from the direction of Ringgold. Before the disposition of the force was completed, General Thomas, with a portion of his command, arrived."

Colonel Gates Thurston, chief-of-staff of McCook's corps, makes the following statement in an official paper : —

GENERAL JAMES S. NEGLEY

LIEUTENANT COLONEL GATES P. THRUSTON

"At the time Bragg's left struck the right of our army, while the latter was in motion, on the morning of Sunday, Sept. 20, 1863, I happened to be sent by General McCook, commanding the Twentieth Army Corps (I was adjutant of that corps and chief-of-staff), with orders to General Mitchell, at Crawfish Springs, to close up toward 'Widow Glenn's house,' and support our infantry on the right, which was moving toward our left. Rosecrans was transferring troops from right to left, and this made a gap between our right and our cavalry. During my brief absence our troops were routed on the right; and on my return to the Widow Glenn's house I found our army gone, and the Rebels in long lines, extending across the open field in front of that house, and far to the south of it, showing that their infantry line extended beyond or south of our right. I knew nothing of the general situation of affairs, excepting that the Rebel troops were in possession of the whole field occupied by our troops when I left, say a half-hour before. . . .

"I then endeavored to ascertain the situation of affairs. After travelling apparently two or three miles around what seemed to be the left of the enemy's lines, I succeeded in finding Generals Sheridan and Davis. Each had collected about half their divisions, in broken and disorganized regiments. The troops were greatly demoralized, and were slowly retiring along a pathway through the woods and over the hills which led in the direction of Rossville, and probably some six miles from there. The battle seemed still raging over on General Thomas's front, and a mile or more east of us. We learned that Generals McCook, Rosecrans, and Crittenden had gone to Chattanooga; and I was desirous that Sheridan's and Davis's troops should go to General Thomas's assistance, and volunteered to go myself and see how they could best assist General Thomas. "After agreeing with Sheridan and Davis on a point where I was to find them on my return, I made several attempts to cross to General Thomas, but was prevented by finding the enemy in my front.

"I finally met General Negley. He said he had been trying to find General Thomas, but was driven back by the enemy, and assured me it was impossible to reach General Thomas ; but a short time afterward I succeeded in reaching him. He was just back on the crest of a hill or rise, in an open field, the battle still raging in his front. I at once informed him of the situation on the right, relating as rapidly as possible the disaster to that part of the army and the present situation of Sheridan's and Davis's troops, and asked him if he wished to use them in any way. I inferred from his conversation that he received from me the first information he had from the right wing of the army after it was routed.

"I do not know with any precision the time of day when I reached General Thomas. I should say it was about four o'clock P. M., but it may have been a little later or somewhat earlier. The General seemed relieved to know that Sheridan and Davis had some troops within reach, and directed me to bring them up on his right at once, and have them ready to be put in position there, or support the right by active operations if circumstances seemed to demand it. Having changed horses for the third time, I ran my horse back to Sheridan and Davis, but found that during my absence they had moved on nearer to Rossville, and I did not find them for nearly an hour at least (say five o'clock). I did reach them along the narrow valley where they were marching, which was much crowded.

" Being adjutant and chief-of-staff of the Twentieth Corps, to which their divisions belonged, I reported to them General Thomas's position and situation, and requested them to return and take position as directed by him. Davis ordered his men to 'right about' at once, and marched back under my guidance, some of Negley's and other troops joining us. General Sheridan said he preferred to go to Rossville, and go out on the Lafayette road. I told him it was getting late, and he could scarcely get on the field by that route before night ; but he insisted on going that way, which was several miles round.

"By the time we reached Thomas's position with Davis's forces, however, General Thomas was withdrawing his troops, the enemy having suspended or given up his attack ; and our troops were being withdrawn, so we did not get into the action.

By that time our troops had in part recovered their courage, and would have done tolerably good service. It was then about dark, — six o'clock P. M., perhaps later. I reported to General Thomas, and remained with him till he went back to Rossville for the night. I followed him there, and remained with him all night."

Sheridan reports upon this subject as follows: —

" On reaching the Dry Creek Valley road, I found that the enemy had moved parallel to me, and had also arrived at the road, thus preventing my joining General Thomas by that route. I then determined to move quickly on Rossville, and form a junction with him on his left flank, *via* Lafayette road. This was successfully accomplished about half-past five o'clock P. M."

And Davis says: —

" General Negley's division at this time passed to the rear in the direction of Rossville, and, I understood, took position at that place. General Carlin and Colonel Martin had also by this time succeeded in re-forming their troops as far as was possible, and reported. Colonel Ward, commanding the Tenth Ohio Infantry, reported to me with his regiment for duty, and after allowing the men a few minutes to procure water, I ordered them again under arms, and moved for the battlefield, with a view of supporting General Thomas's corps, which was still maintaining its position.

" It is proper here to add that several detached battalions and commands reported to me, and accompanied my command to the battlefield, making in all a force of twenty-five hundred to three thousand men. . . .

" While in the act of forming my lines near General Thomas's right I received information from General Garfield that Thomas was falling back, with orders to repair to Rossville."

As to the time the retreat began, General Thomas says: " At half-past five P. M. Captain Baker, commanding my escort, was sent to notify General Reynolds to commence the movement." He nowhere mentions the return to the battlefield of any troops.

There are so many discrepancies in these statements, that the real facts cannot be determined from them. General Davis says that he started to return to General Thomas by the direct route, say two miles away, — when Thurston says it was about five o'clock, — but did not reach him till Thomas was withdrawing. He parted at that time from General Sheridan, who says he went by way of Rossville and the Lafayette road, which is about six miles, and reached General Thomas and reported to him on the battlefield. A board of officers was recently convened to settle these points; but unfortunately the two officers most interested in the question were made members of the board, and no satisfactory conclusion was reached.

But these statements show at least how entirely practicable it was to have brought everything into position for battle on the 20th, with every hope of success.

Negley says that he delayed the movement of his division "one hour" on the morning of the 20th, on account of a "heavy fog." This was at the time he should have placed himself on the left of Baird. This delay, with the following order and its too literal observance in causing Wood to pull out of the line, next to the failure to cause the line to be properly posted during the night of the 19th, before the battle came on, perhaps occasioned, more than anything else, the misfortune of the day.

HEADQUARTERS DEPARTMENT OF THE CUMBERLAND,
Sept. 20, 10.45 A. M.

Brig.-General WOOD, Commanding Division :

The general commanding directs that you close up on Reynolds as fast as possible, and support him.

FRANK P. BOND,
*Major and Aide-de-Camp.*

This order was received from a commander not present, while General Wood's division composed a part of the solid line of battle, and, at that very moment, its skirmishers were about to be engaged by the enemy, whose attack, having commenced on the left, five division-fronts away, had for some time proceeded towards the right, and was then nearly reaching that point.

Reynolds not being next him to the left, Wood pulled out of the line, to move over to where Reynolds was, and the gap thus made let the enemy through, which then swept four divisions to the rear and out of the fight, and lost the day to the Union forces.

The commander-in-chief seems to have been beaten by the sound of battle alone; for, excepting to correct the failure of not putting Negley in place on Baird's left, there was no call for nor need of supports on the left.

The battle finally closed, as narrated by General Thomas in the following report: —

General Garfield, chief-of-staff of General Rosecrans, reached this position (on the battlefield) about four P. M., in company with Lieutenant-Colonel Thurston of McCook's staff, and Captains Gaw and Barker of my staff, who had been sent to the rear to bring back the ammunition if possible. General Garfield gave me the first reliable information that the right and centre of our own army had been driven, and of its condition at that time. I soon after received a despatch from General Rosecrans, directing me to assume command of all the forces, and with Crittenden and McCook take a strong position and assume a threatening attitude at Rossville, sending the unorganized forces to Chattanooga for reorganization, stating that he would examine the ground at Chattanooga and then join me; also, that he had sent out rations and ammunition to meet me at Rossville. . . .

GEORGE H. THOMAS,
*Major-General U. S. Vol's Commanding.*

I have introduced these extracts from official reports, mainly to illustrate phases of the battle which necessitated the different movements of troops. The Government has not yet located the various commands on its map. The recent board of officers at Chicago, on which General Jeff. C. Davis was serving at the time of his death, was ordered for the purpose of deciding the conflicting questions as to time and positions on this battlefield. The map here given is accurate so far as it locates my command and the troops adjoining it. The four divisions on the left on the 20th of September are shown, and the positions where my command fought are marked 1, 2, 3, and 4.

Excepting General Palmer's division, I have not attempted to locate those that fought on the 19th, and accuracy is not claimed for the divisions on the right. On the morning of the 20th Brennan joined Reynolds's right. Sheridan says that in the night his own division was located at "Glenn's." Davis was sent to him, was posted on his left, and Wood's, Negley's, and Van Cleve's, the interior divisions, at some time that morning occupied places in the line as represented between Reynolds and Davis.

As these troops broke back, those of Wood and Brannan are correctly represented as they were able to get footing where they remained the rest of the day, with Steadman's two brigades of Gordon Granger's command, which arrived on the ground and were engaged on Brannan's right for about an hour. Great credit has been rightfully given this force and its commanders, Steadman and Granger, who without orders, but with true soldierly instincts, guided by the sound of battle, came upon the field in time to render most valuable service. But in weighing the comparative merits of the different commanders, it should be remembered that this command was engaged barely one hour, while the other commands were in battle the greater part of two days; and the romance which has been published in connection with this service, wherein it is stated that this command turned cannon upon the retreating enemy at the close of the day, is pure fiction, as no one did this, and the enemy did not retreat.

Those who claim strategic foresight for the movements leading to the battle, and that Bragg was made to give up Chattanooga by reason of our going south of it, which enabled us to seize and hold that place, fail to take account of the fact that the city was gained without the movement. The theory that Bragg fell back for any but strategic purposes of his own is all a mistake. We actually put ourselves in a position so false that for four days we were entirely at the mercy of the enemy; and that we were not totally destroyed by detachments was due to an equally great mistake on his part.

## CHAPTER X.

### THE SIEGE.

AT daylight on the 21st we were posted in front of Rossville, my right resting on the Ringgold road, and remained there till about two o'clock on the morning of the 22d, when we were withdrawn to Chattanooga, and posted on the left of the centre. My command was destined to take a most important and efficient part in the operations that followed here. The whole of Wood's division was on the extreme left flank; then came Palmer, my brigade being on his right flank, and retired just across the railroad. The cut and embankment were fashioned into an excellent defensive line. A line of infantry cover was constructed on the first day along the entire front of the army, practically extending around the town a half-mile from it, with both flanks resting on the river. Its front was cleared of all houses and other obstructions. A large amount of property, including houses, was destroyed and used in the works, and long before night our line was virtually impregnable.

Then the siege came on. The river was closed to us, and our only line of supplies was a wagon-road forty miles long, across Waldon's Ridge, to the little town of Jasper, on which our trains were constantly harassed by the enemy, and several hundred wagons captured and burned. The possibility of permanently holding Chattanooga depended entirely on our own enterprise in disentangling ourselves from the coil around us. Our short rations, the project for withdrawal, and the general condition of despondency have been so much written about that I will not describe them.

Although there were some weeks of half-rations, and men could be seen any day gathering the undigested kernels of grain that had already served as food for horses and mules, still I was not impressed with a sense of much suffering. The whole of the bacon ration was eaten, although, as is well known, our troops, unlike the Germans, who eat it cold with bread, usually fry it, throwing away the fatty and most nutritious part, thus wasting much of it. I do not think there was serious suffering at the siege. Officer's messes were reduced to great simplicity, and at my own we butchered our milch-cow. She was very fat, and proved the sweetest meat I ever tasted. The country across the river, though very poor, was open to us, and we got there, with great risk and effort, some few supplies.

When we reached Chattanooga, the surroundings, and even the skirts of the town, were covered with a fine growth of large black-oak trees. These began to disappear for fuel very early, the men taking merely the branches; later, they used such portions of the trunks as could easily be made into firewood; afterward, they were glad to use the gnarled and tough portions, and when these were gone they assailed the stumps; and finally, with pick and gunny-sacks, they could be seen grubbing out the roots and gathering even the smallest chips and fragments, as one so frequently sees done in foreign countries. This was more expressive of our real straitened condition than any visible sign of short rations.

But the real seriousness of our position constantly weighed upon every one, and more particularly from an undefined want of faith in certain officers of high commands associated with former failures in battle. That it was in our power successfully to raise the siege I never for a moment doubted, in case we could hold on till reasonable aid was sent for co-operation; and I often discussed the plan by which it was finally accomplished, although no one supposed at the time that I would be chosen with my command for so prominent a part in executing it, or that the plan discussed would ever be even seriously considered.

It is an error to consider our position as strictly one of siege, while the whole rear was open; but our final deliverance was one of enterprise. The enemy, although he held us close to our works, and occupied Lookout Mountain, from which he could, and did on a few occasions, throw shells into our camps, did very little damage. There were many people besides our own within the camp, as the town was within our lines, and many had strong reasons for wishing to get out of it. Among them was the family of Mr. Andrew Ewing, whose house I occupied in Nashville on first arriving in that city. Mr. Ewing had gone away with the Confederates, and afterward died. His family occupied a handsome brick house just beyond the line, and it went with the rest to make our breastworks, and almost before the family got out of it. Their position at Chattanooga was very uncomfortable; but General Rosecrans denied them the privilege of passing out. Hearing of this, I saw General Garfield, the chief-of-staff, and finally succeeded in getting authority to pass them through the lines. The difficulty then was how to send them. I set my quartermaster at work, and by getting an old family coach in one place, another somewhere else, and some old horses and mules and harness in as many different places, we soon had two most remarkable travelling outfits. But they promised endurance enough to take their burdens across Waldon's Ridge to the railroad; and so I sent them under charge of a good officer and small escort, and was soon glad to hear of their safe and not very uncomfortable journey and arrival at Nashville. One of

GENERAL JAMES A. GARFIELD

GENERAL JOSEPH J. REYNOLDS

the party, a daughter of Mrs. Ewing, is now the wife of Henry Watterson, of the Louisville " Courier Journal." During the entire war, whenever an opportunity occurred to soften its asperities, no matter in how slight a degree, if it could be done without harm to ourselves I invariably set myself at work to accomplish it, and have never seen cause to regret it.

The great lack at Chattanooga was food for animals, and the horses of our artillery and trains were nearly all dead or unserviceable. Immediate action of some kind could not be deferred much longer.

General Garfield [1] now left to take his seat in Congress; and, as I have always supposed, at the strong intercession of the higher subordinate commanders, General Rosecrans reorganized his entire administrative staff, with Major-General Reynolds as chief; Brannan, chief of artillery; Baldy Smith, who had just reported, chief engineer; and soon after, Whipple became adjutant-general, and Lieutenant-Colonel G. C. Kniffin, of the Twenty-first Corps, chief commissary of subsistence. This was a strong and very competent staff, and gave great encouragement; and the method and style of headquarters was at once revolutionized. The floors were scrubbed, whiskey-bottles put out of sight, business was done by daylight, and every one became hopeful. But the subject of withdrawal was still uppermost in the minds of many, — a movement which, under the most favorable circumstances, must have been fatal in many respects.

It was at this juncture that Mr. Stanton met General

---

[1] Just before General Garfield left for Washington, the election for Governor of Ohio took place. It was arranged for townships to vote separately. Hiram, the town we both lived in, had just two voters, both brigadier-generals, — Garfield and myself. We went together, and put our tickets in a cigar-box with a slit cut in the top. It was the first time in my life that I had voted; and, strange enough, the next time, I voted for Garfield for President.

Grant in Louisville, gave him supreme command in the West, and superseded Rosecrans by Thomas, who sent the famed despatch, "We will hold the town until we starve." With Rosecrans went also Crittenden, McCook, Negley, and Van Cleve.

That these removals were just, on the ground of unfitness, may or may not have been true. The mere fact of being carried to the rear at Chickamauga by the four broken divisions, under circumstances that gave the honest belief that the whole army was retreating, was no evidence of incapacity, and no sufficient cause in itself for such action. Had General Thomas chanced to be in the path of this movement, he must have been carried away from the field of battle, and without fault. That he would have returned, as General Garfield did, and as Generals Sheridan and Davis were doing, no one can know. That the interests of the service and the welfare of the country imperatively demanded the removals that were made, there can be no question; for the disaster at Chickamauga, added to previous ill fortune, had destroyed necessary confidence.

McCook, after Shiloh, where his division fought splendidly, and won great success, seemed at Perryville, Stone River, and Chickamauga pursued by a strange fatality. He assumed a kind of boastful over-confidence that in war always presages failure, because it takes the place of the careful preparation that secures success. It was probably a misfortune to themselves as well as to the country that these officers were given so high commands so early in the war. Crittenden was greatly beloved by his men. He was always genial, kind, just, and brave to a fault; and as he came to my brigade, which was drawn up to bid him farewell, mounted upon his beautiful gray horse "John," usually ridden by his little son (since killed with Custer), and made us an admirable, almost electrical, little speech, if it had been in my power I would have made him commander-in-chief of the armies. McCook possessed a peculiar open frankness of manner and *bonhomie* that made him many friends, and he had many admirable traits of character; he went with the others.

Thus I had seen Buell, Nelson, Crittenden, McCook, Negley, Van Cleve, Jackson, Ammen, and Garfield, — all the general officers I had seen and known most of in the old Army of the Ohio, where we had done our best with the powers God gave us, — all pass out. Some were dead; some were called to other duty; and some were withdrawn from the field. There were left of the officers of Buell's old army, Thomas, Wood, R. W. Johnson, Cruft, Hascall, Harker, and myself; and of those brought in by General Rosecrans, John M. Palmer and David S. Stanley; and a great number of general officers from other armies, then out of employment, were assigned to us.

The army was reorganized at Chattanooga; and in place of giving divisions to those who under ordinary rules had gained promotion in battle, the divisions of the commanders sent to the rear were broken up and the regiments assigned to the different brigades, making them as large as divisions, — that is, of nine and ten regiments, — but their designations were still "brigades." This was done at the recommendation of Gordon Granger, — a new commander, also with the Army of the Cumberland, who was put over the Fourth Corps, then a new designation, while the corps of McCook and Crittenden — the Twenty-first and Twenty-second — passed out, as organizations, with their commanders.

Now came the new regime. But already, before their arrival, and with the assumption of command by Thomas, our hopes went up with a great bound.

## CHAPTER XI.

### RAISING THE SIEGE. — BROWN'S FERRY.

ALMOST immediately after General Thomas assumed command, I was directed to report to General Baldy Smith. Smith told me his plan for opening the line of the river, and informed me that I had been selected for the delicate duty of carrying my brigade in boats at night down the river past the enemy's pickets to Brown's Ferry, nine miles from Chattanooga, there to effect a landing on the south bank, which would be fortified and held as a *tête de pont*. This would enable Hooker's command — the Eleventh and Twelfth Corps, then at Bridgeport — to come up on the south side of the river, make a junction there, and hold Lookout Valley with a bridge secured across the river, without which it would not be safe to bring troops into that valley. The river makes a long bend below Chattanooga, so that, by marching directly across the neck from the town, Brown's Ferry was only two miles away. We rode across that neck, and Smith pointed out the precise spot he had already chosen for the landing, made plain at night by a gap in the hills which lined the south bank of the river; and we selected a point some five hundred yards above, on the opposite side, where, from a line of signal-fires which I should make, I would know when to begin pulling for the other shore. I was to take thirteen hundred picked men of my brigade, in fifty-two parties, in that number of boats, each under the command of a well-known and tried leader; while the remainder of the brigade, about an equal number, under command of Colonel Basset Langdon, First Ohio, joined by Turchin's brigade, were to march to Brown's Ferry across the neck, and as the boats unloaded, be ferried over in them as rapidly as possible.

The manner in which this was all done will be narrated in the official orders and reports made at the time. In selecting leaders, little regard was had to rank. Some were field-officers and some were sergeants.

CHATTANOOGA, TENN., Oct. 25, 1863.

The regimental commanders of this brigade will at once organize parties of picked men as specified below; each squad to be in charge of an officer selected especially for efficiency and bravery. As soon as organized, each colonel will furnish these headquarters with complete rolls of the squads.

Names of men on picket can be used if they are known to be effective.

Commanders of parties will at once muster and drill their squads.

Each squad is to be composed of twenty-five men, including officers and non-commissioned officers. First Ohio Volunteers, seven squads; One Hundred and Twenty-fourth Ohio, seven squads; Sixth Ohio, seven squads; Forty-first Ohio, six squads; Sixth Indiana, six squads; Sixth Kentucky, five squads; Fifth Kentucky, five squads; Ninety-third Ohio, five squads; and Twenty-third Kentucky, two squads, and one squad of seventy-five men, with three officers and complement of non-commissioned officers.

Regimental commanders will themselves take charge of these squads, the next officer in rank commanding the remainder of the regiment.

Lieutenant-Colonel Langdon, First Ohio Volunteers, is detailed to command the remainder of the brigade, and will report at these headquarters.

BROWN'S FERRY, NEAR CHATTANOOGA, TENN., Oct. 30, 1863.

General W. F. SMITH, Chief Engineer, Army of the Cumberland :

I have the honor to report the part taken by troops under my command in the occupation of the left bank of the Tennessee River at this point.

On the morning of the 25th instant I reported, by order of the commanding officer of the Fourth Army Corps, to the chief engineer for instructions, and was then briefly informed for the first time of the duty to be assigned me and the method of performing it; which was to organize fifty squads, of one officer and twenty-four men each, to embark in boats at Chattanooga, and float down the river to this point — a distance by the bend of the river of nine miles — and land on its left bank, then occupied by the enemy, making thereafter dispositions for holding it, while the remaining portion of my brigade and another one should be speedily sent over the river in the same boats.

The movement was to be made just before daylight on the morning of the 27th. My brigade then consisted of the following regiments : Sixth Kentucky, Ninety-third Ohio, Fifth Kentucky, First Ohio, Sixth Ohio, Forty-first Ohio, One Hundred and Twenty-fourth Ohio, Sixth Indiana, and Twenty-third Kentucky Volunteer Infantry, with an aggregate for duty of two thousand one hundred and sixty-six men.

The 25th was employed in organizing my parties, each being placed in charge of a tried officer. On the morning of the 26th, I, in company with the chief engineer, visited the place where it was desired to effect the landing, and from the opposite bank found the position as represented in the accompanying map.

It was desired that I should land, and occupy the two hills to the left of the house. There was a picket post at this point, and also one in the depression between the two hills. It was thought best to organize a party of seventy-five men, who should be the first to land, and at once push out on the road that comes in at the house, clearing and holding it, while half the organized force should be landed simultaneously at each of the two gorges (A and B), who should immediately push up the hills, inclining to the left, and following the crests until they were wholly

GENERAL WILLIAM F. SMITH

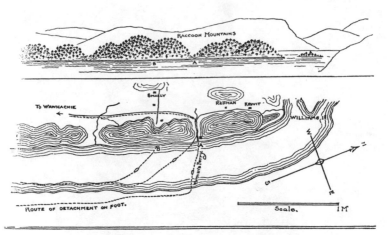

RACCOON MOUNTAINS

SMALLY

RADMAN KRWIT

To WAWHACHIE

WILLIAMS IS

Browns Ferry

ROUTE OF DETACHMENT ON FOOT.

Scale.    I M

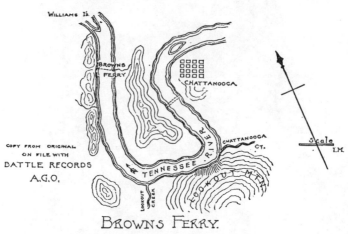

WILLIAMS IS.

BROWNS FERRY

CHATTANOOGA

CHATTANOOGA CT.

TENNESSEE RIVER

LOOKOUT CREEK

LOOKOUT MTN.

Scale    I.M.

BROWNS FERRY.

occupied. Each party of twenty-five was to carry two axes; and as soon as the crest should be reached, a strong line of skirmishers was to be pushed out, and all the axes put to work at once felling a thick abatis. The remainder of the brigade was to be organized; and being ready on the opposite bank, armed and provided with axes, was to be pushed over, and also deployed, in rear of the skirmishers, to assist in making the abatis. Positions were also selected for building signal-fires to guide us in landing.

I afterward selected tried and distinguished officers to lead the four distinct commands, who, in addition to being fully instructed as to the part they were to take, were themselves taken to the spot, and every feature of the bank and landings made familiar to them. They, in turn, just before night called together the leaders of squads, and each was clearly instructed as to his duties; for they were of such a nature that each had in a great degree to act independently, but strictly in accordance with instructions. At twelve o'clock at night the command was awakened and marched to the landing, and quietly embarked under the superintendence of Colonel Stanley, of the Eighteenth Ohio Volunteer Infantry, each squad in its own boat. At precisely three o'clock A. M. the flotilla, consisting of fifty-two boats, — two having been added to the fifty, — moved noiselessly out. I desired to reach the landing at a little before daylight, and soon learned that the current would enable me to do so without using the oars. After moving three miles we came under the guns of the enemy's pickets, but, keeping well under the opposite shore, were not discovered until the first boat was within ten feet of the landing, when the enemy's pickets fired a volley harmlessly over the heads of my men. The disembarkation was effected rapidly and in perfect order, each party performing correctly the part assigned it with so little loss of time that the entire crest was occupied, my skirmish lines out, and the axes working, before the reinforcements of the enemy, a little beyond the hill, came forward to drive us back.

At this time they came boldly up along nearly our entire front, but particularly strong along the road, gained the hill to the right of it, and would have caused harm to the party on the road, had not Colonel Langdon, who commanded the remaining portion of the brigade, arrived with his men at this moment. After a gallant but short engagement he drove the enemy well over into the valley, and gained and occupied the right-hand hill also. The enemy made a stubborn fight all along the hill, but were easily driven away with loss. General Turchin's command now came over, and took position on the hills to the right. My troops were all brought to the left of the road.

The enemy now moved off in full view up the valley. The Fifty-first Ohio, Eighth Kentucky, and Thirty-fifth Indiana Volunteer Infantry, and two batteries of artillery, were subsequently added to my command, and the three hills farther to the left were occupied.

We knew nothing of the country previous to reaching it, except what could be seen from the opposite bank, nor of the forces to oppose us. We found the hill facing the river precipitous, and the face opposite less steep, but of difficult ascent. The top is sharp, having a level surface of from two to six feet in width, forming a natural parapet capable of an easy defence. It is from two hundred and fifty to three hundred feet above the river. Beyond it is a narrow productive valley; and the higher parallel range of Raccoon Mountains is about a mile and a quarter distant. The entire opposite face of the hill we occupy is now covered with slashed timber. The enemy had at this point one thousand infantry, three pieces of artillery, and a squadron of cavalry, — an ample force, properly disposed, to have successfully disputed our landing. Our losses were five killed, twenty-one wounded, and nine missing. We buried six of the enemy, and a large number were known to be wounded, including the colonel commanding.[1] We captured a few prisoners, their camp, twenty beeves, six pontoons, and a barge; and several thousand bushels of corn fell into our hands. My thanks are especially due to Colonel A. Wiley, Forty-first Ohio Volunteer Infantry; to Major Birch, Ninety-third Ohio Volunteer

---

[1] This officer was Colonel W. C. Oates, of an Alabama regiment, now a member of Congress.

Infantry, who commanded and led the parties that took the heights; to Lieutenant-Colonel Foy, Twenty-third Kentucky Volunteers, commanding the party that swept the road ; and to Lieutenant-Colonel Langdon, First Ohio Volunteers, commanding the battalion formed of the residue of the brigade.

Had either of these officers been less prompt, or less obedient to the letter of their instructions, many more lives might have been lost, or the expedition failed altogether.

The spirit of every one engaged in the enterprise is deserving of the highest commendation. My staff gave me the intelligent and timely assistance they have always done; and to Lieutenant-Colonel Kimberly, Forty-first Ohio Volunteer Infantry, and Lieutenant F. D. Cobb, same regiment, I am especially indebted for valuable service.

W. B. HAZEN, *Brigadier-General.*

The following are from the reports of Generals Thomas and Smith : —

CHATTANOOGA, Oct. 27, 1863, 10.30 P. M.

Major-General HALLECK, Washington, D. C.:

General W. F. Smith, commanding Hazen's brigade of Wood's division, Fourth Corps, and Turchin's brigade of Baird's division, Fourteenth Corps, floated boats to form a pontoon bridge down the river from Chattanooga to Brown's Ferry, six miles below ; landed, surprised and drove the enemy's pickets and reserve ; took possession of hills commanding debouche of ferry on southwest side ; laid bridge and intrenched the command strongly enough to hold bridge securely. By the judicious precautions taken by General Smith before starting, and the intelligent co-operation of Generals Turchin and Hazen, commanding brigades, and of Colonel Stanley, Eighteenth Ohio, commanding boat party, this was a complete success, and reflected great credit on all concerned. Our loss, four killed and fifteen wounded ; enemy's, eight killed, six prisoners, and several wounded. Major-General Hooker, commanding troops composing Eleventh Corps and part of Twelfth, marched from Bridgeport at daylight to-day to open road from Bridgeport to Chattanooga, and take some position protecting river. Two brigades of Palmer's division, Fourth Corps, should have reached Rankin's Ferry to-day to co-operate with General Hooker. The Sixteenth Illinois reached Kelley's Ferry to co-operate with General Hooker. If he is as successful as General Smith has been, we shall in a few days have open communication with Bridgeport by water, as well as by a practicable road running near the river on the northern bank.

GEORGE H. THOMAS,
*Major-General U. S. Volunteers.*

The seizure of Brown's Ferry and the splendid defence of Lookout valley by General Hooker's command decided the question of our ability to hold Chattanooga, for steamers began immediately to carry rations from Bridgeport to Kelley's Ferry, leaving but about eight miles of wagon transportation from that point to Chattanooga, and repairs were commenced on the rail-road south of Tennessee River. The enemy made no further attempt to regain Lookout valley after it had slipped from his grasp, and confined himself to an occasional cannon-shot from the top of Lookout as he watched our trains undisturbedly moving from Kelley's Ferry across the valley bearing rations to a grateful army.

To Brigadier-General W. F. Smith, Chief Engineer, should be accorded great praise for the ingenuity which conceived and the ability which executed the movement at Brown's Ferry. The preparations were all made in secrecy, as was also the boat expedition which passed under the overhanging cliffs of Look-out ; so much so that when the bridge was thrown across the river at Brown's Ferry on the morning of the 27th, the surprise was as great to the army within Chattanooga as it was to the army besieging it from without. . . .

GEORGE H. THOMAS,
*Major-General U. S. Volunteers.*

CHATTANOOGA, TENN., Nov. 4, 1863.

GENERAL, — I have the honor to submit the following report of the operations for making a lodgment on the south side of

COLONEL TIMOTHY STANLEY

(Eighteenth Ohio.)

GENERAL JOHN B. TURCHIN

the river at Brown's Ferry. On the 19th of October I was instructed by General Rosecrans to reconnoitre the river in the vicinity of Williams Island, with a view to making the island a cover for a steamboat landing and storehouse, and began the examination near the lower end of the island. Following the river up, I found on the opposite bank, above the head of the island, a sharp range of hills whose base was washed by the river. This range extended up the river nearly to Lookout Creek, and was broken at Brown's Ferry by a narrow gorge, through which ran the road to the old ferry, and also flowed a small creek. The valley between this ridge of hills and Raccoon Mountains was narrow, and a lodgment effected there would give us the command of the Kelley's Ferry road, and seriously interrupt the communications of the enemy up Lookout valley and down to the river on Raccoon Mountains. The ridge seemed thinly picketed, and the evidences were against the occupation of that part of the valley by a large force of the enemy, and it seemed quite possible to take by surprise what could not have been carried by assault if heavily occupied by an opposing force.

The major-general commanding the geographical division and the major-general commanding the department visited with me the ferry a few days after this reconnoissance, and were agreed as to the importance of the position by itself, and especially in connection with the movements to be made from Bridgeport to open the river; and I was directed to make the necessary arrangements for the expedition to effect the lodgments. To do this, fifty pontoons, with oars, to carry a crew and twenty-five armed men, were prepared, and also two flat-boats carrying forty and seventy-five men. The force detailed for the expedition consisted of the brigades of Brigadier-General Turchin and Brigadier-General Hazen, with three batteries, to be posted under the direction of Major Mendenhall, assistant to General Brannan, Chief of Artillery.

Sunday, the 25th of October, I was assigned to the command of the expedition, and the troops were distributed as follows: Thirteen hundred men, under Brigadier-General Hazen, were to embark in the boats and pass down the river, — a distance of about nine miles, seven of which would be under the fire of the pickets of the enemy. It was deemed better to take this risk than to attempt to launch the boats near the ferry, because they would move more rapidly than intelligence could be taken by infantry pickets; and, in addition, though the enemy might be alarmed, he would not know where the landing was to be attempted, and therefore could not concentrate with certainty against us. The boats were called off in sections; and the points at which each section was to land were carefully selected and pointed out to the officers in command, and range fires kept burning lest in the night the proper points should be mistaken. General Turchin's and the remainder of General Hazen's brigade were marched across and encamped in the woods, out of sight, near the ferry, ready to move down and cover the landing of the boats, and also ready to embark as soon as the boats had landed the river force and crossed to the north side. . . . General Hazen was to take the gorge and the hills to the left, while General Turchin was to extend from the gorge down the river. The boats moved from Chattanooga at three A. M. on the 27th; and, thanks to a slight fog and the silence observed, they were not discovered until about five A.M., when the first section had landed at the upper point, and the second section had arrived abreast of the pickets stationed at the gorge. . . . The boats by this time had recrossed the river; and Lieutenant-Colonel Langdon, First Ohio Volunteers, in command of the remnant of the brigade of General Hazen, was rapidly ferried across, and, forming his men, quickly pushed forward to the assistance of the troops under Lieutenant-Colonel Foy, Twenty-third Kentucky Volunteers, already hard pressed. The skirmish was soon over; and General Turchin, who followed Lieutenant-Colonel Langdon, quietly took possession of the hill assigned to him. . . .

W. F. SMITH,
*Brig.-Gen. Commanding Expedition.*

The success of this expedition was complete to the minutest detail. The night was dark, and by keeping well under the shadow of the opposite bank we escaped the observation of the enemy, whose pickets were posted along the bank for seven miles. It was necessary to embark at Chattanooga, for to do so at the ferry would attract the enemy. It was a misty night, with that peculiar stillness felt only just before day, and our progress with the current was in absolute silence. The first three boats, including the large one with fifty men, were under that never-failing soldier, Colonel Wiley, of my old regiment, who was to make the landing at the picket station, which was admirably done. I was in the fourth boat, and landed at the signal-station to direct the boats to their proper landing-places on the opposite side, these being at two gorges in the hill seen against the sky. So admirably was all this executed, that as I reached the crest with the last squad, the entire line was in place just as planned, with the axes sharply at work making abatis, the thin crest forming all the parapet we needed. As the troops that had marched across, including Turchin's, were quickly ferried over and took positions, including the ridge beyond Wiley's position, the morning broke, and the enemy—a full brigade—made a weak attack, but soon drew off along our front and quitted the valley. They were in full view; and except for our utter ignorance of what force there might be near, and our first duty to secure our position, we might have inflicted great damage upon them. As it was, the stillness of morning, with the reverberation from Raccoon Mountain and Waldon's Ridge, both in front and behind us, gave our little battle the noise of a heavy engagement. The enemy did not question our occupation that day; but late the day after a corps, which proved to be Longstreet's, could be plainly seen high up filing around the point of Lookout Mountain to assail us. But before they got ready, Hooker's command, previously ordered up from Bridgeport, had arrived, and received that night the attack meant for us. This fight is known as the battle of Wauhatchie. Steamboats began running that night also; and although fired on from Lookout Mountain, they were not impeded. Our line of supplies for the army was secured, food and forage immediately began to arrive, and the siege was practically raised.

The "Richmond Press," describing this, said : —

"The admirably conceived and perfectly executed *coup* at Brown's Ferry, on the night of the 27th and 28th of October, has robbed the Confederacy of all its dearly earned advantages gained at Chickamauga."

We found in the valley a large bin of corn, some cattle, and a mill. We first began to issue the corn by the ear (five ears a day to each man); and by splitting their canteens and perforating them, the men would grate the corn into meal, and make a coarse but palatable bread. But a neighboring mill was soon running; and our additional supplies, with fresh new camps, and the knowledge of the good work we had done, made us all very happy. We moved down into Lookout valley, and began a very neat and comfortable cantonment, with huts and houses made of small straight pine logs.

Now came in the new regime. General Grant arrived, and General Sherman was approaching. They were new, and different from the commanders we had known before. They wore vests, and coats unbuttoned; and as to military bearing, old Frederick would not have had them in his camp. There was also a sort of outspoken frankness upon military matters that seemed a little strange, and in contrast to the mysterious air that is so apt to pervade military headquarters. But they had from the start, and always retained, the most perfect confidence of the army; and that faith was not misplaced. More accuracy in little things would not, however, have lessened our early faith nor diminished their success. The Emperor William has said, "One button neglected may lead to the loss of an army."

# CHAPTER XII.

## ORCHARD KNOB.

ON the 6th of November we received orders to repair to Chattanooga, where, due to the conformation of the field, was to be enacted the grandest pageantry of real war it was perhaps ever the fortune of man to actually behold. We did not court this order, for we felt a sort of proprietorship in Lookout valley, and very much enjoyed clean camps, pure water, plenty of fuel, and the good things that only the country affords.

On leaving camp a scene occurred that developed the strange want of prescience which sometimes characterized General Hooker, and which at such times seemed to neutralize all his good qualities.

My force had been drawn back from the river a half-mile along the base of Raccoon Mountain. Hooker, on learning that I had been ordered to Chattanooga by General Thomas, and as I was in the act of leaving Lookout valley, rode up to where I was mounted, with my staff round me, and in an excited and petulant manner ordered that I should " not move my men a step; " that it would leave his left flank in the air, and would make his position untenable. The fact was, that for three days his left had rested solidly on the Tennessee River, which was broad and deep, at right angles to it, and a mile to our front; and all beyond that was indisputably held by our forces. To my endeavors to make him understand this he seemed perfectly insensible. His left was as secure as if it had rested on the Ohio River, and my troops bore no relation to his system of defence; but he seemed powerless to comprehend it. I waited till he rode away, and then proceeded to carry out my orders.

Sherman's troops were arriving; Howard's corps had been sent over to Chattanooga from Lookout valley; and Hooker, with the rest of his command, which had remained in Lookout valley since its arrival, was still left to operate from that direction.

On the morning of the 20th I received verbal instructions to hold my command in readiness for active service, and gave the following direction: —

CHATTANOOGA, TENN., Nov. 20, 1863.

There will be no drill this morning. Colonels will see in person that all their arms are put in perfect order ; that one hundred rounds of ammunition per man are procured ; and that the men have two days' rations in their haversacks over what they will eat to-morrow for breakfast. They will report to these headquarters their compliance with this order by six P. M. to-day.

Colonels will at once apply themselves to putting every officer and man in the ranks. All detailed men, provost or other guard, clerks, orderlies, cooks, and officers' servants (soldiers) will be put in ranks, and are relieved temporarily from present details.

All musicians and men without arms will be enrolled for a hospital corps, mustered, and put in charge of the medical officer.

One enlisted man, non-combatant, will be left in charge of each company camp, and one at regimental and brigade headquarters.

The following regiments will be consolidated as battalions, each to be organized into ten equal companies. . . .

At noon, the 23d, by direction of higher authority, I gave the following order: —

CHATTANOOGA, TENN., Nov. 23, 1863.

The division moves out at once upon a reconnoissance. Colonels will immediately form their battalions as indicated for drill, and move out and form on the slope facing the Bald Knob. Front line deployed ; Colonel Wiley on the right, Colonel Langdon on the left. Second line in double column on the centre ; Colonel Christopher on the right, Colonel Pickands on the left. Troops will take sixty rounds of ammunition, and haversacks.

Colonel Berry, commanding the picket line, when he sees the formation to advance being made, will deploy his whole force as skirmishers, and at the proper time advance it as skirmishers with the command, keeping well dressed to the left on those of General Willich.

As it happened, my picket line had been posted exactly in front of the position that fell to my command, and was ready to move forward without any change save to reinforce the line with the picket reserve. It happened also to be in command of Colonel W. W. Berry, of the Louisville Legion, — as fine a soldier and man as the war produced.

The way we executed our part of the work is told in my official report : —

HEADQUARTERS SECOND BRIG., THIRD DIV., FOURTH ARMY CORPS,
IN CAMP NEAR KNOXVILLE, TENN., Dec. 10, 1863.

Act'g-Assist. Adjutant-General, Third Div., Fourth Army Corps :

At twelve M., November 23, I received orders to form my brigade near Fort Wood, and hold it in readiness to move on a reconnoissance in the direction of Mission Ridge (southeasterly), with the remainder of the division. The position assigned me was on the front line. The brigade was formed in five battalions, as follows : —

First Battalion, Colonel Aquila Wiley commanding, was composed of the following regiments ; namely, Forty-first Ohio Volunteer Infantry, Lieutenant-Colonel Kimberly ; and Ninety-third Ohio Volunteer Infantry, Major William Birch.

Second Battalion, Colonel W. W. Berry commanding, — of the Fifth Kentucky Volunteer Infantry, Lieutenant-Colonel Trainor ; and Sixth Kentucky Volunteer Infantry, Major R. T. Whitaker.

Third Battalion, Lieutenant-Colonel E. B. Langdon commanding, — of the First Ohio Volunteer Infantry, Major J. A. Stafford; and Twenty-third Kentucky Volunteer Infantry, Lieutenant-Colonel James C. Foy.

Fourth Battalion, Lieutenant-Colonel James Pickands commanding, — of the One Hundred and Twenty-fourth Ohio Volunteer Infantry, Major J. B. Hampson; and Sixth Indiana Volunteer Infantry, Major C. D. Campbell.

Fifth Battalion, Sixth Ohio Volunteer Infantry, Lieutenant-Colonel A. C. Christopher commanding.

In all, twenty-two hundred and fifty-six effective officers and men.

The First and Third Battalions were deployed in the front line; the Fourth and Fifth formed in double column in the second line. The Second Battalion was on picket, and in position to be used as skirmishers. The entire battalion was deployed as such, and at the sound of the bugle at two P. M. the entire brigade moved forward in exact order, and in two minutes the skirmish line was sharply engaged with that of the enemy, which gave ground after firing their pieces; and no considerable opposition was felt until we reached their first line of rifle-pits, about one half-mile beyond their picket line, where the picket and their reserve endeavored to check our advance. But pushing forward the first battalion, which was immediately in front of their principal force, the work, situated on a rocky hill, was carried in the most handsome manner, and nearly an entire regiment — the Twenty-eighth Alabama Infantry — captured, with their colors, and the position held. This was not accomplished, however, without severe cost to the Forty-first and Ninety-third Ohio. Major Birch, leading the latter, fell here; also eleven of his men killed and forty-eight wounded. The Forty-first Ohio lost eleven men killed and fifty-two wounded. Colonel Wiley and Lieutenant-Colonel Kimberly, of the same regiment, had horses killed under them, and Colonel Berry, commanding the skirmishers, was twice struck.

The position was actually carried at the point of the bayonet, the enemy being captured behind their work, over which our men leaped. During the last half-mile of this advance my right was entirely exposed, and suffered severely from an enfilading fire of the enemy. The night of the 23d was employed in strengthening our position by works, and the 24th was passed without engaging the enemy. . . .

This reconnoissance was ordered for Wood's division, which was to go as far forward as Orchard Knob, while Sheridan on his right should move his division out to Bushy Knob, about half as far, as a support; so that after that distance had been reached my right flank was entirely in the air, and we suffered from it. Willich's brigade was on the left of mine, while Beatty's, the third of Wood's division, was in reserve. Willich's front led him directly on to Orchard Knob, occupied only by a picket post, and this brought me to a little rocky ridge to its right, which was fortified, and manned by the picket reserve, where the only serious resistance was made ; so that while Sheridan in this affair lost but half a dozen men wounded on the skirmish line, and Willich as many more, I had a hard fight, and lost one hundred and twenty-five men out of two regiments, besides other casualties, — a large proportion being killed outright, — and captured a regiment of the enemy. As it was evident that the battalion composed of the Forty-first and Ninety-third Ohio was about to engage in a serious fight, and as we were ordered merely on a reconnoissance, the commander of the battalion, Colonel Wiley, sent word to me, reporting a strong work in his front, fully manned, and asked for instructions. Nothing of this kind was contemplated; but I ordered him to take the work at the point of the bayonet, and in five minutes it was carried.

The entire movement, — the perfect march, as if on drill, taken up by the skirmish line at precisely the right moment, the absolute unfaltering of the line till it marched over the enemy and their works, — as a tactical manœuvre in actual war, has in my experience no parallel.

After this affair was over, General Thomas rode to where the Forty-first and Ninety-third Ohio were, shook hands with most of the officers, and publicly thanked the regiments.

Of this whole movement General Granger says : —

"At half-past one o'clock P. M. I directed General Wood to advance. In a few moments his troops, having passed through the open fields, engaged the enemy in the woods, and drove them back to their rifle-pits. The resistance here met with, especially in front of Hazen's brigade, where we sustained the heaviest loss, was very stubborn, and the enemy were only driven back when his works were cleared by the bayonet.

"In this dash, which was quick and gallant, we lost one hundred and twenty-five officers and men killed and wounded ; and by it we gained Orchard Knob and the ridge to its right, at the same time capturing many prisoners, — the Twenty-eighth Alabama Infantry entire, with the regimental colors."

The number of casualties here given is the exact number that occurred in the two regiments of my command which suffered most. They were the only ones *specially reported* for that day's service as distinct from the three days' fight.

General Wood, in an eight-column article, published July 16, 1876, in the "New York Times," upon these engagements, says : —

"By a bold burst, Willich's brigade carried Orchard Knob. The enemy, seeming paralyzed, made comparatively little resistance. The resistance in Hazen's front was much sharper, and for a moment the advance of the brigade was checked ; but an impetuous dash carried the brigade over the Confederate intrenchments, with the Twenty-eighth Alabama Regiment as prisoners. The casualties of the division in this brilliant movement, chiefly in Hazen's brigade, were one hundred and forty-four killed and wounded."

GENERAL AUGUST WILLICH

GENERAL GORDON GRANGER

The fact was, that there was only a picket station on Orchard Knob, while the whole picket reserve and those driven in were in front of my troops.

The advantage here gained was so important as to decide the changing of the plan from a reconnoissance to one of occupation of the ground gained; and we at once reversed the works and remained there, making the position a starting-point for the final assault two days afterward.

During our advance the guns at Fort Wood, situated at the rear of where our line was formed, kept up a rapid fire over our heads toward Mission Ridge. This I maintained then, as I always have since, was a mistake. The sound of the shot coming through the air behind us was very un-canny and distracting, and caused hundreds of the men to involuntarily turn their heads to see if the shot were com-ing into our line, as the sound seemed to indicate. In fact, several shot did actually fall behind us. There was at one time danger of the line actually breaking from this cause, and everybody felt greatly incensed; and it is doubtful if any benefit whatever resulted from it.

As our right was still exposed, General Granger the corps commander, Wood, and myself rode up to Sheridan's position at Bushy Knob, just before night of the 23d, to prevail upon him to move down his left, to conform to the new plan of occupation, so far at least as to secure the flank of the new position. I say prevail, because for some reason General Granger did not seem inclined to give any command in the matter. It resulted in a long and acri-monious talk, in which Sheridan sharply declined to make the necessary change; whereupon I was ordered to post a part of my command there, which I did, fortifying till past midnight. This crotchet at right angles to the main line is plainly marked on the Government maps to the rear of my right,— at $F$ on my map.

I notice that General Sheridan says in his official report

that he did move down, as "General Wood felt uneasy about his right flank." But I saw no movement nor troops there; and my command, after doing practically all the fighting of that day, was compelled in consequence to fortify much of the night, and no such movement caused any relief to me, which was the purpose of asking for it. Wagner, the commander of Sheridan's left brigade, says in his official report that he moved the 25th, which seems to be the fact in the case.

The 24th was passed in comparative quiet, our great interest being in watching Hooker's movement on Lookout Mountain, which was in plain view after he had crossed the summit. It was a rainy, misty morning; but as it cleared away, and the men and colors came plainly in sight, although some four miles away, the shout that went up from our army in the valley compensated for all the noise the Rebels made as we retired from Chickamauga. This fight on Lookout — for it hardly reached the dimensions of a battle — was one of the preliminary actions that prepared the way for the great battle of Mission Ridge. It was, in a sense, above the clouds, as poetically described, for there were great banks of fog below. The number of troops engaged there was comparatively small; but the action continued into the night, and the discharges of musketry, inaudible at our position, could be plainly seen in the darkness, and resembled a line of fireflies intermitting their light. The effect was exceedingly curious and interesting.

# MISSION RIDGE.

A  Hazen's Brigade, formed Nov. 23.
B  Orchard Knob.
C  Fortified Ridge, occupied by 28th Ala.
D  Hazen's Brigade,
   formed before Assault Nov. 25.
E  Entrenchment by Hazen's Brigade,
   night of Nov. 25.
F  Entrenchment by Hazen's Brigade,
   night of Nov. 23.
G  Sheridan's Division, Nov. 23.
H  Sheridan's Division,
   formed just before Assault Nov. 25.
K  Bushy Knob.

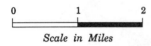

0        1        2

Scale in Miles

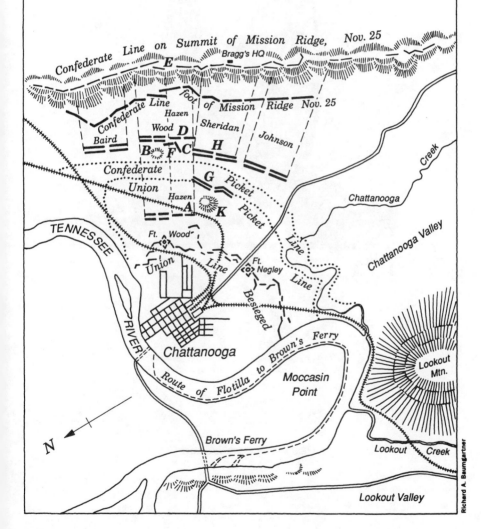

Confederate Line on Summit of Mission Ridge, Nov. 25

Bragg's HQ

E

Confederate Line   Foot of Mission Ridge Nov. 25

Hazen
Baird    Wood  D   Sheridan
B  F  C   H   Johnson

Confederate
Union
Hazen    G   Picket
A   K        Picket

TENNESSEE

Ft.  Wood

Union    Line    Ft.
Negley

Besieged    Line

Chattanooga

Route of Flotilla to Brown's Ferry

Moccasin
Point

Chattanooga

Chattanooga Valley

Creek

Lookout
Mtn.

RIVER

N

Brown's Ferry

Lookout  Creek

Lookout Valley

Richard A. Baumgartner

GENERAL ULYSSES S. GRANT

# CHAPTER XIII.

## ASSAULT AND CAPTURE OF MISSION RIDGE.

EVERYTHING was now ready for the grand battle. On the morning of the 25th Generals Grant and Thomas and many other general officers came down to Orchard Knob, and remained there during the day. It was evident that the enemy had abandoned the positions about Lookout Mountain and his entire left, and was moving to his right in plain view in an almost constant stream along the summit of Mission Ridge, to confront Sherman, who had effected a crossing of the Tennessee River, and was endeavoring to gain a position on the ridge to assail the enemy's right flank. Sherman seemed to make little headway; and we could distinctly see, although three miles away, two assaults of his troops, which were repulsed. At one time, as his men gained a summit, and seemed waiting, — for what, no one at our position could tell, — the enemy, whom we could see just over the crest from his line, suddenly ran away. But still Sherman's men hesitated for some minutes, when all at once the enemy came back, and our people were driven down the hill in great disorder. At this time, about two or three o'clock in the afternoon, Grant directed Thomas to prepare his command to move forward. Thomas called Granger, who had busied himself all day in serving and aiming a field battery posted there, repeated the orders received from Grant, and directed him to prepare Wood and Sheridan to move forward at the quickly repeated discharge of six guns from the Knob, and take the enemy's rifle-pits at the foot of the ridge.  Sheridan's division, somewhat to the rear, was moved up nearly on a prolongation with Wood's, and all the brigade commanders warned, who in turn communicated the order to their colonels ; and just as another and the last unsuccessful effort of Sherman was seen to have failed, like the former ones, Grant, turning, said: " Now, Thomas, is your time ! "[1]  The commanders all quickly mounted, and joined their troops ; the six guns immediately after boomed out the signal; and at the instant the two divisions, Wood's and Sheridan's, were moving forward.

The battle, as to the part taken by my command, was remarkable in this ; that, with the exception of two medical officers, every man in the brigade — but the sick, who took care of camp, and the band — was actually present, armed, and in the fight.   All the servants, cooks, clerks, and detailed men found guns in some way ; for they disliked being stretcher-bearers, — the only alternative.   The musicians, even to their chief, were all present, with stretchers in hand ; and most admirably did they perform their duty.   As we moved across the half-mile of plain before coming to the works at the foot of the hill, although the fire of the mass of guns on Mission Ridge seemed terrific, it had but little effect, on account of the great depression of fire, which made the angle with the plain we were crossing so great that the zone of danger from each shot was very narrow.   One shell took effect directly in a company, — Captain Huston's, of the Fifth Kentucky, — killing and disabling thirteen men.

The following is my official report of the battle of Mission Ridge : —

[1] This scene is literal.

GENERAL PHILIP H. SHERIDAN

Cumberland Gallery Collection

### COLONEL LANGDON

Colonel Bassett Langdon died two years after the war of the wound received
in the battle of Mission Ridge. He was an efficient and trustworthy officer.

HEADQUARTERS SECOND BRIG., THIRD DIV., FOURTH ARMY CORPS,
IN CAMP NEAR KNOXVILLE, TENN., Dec. 10, 1863.

Assist. Adjutant-General, Third Div., Fourth Army Corps :

. . . At about eleven A. M., on the 25th, I was ordered to advance my skirmish line sufficiently to develop the enemy's strength behind his main line of breastworks, at the foot of Mission Ridge, and about half a mile in our front. This was handsomely done under the immediate command of Lieutenant-Colonel Christopher, Sixth Ohio Volunteer Infantry. In this advance Major S. C. Erwin, of the same regiment, was killed by a shell, and eight or ten others killed and wounded. At about three o'clock P. M. I received orders to move forward with the remainder of the division, and take possession of the enemy's works at the foot of Mission Ridge ; then take cover behind them, and there await further orders. The One Hundred and Twenty-fourth Ohio was on picket, and used as skirmishers. The other formation of battalions was similar to that on the 23d instant, — the Sixth Kentucky reporting to Colonel Christopher and acting with the Fifth Battalion, and the Sixth Indiana acting with the Second. Both lines were deployed ; the Third and Fifth Battalion forming the first, and the First and Second, the second line. At the signal the brigade moved forward, and simultaneously a fire from at least fifty pieces of artillery from the crest of Mission Ridge was poured upon us. We moved in good order at a rapid step, under this appalling fire, to the enemy's works, which were situated about three hundred yards below and toward Chattanooga from the crest of the ridge, the enemy fleeing from these works at our approach. The command, on reaching the enemy's works at the foot of the hill, covered itself, as ordered, on the reverse side as best it could, — but very imperfectly, being so near and so much below the crest of the ridge. The musketry fire from the crest was now telling severely upon us ; and as the crest presented its concavity toward us, we were completely enfiladed by artillery from both flanks. The situation was a singular one, and can be best understood by those who occupied it. The command had executed its orders, and to remain there until others could be sent would be destruction.   To fall back would not only be disastrous, but entail disgrace.   On commencing the advance, the thought of storming Mission Ridge had not entered the mind of any one in my command, but now the necessity was apparent to every soldier.   Giving the men about five minutes to breathe, and receiving no orders, and the fire of the enemy being very deadly, I gave the word " Forward!" which was eagerly obeyed.   The forces of Willich,[1] on my left, had begun the movement somewhat in advance of my own; and those of Sheridan, on my right, were a considerable distance in my rear. . . . Not much regard to lines could be observed; but the strong men, commanders, and color-bearers took the lead, each forming the apex of a triangular column of men.   These advanced slowly, but confidently, no amount of fire from the crest checking them.

Lieutenant-Colonel Langdon, of the First Ohio Volunteers, gaining a position where the conformation of the hill gave cover until within three yards of the crest, formed several hundred men there, and checked the leading men; then, giving the command, the column broke over the crest, the enemy at that point fleeing. These were the first men on the hill; and the command moving up with a shout, their entire front was handsomely carried.

Willich's troops, on my immediate left, were still held in check; and those on my right were not more than half-way up the hill, and were being successfully held back.   Hurrying my men to the right and left along the crest, I was enabled to take the enemy in flank and reverse; and by vigorously using the artillery captured there, I soon relieved my neighbors, and carried the crest by this flank movement to within a few hundred yards of Bragg's headquarters, he himself escaping by flight, being at one time near my right encouraging the troops that had checked Sheridan's left.   The heroism of the entire command in this engagement merits the highest praise of the country.

Colonel Aquila Wiley, Forty-first Ohio Volunteers, commanding

[1] Willich told me after the battle that he understood from the first that we were to storm the ridge, and for that reason made no halt at the foot of it.

David Neuhardt Collection

### COLONEL WILEY

Colonel Aquila Wiley succeeded General Hazen as Colonel of the Forty-first Ohio, by whom he was considered the most efficient officer, volunteer or regular, he ever knew. Ever ready, he thoroughly understood his duties and was always successful. He was born in Cumberland County, Pa., and at the beginning of the war was twenty-six years of age.

After leading his regiment at Shiloh, Stone River and Chickamauga, he fell, from a shot in his knee, at the foot of Mission Ridge. After recovering enough to speak, he asked, "Are we going to make it?" (meaning the Ridge), and being assured we would, replied, "Then I am satisfied."

Colonel Wiley is now a lawyer at Wooster, Ohio.

COLONEL BERRY

Colonel W.W. Berry was one of the first in Kentucky to side with
the Union, was the third Colonel of the Fifth Kentucky Infantry
(Louisville Legion), and at the beginning of the war was twenty-five
years old. He was always at the front, always enterprising and
gallant, and the war produced no better soldier.

He was three times wounded at the charge on Orchard Knob, but
again led his regiment at the charge and capture of Mission Ridge
two days later, and when half-way up was struck down by a
grape-shot, and then was borne by his men to the top of the ridge.

Colonel Berry is now a lawyer at Quincy, Illinois. With brigade
commanders like Berry and Wiley there is scarcely a limit to what
may be accomplished in battle.

the First Battalion, was shot through the leg, and amputation became necessary. The loss of this officer to the service cannot be properly estimated. He was always prompt and thorough, and possessed capacity and knowledge of his duties that never left him at fault. I know of no officer of equal efficiency in the Volunteer service, and none whose past services are entitled to better reward. The services of this battalion, composed of the Forty-first and Ninety-third Ohio, also stand conspicuous. Lieutenant-Colonel Langdon, First Ohio, commanding the Third Battalion, was shot through the face just as he had reached the crest of the hill; and after lying prostrate from the wound, again moved forward, cheering his men. The services of this officer in first gaining the ridge should be rewarded by promotion to the grade of brigadier-general. He has previously commanded a brigade with efficiency. Colonel Berry, Fifth Kentucky Volunteers, was again wounded just as he had reached the crest at the head of his battalion, which was the third wound received in these operations. He did not, however, leave the field. A like promotion in his case would be not only fitting, but beneficial to the service. On the fall of Colonel Wiley, Lieutenant-Colonel Kimberly, Forty-first Ohio Volunteers, assumed command of the First Battalion, and through the remainder of the engagement fought it with his usual rare ability. Lieutenant-Colonel Christopher, Sixth Ohio Infantry, and Colonel Pickands, One Hundred and Twenty-fourth Ohio Infantry, commanding battalions, rendered valuable and meritorious service.

I have also to mention Corporal G. A. Kraemer, Company I, Forty-first Ohio Volunteers, for his gallantry in turning upon the enemy the first gun reached on the ridge, which he discharged by firing his musket over the vent. This same man alone ordered and received the surrender of thirty men, with the colors of the Twenty-eighth Alabama Volunteers, on the 23d instant. Sergeant D. L. Sutphin, Company D, Sixth Indiana Volunteers, on reaching the crest captured a stand of colors in the hands of its bearer. Corporal Englebeck, Company I, Forty-first Ohio Volunteers, seeing a caisson filled with ammunition already on fire, with two wounded horses attached to it, cut them loose, and ran the burning carriage down the hill. The colors of the First Ohio Volunteer Infantry, the first on the hill, were carried at different times by the following men and officers : Corporal John Emery, Company I, wounded ; William McLaughlin, Company I, killed ; Captain Nicolas Trapp, wounded ; Corporal Thomas Bowler, Company A, wounded ; Corporal Frederick Zimmerman ; Major Stafford.

The foregoing are but a few of the many instances of heroism displayed on this occasion and deserving especial mention. Major William Birch,[1] Ninety-third Ohio, and Major S. C. Erwin, Sixth Ohio Volunteer Infantry, who fell while leading their men, were soldiers of rare efficiency, and their loss will be severely felt by the service and lamented by their friends.

My entire staff, as has always been the case in the numerous battles in which they have been engaged, conducted themselves with the greatest bravery and usefulness. In summing up the operations of the 23d and 25th, I have to report the capture of three hundred and eighty prisoners, besides a large number of wounded ; of two stands of colors and eighteen pieces of artillery with their appendages, six hundred and fifty stand of small arms, a considerable quantity of clothing, camp and garrison equipage, and eleven loaded wagons. Forty-nine of the enemy, including one colonel, were buried by my parties. . . . My entire casualties are as follows: Officers, seven killed and thirty wounded ; men, eighty-six killed and three hundred and ninety-nine wounded ; missing, seven men : total, five hundred and twenty-nine.

I am, very respectfully, your obedient servant,

W. B. HAZEN, *Brigadier-General.*

General Sheridan received at the time a wrong impression as to the capture of the guns. On learning of this misunderstanding the second day after the battle, I wrote a friendly note to General Sheridan, of which the following is a copy : —

[1] Major Birch afterward recovered.

HEADQUARTERS SECOND BRIG., THIRD DIV., FOURTH ARMY CORPS,
CHATTANOOGA, TENN., Nov. 27, 1863.

Major-General P. H. SHERIDAN, Commanding Division :

DEAR SHERIDAN, — I was informed last evening, greatly to
my surprise, that you had expressed the opinion that I had
claimed and reported a portion of the artillery captured on
Missionary Ridge by your command.    You know that I would
not knowingly do so.    Be pleased to give me any facts you
may have in the matter, so that in case you are correct it can
be rectified.    Please reply by the courier.

> Very truly,
> W. B. HAZEN, *Brigadier-General.*

Instead of defining his claims, he came to my quarters
and insisted rather imperiously upon an unquestioning
giving up of the guns.    I stood upon my written proposition ; and as we left for Knoxville next morning, nothing
further was done.

Except for our sudden move to East Tennessee, there is
little doubt that this question would have been settled
then.    I had personally nothing whatever to do with this
matter.    The guns were voluntarily brought to my headquarters by their captors.    My colonels, hearing of General
Sheridan's demand, came to me in a body before we left
Chattanooga, and in the most positive manner opposed
giving them up, upon the grounds that they were not only
rightfully our own, but captured long before General Sheridan had any troops on the crest.    No further action was
had in the matter, and it is unfortunate that the controversy was not settled in an official way at that time.

General Sheridan, in a report, of which I had no
knowledge until twelve years after it was written, used
the following language :  " General Hazen and his brigade
employed themselves in collecting the artillery from which
my men had driven the enemy, and have claimed it as
their captures."    When called as a witness upon the

Stanley court-martial, General Sheridan testified that he
had no personal knowledge as to the capture of the
guns, but that his information on that point was "gained
solely from his subordinates." In answer to the question, "Did your command reach the crest of Mission
Ridge at that engagement before that of General Hazen?"
General Sheridan testified as follows: "It did. I saw
his troops coming on the hill as I was passing on beyond it."

As all the troops did so well, the question who reached
the crest first is not of itself of vital consequence; but
it is closely connected with the very serious question
whether I have claimed for my command a credit for
the capture of artillery that is not their due. I feel
bound, therefore, to sustain my position by unimpeachable
testimony.

I entertain for General Sheridan's great military qualities
very high admiration; but I feel that in this case he has
formed a hasty and erroneous judgment. He is mistaken
both with regard to the guns and to the priority of reaching the crest. It is susceptible of absolute proof that my
brigade first gained the ridge and broke the enemy's lines;
that they captured eighteen cannon; and that from this
point the ridge was cleared of the enemy to the right and
left.

I will ask the reader to notice upon the map the spaces
moved over by the different commands in the assault upon
the ridge. The positions of my own and General Sheridan's troops are correctly given; also the position of
Bragg's headquarters, which, it will be seen, was opposite
the centre of Sheridan's front.

I will now give portions of the reports of General Sheridan, General Granger, — who was our corps commander, —
and General Bragg, who was present, and reports what he
saw : —

HEADQUARTERS SECOND DIVISION, FOURTH ARMY CORPS,
LOUDON, TENN., Feb. 20, 1864.

COLONEL, — I have the honor to submit to the general commanding the following report of the operations of my division in the valley of Chattanooga, embracing the storming of Mission Ridge and the pursuit of the enemy to the crossing of Chickamauga Creek, at Bird's Mills : —

. . . About twelve o'clock M., of the 23d, I was notified by Major-General Granger that General Wood would make a reconnoissance to an elevated point on his (Wood's) front, known as Orchard Knob; and I was directed to support him with my division, and prevent his right flank from being turned by an advance of the enemy on Moore's Road, or from the direction of Rossville.

In obedience to these instructions I marched my division from its camp about two o'clock P. M., and placed Wagner's brigade on the northern slope of Bushy Knob ; Harker's brigade on the southern slope ; Sherman's in reserve. . . .

Shortly after dark, General Wood feeling uneasy about his right flank, by direction of Granger I moved closer to him. . . .

On the morning of the 25th I directed Colonel Harker to drive in the Rebel pickets on my front, so as to enable me to prolong my line of battle on that of General Wood. . . . Shortly after this disposition had been completed, about two o'clock P. M. orders were received from General Granger to prepare to carry the enemy's rifle-pits at the base of Mission Ridge. . . . After this disposition for attack had been made, my left joined Wood well over toward Orchard Knob. A small stream of water ran parallel to my front. The centre of my division was opposite to Thurman's House, on Mission Ridge, — the headquarters of General Bragg. . . .

While riding from right to left, and closely examining the first line of pits occupied by the enemy, which seemed as though they would prove untenable after being carried, the doubt arose in my mind as to whether I had properly understood the original order; and I despatched Captain Ransom, of my staff, to ascertain from General Granger whether it was the first line that was

to be carried, or the ridge.  He had scarcely left me when the
signal was given, and the division marched to the front under a
most terrible tornado of shot and shell.  It moved steadily on,
and emerging from the timber took up the double-quick and
dashed over the open plain and at the enemy's first line with a
mass of glistening bayonets which was irresistible.  Many of
the enemy fled; the balance were either killed or captured.
The first line of the three brigades reached the first line of pits
simultaneously, passed over them, and lay down on the face of
the mountain.  The enemy had now changed from shot and
shell to grape, canister, and musketry.  The fire was terrific.
About this time Captain Ransom, who had been despatched to
General Granger, as heretofore mentioned, reached the left of
my division, and informed General Wagner that it was the first
line that was to be carried.  Wagner withdrew his men to that
line with severe loss.  One of Harker's demi-brigades was also
retired to the rifle-pits.  Captain Ransom then joined me about
the centre of the line, and confirmed the original order; but
believing that the attack had assumed a new phase, and that I
could carry the ridge, I could not order those officers and men,
who were so gallantly ascending the hill step by step, to return.
I rode from the centre to the left, and saw disappointment in
the faces of the men; told them to rest for a few moments, and
that they should go at it again.

In the mean time the right and right centre were approaching
the partial line of pits, led by twelve sets of regimental colors;
one would be advanced a few feet, then another would come up
to it, each vying with the other to be foremost, until the entire
twelve were planted on the crest of the partial line of pits by
their gallant bearers [the pits half way up].

Captain Avery, of General Granger's staff, here came up and
informed me that the original order was to carry the first line of
pits, but that if in my judgment the ridge could be taken, to do
so.  My judgment was that it could; and orders were given
accordingly, obeyed with a cheer, and the ridge was carried.

The right and right centre reached the summit first, being
nearest to the crest, and crossed it to the right of General Bragg's

headquarters. The contest was still maintained for a few minutes, when the enemy was driven from his guns and the battery captured. Two of the pieces taken were designated respectively "Lady Buckner" and "Lady Breckinridge." The adjutants-general of Generals Breckinridge and Bate, and many other staff-officers, were taken prisoners; the generals themselves barely escaping, General Bragg having left but a few moments before. The whole division had now reached the crest, and the enemy was retiring, but had a well-organized line covering his retreat.

His disorganized troops, a large wagon-train, and several pieces of artillery could be distinctly seen flying through the valley below, within a distance of half a mile. . . .

P. H. SHERIDAN,

*Major-General Commanding.*

General Granger says : —

HEADQUARTERS FOURTH ARMY CORPS,

LOUDON, EAST TENN., Feb. 11, 1864.

. . . At the moment of the advance of these troops Mission Ridge blazed with the fire from the batteries which lined its summit. Not less than fifty guns opened at once, throwing a terrible shower of shot and shell. The enemy, now taking the alarm, began to move troops from both extremities of the ridge for the purpose of filling up the ranks below and around these batteries. In the mean time the troops holding the woods were driven back to the works at the base of the ridge, their pursuers rapidly following. Here they halted, and made a stout resistance; but our troops, by an impetuous assault, broke this line in several places; then, scaling the breastworks at these points, opened a flank and reverse fire upon them, which, throwing them into confusion, caused their precipitate flight. Many prisoners were left in our hands, and we captured a large number of small arms.

My orders had now been fully and successfully carried out; but not enough had been done to satisfy the brave troops who had accomplished so much. Although the batteries on the ridge, at short range, by direct and enfilading fire were still pouring down upon them a shower of iron, and the musketry from the hillsides was thinning their ranks, they dashed over the breastworks, through the rifle-pits, and started up the ridge. They started without orders. . . .

At several points along the line my troops were ascending the hill and gaining positions less exposed to the enemy's artillery fire, though more exposed to the fire of the musketry. Seeing this, I sent my assistant adjutant-general to inquire first of General Wood and then of General Sheridan whether the troops had been ordered up the ridge by them, and to instruct them to take the ridge if possible. In reply to this, General Wood told him that the men had started without orders, and that he could take it if he could be supported. In the mean time an aide-de-camp from General Sheridan had reported to me that the general wished to know whether the orders that had been given to take the rifle-pits " meant those at the base of the ridge or those on top." My reply was that the order had been to take those at the base. Conceiving this to be an order to fall back to those rifle-pits, and on his way to General Sheridan so reporting it to General Wagner, commanding second brigade of Sheridan's division, this brigade was withdrawn from a position which it had gained on the side of the ridge to the rifle-pits, which were being raked by the enemy's artillery, and from this point, starting again under a terrible fire, made the ascent of the ridge. My assistant adjutant-general, on his way to General Sheridan, reported to me General Wood's reply, but by my instructions went no farther with the message which I had given him, as I had already sent Captain Avery, my aide-de-camp, directly to Major-General Sheridan, instructing him to go ahead and take the ridge if he could. I had also, in the mean time, sent all the rest of my staff-officers : some of them to deliver similar messages to Major-General Sheridan and Brigadier-General Wood, — fearing the first message might not get through, — and others to order up the reserves and every man that remained behind to the support of the troops starting up the ridge. Brigadier-General Johnson's division of the Fourteenth Army Corps was now ordered up to the support of Major-

General Sheridan; while Brigadier-General Baird's division of the same corps was pushed up to the support of Brigadier-General Wood, on the left. . . .

G. GRANGER, *Major-General Commanding.*

General Bragg's report is as follows : —

HEADQUARTERS ARMY OF THE TENNESSEE,
DALTON, GA., Nov. 30, 1863.

. . . On Wednesday, the 25th, I again visited the extreme right, now under Lieutenant-General Hardee, and threatened by a heavy force, whilst strong columns could be seen marching in that direction. A very heavy force in line of battle confronted our left and centre. . . . Though greatly outnumbered, such was the strength of our position that no doubt was entertained of our ability to hold it, and every disposition was made for that purpose. . . .

About 3.30 P. M. the immense force in the front of our left and centre advanced in three lines, preceded by heavy skirmishers. Our batteries opened with fine effect, and much confusion was produced before they reached musket range. In a short time the war of musketry became very heavy, and it was soon apparent that the enemy had been repulsed in my immediate front.

Whilst riding along the crest congratulating the troops, intelligence reached me that our line was broken on my right and the enemy had crossed the ridge. Assistance was promptly despatched to that point under Brigadier-General Bate, who had so successfully maintained the ground in my front; and I proceeded to the rear of the broken line to rally our retiring troops and return them to the crest to drive the enemy back. General Bate found the disaster so great that his small force could not repair it. About this time I learned that our extreme left had also given way, and that my position was almost surrounded. Bate was immediately directed to form a second line in the rear, where, by the efforts of my staff, a nucleus of stragglers had been formed upon which to rally.

Lieutenant-General Hardee, leaving Major-General Cleburne in command of the extreme right, moved toward the left when he heard the heavy firing in that direction. He reached the right of Anderson's division just in time to find it had nearly all fallen back, commencing on its left, where the enemy had first crowned the ridge. By a prompt and judicious movement he threw a portion of Cheatam's division directly across the ridge, facing the enemy, who was now moving a strong force immediately on his left flank. By a decided stand here the enemy was entirely checked, and that portion of our force to the right remained intact. All the left, however, except a portion of Bate's division, were entirely routed and in rapid flight, nearly all the artillery having been shamefully abandoned by its infantry support.

Every effort which could be made by myself and staff, and by many other mounted officers, availed but little. A panic, which I had never before witnessed, seemed to have seized upon officers and men; and each seemed to be struggling for his personal safety, regardless of his duty or his character. . . .

The position was one which ought to have been held by a line of skirmishers against any assaulting column; and wherever resistance was made the enemy fled in disorder, after suffering heavy loss. Those who reached the ridge did so in a condition of exhaustion, from the great physical exertion in climbing, which rendered them powerless, and the slightest effort would have destroyed them.

Having secured much of our artillery, they soon availed themselves of our panic, and turning our guns upon us, enfiladed the lines both right and left, rendering them entirely untenable. . . .

As yet I am not fully informed as to the commands which first fled, and brought this great disaster and disgrace upon our arms. Investigation will bring out the truth, however, and full justice shall be done to the good and the bad. . . .

BRAXTON BRAGG, *General Commanding.*

It is not difficult to trace, from the foregoing official utterances written at the time, which all agree as to the essential facts, precisely what did occur at Mission Ridge, and the order of its occurrence.

The accompanying map is accurately reduced from the careful copy drawn from surveys by the United States Government. Wood's was the directing division in that movement; and, as will be seen by the map, on account of the eccentric formation of our line its place was a little in advance of the other troops, and its route to the foot of the ridge somewhat shorter than theirs. It also occupied a position before the advance somewhat in front and not in rear of Orchard Knob, as represented on the Government map. The little ridge carried and occupied by my brigade on the 23d instant is somewhat in advance and to the right of Orchard Knob; and at eleven A. M., when I made the demonstration with the skirmish line, and Major Erwin, Sixth Ohio, was killed, my entire command was moved to the front of it, and remained in the little open wood, and started from there at the general advance, Wood's other troops being advanced to that line just before the movement began. This gave Wood a very decided start at the beginning; so that at the time when, after resting at the foot of the ridge, we started forward again, as stated in my report, General Sheridan's division had not yet all reached the first line. My troops, generally, made no halt after this till the crest was carried. There can be no doubt as to the point from which General Sheridan's division started at the beginning of this movement, — as he says, from "a small stream of water which ran parallel to my front," which the official maps show. General Sheridan says also: "The first line of the three brigades reached the first line of pits simultaneously, passed over them, and lay down on the face of the mountain. About this time Captain Ransom, who had been despatched to General Granger, reached the left of my division, and informed General Wagner that it was the first line that was to be carried. Wagner withdrew his men to that line with severe loss. One of Harker's demi-brigades was also re-

tired to the rifle-pits." He then says : "I rode from the
centre to the left, saw disappointment on the faces of the
men, and told them to rest for a few minutes." And afterward : " Captain Avery, of General Granger's staff, came up
and informed me the first order was to go to the rifle-pits ;
but if I thought I could carry the ridge, to do so." At this
time, he says, " the troops of my left were still held back, and
those of my right not more than half-way up the hill."

We will now see from Granger's report at just what
time this was. It will be remembered that it is considerably more than a mile from this point on the hillside to
Orchard Knob, in the vicinity of which General Granger
was. He says, " after seeing the troops ascending the
hill at several points," he sent Captain Avery " first to
Wood" and then "to Sheridan," to ask "if they had
ordered" that assault, and if they "thought they could
take it [the crest], to go on." In reply, Wood said the
troops had gone on " without orders." " In the mean time
a staff-officer of General Sheridan had reported to me to
know whether it was the line at the foot or top of the ridge
that was to be carried." " My reply was, ' That at the foot.'
Considering this as an order to fall back, Wagner retired to
the foot of the ridge." That is, after Wood says his troops
had "gone on without orders." " My assistant adjutant-
general, on his way to General Sheridan, reported to me
Wood's reply." " I sent him no farther, having already sent
Captain Avery directly to General Sheridan to carry the
ridge if he could." That is, Captain Avery took the message from him (General Granger) nearly a mile away, after
he had seen the troops ascending the hill at several points.
That this distance was considerable, is evident from the
following statement: " In the mean time I sent all my
staff with similar messages to Generals Wood and Sheridan,
fearing the first message would not get through."

It is plain that while I moved directly to the front with

only a halt of five minutes at most, — my colonels say
" but a moment," — General Sheridan, after starting from
a point farther away, made all these stops, half his command falling back to the foot of the ridge after getting
half-way up, and not going on at all till getting orders
from higher authority, sent from a long distance, after
the troops " were seen to be ascending at various points; "
which were Wood's, and he says " were going on without
orders." When I had reached the ridge, made disposition
there, had cleared my whole front and the front of General
Sheridan's left flank, and was enfilading both flanks of the
enemy with the artillery I had captured, I shouted at the
top of my voice to his left to come up to help hold what
we had gained, — Wagner at that moment being far down
the side of the ridge, as already described.

General Bragg, who speaks of what he saw of the breaking of his line, says : " While riding along the ridge
congratulating my troops [for repulsing us], intelligence
reached me that our line was broken on my right, and the
enemy had crowned the ridge."

These troops that had broken the line could not have
been of Sheridan's division; for, as is well known, and as
General Sheridan reports, his extreme right flank, corre-
sponding to Bragg's left, was the first of his troops to reach
the crest, and the Union troops still farther to Bragg's left
were Johnson's, who ascended still later. This of itself is
sufficient to settle the whole question. The only troops
checked, or giving occasion for this demonstration by
Bate's men, were Wagner's, and Harker's demi-brigade,
falling back by order to the foot of the ridge; and Bragg
says this was in his "immediate front," and it was at this
time that he was informed that the ridge had been carried
to his right. It was at this time also that I and many of
my command plainly saw the demonstration about General
Bragg that he refers to, and it is described in my report.

General Bragg says further: "Assistance was promptly despatched to that point under Brigadier-General Bate, who had so successfully maintained the ground in my front, and I proceeded to the rear of my broken line to rally our retiring troops, and return them to the crest to drive the enemy back. General Bate found the disaster so great that his force could not repair it."

This movement of Bate as well as that of Bragg was plainly seen from our position, and is mentioned in Colonel Stafford's statement, yet to be given, who also describes Bate's advance with this line. It is also mentioned in my report.

This was when General Bragg, as is stated in General Sheridan's report, left his front "a few moments before" he (Sheridan) "reached the ridge;" and General Bragg says that "the ridge was first carried" while he (Bragg) was present with his troops "receiving their congratulations," the enemy in his front having been repulsed. "General Bate was immediately ordered to form a second line in the rear." This is the line that covered the retreat, described both by General Sheridan and Colonel Stafford.

Bragg says: "Hardee reached the right of Anderson's division just in time to find it had all fallen back, commencing on its left, *where the enemy had first crowned the ridge.*" Anderson's left is well known to have been in front of my brigade, and is stated by Lieutenant Chalaron, of the Confederate Army, further on, as being a half-mile to the right from Bragg's headquarters, which will be seen by the map to have been in my front.

General Sheridan, in his report, describes the enemy's fleeing troops as plainly seen half a mile away at the moment he reached the ridge; they could be there only because they had been routed by our troops, and this my command did, long enough before General Sheridan saw them, to give them time to get "half a mile" away.

Bragg further says: " Having secured much of our artillery, they soon availed themselves of it ; *and turning our guns upon us, enfiladed our lines, both right and left, rendering their position entirely untenable.*" This enfilading fire would have been impossible had the crest been in possession of our troops to the right and left of those guns; and no troops of ours but mine used, or ever claimed to have used, the captured artillery for this purpose. The Richmond despatch at the time correctly describes how the ridge was cleared. Speaking of the attack upon the left centre, it says : —

" The enemy were confident, and returned to the charge in the handsomest style, . . . when one of our brigades near the centre — said to be Reynolds's — gave way, and the Federal flag was planted on Mission Ridge. The enemy was not slow in availing himself of the advantages of his new position. In a few minutes he turned upon our flanks, and poured into them a terrible enfilading fire, which soon threw the Confederates on his right and left into great confusion. Under this confusion the gap grew wider and wider ; and the wider it grew the faster the foe rushed into the chasm."

This agrees with all the statements from Confederate sources on this subject, and with the accounts given by my own commanders. The testimony is that after reaching the crest we attacked the flanks with infantry and captured artillery, and successively doubled them up and cleared the ridge. Not another commander did or pretended to do this, as will be seen by their reports of the battle; while General Sheridan distinctly says that he " reached the crest with the first portion of his division, its right centre," and that it then moved directly on beyond, or to Chickamauga Creek. That this movement was made as stated by General Sheridan is a perfectly well known fact.

In his official report of the battle General Thomas said, that " the ridge was carried simultaneously at six different points." From his point of view at Orchard Knob, nearly two miles away, he was not able distinctly to see what actually took place, and without doubt reported it just as it appeared to him. This statement, however, is not accurate. In fact, persons at Orchard Knob were not aware that the crest was actually in our possession till they saw the captured guns in my front firing upon the enemy, and this was sometime after we had gained the crest.

The right flank of Baird's division which adjoined the left of Wood's reached the crest about one and a half miles from Bragg's headquarters. Its movement cannot enter as an element into this controversy. I will, however, add a portion of Baird's report, as it shows that Wood's was the directing division, and began the advance sometime before Baird did. This fact, as well as the time when Johnson moved forward, is also fixed by Granger's report.

" . . . I had just completed the establishment of my line, and was upon the left of it, when a staff-officer from Major-General Thomas brought me verbal orders to move forward to the edge of the open ground which bordered the foot of Mission Ridge, within striking distance of the Rebel rifle-pits at its base, so as to be ready at a signal — which would be the firing of six guns from Orchard Knob — to dash forward and take those pits. He added that this was intended to be preparatory to a general assault on the mountain, and that it was doubtless designed by the major-general commanding that I should take part in this movement, so that I should be following his wishes were I to push on to the summit. I gave the necessary orders to the Third Brigade, and passing on to the right, was in the act of communicating them to Colonel Van Derveer, of the Second, when firing from Orchard Knob began. Many more than six shots were fired, and it was impossible to determine whether it was the signal fixed or not ; nevertheless I hastened to the

First Brigade, when I found the troops of General Wood's division already in motion going forward. I at once directed General Turchin to push to the front, and, without halting, to take the rifle-pits; then, conforming his movements to those of the troops on his right, to endeavor to gain the summit of the mountain along with them."

Baird was entirely concealed from Orchard Knob by a forest. The six signal guns were distinctly marked, after which there was a long pause; and the "many more guns" referred to in Baird's report were those that engaged the enemy's artillery after the movement began. Our lines were actually under motion before the sixth gun was fired. In his report Baird further says : —

" I then passed back toward the left to see how things were progressing there, and found the first line of both the Second and Third brigades in possession of the rifle-pits, from which the enemy had been handsomely dislodged; the second line was lying down a short distance in the rear. . . .

" For a time this cannonade was indeed severe. The atmosphere seemed filled with messengers of death, and shells bounded in every direction. It was continued until the guns were captured. . . . Looking toward the right, I saw that General Turchin had passed the line of rifle-pits, and was well upon his way to the top of the ridge. Two of his flags, surrounded by a troop of the bravest spirits, had passed the rest, and remained for some time perched upon the side of the mountain quite near its top. I saw, however, that the troops on the right had halted near the rifle-pits, contrary to my understanding when I gave him my instructions, and that he was unsupported. I was in the act of starting forward my other two brigades for this purpose, when I received orders not to permit my men to go farther, and not to permit them to become engaged. I was at this much perplexed as to how I should best withdraw General Turchin. It was only, however, momentary, as another order came in less than three minutes for the whole line to charge to the top. This order having been communicated, all of both lines leaped forward with a shout, and rushed up the mountain-side. . . .

"The march of General Turchin's brigade was directed upon a prominent knob, on which there were several pieces of artillery, and a small house used afterward as a hospital. . . . This I believe to be the first point carried by my command. It is difficult to determine questions of slight precedence in point of time in a rivalry of this nature, and when all act nobly they are unimportant. The Second Brigade, in line going toward the right, — perhaps that of General Willich, — may possibly have reached its point of aim a little before mine reached theirs, and soon after opened communication with us. The intermediate brigade came up a little later. I particularly mention the first knob taken by General Turchin's command as marking the extreme point toward the right carried by this division." . . .

This shows also that Baird's troops, as well as Sheridan's, and everybody but Willich and myself, were halted by superior authority while making the ascent, and that they were delayed in consequence. The "second brigade to the right" was mine. No order to halt ever reached either General Willich or myself. This is confirmed by Wood; and, in point of fact, after reaching well up the crest, as I looked back to see who would help us to hold whatever might be gained, there was indelibly photographed on my mind the majestic spectacle of Baird's and Johnson's divisions then moving across the open space and nearing the foot of the ridge.

From the foregoing statements the facts as to when and where the ridge was first crowned, and as to the points from which it was cleared in both directions, are easily established, for there were no captured guns enfilading the ridge to the right and left except those captured by my command.

Bragg definitely says that the crest was first crowned in front of Anderson's left. This position is well known;

and from this point the ridge was successively cleared to the right and left. He also says that at the time the ridge was carried — that is, on his right — " he was congratulating his men for repulsing the enemy in his immediate front." There was no repulse except, as we have seen, where Sheridan's troops were drawn back. Sheridan says that when his troops reached the crest Bragg was gone. Bragg says that the ridge was first carried on his right, after the Union troops in his front had been repulsed, and while he was congratulating his men on their success. All this was in plain view of myself and of a large portion of my command already on the ridge.

It was full twenty minutes after this before any of General Sheridan's troops reached the top of the ridge, during which I, with the aid of Colonel Campbell of the Sixth Indiana, formed a strong line facing to the right. I went with it in personal command, and swept the ridge toward Bragg's headquarters, besides directing and managing many of the captured guns, while others of my command were doing similar duty on the other flank.

The report of General W. B. Bate is of great value. He commanded the Confederate troops in Sheridan's front and about Bragg's headquarters. Bate is the only one of all the Confederate general officers of high command at this position in the battle now living. Bragg, Hardee, Breckinridge, and Patton Anderson have passed away.

Bate commanded Breckinridge's division, which composed the front assailed by Sheridan, with Bragg's headquarters at about its centre. This is a well-known fact. Bate says, " In the morning Tyler's right rested on Bragg's headquarters, and Finley's prolonged the line to the left; " and afterward, that his division was moved by a flank till the left of Finley's brigade " rested on the Crutchfield road." And this was the disposition of his command when it received the attack.

It appears that at this time Finley's left was the left of Bate's right brigade; that it rested on the Crutchfield road; and Crutchfield says this road crosses the ridge one hundred yards north of Bragg's headquarters. This, with Lieutenant Chalaron's statement that Bate's right rested on his battery, which was a half-mile north of Bragg's headquarters, definitely settles Bate's position in the Confederate line.

Hindman's division, commanded by Patton Anderson, was on Bate's right and in my front, while Stewart's division was on Bate's left. Bate therefore describes the portion of the battle fought in his front by Sheridan's division. He describes the repulse of Wagner's brigade, and afterward its retiring behind the old breastworks when it was directed to do so, as mentioned by Wagner, Sheridan, and Granger. He then describes how these troops were advanced again; and it is there he says : " During this charge my attention was called to some scattered troops a few hundred yards to my right, making their way apparently without resistance to the top of the hill. Believing these to be Confederates falling back from the trenches, I forbade my right firing upon them, and sent a staff-officer to ascertain who they were."

He then describes how he directed upon them a right oblique fire, and how in a few moments he saw our flag waving in front of Patton Anderson's division, and beyond the depression where Dent's battery was. He says then: " The line in my front had recoiled a second time [meaning when Wagner's brigade was withdrawn by order], but was rallied, and was advancing up the hill in such numbers as to forbid the displacing of any of my command." It was now, he says, that General Bragg ordered him to take a part of his command and dislodge the troops that had already gained the ridge. He says he then took another command, — Major Weaver's, — leaving his own intact to oppose the troops in his front, "and moved it at double-quick some five or six hundred yards to the elevation on the right where the enemy had formed." He then says: "Having made this disposition and opened fire, I left Lieutenant Blanchard of my staff to report the result, and returned to my own line, which was being dangerously pressed." He then goes on to say : " It was but a few moments until the second and third flags were upon the ridge, and the enemy in such numbers as to drive away the command under Major Weaver. The enemy turned our guns upon us, and opened a fire of musketry from right and rear;" and he adds, "this advantage gained, caused my right to give back."

This is the same testimony given by all Confederate authorities, — that this service by us of their own guns on their flanks cleared the ridge. " The enemy formed a line of battle, and moved down upon our right at right angles. Dent's battery was turned upon us, sweeping our lines from right to left. Our men on the extreme right gave back in some confusion." This line at right angles was formed and carried forward by myself personally, with Major Campbell, Sixth Indiana, as described in my official report ; and the first gun was fired by Corporal Kraemer of the Forty-first Ohio, by discharging his musket over the vent under my personal direction, as mentioned in my report.

Bate says further: " Meanwhile the enemy had gained the summit on our left, and was fast enveloping the division, and yet the larger portion of it was on the front line." As yet it is seen that all Bate's front line was in position ; that is, the portion of the ridge Sheridan was assailing had not been carried, except the right thrown back by the flank, where I had attacked it, and the extreme left, where the first of Sheridan's troops reached the ridge.

He goes on to say : " I moved the command, which was

in much confusion, to the rear;" and "we formed a line about one thousand yards from the one just abandoned." This is the line General Sheridan then assailed, when he moved his whole division directly on without halting upon the ridge. The following is Bate's report: —

HEADQUARTERS BRECKINRIDGE'S DIVISION,
DALTON, GEORGIA., Dec. 14, 1863.

COLONEL, — In obedience to General Orders, No. 17, dated "Headquarters Breckinridge's Corps, Dec. 4, 1863," I have the honor to submit the following report of the part taken by Breckinridge's division in the battle of Missionary Ridge on Nov. 25, 1863.

The division I had the honor to command in the recent engagement near Chattanooga, Tenn. (known as Breckinridge's division), was composed of Brigadier-General Joel H. Lewis's brigade (Kentucky), Brigadier-General J. J. Finley's brigade (Florida), and Bate's brigade. . . . When the enemy advanced and took possession of the Knoll, or Orchard Hill, capturing pickets on my right, the two brigades commanded by Brigadier-General Finley and Colonel R. C. Tyler, then encamping at the base of Missionary Ridge, in front of the headquarters of Major-General Breckinridge, were ordered under arms and in the trenches. Assistance being called for on the right, Colonel Tyler was ordered to report with his command to Brigadier-General Anderson as a temporary supporting force. He returned after dark to his designated place in the trenches, with the loss of one man killed and three wounded. Thus located, the entire command remained during the 24th without participating in any of the operations of that day. . . .

About twelve o'clock at night I received an order from corps headquarters to send Lewis's brigade to report to Major-General Cleburne on the right, which was promptly done. Daylight on the morning of the 25th found the two remaining brigades of the division on the crest of the ridge, Tyler's right resting at General Bragg's headquarters, and Finley's prolonging the line to the left; while the enemy, like a "huge serpent," uncoiled

his massive folds into shapely lines in our immediate front.
Fatigue parties were detailed and put to work on the defences
which Lewis had commenced the day previous. . . . . By repeated
application from the front representing the picket force there
without support on the left, and remembering the misfortunes
of the 23d in the picket line to our right, I was induced, upon
consultation with the corps commander, to send the Seventh
Florida Regiment as a reserve to our picket line. This little
force, under the frown of such a " horrid front," remained defiant, and in obedience to orders manœuvred handsomely amid
the peril of capture, until by order it found a lodgment in the
trenches at the foot of Missionary Ridge, with its right resting
at Moore's house, on the left of the Sixtieth North Carolina
Regiment (of Brigadier-General Reynolds's command), and its
left adjoining the command of Brigadier-General Strahls at a
new redoubt, where the main line of defence diverges in the
direction of Lookout Mountain. . . . About one o'clock P. M.
I was ordered by my corps commander to move the division by
the right flank until its right should rest on the left of Brigadier-
General Patton Anderson's line. In the execution of this order
I found Adams's brigade of Stewart's division (Colonel Gibson
commanding) extended on the left of General Anderson's lines,
with a brigade space between. I communicated this fact, through
Captain McCauley of my staff, to General Breckinridge, and
desired to know if in the adjustment of my line this brigade
was to be regarded as a part of Anderson's line. I was answered
in the affirmative, and so made my dispositions. In a few moments, however, I received a message from General Breckinridge
directing me to report in person to him at General Bragg's
quarters, which I did.

General Breckinridge was in the act of going toward Rossville, and directed me to General Bragg, who gave instructions
to let my left rest on the Crutchfield road, where it crossed the
hill, as General Anderson wanted space on his left for Reynolds's
brigade in case it was retired from the trenches, — a fact which
General Anderson had made known to me through Captain
McCauley of my staff and Captain Parker of General Bragg's

staff. My right had under the previous order arrived nearly to the left of General Anderson's brigade, commanded by Colonel Tucker, when the countermanding order caused a left flank movement until the left of Finley's brigade rested on the Crutchfield road.

Cobb's (Kentucky) battery had been detached in the forenoon by General Breckinridge, and by his order detained to the left of General Bragg's quarters in the line subsequently occupied by Adams's brigade of Stewart's division. Slocumb's battery was on an eminence near my right, and Mebarne's battery near the left centre of my line. The temporary earthworks which had been thrown up at these points were a hindrance to the successful use of the pieces, they being too close to the crest of the hill to admit of being placed in front of them ; and being necessarily in the rear, they could not be sufficiently depressed to command the slope of the hill in front. The eminence on which Slocumb's battery was placed projected beyond the general western slope of the ridge, with a slight depression on the right, which gave the advantage of an enfilading fire in that direction. From the top of the ridge to the intrenchments at the foot is six hundred or eight hundred yards, and beyond this was an open field of about nine hundred yards in width. When ordered to move to the right, at one o'clock, I sent a staff-officer to bring that part of Finley's command in the trenches to the ridge to rejoin his brigade. The order was delivered, and the troops commenced ascending the hill ; but upon making the fact known to General Breckinridge, he directed it to remain. When we changed locality our relative position to this command was changed, our left on the ridge not reaching to a point opposite its right at Moore's house. . . .

Hindman's division, commanded by Brigadier-General Anderson, was on my right, and Major-General Stewart's division on my left. These dispositions having been made, we awaited the onset of the foe, who seemed confidently resting as a giant in his strength on the plain below, while volleys on the right told of a conflict being waged. About three o'clock P. M. the enemy initiated a movement along my entire front by advancing a heavy line of skirmishers followed by two unbroken lines of battle, with heavy reserves at intervals.  But a slight resistance was given to this advance by the troops of Reynolds's brigade in the trenches in our immediate front.  They abandoned the ditches on the approach of the enemy's skirmishers, and sought refuge at the top of the hill, breaking and throwing into slight confusion the left of Finley's brigade as they passed through. He rallied and formed these troops (who seemed to be from two or three different regiments of Reynolds's brigade) across the Crutchfield road, a few paces in rear of the main line.  A well-directed and effective fire having been opened on the advancing line handsomely repulsed it, throwing a portion of it behind our vacated trenches, and precipitated others on their second line ; which being out of range of small arms, I ordered the firing to cease and the line to fall back a few paces to replenish ammunition and give the artillery an unobstructed sweep.  This was executed coolly and without confusion.  I took occasion during this interval to push a few sharpshooters forward on the declivity of the hill, in front of the smoke, as videttes.  Order was soon restored in the ranks of the enemy, and another onward movement made in systematic and defiant style.  My infantry was again advanced to the verge of the ridge, and opened a spirited fire, which was constantly replied to.  During his charge my attention was called to some scattered troops a few hundred yards to my right making their way apparently without resistance to the top of the hill.  Believing them to be Confederates falling back from the trenches, I forbade my right firing upon them, and sent a staff-officer to ascertain who they were.  Upon receiving the answer, I directed upon them a right-oblique fire of infantry and artillery from the right of Tyler's command.  It drove them to the left, but did not check their ascent of the ridge.  In a few moments I saw a flag waving at the point in the line of General Anderson's division, beyond the depression in the ridge where a section of artillery of Dent's battery had been firing and was then located.  I thought it a Confederate flag ; but upon a nearer approach and more minute inspection I soon detected the United States colors.  The line in my front had recoiled a second time but was rallied, and was advancing up the hill in such numbers as to forbid the displacing of any of my command.

I was ordered by General Bragg to withdraw a portion of my command and dislodge him if possible ; but upon suggesting that I was without reserves, and the danger of withdrawing when so hard pressed on the front, which would necessarily cause a gap in my line, he directed me to take such as could be best spared. I at once took the command under Major Weaver, — which had come from the ditches, and were aligned across the Crutchfield road, — it being disengaged, and moved it at a double-quick some five or six hundred yards to the elevation on the right and rear of where the enemy had formed near his flag. I was unable, notwithstanding the assistance of Major Weaver, to get this command farther, and could only form it on the hill at right angles to my line, protecting that flank, and seek to dislodge him by a well-directed fire, or hold him in check until the repulsed brigade in Anderson's line could be rallied and retake their lost ground. Having made this disposition and opened fire, I left Lieutenant Blanchard of my staff to report the result, and returned to my own line, which was being dangerously pressed. It was but a few moments until the second and third flags were on the ridge near the same spot, and the enemy in such numbers as to drive away the command under Major Weaver. This command upon the advance of the enemy broke, and retired in disorder. The enemy turned our guns upon us, and opened a fire of musketry from our right and rear. This advantage gained, caused my right to give back.

In seeking to rally the right, I did not see the exact time when the flag went up at the left of General Bragg's headquarters, but refer to the reports of Brigadier-General Finley, Lieutenant-Colonel Turner (who subsequently commanded Bate's brigade), and Colonel Washburn, Lieutenant-Colonel McLean of Florida brigade, and Major O'Neal, commanding Tenth Tennessee. [This shows clearly that the first breach at the right was effected considerably before any troops reached the crest at the left.]

GENERAL WILLIAM B. BATE, C.S.A.

LIEUTENANT J.A. CHALARON, C.S.A.

(Fifth Company, Washington Artillery of New Orleans.)

The enemy formed a line of battle, and moved down upon our right, at right angles with that flank. Dent's battery was turned upon us, sweeping our lines from right to left, and among other effects produced, destroyed two of Slocumb's limbers. Our men on the extreme right gave back in some confusion; and in gallantly seeking to rally them, Colonel R. C. Tyler was dangerously wounded.

Meanwhile the enemy had gained the summit of the ridge on our left, and subjected us to a fire from that source. He was rapidly enveloping the division, and yet the larger portion of it was on the front line with the artillery. I then moved the command, which was in much confusion, to the rear, ordering the batteries and that portion still remaining on the top of the ridge to retire to the line on which we were rallying. There was much difficulty in stopping the debris which had sloughed off from the first line; but through the personal exertion of General Bragg and staff and many subaltern officers, we formed a line about one thousand yards from the one just abandoned, in a most eligible position across the road leading from General Bragg's quarters to the pontoon bridge at Bird's mill. . . .

I am, Colonel, very respectfully yours,

WILLIAM B. BATE, *Brigadier-General.*

I will now give other accounts, from perfectly reliable sources, and from both sides.

The following most graphic and interesting narrative is from an officer of the Confederate "Washington" artillery, Lieutenant Chalaron, some of whose guns and many of whose men were captured by my command. The salient points of his description are easily recognizable as familiar facts; especially the exploded caissons, the road along which many of my command passed up the ridge, and the loss of two guns firing on us after we reached the crest, described by Colonel Stafford.

Attention is again called to the map.

NEW ORLEANS INSURANCE COMPANY.
NEW ORLEANS, May 24, 1879.

General W. B. HAZEN :

DEAR SIR, — Your letter of the 17th instant, asking, upon the recommendation of General R. L. Gibson, for certain information upon the subject of the battle of Missionary Ridge, of Nov. 25, 1864, has been handed to me by my brother, Mr. S. Chalaron, whose name was evidently given to you by mistake, as he was not with the Confederate army engaged on that occasion. With pleasure I submit the following hurried statement : —

The first lodgment made on the crest of the ridge was effected about two hundred yards to the right of the position on which I was stationed in command of the right half-battery of the Fifth Company Washington Artillery (three guns). A depression intervened between my position and the point first carried, and I had a full view of the act. My attention had been riveted on the troops that accomplished it from the moment they emerged from the woods in the valley. Their line in my immediate front had borne away to their left from my fire, seeking shelter behind a large cluster of our log-huts[1] at the foot of the ridge, and from there gained the cover of a swell in the declivity, behind which, protected in a measure, they scaled the slope and massed under this position. Of a sudden, like a wave of blue curling over the crest, the column reappeared, dropping upon a section of artillery posted there. The gunners fought for their pieces and discharged one in the struggle, but were soon overpowered. Two of my guns were immediately turned against the point just captured ; but after the second shot both my limber-chests were exploded by a shell from a battery in the valley, and I was left powerless to molest the fast-increasing numbers of Federals on the ridge. My caissons were ordered up from the rear; but in attempting to reach me by a road passing through the depression alluded to, and the only one available to my position, were fired on by your deploying troops and compelled to retrace their steps. The position I occupied

---

[1] These log-huts gave shelter to my men, many being killed by the splinters.

was half a mile or more to the right of Bragg's headquarters as we faced you. The right of Bate's division (Breckinridge's former division) rested on the left half of our battery. The left of Manigault's and Dea's brigades, of Anderson's division, were reported to me as occupying the position captured, and the two guns, I think, were of Dent's battery. I had been moved from near Bragg's headquarters to the point I fought at only a few minutes before the assault commenced, and had no time to verify the report as to the troops and artillery on my right.

If from the preceding statement you think the position I saw carried was the one taken by your division, I will, from my own knowledge and that of other survivors of that battle residing here, trace upon the map you are willing to send, the position, relatively to Bragg's headquarters, of my battery and that of the troops to the right and left of it.

It will afford me much satisfaction to be definitely informed what commander and what State troops performed the gallant feat I witnessed.

Very respectfully,<br>
J. W. CHALARON.

I add the following note from General Garfield: —

HOUSE OF REPRESENTATIVES,<br>
WASHINGTON, D. C., April 29, 1879.

DEAR HAZEN, — Yours of the 26th came duly to hand. I have talked with several Confederates who were in the battle of Mission Ridge, and find that all agree with the view of General Gibson, who made the enclosed rough sketch, which explains itself.

In haste, truly yours,<br>
J. A. GARFIELD.

The following is General Gibson's letter to General Garfield, sent a few days after the sketch : —

HOUSE OF REPRESENTATIVES,<br>
WASHINGTON, D. C., May 7, 1879.

DEAR GENERAL, — I cannot find the report of the Confederate commanders of the battle of Mission Ridge. I was in command of the front line, with my left resting on Chattanooga Creek, the day before the battle, — in command not only of my brigade, but of the picket line of Breckinridge's corps. I withdrew just as the moon went into eclipse, and about eight o'clock in the morning ascended Mission Ridge. General Breckinridge ordered me to proceed with my brigade to the right, and to occupy a position to be designated by Captain Ellis, of General Bragg's staff, — a brother-in-law of Bragg, a neighbor of mine in Louisiana, and a Yale classmate. I remember passing Bragg's headquarters, and some of his staff saying, " What a grand demonstration below ! But there will be no battle to-day." I had a different impression. I moved a half-mile to the right of Bragg's headquarters, and went into position. I did not like the position at all, and congratulated myself when in a few moments I was ordered to move back again to the left. I rode in advance of my troops. General Breckinridge told me Hooker's corps was marching on Rossville, — a point involving our left flank, — and that he was going to meet him with the handful of troops that could be spared. I rode back again to my brigade and ordered them to march more rapidly ; for our left was weak, and the withdrawal of some of the troops to meet Hooker would leave gaps. Just as I passed Bragg's head-quarters I observed the enemy (our Union friends) moving for-ward, — in fact, making an attack. I was moving left in front, and immediately threw my troops into line. My right rested on the highway descending the ridge, just to the right of Bragg's headquarters, and my left extended the distance of several regi-ments to the left of his headquarters, so that I held his head-quarters. There was a peach-orchard in front of his headquarters, — a depression where I found a battery. The heaviest fighting on my line was just on the right of Bragg's headquarters.

The first break I observed in our line was to the right of Bragg's headquarters, just about where I had been ordered to go early in the day. On leaving the position I understood General Patton Anderson had been ordered to hold it with his division. I would say that the troops of your army who assaulted our lines about half a mile to the left — to your left, on the right of

Louisiana State University - Baton Rouge

COLONEL RANDALL L. GIBSON

(Former commander Nineteenth Louisiana.)

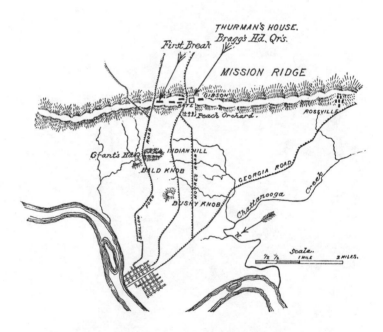

THURMAN'S HOUSE.

Bragg's Hd. Qr's.

First Break

MISSION RIDGE

GIBSON

BATE

Peach Orchard.

ROSSVILLE

Grant's Hd

INDIAN HILL

GEORGIA ROAD

BALD KNOB

Chattanooga Creek

BUSHY KNOB

SHALLOW FORD

BROOKS ROAD

ROAD

Scale.
½  ½  1 MILE        2 MILES.

THIS MAP SHOWS MY POSITION AND ABOUT WHERE THE FIRST
BREAK" OCCURRED, SO FAR AS I COULD SEE.

R. L. GIBSON.

Bragg's headquarters — first gained the summit of the ridge ; for I saw our troops first giving way to my right.   I started to go in that direction to rally the troops, having observed for a few minutes that there was a break and some disorder ; but before I had gone any distance I noticed the support retreating from the battery directly in front of Bragg's headquarters.   I ordered a charge to recover this position, and was urging forward my old regiment (Thirteenth Louisiana) with its colors, when I suddenly perceived that the Federal troops had turned our left, and were marching in line of battle at right angles to ours, sweeping away our lines from the left.   Now Bragg's head-quarters — a farm-house and buildings — shut out my view of the left (my left), and it may be that your troops reached the top of the ridge on the left of the headquarters as soon as those to the right.   But the first Federal troops I saw on the ridge were *several hundred yards to the right* (my right) *of General Bragg's headquarters,* and my opinion has been that they were the first to ascend the ridge.[1]   Mine were Louisiana troops.   I do not recollect the troops on my right or left, the names of their commanders or their States.   I think the Federal troops who came forward on our left reached General Bragg's headquarters before those who made the assault in front of them or to the immediate right of them.   I lost a good many officers and men there, and some were captured.   Colonel Winans was killed, and my colleague, then Lieutenant Ellis, was captured.   The officers with whom I conversed thought our line gave way first about half a mile to the right (our right) of Bragg's head-quarters ; and if I were going to designate the troops on your side who first carried the ridge, I would say the credit belonged to the troops who made the assault several hundred yards to the right of Bragg's headquarters as we faced.   But you must recol-lect I only commanded a brigade, was occupied with my own front, and had limited opportunity for observation, — limited by my position and by obstacles.

Yours faithfully,

R. L. GIBSON.

General J. A. GARFIELD, House of Representatives.

[1] The italics are the author's.

CLEVELAND, OHIO, April 21, 1879.

General W. B. HAZEN :

. . . Fifth. I heard you give the command, or at least I always believed it to be your voice I heard giving the command, " Forward ! " at the base of Mission Ridge, on the 25th of November, 1863, whereby we charged up said hill; and when they say that they gained the summit of the hill to the right of your brigade first, they are mistaken. When I got on top of the hill a company of Rebels came down the crest of the hill from our right to attack us. Major Williston and myself, the only officers I saw, ordered all the men to fall in; and about one hundred fell in, and the Rebels opened fire on us. But we returned it, and drove them over the hill. Our men fired the Rebel cannon along the crest of the hill toward Bragg's headquarters, and the Rebels fell back down the hill, and then those troops came up; and I believe the artillery collected and placed around your quarters by myself and our men rightfully belonged to your brigade. I saw you on the hill immediately after the fight, and you spoke to me. . . .

Yours respectfully,

JAMES McMAHON,

*Late Captain* 41*st Regiment Ohio Vet. Vol. Infantry.*

From the mass of letters that I have received I select the following : —

CINCINNATI, OHIO, Jan. 9, 1880.

General W. B. HAZEN :

MY DEAR SIR, — Your letter of the 28th, in reference to General Sheridan's report of the battle of Mission Ridge, is at hand.

I was then the adjutant of the Sixth Ohio Volunteer Infantry, with rank of first lieutenant. My position was on the right of my regiment during the assault on Mission Ridge. The regiment was in the first line of battle, with the Sixth Kentucky on our left, and Colonel Basset Langdon's battalion on our right. When our (your) brigade gained the top of the ridge and drove the enemy out of their works, neither General Sheridan's command on the right nor General Willich's on the left had gained the top.

General Sheridan's command was, as I now remember, two thirds or so of the way up, and it was several minutes before he gained the top. Our regiment, with the Sixth Kentucky, turned to the left and cleared a part of General Willich's front, while the regiments under Colonel Langdon turned to the right and attacked the flank of the enemy in front of General Sheridan. How much of his front was so cleared I cannot tell. General Sheridan's left was then considerably below the brow of the ridge. How much time it took for him to come up one can hardly tell. We cannot estimate time very correctly in the midst of such affairs. But the facts that your brigade first gained the top of the ridge, attacked the enemy in General Sheridan's front in the flank, and relieved him so that his command came up, and that his left came up after we did, cannot be disputed by any one who was in that part of the line. As to the guns captured, — in front of the right of my regiment and the left of Colonel Langdon's was a six-gun battery, which we captured and turned on the enemy. Critchell was very active in this capture, and in handling the guns afterward. (You had some friction primers in your pockets, and used a handkerchief for a lanyard.)

In front of the Sixth Kentucky, reaching over partly in Willich's front, was another battery. The enemy began hauling off the guns, when I ordered our men to shoot the horses. The drivers and men abandoned the battery, and our men, with the Sixth Kentucky, captured three guns before General Willich's command reached them. General Willich always claimed two of them, as they were in his front; but our men had them first. If this was "gleaning," we "gleaned" them from the battlefield. The other battery was farther to the right, I suppose, — that is, if there was another. My recollection is that we captured sixteen pieces. I saw the capture of twelve of them myself.

Yours truly,

E. S. THROOP,
*Late Adjutant Sixth Ohio Vol. Infantry.*

P. S. Colonel Langdon was wounded in the assault, and many years afterward died from the effects of the wound.

CINCINNATI, OHIO, Feb. 23, 1880.

General W. B. HAZEN :

DEAR SIR, — . . . I was the acting sergeant-major of the Sixth Ohio Infantry at the battle of Mission Ridge, and took part in the whole affair, from the time we started from Fort Palmer until the fight was over. The Sixth Ohio was consolidated with the Sixth Kentucky (Whitaker's), and was in the skirmish in the morning and in the advance in the afternoon. We crossed the level up to the road that ran across our front going to Sherman's right. The line kept well up until about half-way up the ridge, when both of our flanks were stopped by a heavy cross-fire from the Rebels at the head of the road (before mentioned) and the knob that the Rebs held on our right. We got into a cut, or ravine, and pushed up without much trouble until near the top. Willich, I think it was, on our left, was all mixed up, and his brigade stopped. When we got to the top of the hill we had quite a hot time over a four-gun battery posted so as to sweep the front of the ridge that the troops on the right were covering. We turned them on the wagon-train that was just getting off the hill, when the guns on Tunnel Hill, over by Sherman, opened on us and took their own battery in flank which was in front of the troops on our right. We then had full possession of our entire front, and were firing on the Rebels right and left. A party from my company (A, of the Sixth Ohio), with the assistance of others, took the guns (the four before spoken of), and commenced firing up the face of the ridge to the headquarters of some Rebel general where there were quite a number of guns that they were trying to get down the back of the ridge by the road. My party killed the horses as fast as we could, and were firing on the retreating Rebs as the line of troops from the right came over the hill behind us. The guns that were in front of Sheridan had been limbered up, and were on the retreat before he got up the hill. We fired over one hundred rounds at the wagon-train that was going off to Chickamauga Station, and exploded quite a lot of ammunition wagons. . . .

As soon as the firing ceased I got a train of horses from a

caisson down at the foot of the hill, and hauled the guns that
were in our front (four) and the guns from the battery of which
we shot the horses, on the road up to the top of the hill, where
I had a fuss with General Willich, who threatened to shoot my
party; he claiming that the guns were captured by his men.    I
told him that the guns were ours, and that we intended to keep
them, when he rode off.    The guns that we got up to your headquarters that night were the ones that were in our own front,
and the same ones we were firing when you were present, which
was as soon as we got the ridge.    We had full possession of
the entire front before any of the troops on either flank got up.
I send with this a rough sketch of the face of the ridge and
top, showing where the guns were located.

Yours truly,

B. P. Critchell.

Greencastle, Indiana, Jan. 12, 1880.
General W. B. Hazen :

Sir, — I was First Lieutenant, Company G, Sixth Indiana Volunteers, the regiment being on the left of the front line of your
brigade when it was moved forward to attack the rifle-pits at
the base of Mission Ridge.    When within about one hundred and
fifty yards of the rifle-pits I was wounded in the left knee, and
sat on a stump until the rifle-pits and ridge had been carried by
your brigade and other troops.    The first troops to reach the
top of the ridge were a squad of about a dozen men from the
Sixth Indiana or the Fifth Kentucky, or both, followed immediately by other troops to the right and left of them, all from
your brigade.    Within a few seconds, and when about two hundred or three hundred men had gained the top of the ridge,
they parted to the right and left and began clearing the ridge of
the Rebel troops, — that portion going to the left being joined
by the right of General Willich's brigade after they had cleared
away a Rebel force by a flank fire, thereby allowing the remainder
of General Willich's brigade to reach the top of the ridge.

I know but little of the work performed by that portion of
the brigade which faced to the right, as most of the fighting was
on the south slope of the ridge ; and I could only see the right

of our line as it advanced against a Rebel battery stationed near a house said to have been General Bragg's headquarters. Who of your command captured that battery I cannot say, except from hearsay. I heard it was done by the First and Ninety-third Ohio regiments.

At the time the first troops of your brigade gained the top of the ridge General Sheridan's division, so far as I know it to have been his, — that is, the one on your right, — was about two thirds of the way up the ridge; and the battery I have spoken of had been silenced before the troops climbing the ridge in front of General Bragg's headquarters had reached the top of the ridge. It is my opinion that fully three or four minutes elapsed after your brigade had gained the ridge before any part of General Sheridan's division reached the top; at all events, it was some minutes after. In my opinion, your brigade cleared about two hundred yards of his front. I have no personal knowledge of the capture of any guns; but my position gave me a clear view of the entire line of the ridge, from the left of General Willich's brigade across your front to the right of General Sheridan's division.

Very respectfully, your obedient servant,

W. N. WILLIAMS,
*Second Lieutenant U. S. Army, Retired.*

DAYTON, OHIO, May 2, 1879.

General W. B. HAZEN :

SIR, — A gentleman in this city — Mr. Charles H. Ware, formerly private in Company A, Ninety-third Regiment Ohio Volunteer Infantry — says, that at the battle of Mission Ridge, after you carried the breastworks at the foot of the hill, the fire was so hot that the troops all huddled down on the ground, behind the Rebel works, and that you lay down across his legs; that as you lay there the fire was exceedingly severe, and that you rose up, drew your sword, waved it in the air, and shouted, " Forward ! forward ! " that you and the boys near you rose up and went ahead and gained the top.

Mr. Ware is a prominent business man here, and is thoroughly reliable and trustworthy, enjoying the confidence of the whole community.  I thought the evidence might be of use to you.  Any further information I may be able to send will be cheerfully given.

Yours truly,

CHARLES WINCHET.

OFFICE ASSISTANT QUARTERMASTER U. S. ARMY,
FORT WORTH, TEXAS, Jan. 19, 1880.

General W. B. HAZEN :

. . . I was an officer of the Forty-first Ohio Infantry (of which you were the first colonel) from Jan 21, 1862, until Nov. 27, 1865.  I was an officer of your staff from Dec. 8, 1862, until Jan. 5, 1864. . . . I distinctly recollect your giving the command " Forward ! " for your troops to ascend Mission Ridge from where they rested at the enemy's abandoned rifle-pits, the fire of the enemy being so hot that they were obliged to move either forward or backward. . . .

Very respectfully, your obedient servant,

E. B. ATWOOD,
*Captain and Assistant Quartermaster.*

INDIANAPOLIS, INDIANA, April 18, 1879.

General W. B. HAZEN :

MY DEAR GENERAL, — . . . I was in your brigade, and second in command of left wing of battalion formed of the Sixth Indiana and Fifth Kentucky, under Colonel Berry.  I know you were with us when we reached the foot of the hill of Mission Ridge ; and when you spoke to Colonel Berry, asking whether we could hold the position, he informed you it was not tenable, and at once a forward move was made.  When we reached the top of the ridge the color-sergeant of the Sixth Indiana mounted a captured gun and waved the colors, and was shot.  I took the colors and jumped on the gun, and looked up and down our lines.

Wagner to the right and Willich to the left were struggling nobly forward, but had not reached the top yet ; nor could I see any part of our line that had broken through the enemy's intrenchments save our own.  I know still further that just as I sprang from that gun I met Major Stafford, First Ohio ; and he and I taking in the situation, he formed to the right and I to the left, and sweeping down, he in front of Wagner, I in front of Willich, we broke and doubled back the enemy, until I was met by the retreating foe, who sought the road as an outlet from their position and nearly overwhelmed me. Stafford met with resistance from Louisiana troops, and had a hard fight, but charged them, and they went flying in retreat. I have not forgotten the two guns of the many we captured that General Willich claimed as trophies, and how I contended that they were captured by men of my command and of the Fifth Kentucky. Those men are still living. Those guns were captured in General Willich's front; but it was two hundred yards in his front, and before he had crossed the enemy's lines. I turned on the enemy six guns captured near Bragg's headquarters; and while I was directing their use, you came up with a large lieutenant who was on your staff, and almost immediately Captain Simonson came up, and you put him in charge of the captured artillery. . . .

Yours respectfully,
A. W. PRATHER,
*Late Colonel* 120*th Indiana Vols., Brev. Brig.-Gen.*

COLUMBUS, OHIO, Feb. 1, 1880.
General W. B. HAZEN :

. . . The following is the truth, without any exaggeration whatever, and what I am willing to swear to at any time. But I wish it understood that *personally* I claim no honor above any man in the brigade, for I considered them all heroes, but am very anxious the brigade and its commander should receive the honors justly due them on that occasion. . . .

At the battle of Mission Ridge I belonged to General Hazen's brigade, General Wood's division, Army of the Cumberland, and was in command of the First Ohio Infantry ; Colonel Langdon, my senior, being in command of the first line of battle of our brigade. My regiment was on the right of the brigade in the front line. The brigade was on the right of Wood's division, and immediately to the left of Sheridan's division. In this manner we advanced, and captured the enemy's works at the foot of Mission Ridge. It being impossible to remain here on account of the plunging fire from the enemy's guns at the top of

the ridge, I got over the works and went a short distance up
the ridge for the purpose of finding better protection for my
men.  General Hazen was but a few feet from me at the time.
Colonel Langdon, seeing me, signalled, as he afterward told
me, to know what the orders were.  My men had commenced
getting over the works, and I turned to look at General Hazen
as if for orders, when I saw him urging the brigade over the
works, and by his gestures approving and urging our advance.

This was the first break in all that long line of battle for the
top of Mission Ridge.  The fire of the Rebels was terrible;
orders could not be heard ten feet, so almost all orders of officers
were given by the motion of the hand or sword.  Near the crest
of the ridge, and under a slight embankment made by a roadway,
we halted for breath, and to let those behind close up before
making a final charge.  At this point Colonel Langdon was badly
wounded, and fell.  General Hazen was close up with us ; and as
soon as we had a tolerably good line we made the break for their
works, tramping over Rebels that lay behind logs in rear of their
works, going over their main works, capturing many prisoners and
two guns at the point that my regiment went over.  We (the brigade) were considerably mixed up by this, all going over about the
same time, followed shortly after by Willich's brigade on our left.

Hazen's brigade was the first on top of the ridge.  Sheridan's
division at this time was about half-way up the ridge, lying
down.  As compared to General Bragg's headquarters, I was
then about three hundred yards, I think, to the left of it.
There was no break in the Rebel lines to the right of us ; and
about one hundred yards to our right the enemy had turned
two guns, and commenced firing along the ridge at us.  I immediately formed as many men of my own regiment as I could get
hold of, some of the Ninety-third Ohio (Colonel Smith's regiment), and some of the Sixth Indiana (Colonel Prather commanding), across the ridge, facing these guns.  I ordered a
charge, struck the enemy's flank, doubled them back, and captured the two guns.  About this time I saw Hazen; he was
on the ridge, forming the brigade and repelling an attack of the
Rebels.  We turned one of these guns and fired at the enemy ;

and as soon as the smoke cleared away I saw them forming a regiment — one of Bragg's reserve regiments — across the ridge. They also turned four guns that were near his (Bragg's) head-quarters, and commenced firing at us.

I was then immediately in front of Sheridan's left brigade. The firing of these four guns created a great deal of smoke. I ordered a charge toward them, but inclining toward the left, so as to keep out of the fire of the regiment that was forming across the ridge. As we emerged from the smoke we struck this regiment on their right flank just as their colors were coming into line. They broke, and ran down the ridge. We captured only one man, — a sergeant of this regiment. This brought us to within a few paces of those four guns that I spoke of, and in a very short time we had them in our possession. At this time the retreat was sounded, and the balance of the enemy along the ridge, as far as we could see to the right of us, retreated in tolerably good order. We were now at Bragg's headquarters. At this time I ordered *Captain Hooker, of the First, to go down and tell General Sheridan to come on up; that the Rebs had gone.*[1] We then followed the enemy down the ridge; stopped a long train of caissons and ammunition wagons trying to get out of a pass that went through a second ridge about one third the height of Mission Ridge; then to the top of the second ridge, where we captured one gun that was firing at us. There in the second bottom I saw the Rebel army, not over twenty-five yards from us, retreating in good order. We stopped here, but in a few minutes received an order from General Hazen to return to the command at the top of the ridge; and as we arrived near the top we met General Sheridan's division that had just come across the works. I here met General Hazen, who inquired of me what guns I had captured. I pointed them out. He asked me if I was sure of it. I told him there could be no mistake about it, and called Captain Hooker, who said the same. We took only six guns from Sheridan's front, and hauled them to our regimental headquarters. . . .

J. A. STAFFORD,

*Late Colonel* 178th *Ohio Vols., Brev. Brig.-Gen.*

[1] The italics are the author's.

The following is an extract from a letter of Major S. B. Eaton, late president of the Edison Electric Light Company, dated New York City, Feb. 23, 1880: —

" With reference to the battle of Mission Ridge, at Chattanooga, I was present, serving at that time upon General Hazen's staff.  Just before the battle Hazen's brigade rested upon Orchard Knob, — an eminence where the general officers who directed the movements of the day were assembled to survey the battle.   Our brigade knew of this fact ; namely, that the leading generals — including, I think, General Grant himself — were occupying the knob ; and every soldier seemed to feel an exultant pride in thus marching to battle under the immediate eyes of these distinguished officers.   Perhaps this very fact may partly account for the impetuous gallantry immediately afterward displayed by our brigade.

" The signal to advance was the discharge of the cannon placed on Orchard Knob.   It was a grand sight.   The long lines could be seen moving forward at the same moment, and in almost perfect order.   As our line advanced, its path was across the plain that separated Orchard Knob from Mission Ridge ; and as we crossed that plain the artillery of the enemy opened upon us with a continuous discharge of shot and shell.   Fortunately, however, owing to the elevation from which the guns were fired, this did but little damage while we were crossing the field. Experience had already taught our men that artillery, at least when fired from an elevation, makes more noise than slaughter. After crossing the plain we found at the foot of the hill the empty rifle-pits of the enemy.   They were so constructed as to be under cover and protection of the Confederate artillery placed along the heights ; and when our troops reached these rifle-pits they found themselves enfiladed from both directions by a murderous cross-fire of shot, shell, and grape, which not only made the rifle-pits of no protection to us, but made them, if anything, more dangerous than the open plain itself.

" The orders issued to our brigade when the advance began were, to take possession of these rifle-pits and the foot of the hill, and there remain. No sooner, however, were these pits reached than, as I have said, the cross-fire of the enemy made it almost certain death to remain, and every man saw that he must either press on up the hill or retreat. Immediately, and without orders, our men here and there stepped over the rifle-pits and began climbing the ascent, their officers accompanying them, calling also for the remaining troops to advance. Thus began the attack upon the ridge.

"When this advance up the ridge took place I remained, by order of General Hazen, in the rifle-pits at the base of the hill, in charge of a small body of men selected for special service. As our men climbed the slope, the cannons on the heights ceased their deadly cross-fire upon the rifle-pits, and were turned upon our advancing soldiers. In this way it happened that I was all at once largely removed from danger, and from my position was afforded a full view of the advance, not only of our own brigade, but of the entire line, especially upon our right, where the formation of the ground gave me the best possible view. The advance up the heights was in the first instance begun, as I saw, by the soldiers belonging to General Hazen's command; and, as I have already said (so far as I knew), it was begun without orders, or rather in the face of orders to the contrary. It was, as I have said, certain death to remain in the rifle-pits, and our men seemed to think there was nothing else to do but to scale the heights. The advance beginning thus, and not simultaneously, there was no line of battle, and indeed no regular formation whatever. In fact, the movement was quite the reverse of this. For the moment, each man seemed to be acting for himself; the bravest and strongest getting the start, and the others crowding along behind.

"This advance of our brigade, instantly observed by the soldiers of the adjoining commands, inspired them, and they also stepped over the ditches, and began to go up the ridge. Our brigade, however, having started first, maintained its lead, and reached the top while the other troops farther along the line were still ascending. By the time our brigade had thus reached the crest the cannonading had partially stopped; and as soon as our men were fairly on the top, the artillery in our front ceased altogether. I could see our men branch off to the right and left as they reached the top of the heights, moving along on the crest over the space lying in the immediate front of the other brigades. In this way, for some distance along the crest the enemy was driven from his cannon by our brigade before the troops of the other brigades had themselves gained the top. In a short time, and after the firing had ceased, several of the general officers, who had remained on Orchard Knob for the purpose of directing the battle (including the division and corps commanders Wood and Granger), rode across the field and, passing within speaking distance of myself, went up the ridge, following the exact path up the slope that had been taken by a portion of our brigade. As these general officers ascended, large numbers of prisoners, who had surrendered to our brigade, came pouring down the side of the ridge, and were taken charge of by the men under my command.

" As regards the number of pieces of artillery captured on the heights by Hazen's brigade I have no personal knowledge, and none as to their location when they were captured. On this point all I can say is, that the troops of our brigade were the first on the crest of the ridge ; that upon reaching the crest they immediately advanced along it, especially to the right, silencing the artillery which up to that time was diagonally raking the sides of the ridge from the very top down even to the rifle-pits, where I still remained, and upon other troops to the right and left ; that this was done before any of the troops on our right had gained the crest ; and that from the appearance of things at the time I then thought and believed, as I now do, that the artillery captured on the ridge in front of our own brigade and in front of the lines of the other brigades on both sides of us, and more especially on our right, was fairly captured by, and should be credited to, General Hazen's command."

CINCINNATI, OHIO, Feb. 14, 1880.

I was present and took part in the battle of Mission Ridge, Nov. 23, 24, and 25, 1863, as acting major and in command of the left wing of the Sixth Regiment Ohio Volunteer Infantry.

The position of our regiment before advancing in the general attack was in front and a little to the right of Orchard Knob. In advancing we moved straight across the open space in our front to the foot of the ridge, passing over a road that ran diagonally across the face of the ridge, on our way up; the road commencing at a point about opposite the left of our regiment, and passing to the foot of the ridge on our right. We had considerable difficulty in crossing the road, the enemy having two pieces of artillery posted at the top of the ridge firing grape and canister down this road. When we reached the top of the ridge we found the enemy in our front in full retreat on our left; and on a line with the position we then occupied the enemy were still holding their own against the troops under General Willich. I proceeded with my command about three hundred yards beyond the crest and a little to the left, to a ravine that ran perpendicular to the ridge. The enemy were endeavoring to escape with a battery of artillery (four or five pieces) along a road in the ravine. I ordered my command to fire at the horses, killing and disabling several; the artillerymen mostly escaped in the woods. The number of pieces of artillery captured on our front I do not at this late day remember, but I am sure *we captured all there were to take.* The pieces taken were turned on the enemy with very good effect. My attention was now particularly called to our troops on the left. I noticed that they had great difficulty in pressing their way to the top of the ridge, and only reached it some twenty or thirty minutes after we had, and then only with the assistance we rendered in attacking the enemy in flank and rear. I do not know of, nor did I see, any rifle-pits constructed by the troops of our division on the ridge. . . .

Respectfully submitted,

CHARLES B. RUSSELL,

*Late Captain Company D, Sixth Ohio Vol. Infantry.*

COLUMBUS, OHIO, Jan. 24, 1880.

General W. B. HAZEN:

. . . The victory gained by the Army of the Cumberland on the 25th of November, 1863, was so complete, and the result so decisive, that all the incidents of the battle are vividly impressed

upon my mind.   On the 23d of November the brigade to which
I was attached (Second Brigade, Brigadier-General W. B. Hazen)
was engaged in the attack on Orchard Knob, which was taken at
the point of the bayonet, the greater part of the Twenty-eighth
Alabama Regiment, with its colors, being captured by the Forty-
first and Ninety-third Ohio Infantry, both of which regiments
suffered severely, the latter by the death of its commanding officer.   In the advance against the fortified position of the enemy
at Orchard Knob both regiments, being confronted by a strongly
intrenched enemy and suffering from a galling fire, were inclined
to falter at the foot of the hill, when General Hazen, who was
mounted and immediately in rear of the regiments named, himself gave the order to advance, and urged them forward.   On
the afternoon of the 25th, at the preconcerted signal for the
charge, General Hazen's brigade (with the other brigades of
the Third Division) advanced in two lines.   When the timber
about Orchard Knob had been cleared, and the brigade had
reached the open ground, it was assailed by the most terrific
storm of shot and shell I ever witnessed.   The fire from the
batteries at the summit of the ridge, together with that of the
infantry at its foot, was so severe, and so rapidly reduced our
ranks, that an order was given to "double quick," which soon
changed to a full run, the two lines reaching the rifle-pits at the
foot of the ridge at the same moment.   Immediately after the
brigade reached this position I saw General Hazen dismount
and endeavor to drive his horse to the rear.   The advance had
been so rapid, the distance being about a mile, that a halt was
absolutely necessary to enable the men to recover their wind.
The line at the foot of the ridge was enfiladed from both flanks
by the Rebel batteries, and men and officers crowded closely
together in front of the captured Rebel earthwork, to gain from
its parapet what shelter they could from the storm of grape and
canister with which they were assailed.

    Some minutes after the position at the foot of the ridge was
gained, General Hazen's attention was called to the fact that a
portion of the First Brigade (General Willich) had commenced
to ascend.   He immediately ordered his brigade forward . . .

General Hazen's brigade was the first to reach the top of the ridge. General Willich's brigade, which was the first to commence the ascent, did not reach the summit until some minutes after it had been gained by General Hazen's; the delay being caused by the fact that the ridge in its front was higher and steeper than in front of General Hazen's brigade. The latter was considerably assisted by two roads which wound up the sides of the ridge and materially lessened the labor of the ascent. General Hazen walked up the ridge (its precipitous sides prevented the use of a horse, except on one of the roads above mentioned), and gained the summit in advance of a considerable portion of his command.

The position occupied by General Hazen at this time (which was the only space on the summit of Missionary Ridge occupied by Union troops) was but a short distance to the left (Rebel right) of General Bragg's headquarters. Immediately upon gaining the crest the regiments of the brigade were engaged in clearing the enemy from the top of the ridge both right and left, in which work they were assisted by the other brigades of the Army of the Cumberland as they successively gained the summit. . . . A considerable number of captured guns were in position in our immediate front, but a portion (how many, I am unable to say) were taken in the movements to the flanks above mentioned. It was always a well-understood fact with the officers of the army of my acquaintance, that no order to advance beyond the Rebel works at the foot of the ridge was given by any one until after the rifle-pits had been carried. I believe General Hazen gave the first order to assail the summit.

Very respectfully,

SAMUEL B. SMITH,

*Late Major Ninety-third Ohio Vol's, A. A. G. Ohio.*

General Wagner's report will be introduced here, which, followed by statements of officers in my brigade who commanded on the flank adjoining him, will show how the conflict about the guns originated : —

HEADQUARTERS SECOND BRIGADE,
FOURTH DIVISION, FOURTH ARMY CORPS,
LOUDON, TENN., Feb. 22, 1864.

SIR,— I have the honor to make the following report of the part taken by my command in the battle of Missionary Ridge. . . . On the 23d of November I received from General Sheridan orders to move to and form my command in order of battle near the picket lines to the right of Fort Wood. Soon after, I was ordered to advance and drive in the Rebel pickets, which was done, advancing about one thousand yards with the loss of only six men. Colonel Harker was on my right and General Hazen on the left. I remained in the position thus gained until the 25th, with but slight skirmishing with small arms, and a few shots from Battery G, Fourth United States Artillery, which had reported for duty temporarily.

About two o'clock P.M., on the 25th, I was informed by General Sheridan that we were to carry the enemy's works at the foot of the ridge, and possibly storm the heights, and was directed to make dispositions accordingly. I moved my command forward some eight hundred yards, formed in order of battle, and lying on our arms awaited the signal to advance. . . . About three o'clock the signal to advance was given; the command at once moved forward in conjunction with other commands on the right and left respectively, and was met by a terrible fire which the enemy immediately opened from his artillery posted on the ridge. Lieutenant-Colonel Lennard carried the lower works with his regiment, and pushed forward to the foot of the ridge, some two hundred yards in advance, where he was joined by the second line, which had moved rapidly forward without halting.

At this time I was informed by a staff-officer that it was General Granger's order not to go beyond the works at the foot of the ridge. Part of my command was already beyond that point; but I directed it to return to the works, and sent an officer to General Sheridan, asking permission to carry the heights, as I saw we must do that or we could not remain in the works, the enemy having complete control of them with his artillery.

However, before hearing from him I ordered the command to storm the ridge, bringing up the Fifteenth Indiana and Ninety-seventh Ohio, which had not yet been engaged, although suffering from the enemy's artillery.

The result is a matter of history, as we gained the ridge, capturing artillery, prisoners, and small arms ; to what amount, however, I do not know, as we pushed on after the enemy as soon as I had re-formed the command. The enemy was immediately in my front, retreating in the direction of Chickamauga Station, and attempting to get off a portion of his artillery and train. I immediately pushed forward in pursuit all the troops I had formed, sending the Fifteenth Indiana and Twenty-sixth Ohio under Lieutenant-Colonel Young to the left to capture a battery (that was trying to escape with a small guard), which was done. . . . Lieutenant-Colonel Neff, Fortieth Indiana, after several color-bearers had fallen, took the colors and bore them up the hill and in pursuit of the enemy, passing directly by Bragg's headquarters. Captain Tinney, with his usual gallantry, dashed up the hill with the first troops, and with the aid of an orderly (George Dusenbury, Fifteenth Indiana) turned the loaded guns of the enemy on his retreating ranks. . . . I am, sir, very respectfully,

Your obedient servant,

G. D. WAGNER,
*Brig.-Gen. Commanding.*

To Captain GEORGE LEE, A. A. G. 2d Div., 4th Army Corps.

A true Copy.

R. C. DRUM, *Assist. Adj.-Gen. U. S. A.*

Adj.-General's Office, May 13, 1880.

General Wagner's report is pertinent, since he commanded that flank of Sheridan's division that was nearest my own, and his were the only troops between my right and Bragg's headquarters; as Wagner says, " Colonel Neff passed directly by Bragg's headquarters."

He relates that he, with his brigade, was halted after reaching the foot of the ridge, and then fell back to the works, and sent for authority to go on, which General Sheridan says he gave him. He then describes reforming his lines by bringing up the regiments from the rear, — the "Fifteenth Indiana and Ninety-seventh Ohio." This clearly accounts for the time which enabled my troops to advance so far beyond them. He does more. He states that on reaching the top of the ridge (and he makes no mention of any fighting there) he "re-formed the command." "The enemy was immediately in my [his] front, retreating in the direction of Chickamauga Station." That is, the enemy had already left the ridge and was retreating. He says further: "I immediately pushed forward, sending Lieutenant-Colonel Young to the left to capture a battery that was trying to escape with a small guard." This battery, its capture, and the sending of troops from Sheridan's division are described in several statements in this narrative, particularly by General Stafford and Sergeant-Major Critchell, and in statements by officers of the One Hundred and Twenty-fourth Ohio. It is probable that these guns gave rise to the controversy.

Speaking of Captain Tinney, Wagner says: "With his usual gallantry, [he] dashed up the hill with the first troops, and . . . turned the loaded guns of the enemy on his retreating ranks." This is the only mention by any commander, not under my orders, of using the enemy's guns; and he says the enemy was then "retreating," and that Tinney was with the "first to reach the ridge," and that these guns fired upon the "retreating enemy;" but says nothing of "sweeping the ridge to the right and left," which, as is seen all through this narrative, was done by my troops.

This report fixes another point, — that General Sheridan did not move his troops forward to fill the gap that exposed Wood's right (my right) the night of the 23d, for Wagner says: "About two P.M., the 25th, I was informed by General Sheridan, . . . I moved my command forward some eight hundred yards, to join Wood's right formed in order of battle, and awaited the signal to advance." The point where he halted was still considerably to the rear of my right, and his estimate of the distance corresponds to that separating the lines of Sheridan and Wood.

I will now give the statements of officers in the regiments of my brigade adjacent to General Wagner's troops.

CLEVELAND, OHIO, Jan. 22, 1880.

General W. B. HAZEN :

DEAR SIR, —. . . On the afternoon of Nov. 25, 1863, when our brigade lay on or near Orchard Knob, our regiment, the One Hundred Twenty-fourth Ohio Volunteers, of which I was at that time the adjutant, was deployed upon the skirmish line, and initiated the movement upon Mission Ridge by charging and capturing the rifle-pits at the foot of the ridge. After waiting at that point a few minutes until our line was joined by the other regiments of the brigade, we ascended the ridge, drove the enemy in our front, capturing their line of works at the top, and then cleared our right to the distance of musket-range by firing into the enemy's right flank. It was after this circumstance that, while some of our men were engaged in turning and firing upon the retreating enemy several of their guns, I appropriated a horse attached to one of the captured guns, having lost my horse the previous day, and rode to the right to assist in collecting our scattered regiment and to note our prizes, and then saw General Wagner's column approach and cross the enemy's line of works. Remembering my own movements after reaching the top of the ridge, I judge that between five and ten minutes must have elapsed before I saw Genaral Wagner's men as stated above.

My recollection is that our regiment claimed seven pieces of artillery, two or three of which were captured by the right wing of the regiment under my immediate observation, and were used upon the retreating enemy before any portion of General Wagner's troops appeared at the top of the ridge. . . .

Yours very respectfully,

C. D. HAMMER.

The statement of Captain Haskell F. Proctor, late of the One Hundred and Twenty-fourth Ohio Volunteers, is as follows: —

The One Hundred and Twenty-fourth Regiment Ohio Volunteer Infantry at the battle of Mission Ridge occupied a position deployed as a heavy line of skirmishers or a single line of battle, connecting the balance of the brigade (Hazen's) on its left with Sheridan's division on its right. The advance upon the Rebel works at the foot of the ridge was a grand and complete victory, and almost simultaneous with its capture came the cry of "Forward!" and we started with a will, receiving a continuous fire from the enemy on the ridge; but we kept on until we gained the Rebel works on the top of the ridge, driving the enemy from their position and cannon and capturing many prisoners. Sergeant Shaughnessy of Company C, and those in his immediate vicinity, captured two pieces of cannon which were loaded, and turned them upon the retreating foe.

The position of Company F, which I commanded, was perhaps three hundred feet to the right of Company C, but I gained the summit about the same time. The extreme right of the regiment was a little later in getting up, and the troops still to the right (Sheridan's), I am positive, were behind our brigade in reaching the top of that ridge. On gaining the summit and seeing the situation, I gave the command, or rather said, "Come on, boys!" and proceeded over the slope. At first we were a little disorganized; but I soon got what men followed me (about forty in number) deployed as skirmishers, the centre being on a wagon-road that General Bragg reached beyond us and took his departure on. About a quarter of a mile from the summit we captured one cannon, two limbers or caissons, and a number of prisoners. We advanced at least one half-mile farther, when we came upon a large wagon-train in park, guarded by about two companies of cavalry, with which we kept up a lively skirmishing. I sent word to the rear for reinforcements, and that I could capture the most of the train. After remaining sometime and taking two of their wagons, I deemed it best, on not receiving help, to withdraw with the spoils I already had.  In falling back to my command I found that General Wagner had advanced with his brigade within a quarter of a mile of my advanced position, and he afterwards claimed the right of capture of the guns and wagons that I took with a handful of men of Hazen's brigade.  Our brigade gained the summit of Mission Ridge some little time before the division on our right, and then cleared the Rebel works for some distance to our right and their front (Sheridan's).

The guns, etc., claimed by General Sheridan as his capture were taken by us before his troops were on the ridge.

At the time of the battle I was a lieutenant commanding Company F.

HASKELL F. PROCTOR,
*Late Captain 124th Ohio Vol. Infantry.*

MARQUETTE, MICHIGAN, Aug. 12, 1880.

General W. B. HAZEN :

. . . At the storming of Mission Ridge I was in command of my regiment, and clearly remember all the details of that engagement.  At about noon you sent me to the skirmish line to relieve the Sixth Ohio and the Ninety-third Ohio.  Immediately after my regiment was deployed you ordered me, through an aide-de-camp, at a signal of six guns from Orchard Knob to charge and capture the line of intrenchments at the foot of the ridge, then to re-form my regiment and join the brigade. We captured the intrenchments as directed; but the brigade in mass followed us so closely that there was no time to re-form before the movement was made upon the ridge, and my command went forward as a skirmish line, slightly overlapping the left brigade (Wagner's, of General Sheridan's division) and in front of it.  We gained the summit in advance of that brigade by some minutes.  I went up by the main road to the north of the Mission Ridge House (Bragg's headquarters), and on reaching the summit of the ridge found Sergeant Shaughnessy, of Company C, immediately on my right, with about twenty men of his company, moving stealthily upon an unsupported section of artillery, which they rushed upon and captured.  I was with them in a moment, and finding the guns (two in number) loaded, we wheeled them about and discharged them at the retiring enemy.  We then discovered the remainder of the battery at a short distance to our right, and mustering as many men as possible (probably one hundred in all), we charged and captured these pieces, making in all six guns.  The enemy had succeeded in getting away with the caissons and battery wagons. We charged down their side of the hill, and captured not only the caissons but the battery-wagons loaded with small arms. On returning to the ridge I found a regiment of General Sheridan's division in possession of the guns we had captured, and they laid claims to their capture.  I said to the commanding officer that my men had captured the guns from the enemy, and we could take them from his regiment just as easily, and would do so if they persisted in keeping them ; whereupon he allowed me to drive them off and park them in the lines of my division, and my report of their capture was made to you.  Now, in conclusion, I submit that General Sheridan had not a regiment in his division so weak in courage as to allow another regiment to take from them the fruits of their capture.  The fact that we parked these guns is evidence beyond dispute of who captured them.

Respectfully,<br>JAMES PICKANDS,<br>Late Colonel 124th Ohio Vol. Infantry.

I have received the following letter from Corporal Englebeck, the soldier of the Forty-first Ohio who, after reaching the top of the ridge with his regiment, and seeing the smoking caisson, ran it down the hill, as mentioned in my official report of the battle : —

GYPSUM, OHIO, March 25, 1872.

GENERAL HAZEN, — I have been away, and on my return found your letter requesting me to state where General Sheridan's troops at Mission Ridge were when I turned the limber down the ridge.  They were down at the foot yet.  The gun was in our direct front, and just to the right of where the flag of the Forty-first Ohio came on to their works. I did this the first thing after crossing the enemy's works. It must have been about ten minutes before the right and left beyond our brigade reached the crest.

Very truly,

H. J. ENGLEBECK.

The following is from Sergeant Kraemer, the man who discharged the first gun captured on the ridge by firing his piece over the vent : —

FORT WORTH, TEXAS, Jan. 27, 1883.

W. B. HAZEN, Washington, D. C. :

DEAR OLD GENERAL, — . . . I know that your orderly took your horses back, and that after taking the line to the foot of the ridge and lying a short time to get our breath, we went forward, — you in front, — and that when I fired the captured gun, the enemy were in force on the line on our right and at General Bragg's headquarters, and that there were none of the Union troops on the ridge to the right of them or of us.

Wishing many happy days in the future, I remain,

Yours truly,

G. A. KRAEMER,

*Company I, Forty-first Ohio Vol. Infantry.*

The following is Crutchfield's letter : —

MIMOSA, GEORGIA, Sept. 2, 1882.

General W. B. HAZEN :

MY DEAR SIR, — The locality of Bragg's headquarters during the Mission Ridge fight was the Thurman house. The road running east and west from Tennessee River across the ridge, which you call the Crutchfield road, passed by my brother's house, near Fort Negley, close to the Stanton house. It is now called Montgomery Avenue, running, in accordance with the land survey, N. 70 degrees E., S. 20 degrees W. The road is directly on this line from the river, running east until it strikes the foot of the ridge ; then it curves to the left for easy grade, passing over the ridge about one hundred yards north of Bragg's head-quarters. At the Thurman house Sheridan's column passed up the ridge.

Sincerely,<br>W. CRUTCHFIELD.

I add the following valuable letter from Governor Harris : —

MEMPHIS, TENN., March 25, 1883.

General W. B. HAZEN :

DEAR SIR, — In answer to your note of the 21st instant ask-ing a statement of what I saw of the battle of Missionary Ridge in front of Chattanooga, I have to say that being at that time Governor of Tennessee, I was acting as volunteer aide to General Braxton Bragg, and was with him all of that day. The left wing of the Confederate line of battle occupied the crest of the ridge, and the position occupied by General Bragg and myself most of the day was from a quarter to a half mile to the right (north) of the house used by General Bragg as headquarters. The battle commenced early in the morning on our (the Con-federate) right, near the railroad tunnel; and for several hours in the early part of the day we could see with our field-glasses heavy bodies of Federal infantry moving in the direction of our extreme right where the battle was going on. That movement on the part of the Federal army induced General Bragg to send most of his available force to strengthen our right wing, and thus to reduce our left wing (not engaged or even threatened with assault) to a single file of men at the distance of about five feet apart.

At about three o'clock in the evening, when General Bragg and myself were about midway between his headquarters and the point at which the Shallow Ford road crosses the ridge, we saw a heavy column of Federal infantry move out from Chatta-nooga toward the centre of our left wing, and when it reached a point near the foot of the ridge deploy into line of battle and charge up the ridge. They were repulsed and driven back in disorder, but very soon re-formed their line of battle in the valley and made a second charge. The Confederate line in the position occupied by General Bragg and myself vigorously and stubbornly resisted the advance of the enemy; and I felt confident would do so successfully, until General Bragg was informed by a staff-officer that our line had given way at the point where the Shallow Ford road crosses the ridge, which was from a quarter to a half mile to the right of where General Bragg and myself were stationed. General Bragg immediately ordered General W. B. Bate, who occupied the ridge in our front and to our left, to move his division to the right at a double-quick, and re-establish our line at the crossing of the Shallow Ford road. General Bate moved to the right to execute the order, leaving a gap in our line in front, and to the left of the position occupied by General Bragg and myself.

General Bate's troops, on approaching the crossing of the Shallow Ford road, were repulsed and driven back by a fire which enfiladed the remaining line of our left wing, under which our line crumbled rapidly from right to left. The crest of the ridge being thus vacated, it was very soon occupied by Federal troops.

I write from memory, having preserved no notes of the events of that day; and while I may be inaccurate as to time and distances, I am confident as to the events stated.

I send herewith a very rough pencil sketch of relative positions, which may aid you in understanding a little more clearly; but in drawing this sketch very little attention was given to distance from point to point.

Very respectfully,

IsHAM G. HARRIS.

I regret the length to which this subject has extended, but its importance justifies full discussion. The one statement in General Sheridan's report, that in his division the "right and right centre reached the crest first, and crossed it to the right of Bragg's headquarters," taken in connection with the universal testimony of both sides that the crest was first carried at a considerable distance to our left of Bragg's headquarters, settles the whole question as to what troops did first carry Mission Ridge.

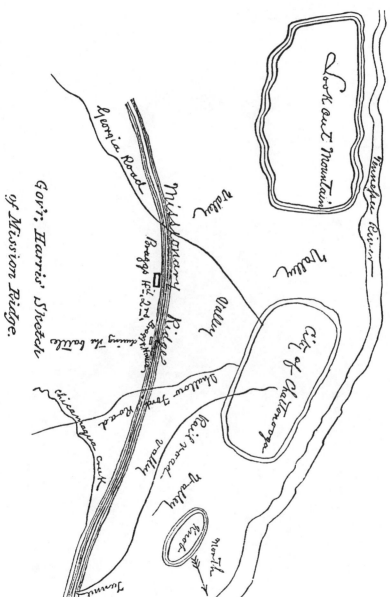

Gov'r. Harris' Sketch
of Mission Ridge.

MAJOR SETH B. MOE

This account of Governor Harris leaves no possible doubt as to the point of the ridge first carried. Since receiving it I have visited Chattanooga, and with Major Moe — a staff-officer of General Gordon Granger at the battle, and since the war a resident of Chattanooga, and a civil engineer who has surveyed and remapped the battlefield, and is familiar with every part of it — went over and carefully examined the ridge where the battle was fought.

The Shallow Ford road leaves Chattanooga, passing eastward between Orchard Knob and Indian Hill; thence along, nearly bisecting the ground passed over by my brigade in the advance on Mission Ridge, till it reaches the foot of the ridge, and then divides into two branches, — just as is shown on the map, — one branch passing directly across the ridge, and the other passing obliquely to the left. The distances of the two crossings from Bragg's headquarters are given as follows by Major Moe from his official surveys : —

From Bragg's headquarters to first branch Shallow Ford road is three quarters of a mile; to second branch, one mile and sixty rods.

Moe, *Civil Engineer.*
CHATTANOOGA, May 7, 1883.

These are the roads my command chiefly followed in ascending the ridge; and the *direct* crossing is the one referred to by Governor Harris, — since the other one is not in view from where he was situated, — and the direct one is where the first break took place.

By referring to the map, which was prepared by me two years before I visited the battlefield, it will be seen to correspond accurately with the distance given by Major Moe. The little intrenchment at *E*, referred to in General Sheridan's report, is still fully defined, and has the form of a semicircle; it is large enough to contain a division, and is

so situated on a shoulder of the hill of the same slope as to
have been defensible in any direction, had not other troops
reached the crest, — which seemed very uncertain when
the order to make it was given.   The crotchet *F*, at Indian
Hill, constructed in the night of the 23d, is also still in
good preservation.

The accounts of Lieutenant Williams, of the army (who,
being wounded, halted before reaching the first line), and
of Major Eaton, my provost-marshal, — both of whom saw
the assault from points so far to the rear as to be away from
danger, — are entitled to the greatest consideration.   Their
positions in the valley brought the whole line — to the
right and left as well as the top of the ridge — completely
within their vision, and gave them such advantages for
observation as to make any mistake on their part very
improbable.   Nor can I be mistaken in what I saw, for
I was where I saw all of what is here in question.   From
the time his division was about to begin the ascent till he
had reached the top of the ridge, General Sheridan was not
so situated with respect to the slopes of the ridge as to
have seen anything that occurred in my front.

After the forward movement began at Orchard Knob I
received no direction and saw no general officer till about
fifteen minutes after the ridge was gained, when I saw
General Wood near the foot of the ridge moving rapidly
toward the left of Willich's brigade.   Some fifteen or
twenty minutes later he came to the top of the ridge by
the Shallow Ford road.   On reaching the top, and in my
presence, he — and not Granger, as is published — said :
" Boys, I will have you all court-martialled ; you were
ordered to go only to the foot of the ridge, and here you
are at the top !"   About twenty minutes later General
Granger came up the same road, and turning to his right
went to Bragg's headquarters, — I riding with him, —
where General Sheridan then was, when Granger wrote

his despatch to Mr. Stanton that he had gained Missionary Ridge.

My headquarters were established for the night on the crest of the ridge, and the eighteen guns we captured were by their captors drawn up in front of it without any direction from me. General Willich then rode over to where I was, and said that his command had captured two of them, and I at once, without question, gave orders to turn them over, as I would have done the whole lot had any one made reasonable claims to them. We then completed the defensive work already noticed looking down the main road the enemy retreated on, — the only "constructing of rifle-pits" done in Wood's division. This work is plainly indicated on the official map.

In the experience of every man there are some moments so marked with distinct impressions as never to fade from the mind. This part of the battle of Mission Ridge is indelibly stamped upon my memory. I can make no mistake about it. The splendid success of the day was due to the men rather than to the generals. I have tried to present evidence that will settle all questions as to the important service of my own command and as to my personal agency in the struggle of the day.[1]

[1] The following is an extract from the report of General Sheridan which gave rise to this controversy : —

"While we were thus pushing the enemy, and forcing him to abandon his artillery, wagons, and stores, the division of General Wood remained on Mission Ridge constructing rifle-pits ; and General Hazen and his brigade employed themselves in collecting the artillery from which my men had driven the enemy, and have claimed it their capture.

"General Wood, in his report to General Thomas of artillery taken, claims many pieces which were the prizes of my division ; and when told by me that the report was untruthful, replied 'that it was based upon the report of General Hazen,' who, perhaps, will in turn base his on those of the regiments. But whether Wood, Hazen, regimental or company commanders are responsible, the report is untrue. Eleven of these guns were gleaned from the battle-field and appropriated while I was pushing the enemy on to Chickamauga Station."

## CHAPTER XIV.

### EAST TENNESSEE.

TWO days after the battle of Mission Ridge the Fourth Corps and the Army of the Tennessee, all under General Sherman, set out for Knoxville to the succor of Burnside, who had not come down to join our army before the battle of Chickamauga, but after reaching Kingston had returned to Knoxville. When the siege of Chattanooga had fairly begun, just after the affair at Brown's Ferry, Longstreet, with a large force, had been detached to operate against Burnside, whom he drove within the town of Knoxville, assailing his advanced works, but without success. Great fears were entertained that Burnside could not hold out until relief reached him.

We set out with one wagon to a regiment, carrying seven days' small rations. No more regular issues were made for many weeks. We marched rapidly, and reached Knoxville in seven days. Two days before our arrival Longstreet withdrew. We found that the city had been all along open to the east, toward the rich Holston valley, where large quantities of supplies were within reach of the garrison.

The series of partial campaigns that consumed the remainder of that winter are only interesting as showing the great disadvantage of constantly shifting the head of so important a command. Sherman, after taking command and assuring himself that Longstreet had actually retired, and that the country could supply such food as the

commissary could not provide, relinquished the command
to Burnside, and returned with his army to Chattanooga,
leaving the Fourth Corps, under Granger, to aid in holding
East Tennessee until spring. We at once organized a system of foraging, putting it in charge of enterprising officers, and by running the mills of the country soon had
ample and wholesome food, with about the same certainty
as when supplied by the regular department. This duty
in my brigade was put in charge of Lieutenant Whalley,
of the Sixth Indiana, who performed his novel task with
remarkable enterprise and success, and showed great gallantry in many encounters with the enemy's patrolling
parties.

Before reaching Knoxville I witnessed one of these
scenes of war-robbery, made necessary by our vocation,
the harshness of which we endeavored to soften by calling it "foraging" and "living on the enemy." Seeing a
country house a mile ahead well supplemented by barns,
stables, out-houses, stacks of fodder, and all evidences of
thrift and abundance, the foraging officer was called to
the front with his party, and directed to take the wagons
available for this purpose, and by going forward at a rapid
pace take whatever he found coming within his authority,
particularly the transportation. A full regiment was sent
on with him at double-quick to aid and guard his party.
The place proved a real magazine of teams, grain, meat,
fodder, chickens, and cattle. So dexterously was this all
gathered by the many hands, that on the arrival of the
command the new supplies fell into line, and moved on
without a halt of the column; receipts even having already
passed. The distress of the household can be imagined,
and I trust that long since they have been fully remuner-
ated, if their status for loyalty permitted it; but such
scenes are not entertaining.

So far as the troops were concerned, our winter's service

in East Tennessee, without a commissariat or tents, and
with but few regular supplies, although very severe, was
remarkable for its good sanitary condition and abundance
of good living.  In a single day the men would impro-
vise comfortable shelters, and the officers would colonize
in the country houses; and the contentment that comes
with the comforts that cost their full value in labor was
wholesome.

The historian of the operations in East Tennessee that
winter has not yet been found.  He will fill a volume;
and space permits to me but a mere sketch.  On our arrival, Burnside almost immediately sent out his whole army
with the Fourth Corps in pursuit of Longstreet, with his
chief-of-staff, Park, in command.  We got no farther than
Blaine's Cross-Roads, near Strawberry Plains, eighteen miles
from Knoxville, where we halted from the 15th of December
to the 14th of January, the advance troops being drawn back.
The reason for this I never quite knew; but it was said to
be necessary in order to repair the railroad bridge across
the Holston at that point.  During this time Burnside was
superseded by Foster, and the bridge at Strawberry Plains
was completed.  Foster renewed the pursuit, and we
moved on to Dandridge, two days beyond Strawberry
Plains, where we were resisted by a portion of Longstreet's
force.  Foster was suffering from an old wound received
in the Mexican War, and remained in Knoxville, sending
Park in command, who stopped at Strawberry Plains and
turned the command over to Granger, who also remained
behind two days, as alleged, to hurry up supplies; so the
army in fact went forward under the command of Sheridan,—a division general, and four removes from the proper
commander.  There was no end of talk and fun about this
shifting of command.  Not that every one was not glad
enough to have Sheridan at the head, for he had already
gained the confidence and respect he afterward proved

himself so worthy of; but this shifting was not calculated to increase confidence in the direction of affairs.

With General Willich, who had been an officer in the Prussian service, the matter was a more serious joke, and he insisted that the plan ought to have been carried out to its utmost limit, when we should have had the anomalous spectacle of an army in the field in the command of a corporal.

On arriving at Dandridge the troops were immediately posted in line, and information gathered of the movements of the enemy, who was very active and threatening. The cavalry of the two armies skirmished sharply, and ours, under Sturgis, was drawn back, when the impression got abroad that Longstreet with a superior army would assail us. At this time, the evening of the second day, Granger arrived on the scene and at once called a council of war. It appears that he was not able to gain readily all the information he desired of his front and the real disposition of the enemy, or that he might have done had he come on with his army; and an interview with the general officer of the pickets failed to elicit from him an entire elucidation of the whole problem. At all events the officer of the pickets was relieved in a summary way, and sent to his quarters, and at midnight I was summoned from my bed to report to General Granger for orders as general officer of the day. On reporting, I found the council had just broken up, and only Generals Granger, Sheridan, and Granger's chief-of-staff, Colonel Fullerton, were present. Showing great annoyance, General Granger at once turned to me in a rough, imperious way, and began a sort of catechism upon the entire subject of the front in a petulant, rapid way, as a pedagogue might do with a class of derelict children. I was not able to answer, nor had he any reason to expect that I would or could answer one half his questions, and his petulance turned to anger. I then demanded

that his tone and manner be corrected. The invariable
weapons of a commander, arrest and quarters, were applied
to me, and a third officer of the pickets, Colonel N. L.
Anderson, Sixth Ohio, was sent for. As this was the first
and only time in my life that I was ever under arrest, I
have mentioned it here. Next day I received a note from
General Elliot of the cavalry service, formerly an officer of
Granger's old regiment, looking toward a pacific settlement; and I selected Captain Eaton of my staff to arrange
matters. Elliot said that his friend only wished an expression from me that I did not intend disrespect; and
Eaton replied that I had intended nothing beyond the
proper protection of my own dignity as an officer, and that
my action was called out by Granger's manner. I was
then released, and ordered in command of the rear of the
army in its withdrawal, which was to take place at once.
Our army retreated at dark, but the roads were not cleared
so that my brigade as a covering force could take up its
march until midnight. It rained, and the roads immediately
became very muddy. The enemy was very annoying, the
army straggled to an unusual degree, and the first twenty-
four hours of our retrograde march was one of the most
annoying episodes of my life. General Granger was soon
after superseded as commander of the Fourth Corps by
General O. O. Howard, and he never returned to our army.
Whatever may have been his faults as a commander, he
was genial, brave, and generous. After a short rest we
were again sent with the other brigades of the division on
a reconnoissance to New Market, and then returned and
were disposed about Knoxville, and I was sent to Lenoir's
Station, toward Loudon, and six miles from it. Here we
passed through the process of re-enlistment, known as
veteranizing, all of my nine regiments remaining in service. Lenoir's is a pleasant place on the Tennessee River,
and the seat of valuable cotton-mills. Mrs. Lenoir was a

sister of Postmaster-General Key. The family were at home, and while not partial to our cause, were courteous and refined people. We did all that we could to protect their interests and relieve them from the vexations of their situation.

While here, General Foster was superseded by General Schofield, and the command was designated the Army of the Ohio. General Schofield at once organized another campaign against Longstreet, now in winter-quarters near Rutledge, and on the 16th of February we set out again for Knoxville, passing through Campbell's Station, the birthplace of Farragut, where Burnside had his first fight on Longstreet's approach. From this time until the 18th of April the command was almost incessantly on the march. At the latter date it found itself at McDonald's Station, Tennessee, not far from Cleveland, where we began preparing for the Atlanta campaign. During most of this period in East Tennessee we were actually on the road, marching to New Market, Bean Station, Rutledge, Strawberry Plains, Blaine's Cross-Roads, and Powder Springs, and visiting each of these places two or three times.

Whatever the real results of this remarkable winter's work may have been, its visible fruits were not great. Instruction was still kept up as opportunity offered. The following order upon the subject of foraging upon the country was formulated for the first time here, and was generally adopted in my command as the regulation of that extensive system of gathering supplies, up to the close of the war:

IN THE FIELD, TENNESSEE, Dec. 4, 1863.

Foraging, except as prescribed below, is prohibited.

A trusty officer and five men from each regiment will at once be detailed to procure food. They will receive their instructions from and make all their reports to Lieutenant Chilton, Acting Commissary of Subsistence of the brigade, and at once, and until further orders, proceed to procure rations for their regiments.

They are directed to impress transportation. Each regiment will need one good team, and riding animals for the party. The name, political status, and amount received will be reported in each case, and memorandum receipts given. The parties will go armed, and take every precaution against bushwhackers. All other foraging, except as may be personally directed by commanders for their own messes, is prohibited. All officers are directed to assist in the enforcement of this order. Proper remuneration will always be given where foraging is procured for officers' messes, unless they take advantage of the regimental party.

W. B. HAZEN, *Brigadier-General.*

IN CAMP NEAR KNOXVILLE, TENN., Dec. 10, 1863.

It is probable that the command will march for Chattanooga to-morrow or next day. In view of the fact that many of the men are without shoes, regimental commanders are informed that moccasins can be made that will enable us to take back our barefooted men. Regimental commanders will attend to it, having the moccasins made for all such men this afternoon. For that purpose detail at once all shoemakers, tailors, and handy men. Hides can be procured at the brigade butcher-shop. Doctor Hart, Forty-first Ohio Volunteers, will give any information desired about making them. They can be sewed with thongs of thin hide, and a pocket-knife is the only implement necessary. . . .

LENOIR'S STATION, TENN., Feb. 3, 1864.

Brigade Officer of the Day:

Until further orders there will be battalion drill from half-past two to four P. M. daily, Saturdays and Sundays excepted.

1. Sixth Ohio Volunteers, Colonel Anderson drill-master; 2. Fifth and Sixth Kentucky and Sixth Indiana Volunteers, Colonel Berry drill-master; 3. First and Ninety-third Ohio Volunteers, Major Stafford drill-master. All guards and pickets relieved in the morning will attend. Commanders will see that every available officer and soldier attends. The drills will be held between the railroad station and the camp of the Fifth Kentucky Volunteers.

The officer of the day will attend with a bugler, and cause the recall to be sounded at the proper time, as well as the hour for commencing the drill. . . .

LENOIR'S STATION, TENN., Feb. 13, 1864.

The following-named officers are relieved from the charges against them, with the consent of the division commander, and the charges are hereby withdrawn. . . .

Obedience and regard for discipline are soldierly qualities that are seldom violated without disgrace, from which the above-named officers are rescued only by their recent valuable service and general good conduct. In future they will sedulously avoid all causes of complaint, remembering that the honor and efficiency of the army are in the hands of its officers, who can elevate or degrade the service, and bring credit or shame on our arms. Too great caution in this respect cannot be practised, and it is hoped these officers will prove themselves fully worthy of this mark of esteem and confidence. . . .

## CHAPTER XV.

### ATLANTA CAMPAIGN.

WE at once began our preparations for the new campaign. I had hoped, and with good reason, to be given a division. By the rules of succession, so scrupulously and justly maintained in the Army of the Tennessee, I should have been so assigned after Shiloh. But since then I had seen the old second division of Nelson go successively to the command of Ammen, Sooey Smith, Palmer, and Stanley, and was still to see it given to Kimball, while I was kept with my brigade, which formed a part of it at the beginning. It was perhaps from this fact that my brigade came to have a special character, and was so frequently selected for delicate and important duties. It was understood and wished by the officers of Van Cleve's division, after Chickamauga, that I should command it ; but in the reorganization it was, at the last moment, and at the strong appeal of Gordon Granger, deemed better to enlarge the brigades, and Van Cleve's, with other divisions, was broken up. Granger had not, previous to the reorganization at Chattanooga, commanded in that army, but was then assigned to the Fourth Corps. Brigades were, in consequence, increased to the size of divisions, without that designation. I was also offered a division in the Army of the James ; but the expected change in the command of that army, as will be remembered, did not take place, General Butler being retained in command, and I in consequence remained with my old brigade. General Thomas was a strict observer of rank, and by yielding everything to the one idea of date of commission lost sight of the claims of service in actual battle; and in doing so, I believe, made a grave mistake. The great numbers of general officers sent to his army from the supernumeraries of the Army of the Potomac, instead of being assigned to posts, as was done in the Army of the Tennessee, were invariably given command of troops according to their rank. A wiser course would have been to advance junior officers who had earned promotion in battle. Thus it came about that thirteen general officers, including those brought in by General Rosecrans when he came to the army, were placed in command of divisions in that army at different times, while but one of our own brigade commanders (Carlin) was advanced to a division; and this during a period embracing the great battles of Stone River, Chickamauga, and Chattanooga. The result was, that very many of the best colonels of that army, such as Wiley, Berry, and Payne, never arrived at the rank where the Government could fully avail itself of their high qualities and youthful vigor; while the commands they had earned in battle were given to others less worthy, less efficient, and who had no claims to them. In a service like ours, where general officers must be largely chosen experimentally, an early commission should be no charter to command troops after failure ; and the chances of efficiency are much smaller in such cases than with the young men who come up from lower grades through successful service in battle. This most valuable principle was not sufficiently considered, and least of all in the Army of the Cumberland.

Drills and instruction of all kinds were taken up and pushed to their utmost in my command, while the refitting and reclothing, so much needed, were hastened with all vigor. The following orders will illustrate our work : —

IN THE FIELD, TENNESSEE, April 19, 1864.

I. The following calls and duties are prescribed until further orders : 1. Reveille, daybreak ; 2. Police-call, 5.30 A. M. ; 3. Breakfast, 6 A. M. ; 4. Sick-call, 6.30 A. M. ; 5. Drill-call (company), 6.50 A. M. ; 6. Recall, 8 A. M. ; 7. Guard-mounting, 8.15 A. M.; 8. Drill-call (battalion), 8.50 A. M.; 9. Recall, 10 A. M.; 10. Dinner roll-call, 12 M. ; 11. Drill-call (brigade), 3.45 P. M.; 12. Recall, 5 P. M. ; 13. Police-call, 6 P. M. ; 14. Dress-parade, sunset; 15. Tattoo, 8.30 P. M.; 16. Taps, 8.45 P. M.   From ten to eleven A. M. the recruits of the brigade will be drilled by competent drill-masters.   There will be a special call for this drill, and the brigade-officer of the day will see that all recruits are out promptly.   He will also see in person that all the above duties are promptly and properly attended to.   He will attend drills with a bugler, and indicate rests of five minutes every twenty minutes.   Colonels are referred to division general orders which deprive all persons of the power to excuse any from drills excepting those coming off duty, who will be excused from all morning drills of that day.   The order of precedence in the book of Tactics will be followed in all drills.   It is hoped that all officers of the brigade will share with its commander the interest felt in these exercises, and will exert their best abilities in their proper execution.

II. Commanding officers will see that the hair of men and officers of the command is neatly and properly cut before the next Sunday morning inspection. . . .

APRIL 25, 1864.

Lieutenant-Colonel BOWMAN, Ninety-third Ohio Vol's ; Major CAMPBELL, Sixth Indiana Vol's:

Be pleased to institute schools of instructions in Tactics for the officers of your regiments.   Many of them are sadly in need of it.   Report to me on Tuesday what you have done in the matter.

MCDONALD'S STATION, EAST TENNESSEE,
April 26, 1864.

Hereafter at target-practice the system furnished and prescribed by the War Department will be strictly observed.

The general commanding the brigade was much annoyed this morning to notice that with many regiments the practice was permitted to run into a meaningless fusilade, and was surprised that officers who had been in service so long should have learned so little of some portion of their duties. The book of Practice has often been furnished the troops of this command, but, judging from this morning's exercises, has probably never received much attention, and I am now able to find only three copies in the entire command. One will be given to each two battalions, and will be left with the odd numbered one.

Colonels will at once attend to the making of targets, rests, etc., and make every preparation necessary to carry out the system. No firing will be practised until further orders from these headquarters, but preparations leading to it will be rigorously observed. Colonels will in person superintend these instructions.

McDONALD'S STATION, EAST TENNESSEE,
April 27, 1864.

During the coming campaign but one wagon will be allowed each regiment. In this must be carried ten days' forage for the team and horses of officers, and such cooking utensils and officers' blankets and clothing as are indispensable. Officers will at once see that there are no trunks, mess-chests, or boxes carried, excepting one box for each regiment, in which there must be blanks and stationery sufficient to make the required company and regimental reports and returns, which in future will be required on the march. Extra ammunition and rations will be carried on an extra train detached from the troops. Regimental commanders will at once set themselves upon preparing their regiments as above indicated, with a view to marching at thirty minutes' notice.

Regimental adjutants will at once prepare their desks or boxes, and procure proper stationery and blanks for the purposes above named. Officers can carry in their wagons a few shelter-tents or flies. It is suggested, with a view to economize room, that regimental messes among the officers be formed, when agreeable to them ; in which case one box or chest can be taken for mess purposes.

This circular means nothing more than speedy preparation. All extra property will be stored at some place yet to be indicated, and a trusty non-commissioned officer from each regiment left to take charge of it.

IN THE FIELD, May 5, 1864.

. . . For the coming campaign, and until further orders, the following will be the organization of battalions for fighting, marching, and campaigning purposes. First Battalion : One Hundred and Twenty-fourth Ohio and Ninety-third Ohio Volunteer Infantry, — Colonel O. H. Payne, One Hundred and Twenty-fourth Ohio, commanding. Second Battalion : Fifth Kentucky and Sixth Indiana Volunteer Infantry, — Colonel W. W. Berry, Fifth Kentucky Volunteers, commanding. Third Battalion : Twenty-third Kentucky and Sixth Kentucky Volunteer Infantry, — Lieutenant-Colonel J. C. Foy, Twenty-third Kentucky Volunteers, commanding. Fourth Battalion : Forty-first Ohio and First Ohio Volunteer Infantry, — Lieutenant-Colonel R. L. Kimberly, Forty-first Ohio, commanding. This organization will be made on moving from this camp, except that the Fifth Kentucky, Sixth Kentucky, and Sixth Indiana Volunteers will remain as now until the arrival of the Twenty-third Kentucky Volunteers.

In action it is directed that volley-firing be that habitually employed either by wing, rank, or battalion ; and in order to be perfectly prepared to execute these fires correctly, battalion commanders will exercise their commands in firing without cartridges at least once a day until further orders. . . .

IN THE FIELD, May 6, 1864.

Regimental commanders will direct that a minute inspection be made of every company in their regiments, to see if every man has forty rounds of ammunition in good order in his cartridge-box. . . .

My journal and official report will furnish my description of our part in this remarkable campaign up to the time I relinquished the brigade to command a division in the Army of the Tennessee.

*May* 6, 1864. Still occupying same camp. Baggage reduced to one wagon each, for corps, division, and brigade headquarters.

*May* 7. Moved at 5.30 A. M. in the advance of our division (Stanley moving in advance of us) down old Alabama road, six miles, to Tunnel Hill, which we reached at two P. M. Tunnel Hill occupied only by enemy's cavalry, who were easily driven away. First artillery firing at 8.55 A. M. Our brigade not engaged. Colonels Berry and Payne, with their battalions, sent to occupy a ridge between Tunnel Hill and Rocky-Faced Ridge, forming a line facing down the valley toward the approach from Buzzard's-Roost Gap.

*May* 8. Colonel Kimberly's and Colonel Foy's battalions moved over and formed in rear of Payne's and Berry's. Moved with the entire corps and took position near the base of Rocky-Faced Ridge.

*May* 9. Reveille at 3.30. Advanced up the ridge, two thirds of the way (General Willich being on our left) in double lines, Colonel Payne's battalion on the right of front line, Colonel Berry's on the left. Colonel Foy's battalion furnished the skirmish line and Colonel Kimberly's in reserve, in column doubled on the centre. Remained until four o'clock, our skirmishers near the top and losing heavily. The object of this advance was a diversion in favor of Stanley's division, which had gone to the left to occupy the ridge. Moved off at four o'clock to join Grose's left ; but owing to error in Stanley's lines we did not find it, and went into bivouac near camp of last night at six o'clock. Sharpshooters very troublesome, striking groups of men at the distance of a mile from the ridge.

*May* 10. In same place. Much worried by sharpshooters.

*May* 11. Moved a few hundred yards to the rear under cover of a crest out of reach of sharpshooters. All the army, except one corps, moving to-night. One corps will be left to occupy this valley.

*May* 12. Remaining quiet. News from General Grant very cheering. Reported that a Rebel column is moving around toward our left in Ringgold. General Wood gone with Willich's and Beatty's brigades to ascertain, and if true, to intercept it.

*May* 13. Enemy retreated last night through Dalton.  Moved at two P. M., passing through Buzzard's-Roost Gap.  Dalton, one of the oldest places in Georgia, we found almost abandoned, and much dilapidated, owing to long occupation by Rebel troops. I saw here, the only time in my life, a row of whipping-posts. Went into bivouac about dark, but at ten o'clock were ordered forward to join the division, two miles toward Resaca.  Delayed by moving trains, and did not come up with the division until midnight, when we formed on Willich's left, and the men bivouacked near their arms.  Marched eight miles to-day.

COLONEL OLIVER H. PAYNE

(One Hundred Twenty-fourth Ohio.)

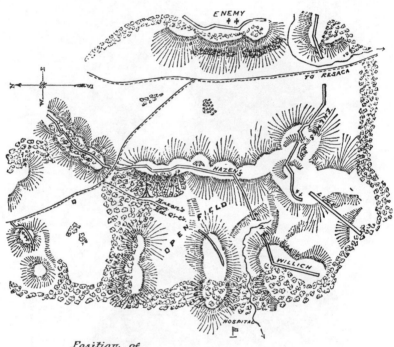

Position of
HAZEN'S BRIGADE
AT RESACA.

A. G. Bierce
Lt.&Actg. Top. Engineer

Scale—Yds.
100     200

Traced in Adjutant General's Office.
From Original Records.

## CHAPTER XVI.

### RESACA.

EARLY on the morning of the 14th of May we advanced on the Resaca road. About eleven o'clock A. M. the cavalry came upon the enemy's infantry, and the head of the column was halted. The brigade was placed in position on the left of Willich's (Stanley being on our left), with a strong skirmish line deployed, and at noon began to advance in two lines, as follows: Colonel Kimberly on the right and Colonel Foy on the left of the first line; Colonel Berry on the right and Colonel Payne on the left of the second line. The advance was a difficult one, through thick woods and tangled undergrowth. The skirmishers drove those of the enemy before them for about three miles, when Colonel Payne, who had relieved Colonel Foy in the front, drove a Rebel line handsomely across a cornfield into their works beyond, and gained a strong position within two hundred yards of their intrenchments. His line was here exposed to an enfilading fire from a battery, but Colonel Kimberly's battalion, charging across the field and forming nearly at right angles with Colonel Payne's, soon silenced it, and held the position within seventy-five yards of the enemy's main line. The cannoneers were driven away from their guns, and only succeeded in recovering them after dark. Grose's brigade, of Stanley's division, formed on our left, and Willich, of ours, upon our right. Colonel Foy's battalion was placed in the front line on Kimberly's right. The sketch of this position, drawn on the spot, shows this salient quite in advance of anything on either flank of it, and it dominated the enemy's lines for a long distance on both flanks. It was just at the apex of the elliptical-shaped position of the enemy, on the side opposite Resaca.

The two days we were here afforded an uninterrupted practice of sharpshooting at close range. On the second day orders were received that at twelve M., when Hooker should attack on the left, and we saw the enemy uneasy or falling back, a general attack was to be made. At the hour indicated, Hooker did attack, and the enemy's skirmishers in our front could be seen rapidly retreating, and I commanded, " Forward ! " My entire brigade leaped the works and went forward ; but as no other troops did so on either of our flanks, they drew a concentrated fire of great violence and were recalled. This cost us a hundred men in less than a minute. Sixty were lost the day before in the dash to gain the ground here occupied. An amusing *contretemps* occurred the previous evening. A Rebel brigade commander, Colonel McSpadden of an Alabama regiment, returning from a visit to his division commander, mistook our advanced position for his own, and deliberately walked into my lines, and was at my headquarters a moment afterward, not thirty yards in rear of the main line. His confusion and disgust can be imagined. I had gone to bed; and after a few minutes' pleasant chat, which in a measure reassured him, I dismissed his guard and asked him to share my blankets for the night, and we were soon both sleeping fraternally. After breakfasting with me, I gave him a horse and sent him with an officer to corps headquarters with my best wishes, and never heard of him afterward.

Under cover of a heavy musketry fire, which our army supposed was an assault, the enemy retreated during the night of the 15th and 16th, leaving many of their wounded on the field. Evidence of the destructive fire by our men was everywhere apparent. We moved in pursuit about eight o'clock A. M., passing through Resaca, across the Oostenaula, to within two miles of Calhoun, and reached there about dark and bivouacked. The enemy had contested Newton's advance at Resaca and burned the railroad bridge. We marched seven miles that day.

*May* 17. Marched at seven o'clock in advance of the division, moving down the railroad parallel to General Stanley on our right. Skirmishing by Colonel Kimberly's battalion all the way to within two miles of Adairsville, where the enemy, showing a heavy front and reported to be advancing, threw us into a defensive attitude. The brigade formed in order as follows, and threw up a breastwork : Colonel Foy on the right of front line ; Berry in the centre, and Colonel Kimberly on the left ; Colonel Payne in reserve. Marched nine miles to-day.

*May* 18. Moved into Adairsville, and rested until two P. M., when we moved forward on Kingston road to within two miles and a half of that place. Halted, and bivouacked for the night. Marched ten miles to-day.

*May* 19. Marched through Kingston, taking the Kingston and Cassville road. The enemy being found in force on Best's plantation, a line was formed, our brigade on Stanley's right, and moved cautiously forward. Sharp skirmishing and artillery practice until night closed, our skirmishers having driven those of the enemy, and our main line having advanced nearly two miles. Owing to the Fourteenth Corps not getting into position, we were unable to press them any farther. Colonel Payne and Colonel Kimberly, whose battalions had been in the front line during the day, were relieved by Colonels Berry and Foy, who were ordered to throw up a slight breastwork. Marched ten miles.

*May* 20. Had a quiet night's rest. Enemy worked until midnight upon their intrenchments, when they retreated. Army very tired and needing rest.

*May* 21. Still in camp near Cassville. Heat oppressive.

*May* 22. Still remain in camp, enjoying the quiet. A man killed in camp to-day by a stray bullet, no one knowing whence it came nor hearing any report.

*May* 23. Marched at eight o'clock, crossing the Etowah at Gillam's bridge, going into bivouac at half-past eight. Distance, eight miles.

*May* 24. Moved at eight o'clock. Proceeded south by Stittsboro' road, and camped at night near Burnt Hickory. Road lies over the Burnt Hickory range of hills, a spur of the Alatoona Mountains. Plenty of water, but a scarcity of forage. Poor country generally. Marched eight miles to-day.

*May* 25. Moved about noon on Dallas road. About dark heard heavy artillery and musketry firing in front, and ascertained that Hooker had come upon a column of the enemy and was engaging them. Crossed the Pumpkin-Vine Creek, and went into bivouac beside the road after ten o'clock. Raining hard since dark. A very severe, trying day. Marched seven miles.

*May* 26. Moved into position at daybreak on Willich's left, in rear of an open field, the Rebel skirmishers on the opposite side. In the centre of the field was a house, with the family still in it. About seven o'clock our skirmishers, with Willich's, moved over the field and drove those of the enemy, gaining a good position for artillery. As was afterward ascertained, this had been the enemy's extreme right, and they, finding themselves in danger of being flanked, retired their right across a creek in our front. Our brigade was thrown over the stream, and formed, facing the enemy's new line, our right resting on the stream, Colonel Berry on the right and Colonel Foy on the left of the first line. General Cox's division formed on our left about dark. A section of artillery was got into position and developed a battery on our left, commanding and enfilading our guns.

Major Hampson, One Hundred and Twenty-fourth Ohio, aide-de-camp to General Wood, was killed on the morning of the 27th. About nine o'clock our division was relieved by Stanley's division, our brigade by General Whitaker's. Supported by Willich's brigade in close column, and by

MAJOR HAMPSON

Major James B. Hampson was born at Carrollton, Ohio, in 1838, and
was killed at twenty-six. He was a fearless and accomplished officer.

LIEUTENANT COLONEL ROBERT L. KIMBERLY

(Forty-first Ohio.)

General Johnson's division on the left, we moved to General Schofield's left, and were ordered to find the enemy and attack him. After moving four miles through thick wood and undergrowth, we found ourselves in position for attack, and went forward, Colonel Kimberly on the right and Colonel Payne on the left of the front line. After advancing about three hundred yards we found the enemy posted behind works on the crest of a commanding ridge, and were immediately hotly engaged in what is known as the battle of Pickett's Mills.

## CHAPTER XVII.

### PICKETT'S MILLS.

THIS engagement was fought toward evening on the 27th of May, 1864, near Dallas, Georgia, and has generally been confounded with the action at New Hope Church, fought two days before. It takes its name from a mill situated half a mile in rear of where the action took place, and was fought under the chief command of Major-General O. O. Howard. It is scarcely noticed in any of the reports of the Union commanders, and is ignored by Sherman in his memoirs; but it was the most fierce, bloody, and persistent assault by our troops in the Atlanta campaign, and the Confederates, who were victorious, have described it at length. The purpose of this engagement was to find the enemy's right flank, and then drive it in, double it back, and assail the Confederate rear. Unfortunately the day was too far spent when the attack was made, to give the best promise of success.

My command was withdrawn for this attack from a position in the line where for forty-eight hours it had been very actively engaged. Many felt that this imposed on us an additional service of very great severity out of our turn. General Wood's report shows that he protested stubbornly. In a conversation with General Howard, our corps commander, when we were given the advance, he said to me that he had selected the force he thought gave the greatest promise of succeeding in the work in hand. This remark forestalled any objection on my part. We

GENERAL OLIVER O. HOWARD

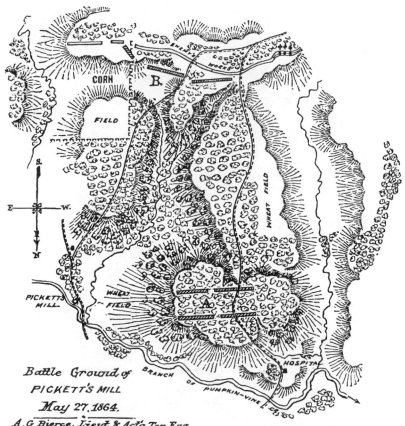

CORN

B.

FIELD

ENEMY'S WORKS

WHEAT FIELD

PICKETT'S MILL

WHEAT FIELD

A

HOSPITAL

BRANCH OF PUMPKIN-VINE C*

Battle Ground of
PICKETT'S MILL
May 27. 1864.

A. G. Bierce, Lieut. & Ac'g Top. Eng.
A. & B. positions of 2$^{nd}$ Bgd. 3$^{rd}$ Div. 4$^{th}$ Corps.
W. B. Hazen
Brig. General.

Scale—Yds.
100    200              400

Traced in Adjutant General's Office April 22$^{nd}$ 1879.
From Original Records.

proceeded from ten in the morning through a dense wood till two P. M., and then halted for two hours and a half. I was then ordered to form for the attack at the point *A*, as shown in the sketch, the other two brigades forming similarly in my rear; in all, six lines.

The accompanying map was accurately drawn by my topographical officer on the spot, two or three days after the battle. It represents only my own command and the enemy in our front. The attack was to have been by column. Our approach was through a dense wood, and our advance in the attack was through a wood so thick that we could keep our direction only by the compass; and in moving, the rear line made distance to the left by just its front, and came into action on the prolongation of the front line. No attack could have been made in better form, nor persisted in with more determination; but as a column attack it was a failure. The several brigades, instead of striking in such rapid succession that each might benefit by the advantage gained by those before it, were put in at intervals of forty minutes. This resulted in separate attacks by detachments, with ample warning to the enemy to get ready and repair damage. Just as I was about to move, General Wood in my presence remarked to General Howard, " We will put in Hazen, and see what success he has." This was a revelation to me, as it was evident there was to be no attack by column at all. The attack was made, however, with the belief on the part of the men that it was by column, which made the long interval before relief came seem inexcusable to many. When my command had worn itself out in a close fight of just forty-five minutes, losing over five hundred men, and I had sent back all my staff and several other officers to hurry up the other lines, we began to fall back man by man, company by company, and regiment by regiment, from sheer necessity; for, as General Wood said in his report, " no troops could stay there and live." The command all fell back in this manner, sifting through the dense wood, except about three hundred men, who, as it proved afterward, could not get away without uncovering from positions they had taken in the immediate front of an overpowering enemy, who had by this time been reinforced by Cleburne's division. The brigade mostly fell back along the depression where the little brook is shown on the map as emptying into Pumpkin-Vine Creek, just below the mill. I had taken my position, and had remained during all the fight at *B*, on the map, under very great exposure, where I could see all the left of the line and some of the right. The whole fight was terrific and the slaughter immense. The left flank fell back along the fence near my position running at right angles to the line of battle, as shown on the map, and here fired with great execution upon the enemy advancing across the cornfield from our left. The enemy came on in fine style, coming up from the ravine beyond; but after one volley from our men along the fence they were out of sight, to a man, in twenty seconds. Our next brigade to advance (Gibson's) was met as we fell back about two hundred yards from the front line as represented on the map. My command was re-formed with great difficulty near Pumpkin-Vine Creek. I rode rapidly to each place where I saw a regimental color, and halting it would order the bearer to stand in his position, and then, with my aides, orderlies, and the staff of other officers, would direct the men one by one to their colors. It was slow work, as the men were in bad humor, and felt that they had not been properly supported. They went into the fight with the implied promise of immediate support that a column attack always gives, and they felt, as they expressed it, that they had been " sold out." As soon as I had gotten together a small fragment of three or four of my nine regiments, I was taken, by General Howard's order, to a new position on the right. Everybody was morose, and found fault with his superior, — the men with their captains, the captains with their colonels, and so on all the way up.

This battle was the subject of a great deal of criticism and fault-finding. The two fatal mistakes, as they appeared to me, were the two hours' halt after arriving on the flank of the enemy — who were alert, and knew what we were doing — and the abandonment of the column movement in attacking, after the two hours had been wasted in getting ready for it. In confirmation of this opinion, and to show the desperate character of the assault, I quote the following extracts from the account of the engagement by General Joseph E. Johnston, our opposing commander-in-chief : —

"The Federal troops extended their intrenched line so rapidly to their left that it was found necessary, on the morning of the 27th, to transfer Cleburne's division of Hardee's corps to our right, where it was formed on the prolongation of Polk's line. . . . Between five and six o'clock in the afternoon Kelly's skirmishers were driven in by a body of Federal cavalry, whose advance was supported by the Fourth Corps. This advance was retarded by the resistance of Kelly's troops fighting on foot behind unconnected little heaps of loose stones. As soon as the noise of this contest revealed to Major-General Cleburne the manœuvre to turn his right, he brought the right brigade of his second line (Granberry's) to Kelly's support by forming it on the right of his first line, when the thin line of dismounted cavalry, that had been bravely resisting masses of infantry, gave place to the Texan brigade.

"The Fourth Corps came on in deep order, and assailed the Texans with great vigor, receiving their close and accurate fire with the fortitude always exhibited by General Sherman's troops in the actions of this campaign. They had also to endure the fire of Govan's right, including two pieces of artillery, on their right flank. At the same time Kelly's and a part of Humes's troops, directed by General Wheeler, met the Federal left, which was following the movement of the main body. . . . The united forces continued to press forward, however, but so much delayed by the resistance of Wheeler's troops as to give time for the arrival on that part of the field of the Eighth and Ninth Arkansas Regiments under Colonel Bancum, detached by General Govan to the assistance of the cavalry. This little body met the foremost of the Federal troops as they were reaching the prolongation of Granberry's line, and charging gallantly, drove them back, and preserved the Texans from an attack in flank which must have been fatal. Before the Federal left could gather to overwhelm Bancum and his two regiments, Lowry's brigade, hurried by General Cleburne from its position as left of his second line, came to join them ; and the two, formed abreast of Granberry's brigade, stopped the advance of the enemy's left, and successfully resisted its subsequent attacks. The contest of the main body of the Fourth Corps with Granberry's brigade was a very fierce one. The Federal troops approached within a few yards of the Confederates, but at last were forced to give way by their storm of well-directed bullets, and fell back to the shelter of a hollow near and behind them. They left hundreds of corpses within twenty paces of the Confederate line. When the United States troops paused in their advance within fifteen paces of the Texan front rank, one of their color-bearers planted his colors eight or ten feet in front of his regiment, and was instantly shot dead. A soldier sprang forward to his place, and fell also as he grasped the color-staff. A second and third followed successively, and each received death as speedily as his predecessors. A fourth, however, seized and bore back the object of soldierly devotion.

" About ten o'clock at night Granberry ascertained that many of the Federal troops were still in the hollow immediately before him, and charged and drove them from it, taking two hundred and thirty-two prisoners, seventy-two of whom were severely wounded.

" The Federal dead lying near our line were counted by many persons, officers and soldiers. According to those counts there were seven hundred of them.[1] . . . We found about twelve hundred small arms on the field. . . . In the affair at New Hope Church, two days before, greater forces were engaged."

The following is from General Hood, commanding the Confederate corps on their left : —

HEADQUARTERS HOOD'S CORPS, IN THE FIELD, 1864.
General JOSEPH E. JOHNSTON, Macon, Georgia:

GENERAL, — Agreeable to the directions of the commanding general, I have the honor herewith to submit the operations of my command since the 7th of May. . . . On the morning of the 27th the enemy were known to be rapidly extending their left, attempting to turn my right as they extended. Cleburne was deployed to meet them ; and at half-past five P. M. a very stubborn attack was made on his division, extending to the right, where Major-General Wheeler with his cavalry division was engaging them. The assault was continued with great determination upon both Cleburne and Wheeler. . . . About ten o'clock at night Brigadier-General Granberry, with his brigade of Texans, made a dashing charge upon the enemy, driving them from the field. . . .
Respectfully,
J. B. HOOD.

I witnessed the attack of the two brigades following my own, and none of these advanced nearer than one hundred yards of the enemy's works. They went in at a run, and as organizations were broken in less than a minute.

*May* 28. Remained in position of last night, strengthening our lines. Annoyed somewhat by Rebel artillery. Willich is on our right, and King's brigade, of Johnson's division, on our left.

*May* 29. Still occupying same position. Fusilade last night. Artillery continued to annoy us.

*May* 30. No sleep last night, the pickets keeping up a constant fusilade. Our skirmishers moved forward about fifty yards this evening, and dug pits for their protection.

[1] This estimate is too great, although Wood's division lost in killed and wounded about fifteen hundred.

*May* 31. Shortly after daylight this morning the enemy's pickets were advanced, apparently for the purpose of occupying the crest, which our troops fortified last night. Meeting with a fire from our main line, they hastily retreated. Two prisoners fell into our hands.

*June* 1. Still occupying same works. Brigade lost last month 726 men, of whom 142 were killed and 537 wounded.

*June* 2. All quiet. Less picket-firing than usual. Severe thunder-storm about noon, during which two men of the First Ohio were killed and two disabled by lightning. The two disabled were sent to hospital.

*June* 3. Withdrew our pickets and struck tents. Troops close behind their works. Object, — to deceive the enemy into the idea that the works were evacuated. Not successful.

*June* 4. Nothing of importance transpired to-day.

*June* 5. Enemy retired last night. We are remaining quietly in camp to-day.

*June* 6. Moved at about eight o'clock in the direction of Acworth. Went into camp at noon, having marched seven miles. Roads very muddy, and marching difficult.

*June* 7. Remained in camp to-day.

*June* 8. Full rations for two days. Brigade inspected by brigade acting-inspector-general.

*June* 9. Ordered to march at six o'clock to-morrow morning.

*June* 10. Reveille at four o'clock. Enemy contesting our advance. Did not get out of camp until two o'clock. Very warm, with frequent showers. Progress very slow ; halts long and frequent. Went into camp just before dark, having marched only about four hundred yards.

*June* 11. Reveille at daylight. At nine o'clock received orders to relieve General Wagner's brigade on front line. Order countermanded. Moved at eleven o'clock three hundred or four hundred yards, and went into position, in reserve to Stanley's division. Raining hard this evening.

*June* 12. Rained hard all night ; still continues. Roads nearly impassable for artillery. Quiet in front. Only an occasional picket-shot.

*June* 13. Rain continues. Roads from Big Shanty, over which the subsistence stores for the corps are transported, nearly impassable.

*June* 14. Ceased to rain. The brigade moved forward about two miles, and into reserve again.

*June* 15. Moved out at half-past two P. M., following Beatty's brigade, General Newton, to assault enemy's work, supported by Stanley and one division in column. Assault not made. Rebel General Polk's death reported by deserters.

*June* 16. Still occupying position in reserve. Continual shelling going on in front. Enemy opened their batteries from Lost Mountain to-day.

*June* 17. Moved at seven o'clock A. M., the enemy having left our front during the night. Moved into position on the left of General Williams's division, Hooker's corps. After advancing a few hundred yards the enemy's pickets were found and driven slowly, Major Stafford commanding the skirmishers, Colonels Kimberly and Foy in the front line. The skirmish line arriving at an open field, we were unable to advance farther on account of an oblique fire from both flanks. Captain Kile, of the Forty-first Ohio, was sent to the left with four companies of his regiment, and having deployed them as skirmishers, charged across the field and gained possession of a house from which the enemy had been firing upon the left of the skirmish line, thus enabling the line to cross the field in our front. This without firing a shot. The front line was relieved during the evening by Colonels Payne and Berry ; Colonel Campbell, Sixth Indiana, relieving Major Stafford on the skirmish line. At half-past ten P. M. an attempt was made to drive in our pickets, which was unsuccessful. Pioneers threw up an earthwork for skirmishers during the night.

*June* 18. An advance of the skirmish line at four o'clock A. M. was ordered ; but owing to the formation of the lines, as yesterday, our right was exposed to an enfilading fire. This being corrected, the line was advanced slightly. Continued skirmishing during the day.

*June* 19. Reveille at half-past three. Enemy retreated during the night. Moved in pursuit at nine o'clock A. M. After advancing about one mile, went into column in rear of Stanley's division.

*June* 20. Reveille at three o'clock. Moved at seven o'clock into front line, relieving Williams's brigade, General Hooker's corps ; Colonel Berry's and Colonel Payne's battalions in the front line ; Colonels Kimberly and Foy in the second line, the Ninety-third Ohio on the left of front line. Continued the works which General Williams had not completed. Sixth Kentucky on the skirmish line. Very little firing in our immediate front. Moved about one mile, to a new position.

*June* 21. During the night our line was extended to the right by the Sixth Indiana, from Colonel Berry's battalion, and the pickets advanced, the pioneers digging pits for their protection within fifty yards of the enemy's skirmish line. Main line occupied this morning by Forty-first Ohio, Sixth Kentucky, Twenty-third Kentucky, and Ninety-third Ohio front line ; Fifth Kentucky, Sixth Indiana, and One Hundred and Twenty-fourth Ohio second line, the front line covering its own front by skirmishers from each regiment. At two o'clock the skirmishers advanced across the open field in their front, driving those of the enemy about four hundred yards. They were quickly supported by the front line and Colonel Berry's battalion, which formed upon the left, Neffler's brigade moving up on the right. Breastworks were immediately thrown up, and the second line moved up.

*June* 22. Colonels Berry and Payne, with battalions, in front line. About four P. M. General Hooker's lines were attacked, and Colonel Kimberly's battalion was sent to fill up a vacancy in his line. Brisk skirmishing all along the front.

*June* 23. Colonels Berry and Foy in front line. At two P. M. orders were received to be in readiness to advance the skirmish lines. At four o'clock the pickets of the entire corps were moved forward, one portion of the line supported by the Ninety-third Ohio. After advancing seventy-five yards the troops came under fire from the enemy's main works. A temporary cover was thrown up, which enabled them to hold the ground, and a good work was built after dark. Loss heavy. Lieutenant Bierce, acting topographical engineer, wounded in the head.

Betty F. Strauss

LIEUTENANT AMBROSE G. BIERCE

(Ninth Indiana and Hazen's topographical officer.)

Gary Delscamp Collection

CAPTAIN EASTMAN

Captain John Eastman was born in New Hampshire, and when killed,
was thirty-three years old. He was an officer of great efficiency and merit.

Casualties : Sixth Kentucky, — officers killed, 1; wounded, 1; men killed, 2; wounded, 12. Ninety-third Ohio, — officers killed, 1 (Captain Eastman); men killed, 2; wounded, 36. One Hundred and Twenty-fourth Ohio, — men wounded, 2. Fifth Kentucky, — men killed, 1; wounded, 2. Sixth Indiana, — men wounded, 7. Headquarters, — officers wounded, 1 (Lieutenant A. G. Bierce); officers killed, 2; wounded, 2; men killed, 5; wounded, 59 : total, 68.[1]

*June 25.* Colonels Berry and Foy on the front line. But little skirmishing. Four Rebels killed and two wounded in one rifle-pit.

*June 26.* Colonels Kimberly and Payne in front line. No firing in our immediate front.

*June 27.* Moved to the right at eight o'clock A. M., and formed behind works just vacated by Wagner's brigade, as a support to Newton's division in an assault upon the enemy's works. Beatty on our right. About two o'clock, the signal being given, the advance commenced; but the assaulting column coming upon strong abatis, and under fire from the enemy's main works, retreated, and the brigade moved back to its position of yesterday. Lieutenant Siddall, aide-de-camp, had his horse shot while on the skirmish line. General Harker killed, and General Daniel McCook severely wounded.[2]

This open assault, known as the attack at Kenesaw Mountain, made by a small detachment upon the centre of the enemy's fortified position, has been severely criticised. It is doubtful if it will stand the criticism of the future.

---

[1] Eastman was a man of rare qualities, and with opportunity would have filled with credit almost any position in the army. Bierce, a brave and gallant fellow, recovered, and is now well known in California for rare literary abilities. It was a mistake to require us to advance closer, being already so near.

[2] Harker was a young and very promising officer, a graduate of West Point, and a general favorite. McCook, who died from this wound, was the youngest son of the famous Ohio family of that name, and the third in order of the four to lose their lives in the war.

*June* 28. All quiet in front all day.

*June* 29. Colonels Berry and Foy in the front line. All quiet. Pioneers constructing abatis in the brigade front.

*June* 30. An assault was made upon General Davis's line at two o'clock this morning, and the brigade was ordered under arms; but the assault upon the right being repulsed, all soon became quiet. Inspection and muster of regiments to-day. Casualties for the month of June : officers, — killed, 2; wounded, 3; aggregate of officers, 5. Men, — killed, 12; wounded, 104; aggregate of men, 116.

*July* 1. Colonels Berry and Foy in the front line. All quiet in front. The brigade ordered to be held in readiness to relieve General Carlin's brigade, Johnson's division. Pioneers cutting road to his lines, cutting head-logs, and making other preparations to repair and improve the works.

*July* 2. At daylight the picket line was ordered to fire for ten minutes, which, after giving the enemy due notice (firing on the picket lines having ceased by mutual understanding), they proceeded to do. Pioneers preparing stakes for a palisading to be put out to-night. General Wagner's brigade relieves us, and we move to relieve Carlin's brigade. Colonel Berry, commanding second line, moves at half-past seven P. M., relieving General Carlin's first line. Colonel Payne, commanding front line, was relieved by Wagner's second line about midnight, and proceeded to the new position. Headquarters not to be moved until morning.

*July* 3. At two o'clock this morning a Rebel deserter, a mail-carrier, came into our lines, and reported the enemy gone from our front. He had met them half-way between their deserted works and Marietta. At daylight strong reconnoitring parties were sent out, and prisoners who had straggled behind their column were captured. The deserted works were very strong, with abatis, chevaux-de-frise, traverses, advanced works, and lunettes for artillery commanding the entire front. The lines at my position were very near together. A few days before we occupied them, a severe assault of the Rebels had been repulsed, they leaving a great many dead. Among them I found a Major

Gordon, of a Georgia regiment. In the few days the corpses seemed to have settled away into the ground, the grass growing upward so that they seemed perfectly flat with the earth; but Major Gordon's long blonde hair lay upon his temples as perfectly arranged as if just from his chamber.

At an early hour the troops were put in motion toward Marietta, Stanley in advance, followed by Newton and next by Wood, the division marching in regular order; first, second, and third brigades in order. Arrived at Marietta about one o'clock, passed through town, and a mile out halted forty minutes for dinner, and proceeded, our division marching on the left of the railroad, and went into bivouac just before dark, four miles from Marietta. Marched to-day seven miles and a half.

*July* 4. At eight o'clock moved about one mile to the left, took position on the extreme left of the army and somewhat retired, and threw up works. At noon the picket line, composed of the Ninety-third Ohio, was strengthened by four companies of Colonel Berry's battalion, commanded by himself, and the line moved forward to correspond with movement of troops on our right. After advancing three fourths of a mile a dense swamp was encountered, which was crossed with difficulty. Colonel Berry lost two men killed, — one from Fifth Kentucky and one from Sixth Indiana. The line advanced to within sight of the enemy's main line, driving in his pickets. They were relieved at night by troops of the Third Brigade.

*July* 5. Enemy left our front during the night. Started in pursuit about eight o'clock, the Fourth Corps moving on the left on the railroad. Fourteenth Corps on parallel road on our right, this brigade moving in advance of the corps. Came up with the enemy's rear-guard, consisting of cavalry, about two miles out, and skirmishing with them, drove them rapidly. When within a mile of Vining Station, Colonel Payne relieved Colonel Berry's battalion and Twenty-third Kentucky on skirmish line, and Kimberly's battalion was detached and sent to the left to intercept, if possible, a portion of the enemy's train, reported by a captured station-agent as crossing the Chattahoochee River by a pontoon bridge. Just at this time Palmer's

advance was met by the enemy at a point where the road inter-
sected the railroad, and his artillery from a commanding hill
accelerated the Rebel movement across the bridge. When our
skirmish line reached the river, the last cavalryman had crossed
and cut the bridge loose from our side, allowing it to swing
around with the current. They are, however, unable to remove
it, and the pickets are ordered to fire volleys during the night
when any noise is heard in that direction.

Major Williston of the skirmishers, First and Forty-first Ohio,
slightly wounded in the shoulder. Sixth Kentucky sent out on
picket to-night. Marched five miles to-day.

Among the captures at Vining's Station to-day was a
negro named Jess. But for this capture I might never
have known the luxury of owning slaves. When taken,
he was making good time to the rear, with a washtub on
his shoulder. It was full of a large washing, and the
darky, tub, clothes, and all were brought to me. Jess
was not disconcerted, nor was he pleased with his captiv-
ity. He at once gave an account of himself, and, as it
proved, was a sort of general striker for the Southern Chris-
tian Commission, and his tub constituted the laundry of
that most worthy body. He was very black, with a dished
face and high head. I at once took him into my service,
where he continued till long after the war. His accom-
plishments proved to be more varied and perfect than I
ever knew possessed by any other individual. He was a
thorough groom, valet, cook, laundry-man, and butler. He
could darn my stockings, mend my clothing, sew on my
buttons, forage from the country, keep my mess-accounts,
and take full charge of arranging my headquarters; and
he actually did or caused all this to be done excellently,
and with the least amount of care on my part. It was only
necessary to let him know the number expected at dinner
and the desired quality of it, and at the appointed moment
the soup would be smoking on the table, which would be

COLONEL JAMES C. FOY

(Twenty-third Kentucky.)

JESS

accurately arranged to the last detail, with cloth and napkins snowy white and glass so polished that it glistened, while Jess with napkin stood ready to serve. After the war, when his wages had accumulated, he left me at Murfreesboro', to go to Alabama, where his family was. I afterward wrote him asking if he would come back, and he answered, "Certainly;" but added that he was living happily with his family in his own house, his children going to school; that he had two transport-wagons, which earned him sixty dollars a month, and that I could understand about what it would be necessary to pay him. This was above my figure, and I never expected to find the like of Jess again.[1]

Jess possessed a rare fund of the best sort of darky wit; but he formed no exception to all the colored men I knew in the South in this, — that while he was perfectly upright and trusty in all matters about headquarters, he had no respect for the rights of the inhabitants of the country. One of his most expressive avowals of good intentions, when warned not to forage bedding, towels, table furniture, and such small matters, was the declaration, with an air of injured innocence, and an irresistible gravity, that sooner than do such a thing he would "go to h—ll uphill on his knees backwards."

*July* 6. Sixth Kentucky relieved by Sixth Indiana on picket line. Brigade in camp on left of road. Works for pickets and sharpshooters and an epaulement thrown up by pioneers. Cars came to within two miles of our lines to-day.

*July* 7. One Hundred and Twenty-fourth Ohio on picket. Pioneers cutting a road from headquarters to main road. At eight o'clock this afternoon a demonstration was made in our front in favor of Schofield's corps, which was ordered to cross the river above. All the artillery opened and all the wagons of the

[1] Twenty years has made Jess an old man, and he is a messenger in my office now.

brigade were sent down to near the river and driven furiously about. Colonel Frank Sherman missing to-night. Supposed to have been captured, as a pass (break in the line) was discovered between this and Fourteenth Corps, and one man from Twenty-third Kentucky was captured there to-day.

*July* 8. Twenty-third Kentucky on picket. Rebels thinking our demonstration last night an actual attempt to cross the river, cut loose their pontoon bridge, trusting to the current to carry it beyond our reach. Instead, however, it floated over to us. Captains Jones and Eaton inspecting the brigade to-day. All quiet along our front, except an occasional shot by the pickets.

*July* 9. Forty-first Ohio on picket. General Schofield across the river and General Stanley reported as crossing this afternoon. Rebels opened with artillery on our camps this afternoon. Colonel Foy, commanding Twenty-third and Sixth Kentucky Battalions, wounded by a piece of shell.[1] Pickets succeeded in securing pontoon bridge last night.

*July* 10. Struck tents at ten o'clock, and marched about eleven o'clock up the river, following Stanley's division; this brigade in rear of First and Third brigades. Road obstructed with troops moving slowly. Went into camp near ferry. Marched about eight miles.

*July* 11. Still in camp. One division of Schofield's corps over the river.

*July* 12. Moved at ten o'clock, following Third Brigade in direction of Power's Ferry, where, after two hours' delay for completion of pontoon bridge, we crossed, and went into position about two miles from the river, on the left of First Brigade, at three o'clock P. M. Pioneers immediately set to work building works and constructing abatis. Marched four miles.

*July* 13. Moved forward to next ridge this morning, and constructed works. Troops in front line : Twenty-third and Sixth Kentucky, Major Northrup commanding battalion ; Fifth Kentucky and Sixth Indiana, Colonel Berry. In second line : One Hundred and Twenty-fourth and Ninety-third Ohio, Colonel Payne ; First and Forty-first Ohio, Lieutenant-Colonel Kimberly. Nothing but light cavalry force in front. At ten o'clock P.M.

1 Colonel Foy's wound was fatal. He was a fearless, trusty soldier.

an order was received requiring the brigade to be in readiness to move at five o'clock A. M. to-morrow.

*July* 14. Order of last night countermanded by order received at two o'clock this morning. All quiet in front. Troops making themselves comfortable in camp.

*July* 15. Remaining quietly in camp. Court-martial went into session to-day.

*July* 16. Reveille at four o'clock. Sixth Kentucky on picket. Captain Beebe reported to General Howard to-day as aide-de-camp. General court-martial in session. All quiet on the line all day.

*July* 17. Orders received last night to move to the front at half-past four this morning, leaving the tents standing. Reveille at three o'clock, First Brigade in advance. Started about half-past five, and formed on the right of First Brigade, just outside the picket line, then moved down the river-bank by the flank, throwing us in front. Drove the enemy's cavalry before us without difficulty, and reached Pace's Ferry (our destination) about ten A. M. Distance three miles and a half. Threw up slight works, to make our position sure. The Fourteenth Corps on the opposite bank waiting to cross, threw a pontoon across by twelve M. and Davis's division crossed to relieve us. There being some delay in getting our skirmishers relieved and Davis's troops into position, we did not get back to camp until six P. M. In the mean time General Stanley occupied our works with one of his brigades, fearing an attack. The Fifth Kentucky, being on picket, did not go out.

*July* 18. Reveille at four o'clock. Sixth Indiana Volunteers went on picket at daylight. Orders to move at five A. M. to follow Stanley's division, Newton in advance, Second Brigade in advance of the division ; and started about nine o'clock, making numerous halts. Skirmishing in front. Marched about six miles to Buckhead, getting there at three P. M. Formed on the right of Newton's division and threw up works. One Hundred and Twenty-fourth Ohio on picket. Hooker's corps joined us on the right at half-past five P. M. Front line moved out about three hundred yards, to a ridge, at nine P. M. Threw up new works

and cut timber in front, working nearly all night. Twenty-third
and Sixth Kentucky on the left; Fifth Kentucky and Sixth
Indiana in the centre; First and Forty-first Ohio on right of
front line; Ninety-third Ohio in reserve. No enemy in our
front.

*July* 19. Reveille at three o'clock. Twenty-third Kentucky
went on picket just before daylight. Brigade moved to the front
to Peach-tree Creek at one P. M., where the First and Third brigades went on a reconnoissance at daylight this morning. The
pioneers under Captain Zoller, Fifth Kentucky, were set to work
to repair the bridge over the stream, and had the greater part done,
when they were relieved by General Newton's pioneers, the brigade being ordered across the creek to relieve the First and Third
brigades, which was accomplished just about dark, occupying
their works and strengthening them. Enemy in force in our
front. Each regiment picketing its own front. Captain Eaton,
provost-marshal, was severely wounded while assisting the work
at the bridge. Other casualties: Forty-first Ohio, 1 wounded;
Sixth Indiana, 1 wounded: total, 2.

*July* 20. Reveille at three o'clock. Brigade relieved by
Colonel Bradley's brigade of Newton's division at eight o'clock
A. M. Joined the First and Third brigades, and marched up the
creek on the north side, following Stanley's division. Major
Stafford, First Ohio, went to division hospital sick. Considerable skirmishing in front during the afternoon; consequently
moved very slowly. Crossed both branches of Peach-tree Creek,
and finally went into camp in reserve between the two branches,
about a quarter of a mile in rear and right of Stanley's line,
about four miles from Atlanta. Several wounded by stray shots
while waiting to get into position.

*July* 21. Reveille at half-past three A. M. Brigade moved
out on front line, between First and Third brigades, at eight A. M.
Pioneers built a bridge across the south branch. Built works
as usual. First and Forty-first Ohio and Sixth and Twenty-
third Kentucky in front line. About noon, Fifth Kentucky
and Sixth Indiana, Colonel Berry, were sent to the right of
First Brigade; and at four P. M. Colonel Payne's battalion,

Ninety-third and One Hundred and Twenty-fourth Ohio, was sent also to protect an opening in the line, each regiment picketing its own front. Considerable skirmishing in front of left of brigade. Lookout in a large pine-tree, from which the streets of Atlanta can be seen distinctly. Lieutenant-Colonel Langdon, First Ohio, who was wounded in the assault of Mission Ridge, returned to-day, looking well.[1]

*July* 22. Reveille at daylight. The enemy fell back from their works in our front during the night to a position about a mile and a half from Atlanta. The First Ohio, under Captain Hooker, was sent out at daylight, and came up to the enemy's skirmishers in rifle-pits. Captured two prisoners. The brigade was moved to the front at half-past seven, following First Brigade, and was formed on right of Stanley's division, with Third Brigade on our right. Built breastworks. Colonels Berry and Payne in the front line. Bridge's battery posted in the rear of Colonel Berry's battalion, firing occasional shells into the city.

The enemy turned our left about noon to-day, killing Generals McPherson and Force,[2] capturing a number of prisoners of the Seventeenth Corps, and taking ten pieces of artillery, six of which were retaken by our troops. Marched one mile to-day.

*July* 23. Reveille at 3.45 o'clock. Picket-firing commenced very early, and continued at intervals. Bridge's battery fired occasional shots into Atlanta, getting some replies from the enemy's batteries.

*July* 24. Reveille at early daylight, 3.45 o'clock. Considerable skirmishing along the line, and some artillery-shots exchanged. A soldier of Sixth Kentucky killed by premature explosion of shell from Bridge's battery. Regiment moved from front of guns.

*July* 25. Reveille at 3.45 o'clock. Pioneers making an abatis and palisade. Drew new axes and spades for pioneers. First Ohio and Fifth Kentucky relieved from this department. Colonel Langdon to report at Chattanooga to General Steadman. Colonel Berry to report at Nashville to General Rousseau. Orders

---

[1] After the war Langdon died from the same wound.
[2] Force was not killed, but seriously wounded.

received this afternoon, and they with their regiments will start to-morrow morning. One casualty.

*July* 26. Reveille at 3.45 o'clock. Ninety-third Ohio detailed for picket at daylight, to relieve whole line. Fifth Kentucky and First Ohio drew rations and started back at half-past seven o'clock. All quiet in front except picket-firing.

*July* 27. Reveille at 3.45 o'clock. Sixth Kentucky on picket at daylight. Major Northrup's battalion, Sixth and Twenty-third Kentucky Volunteers, went on front line to left of the brigade, in works made by Grose's brigade. Brigade all in front line now. General Howard placed in command of the Army of the Tennessee. General Stanley assumed command of the Fourth Corps, and Grose of the First Division. One casualty.

*July* 28. Reveille at 3.45 o'clock. Sixth Indiana on picket at daylight. Forty-first Ohio carried Rebel skirmish-pits in our front, in conjunction with Colonel Suman, Ninth Indiana, on the left, and Colonel Kneffler on the right. Captured three prisoners. Rebels attacked General Howard's army just after getting into position, on the right, and were repulsed with a loss of 5,000 to 6,000 (estimated). Our loss stated at 528. General Hooker relieved from Twentieth Corps. Captain Crawford, Sixth Indiana, detailed as acting-assistant inspector-general, and Captain Jones relieved. Lieutenant Galbreath, One Hundred and Twenty-fourth Ohio, detailed as provost-marshal. Five casualties.

*July* 29. Reveille at 3.45 o'clock. One Hundred and Twenty-fourth Ohio on picket at daylight. All quiet along the lines all day, excepting an occasional shell from the Rebel forts.

*July* 30. Reveille at 3.45 o'clock. Twenty-third Kentucky on picket at daylight. Pioneers getting out abatis and palisades. One casualty.

*July* 31. Reveille at 3.45 o'clock. Forty-first Ohio on picket at daylight. All very quiet all day. Entire brigade at work laying abatis and palisades along entire front. Casualties for the month of July: officers killed, 3; men killed, 6; men wounded, 33; men missing, 3: total, 45.

*August* 1. Reveille at four o'clock. Ninety-third Ohio on picket at daylight. All quiet during the entire day. Pioneers and Sixth Kentucky at work on new line of works in the rear.

*August* 2. Reveille at four o'clock A. M. Sixth Kentucky on picket. Pioneers hard at work all day.

*August* 3. Reveille at four o'clock. Sixth Indiana on picket. All quiet until evening. At five P. M. the Sixth Indiana, supported by Twenty-third Kentucky, took the Rebel skirmish-pits and four prisoners, who were taken to the rear by Neffler's men. As Gibson's line on our right did not advance, the pits were given up, the enemy flanking the line. No loss in Sixth Indiana; one man of Twenty-third Kentucky, in reserve, killed by grapeshot.

*August* 4. Reveille at four o'clock. One Hundred and Twenty-fourth Ohio on picket. Pioneers and details were again at work on obstructions in front. The new line of works about completed.

*August* 5. Reveille at four o'clock. Twenty-third Kentucky on picket. All quiet until evening. Twenty-third Kentucky made a demonstration, advancing the line, and regiments marched out from works. One man wounded.

*August* 6. Reveille at four o'clock. Forty-first Ohio on picket. Programme same as yesterday. Demonstrating all along the line.

*August* 7. Reveille at four o'clock. Programme same as yesterday. Ninety-third Ohio on picket. All very quiet all day on the lines. Cloudy nearly all day.

This gives the merest sketch of our work to the close of my service with the Army of the Cumberland; but the life and spirit of which that service was full, is not found in formal utterances. The following letter gives some idea of it at this stage of the war: —

NEAR ATLANTA, GEORGIA, Aug. 2, 1864.

You are at home, without doubt, as I would like to be for a short time. The campaign is running into its fourth month, with scarcely a day but a large part of the command is under fire.

My losses in killed or wounded are already over a thousand; but this is no fair proportion of the losses of our army, as the Fates, as usual, have put us in warm places.

Will the people at home keep up their pluck and fight this thing out? It all depends upon their steadfastness. If Richmond does not fall, the Army of the West will finally make its way to the back door. If none of the Eastern Rebel army comes here, we will wear this one out before the close of the season, and it is but a matter of time when the entire force of the enemy must waste away. Will the people remain steadfast? Johnston's veteran army, by his official report of the 25th of June, contained 46,628 arms-bearing men, including 6,631 of Wheeler's cavalry. They have lost since that time 5,000 prisoners, and in their three assaults upon our works since arriving in front of this place at least 20,000 men. They have received from Mississippi 3,500 men with Stephen D. Lee, and are receiving from Governor Brown's proclamation about 8,000 militia. This gives them to-day an army of about 25,000 veterans and 8,000 militia; 33,000 in all.

These figures are substantially correct. The hope of being reinforced by Kirby Smith is at last given up; and after exhausting the militia of Alabama and Eastern Mississippi, — which may amount to ten thousand more, if they have the power to force them out, — I cannot for my life see how the enemy can make up the wastage of their army. I do not pretend to say what our losses have been since leaving Chattanooga. But I know the Rebel army, when it was joined by Polk just before the fight at Resaca, was 71,000 strong (this included Polk); and that, besides the additions before mentioned, it has received a brigade (Harting's) of at least 3,000 from Mobile. This gives the enormous loss to them, since the campaign, of 52,000 men.[1] What possible chance is there for these 33,000 men now before us? These figures may seem exaggerations, but they are not. And when the large number of captures is remembered, — that there have been no less than twelve engagements where from one to three corps have been in battle, with

[1] Some of these returned after recovering from wounds.

the ordinary desertions and losses from disease, — their immense losses are readily accounted for. And what will hinder the daily attrition of the next three months from completing the overthrow of the foe before us?

You will say, perhaps, Why not assault so contemptible a foe, and put him out of his misery at once? The art of war here is no longer one of chances. Both armies carry a full supply of intrenching tools; and no force on either side ever rests till it has before it a complete line of works strong enough to resist the heaviest field ordnance, with obstructions in the front in the way of abatis, palisades, and intrenchments that puts the matter of direct assault quite out of the question. I think the battle of Chickamauga, on the left flank, taught both armies the value of these works. No assault by either side in this campaign has been successful. It would surprise you to see how quickly and willingly these men construct their works. None appreciate their value more than the men themselves.

We are losing some good officers, and of course some men; but I wish all could understand how vitally this campaign is striking the Rebellion. Did you read Governor Brown's proclamation, calling out the militia and detached men?[1] There was no blooming palmetto about that, but a plain and open groan, showing clearly how deep the travel of our army is moving down upon the tender places of the Confederacy.

You know, of course, that Johnston has been relieved by Hood, a man of much less ability. Gossip has it that his Government was dissatisfied with Johnston's continued retreating, and sought a man who believed their army could check us. Hardee is said to have been of Johnston's opinion, — that the endeavor to hold Atlanta would be the destruction of the army. Hood was then proffered the command, and accepted the conditioned task. He has commenced it well, — has already assaulted us three times. We, being behind our works, have lost in all 9,500 men, while he is known to have lost 20,000.

I have never believed the foregoing the true reason for the

[1] These detached men were invalid soldiers assigned as laborers throughout the State.

change of army commanders, but that Johnson was taken East to assist in planting a column in Pennsylvania. He knows that country thoroughly. It is the theatre of his first operations in 1861. Besides, he is their best general; and this is to me the only reasonable theory of their action.

The greatest victory for them — greater than fifty " Manassases," and the only one that can give them a ray of hope — will be for you at home to defeat the war-party in the coming campaign. If they can by any possibility keep their army in the field, — no matter whether victorious or not, — and a little before election place a strong army upon the soil of a Free State, with a fair play of sharp diplomacy on their part carelessly met by us, then let the question go flat before the people, " Peace, or war?" and who can tell what will be the fate of our last three years of blood and victory? I fear nothing in Ohio; but our first great battle must be at the ballot-box, and the war-power must be sustained at all hazards.

I am, very respectfully, your obedient servant,

W. B. HAZEN, *Brigadier-General.*[1]

My separation from that army was a sad event to me; and after issuing the following order I rode away, with a single orderly, never again to see as soldiers many of those who for three years had stood bravely by me in so many battles and in so much danger. On five occasions we had seen a third of our force go down; but others came to take their places, and we who were left labored on. The ties of comradeship in the deadly strife of battle, when there is honest effort, faith, and trust, are so strong that nothing can sever them; and this was my strength. The following is the order : —

NEAR ATLANTA, GEORGIA, Aug. 17, 1864.

In obedience to orders from headquarters Military Division of the Mississippi, the undersigned hereby relinquishes command of this brigade.

---

[1] Without writing this letter for such a purpose, it came to have a wide publication.

GENERAL JOSEPH E. JOHNSTON, C.S.A.

COLONEL P. SIDNEY POST

(Fifty-ninth Illinois.)

With many regrets at separation from the old soldiers, some of whom have fought with him in every battle of this army, he trusts the same readiness and zeal will still actuate them in the performance of every duty as in times past.

I turned the brigade over to the senior colonel then present, O. H. Payne of the One Hundred and Twenty-fourth Ohio, — a most gallant and worthy officer, son of one of the best citizens and most distinguished men in the country, Hon. H. B. Payne, of Cleveland, Ohio. Colonel Payne had been in the war from the first, and was entitled to the command, and I never doubted for a moment that he would be confirmed in it. Soon after, I learned that the same influences that had at times antagonized me had secured the brigade for an officer who had never served with it nor with the division or corps, — Colonel Philip Sidney Post, an excellent officer, and worthy of every consideration, who afterward had so distinguished a part with the old brigade at Overton's Knob, in the battle of Nashville. He was subsequently for twelve years consul-general at Vienna.

The losses of the brigade in the campaign up to this time were eight hundred and sixty-four.

## CHAPTER XVIII.

ATLANTA CAMPAIGN TO JONESBORO'.

ON the 17th of August I reported to Major-General
Logan, the commander of the Fifteenth Corps, for
assignment to the command of a division. He was just
sitting down to supper with his staff, and I joined them.
The staff was very numerous, and, as I found afterward,
very efficient. Most of them were young men. It was the
first time I had met Logan, and I was most agreeably impressed by him, both as a soldier and a man, and have
never had reason to change that first impression. Dodge
and Ransom soon came in, both new to me. They and all
the officers seemed remarkably young, as in fact they were.
This was a result of the system of promotion in the Army
of the Tennessee, where commands were given to their own
officers who had earned them. General Howard and myself were perhaps the first importations and infringements
upon this rule. I had been a brigade commander of low
comparative rank, and now found myself, with the exception of General Osterhaus, who was absent, the officer next
in seniority to the corps commander. Of my brother officers, Ransom, who was soon promoted to the command of
the Sixteenth Corps, was born in Norwich, and Mower, who
next received a similar promotion to the Twentieth Corps,
at Woodstock; while I, who afterward succeeded to the
Fifteenth Corps, was born in Hartford. All three places
are in Windsor County, Vermont, within a radius of eight

GENERAL JOHN A. LOGAN

GENERAL PETER J. OSTERHAUS

COLONEL WELLS S. JONES

(Former commander Fifty-third Ohio.)

Cumberland Gallery Collection

COLONEL THEODORE JONES

(Former commander Thirtieth Ohio.)

miles. I can hardly describe my feelings at first reporting among entire strangers. I was young, and naturally expected criticism, but determined to fulfil the implied promise of good service, which alone carried me there. I was assigned to the Second, Sherman's old division, which fought under him at Shiloh, and had since been under McPherson, Blair, and other able and favorite officers. But recently it had been unfortunate. Under General Morgan L. Smith on the day of McPherson's death it was badly broken, and considerably damaged. Lightburn afterward commanded it, and at an affair of pickets a few days before my assignment to it there was great complaint of misconduct, and one of the brigade commanders — Colonel Martin of the One Hundred and Eleventh Illinois, a most worthy man — was seriously blamed, and unjustly so, as I afterward learned. Lightburn resumed his brigade ; but the day I took command he was wounded in the head and obliged to leave the field, and I have never seen him since.

My brigade commanders were then Colonels Wells S. Jones and Theodore Jones, both of Ohio; and I will say of them, that no more loyal, ready, and efficient service was ever rendered than they gave to the country and to me from that time to the close of the war. The division, as compared with the troops I had commanded, was in a wretched condition, as will be seen by the following orders, which I found imperatively necessary. Many men were absent or non-combatant, and the number in ranks was about seven hundred less than in the brigade with which I had entered the campaign, and but two hundred more than I left with it. While the soldiers of the Army of the Tennessee and of the Cumberland were equally good, the following orders were necessary to bring this division up to the standard of discipline and administration I had known in the latter.

NEAR ATLANTA, GEORGIA, Aug. 18, 1864.

When in camp or bivouac the following requirements will be strictly carried out : —

I. Roll-calls at reveille, at twelve o'clock M., at retreat (sunset), and at tattoo, and a thorough policing of camp at six A. M. and five P. M.

II. There will be officers of the day detailed for regiments, brigades, and division, who will under their respective commanders be held responsible for the proper execution of the above, and when calls are not sounded on the bugle, will notify their commands at the proper hour.

III. Each regiment and battery will cause a proper number of sinks to be made, and will take proper steps to compel their use.

BEFORE ATLANTA, GEORGIA, Aug. 23, 1864.

I. The great disproportion of the non-effective to the effective strength of this division as reported by regimental commanders requires the attention of all having the good of the service at heart, to effect a more economical disposition of strength.

1. The brigade quartermasters will at once assemble and park all the transportation of their respective brigades in some proper place, at least one mile in rear of the lines, and will be prepared to do with their force all mechanical work now done by regimental blacksmiths, carpenters, etc. All regimental mechanics, wagonmasters, forage-masters, and wagon-guards will then be returned to the ranks of their regiments. A proper guard for the trains, not to exceed twenty men to a brigade, can be detailed from day to day.

2. It is the duty of the commissary of subsistence to prepare the fresh beef to issue to regiments, and he will attend to butchering it. All regimental butchers and commissary men will be returned to duty in the ranks. Each regiment should provide itself with a competent commissary sergeant, to receive and issue to companies, temporary details being furnished to assist him.

3. Regimental ordnance sergeants and postmasters will be returned to the ranks. Each regiment will provide itself with a sergeant-major, who will attend to all these duties. But one

clerk will be allowed a regiment, and he must at all times be completely armed, equipped, and reported effective. All cooks in excess of one to a company will be at once returned to the ranks, and also all teamsters in excess of the number of authorized teams. No company clerks will be excused from general duty.

4. The number of men allowed at higher headquarters, and with the various departments of division headquarters, will be announced hereafter.

II. Regimental commanders will at once make requisitions for arms, and without delay completely arm and equip all men in their commands needing them.

BEFORE ATLANTA, GEORGIA, Aug. 23, 1864.

. . . Regimental commanders will forward without delay to these headquarters, through brigade commanders, a detailed report of all officers and men detached, absent sick, or absent without authority; giving name, where, how long absent, and if authorized, by what authority.

BEFORE ATLANTA, GEORGIA, Aug. 25, 1864.

. . . Non-veterans of this command will perform all duties of soldiers in the field till they are mustered out of service, which will in every case be as soon as they are by law entitled to such muster-out.

Commanding officers of regiments and brigades will see closely to the execution of this order.

The condition of the division at this time was deplorable. The brigade trains were not parked, but the teams were scattered all about the country, scarcely two in a place. Every teamster, wagon-master, cook, or other regularly detailed man had his assistant, who, with a great number of clerks, acting ordnance-sergeants, and postmasters, were not armed. Besides, the men who had not veteranized, and whose time was unexpired, had by some means gotten out of line, and were mostly back with the division train, waiting for their discharge. The foregoing orders had a magic effect. The brigade commanders came over to thank me for them, expressing in the warmest terms their appreciation of the spirit they saw in them, and the promise of their loyal aid in carrying them out; and their assurances were never violated. A constant stream of men began to pour in from every quarter, and the effect was within a week to bring the number of men with muskets from seventeen hundred up to twenty-two hundred. From the first, there was the most hearty desire upon the part of all officers to aid these reforms, and they were successfully carried out.

We were now preparing for the final swing around Atlanta. If I could only get the division to keep well closed up, and without straggling in marching, I felt confident of success with it; for the men and officers were both admirable, and largely made up of Ohio troops. To effect this, the following order was issued : —

ON WEST POINT RAILROAD, GEORGIA, Aug. 28, 1864.

. . . In order that the troops of the division may march uniformly and in a military manner, the following directions are published : —

I. When orders are given to be prepared to march at a certain hour, the command should be ready at the prescribed time to be put in motion by formal command.

II. The troops will be formed when facing by a flank in four ranks, and company commanders will see strictly that their men retain this formation, and in marching keep properly closed, as strict compliance with this will obviate nearly all the faults in marching. Regimental and company commanders will frequently place themselves on the flanks of their commands to rectify the position of their men. When officers march at the head of a command without paying attention to the rear, they fail to do much of what is their duty. Company commanders who fail to cause their companies to march properly and in accordance with the above will be recommended for dismissal. When regiments and companies are put in motion, the command should be given in a loud voice, and the entire column made to take up the march simultaneously, and not successively from front to rear.

III. Whenever a command has to pass a defile of any kind, the commander will remain to see that all of his command is passed expeditiously.

IV. Each regiment and brigade will have a rear-guard under an efficient officer to march in rear to prevent straggling, and in case of regiments will be particular to keep the servants and led animals well closed up. This guard will march in a military manner, with bayonets fixed.

V. A general staff-officer will always accompany the column, frequently inspecting it, and in finding any violation of this order will at once report the same to the proper commander of the brigade in which it occurs, who will proceed in person to correct the irregularity.

VI. All teams and artillery will be kept closed to one yard. The provost-marshal of the division will habitually march in the rear with a sufficient guard, and will arrest all stragglers, reporting the same to the division commander at the close of the march, who will hold them for trial by regimental provost, it being the duty of regimental commanders to at once appoint these officers in accordance with act of Congress. At the close of a march, before breaking ranks the rolls will be called, and all absentees reported to the regimental provost for trial.

VII. The officer commanding the two regiments that march in rear of the artillery will personally attend to assisting with his men in passing it over bad places in the road.

The effect of this order was all that it contemplated. There were no stragglers and no courts. We moved out of the works at half-past eight o'clock P. M., the 26th of August, marching till eleven A. M. next day, and on the 28th reached the West Point Railroad, about thirty miles to the southwest of Atlanta.

The following extracts from my journal show our daily

routine in the trenches, and on the march as far as Lovejoy's Station, where the movement terminated : —

*August* 18, 1864.   At four P. M. made a demonstration for
the purpose of drawing the enemy from his works if possible.
Colors were displayed, skirmish line opened a brisk fire and
the artillery a furious cannonade, the troops cheering loudly.
This continued for perhaps half an hour, but without producing anything important except a desultory fire from enemy's
skirmishers.   Troops were kept well in hand until all became
quiet.   Afterward General Charles R. Woods reported that his
skirmish line had advanced a short distance, and the right of
ours was immediately thrown forward until the lines connected
properly.   At about nine P. M. the enemy's skirmishers opened
a brisk fire, which was returned by our men.   Nothing of importance occurred.

*August* 19.   Made another demonstration to-day at twelve M.
Artillery and skirmishers opened fire.   Colors displayed, troops
cheering.   Supports were thrown forward to skirmish line.   Succeeded in drawing the fire of the enemy.   He opened three
batteries in front of our division, and apparently expected an
assault.   Demonstration lasted for half an hour.   Troops well
in hand till all became quiet.   Nothing else of importance occurred.   Established headquarters this afternoon farther to the
right and nearer the centre of the division.

*August* 20.   In same camp to-day, with no occurrences of
particular interest.   The casualties of the division during the
month to this date are two officers and sixteen men killed ; one
general officer, eight commissioned officers, and seventy-eight
men wounded : total, one hundred and five.

*August* 21.   Nothing of interest occurred in camp to-day.
Still in the same position.

*August* 22.   All quiet to-day.   At about ten P. M. an order
was received from corps headquarters requiring increased vigilance on the picket line to guard against surprise and prevent
the enemy from evacuating his line.

*August* 23.   To-day cut timber for the construction of a palisade about one hundred and fifty yards in front of the main

GENERAL HARKER

General Charles G. Harker was born in New Jersey and, when killed, was
twenty-seven years of age. He was a graduate of West Point, and a gallant,
fearless and accomplished officer, with an uprightness of character and
gentleness of manner that won him the love and friendship of all.

ESCAPED UNION PRISONER OF WAR

(Photographed in Huntsville, Ala.)

line of works.   One commissioned officer and one enlisted man were wounded, and two enlisted men killed.

*August* 24.   General Woods, in preparing to advance his troops (on our right) into a new line of works, attracted attention of the enemy, who reinforced his skirmish line, causing an exchange of shots between the pickets, which extended to our right.   The movement was deferred, and all became quiet.   General Lightburn started North to-day.   Two men were wounded.

A large number of escaped prisoners from Andersonville came into our lines while we were before Atlanta, all showing, by their condition and by their statements, the wretched state of our men confined there.   It seemed to me that so long as it was possible by any sort of arrangement between the two belligerents for us to reach that camp, — by commissioners, humane persons, or in any other way, — to give aid to our men, it was the most urgent possible duty to do it; and I shall always believe that some way might have been devised to save those poor fellows from the dreadful suffering and death they met there.   I consider this failure upon our part a blot and a reproach.

# CHAPTER XIX.

### JONESBORO'.

AUGUST 25. The Army of the Tennessee to-day commenced the movement intended to place it southwest of Atlanta. The Sixteenth and Seventeenth corps, or a portion of them, fell back to a new line of works in the rear, the Fourth Corps having previously withdrawn from its position. We received to-day the order for the movement, which required fifteen days' rations and a large amount of ammunition. The day was spent in preparation for the march. Nothing of interest transpired on our part of the line. Four enlisted men were wounded.

*August* 26. The day was also spent in preparation. Trains were sent away in the afternoon, and rations for three days issued. The troops were withdrawn from the main line at eight o'clock P. M., and marched in a southerly direction, passing Wilson's house after midnight, and continuing the march all night in a drenching rain. The pickets of the division were withdrawn simultaneously with those of the First and Fourth divisions and Sixteenth and Seventeenth corps at near two o'clock A. M. on the 27th instant, and joined the division three or four miles beyond Wilson's house. The sergeant-major of the One Hundred and Twenty-seventh Illinois was wounded while withdrawing main line at night.

*August* 27. March continued this morning in same order as yesterday, — First Division in advance, followed by Second and Fourth divisions respectively. Crossed Camp Creek at ten o'clock A.M. ; then on to Wolf Creek, where we halted and went into position on surrounding ridges, Second Division in centre of corps. Threw out pickets about half a mile in advance, connecting properly on right and left. Works were laid out and built during the afternoon and night. Beautiful position for a camp, — water and forage in abundance. Distance marched, about sixteen miles. No casualties. No enemy in our immediate front.

*August* 28. Marched this morning at seven o'clock in same order as yesterday, and in a direction nearly south. At nine o'clock a small force of the enemy was reported to be in front of the First Division, which went into position; but a reconnoissance developing nothing, the column moved on. Struck the West Point Railroad after twelve M. near Spadua Church, thirty miles from Atlanta and a mile and a half from Fairborn. Fifteenth Corps took position across the railroad; Second Division on the left and First on the right of road, the Fourth Division being employed in destroying the road. At night connected our pickets with those of the Fourteenth Corps on our left, thus throwing the picket line along the railroad. Had a slight skirmish with a party in our front, killing one Rebel. No casualties to-day.

*August* 29. This division in same position to-day. Sent out one regiment this morning (Sixth Missouri) on a reconnoissance, but found nothing. Afterward Captain Crane, Company A, Eighth Missouri Infantry (mounted), with his command, captured one lieutenant and nine men (Texas Cavalry), with horses and equipments complete. Non-veterans of Thirtieth Ohio mustered out. Water and forage very scarce at this point. No casualties to-day. Our division assisted this afternoon in destroying the railroad.

*August* 30. Marched this morning at seven A. M., this division in advance of corps, the Second Brigade (Colonel W. S. Jones) in advance of division. The enemy was found within about three miles and a half. Formed line and deployed skirmishers; then pushed forward, driving them from their skirmish-pits and barricades. The force was found to consist of Ross's and Armstrong's brigades of cavalry and a brigade of infantry. We continued to drive them from position to position, passing Bethesda

Church, crossing Plain Creek, then on to Renfro, where it was designed we should halt; but the scarcity of water at this point made it necessary to move on. We reached Flint River at about five P. M., and after a temporary check succeeded in flanking the enemy from his position behind it; then pushed on to within half a mile of Jonesboro', where we found a strong infantry force intrenched. Night coming on, we halted, formed line, and commenced intrenching. This division was formed on left, and the Fourth on right of road. Eighteen men were wounded, — all of the Second Brigade except Captain Crane,[1] Eighth Missouri Infantry (mounted). Distance marched, twelve miles.

*August* 31. This morning the First Brigade (Colonel Theodore Jones) was thrown forward in advance of the left, and after sharp skirmishing succeeded in taking possession of an eminence commanding the enemy's position and overlooking the Macon Railroad. The movements of the enemy made it necessary to extend the skirmish line so far to the left that the brigade was much weakened, only two regiments remaining in the original line. Reinforcements were sent from the First Division (two regiments) and from Seventeenth Corps (three regiments). As soon as this position was secured, temporary works were commenced, and were but half completed when the enemy charged our whole line, the action lasting about an hour and a half. The enemy made two distinct assaults with great gallantry, but met with a bloody repulse each time, — the result not of a strong line or superior numbers, but of the calm, steady, and persistent courage of our troops. Major-General Anderson, of Lee's corps, with his staff, rode up to within seventy-five yards of our works. He was twice wounded (but not captured); two of his staff were killed and two wounded. Great credit is due to all, but especially to the First Brigade, for sustaining themselves so well during the engagement. Our casualties were fourteen killed and sixty-eight wounded. We buried inside of our picket lines two hundred and eleven of the enemy; captured ninety-nine prisoners unhurt, seventy-nine wounded, two stands of colors, and over one thousand stands of small arms.

[1] Crane finally died of this wound.

Spent the night in carrying away the dead and wounded of the enemy.

*September* 1. This morning advanced picket lines, and found the enemy in force. Nothing of importance on our front to-day, except that in the afternoon we kept up an incessant demonstration in favor of the Fourteenth Corps (General Jeff. C. Davis commanding), which attacked the enemy on our left. Two commissioned officers and twenty-four enlisted men were wounded.

*September* 2. This morning advanced picket line, and found that the enemy had retreated. Occupied Jonesboro' at daylight. Column marched at eight o'clock in pursuit, taking the road to Lovejoy's Station, this division being in rear of the corps. The enemy was found within about five miles, when the Fourth Division and First, or parts of them, formed line, advanced, and engaged the enemy; this division in reserve. Three enlisted men were wounded.

*September* 3. In same position. One enlisted man was wounded.

*September* 4. To-day laid out line for works in rear of position. Commenced work on them at twelve M., the First Brigade working on the left and the Second on the right of railroad. Finished works by night.

Received congratulatory order from General Sherman, announcing the occupation of Atlanta on the 2d instant, the enemy beginning to evacuate the city as soon as the result of his assault of our position on the 31st was learned.

On reaching Flint River I saw for the first time the use of the magazine gun. An advanced force from the enemy at Jonesboro', two miles beyond, occupied a barricaded position on the opposite side of the river, to dispute our crossing. A regiment of Kilpatrick's cavalry, armed with these guns, was dismounted, and advancing to within range, opened fire, the sound of which was continuous, like that of a large force. The enemy at once took to their heels and gave us the bridge, but we found no killed or wounded.

We arrived in front of Jonesboro' too late to make suitable disposition for battle. But in the early morning next day, as I saw the absolute necessity of at once occupying and holding a hill to my left and front, Colonel Theodore Jones was directed to move his brigade over and occupy it. In doing so he met the enemy coming for a like purpose. But we got it, and luckily; for it not only dominated our line in flank, but overlooked the town and all the ground held by the enemy.

The following is my report of the battle of Jonesboro':

EAST POINT, GEORGIA, Sept. 10, 1864.

Lieut.-Colonel R. R. TOWNS, Assist. Adj.-Gen. 15th Army Corps:

This division, leading the corps, took up the march at seven A.M., the 30th, in the direction of Jonesboro', distant thirteen miles. After moving about five miles we came upon a portion of Kilpatrick's cavalry that had been checked by two brigades of the cavalry of the enemy. Forming two regiments as a support to the skirmishers, already strong, they all advanced, in conjunction with some troops of the Sixteenth Corps on the right, the enemy giving way. Whenever the enemy found time he endeavored, by making temporary barricades and by the use of artillery, to check our column; but the march was kept up with but little delay the entire day. We crossed Flint River, drove the enemy from the other side, repaired the bridge, and pushed on to within half a mile of the town before dark. At this time we captured an infantry soldier from the enemy, who told me that two divisions of Hardee's corps were before us, and that our lines were not over two hundred yards apart. This was also made probable by the character of the musketry fire. The troops were here formed in line, the right resting on the Fairborn and Jonesboro' road, and extending north. A good barricade was made along their front.

Early in the morning of the 31st Colonel Theodore Jones, commanding the First Brigade on the left, was directed to seize and fortify a commanding eminence about one quarter of a mile to the front of his left. He had just gained it, when the enemy

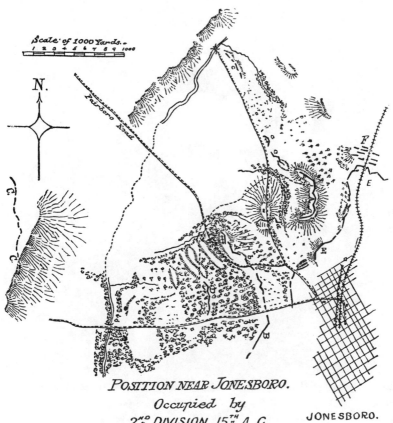

Scale of 1000 Yards.
1 2 3 4 5 6 7 8 9 1000

N.

*Jonesboro Road*

F

E

E

*POSITION NEAR JONESBORO.*
*Occupied by*
2ⁿᵈ *DIVISION* 15ᵗʰ *A. C.*
*From Aug't 30ᵗʰ to September 2ⁿᵈ 1864.*
*GENERAL W.B.HAZEN* COM'G.

JONESBORO.

EXPLANATION.
A. Positions of 2ⁿᵈ Division.
B. " 4ᵗʰ "
C. " " 17ᵗʰ A.C. Aug. 31ˢᵗ
D. Works constructed by 1ˢᵗ Div'n.
E. Enemy's Line.
F. Attack of 14ᵗʰ Corps Sept.1ˢᵗ

Drawn Sept. 3ʳᵈ 1864.
By J.R.Scupham
Div Engineer

TRACED IN
ADJT. GEN'LS OFFICE.
From Original Records.

EXPLANATION.
a. Positions of 1ˢᵗ Brigade
b. " " 2ⁿᵈ "
c. Final position of 11ᵗʰ A.
d. Col. W.B.Woods 2 Regiments
e. Col. Bryant's 3 "

COLONEL WILLIAM B. WOODS

(Seventy-sixth Ohio.)

came also to occupy it. He held his ground, however, with a portion of his command, while the remainder fortified the position, which was found to be of great importance, as it overlooked the entire front occupied by the enemy.

A column of Rebel troops was now seen to be extending to our left, placing artillery, and making all disposition necessary to attack. As he extended beyond my left, and as my troops were formed in a light line with considerable intervals, a brigade from the Seventeenth Corps, under Colonel George E. Bryant, Twelfth Wisconsin Volunteers, and two regiments under Colonel William B. Woods, Seventy-sixth Ohio Volunteers, were sent to me, and posted where most needed, and where they afterward performed good service. I now had sixteen regiments in the line and one in reserve. No point of the line could be given up without endangering it all. At two P. M. the enemy began a vigorous fire of artillery all along his line, and was soon after seen advancing his infantry. We had good works, and the attack was met with the most perfect confidence. He came with two full lines, supported by troops in mass coming in one place, — the advanced salient on the hill, — quite inside the works, and persisted in the attack for about three quarters of an hour, when he was completely repulsed at all points, and those who came too near were captured. We lost quite heavily in the trenches before the fight took place; but during the fight we had but eleven killed, fifty-two wounded, and two missing. Of the enemy, we buried two hundred and eleven, and captured ninety-nine unhurt and seventy-nine wounded. We took also two stands of colors and over a thousand stands of small arms. I have reason to believe that over a thousand of the enemy were wounded. The division remained in this position during the fight of the Fourteenth Corps on the 1st instant, participating in it from behind our works, and on the 2d moved forward to near Lovejoy's Station.

The extended front, caused by occupying the hill, made my line a very long one, a portion of it consisting of but a single rank. The two regiments sent under Colonel W. B.

Woods filled the gap between this and the old line, the right of which rested on the Fairborn road; while Colonel Bryant, with three regiments, was retired from the left flank of the advanced position. The attack was made by the whole corps of Stephen D. Lee, which made two successive efforts. The enemy first made a light or feigned attack upon the division on my right; and Lee then threw his entire corps on my front, endeavoring mainly to drive us from the advanced hill seized in the morning. The attack was received by this thin line with perfect coolness and confidence. No men could possibly have behaved better. The enemy came over our works at the salient on the hill, and a hundred of them were captured before they could get back.

The conduct of Colonel Woods — now of the Supreme Court of the United States — was admirable. Although he occupied an important place in the line, I was compelled to withdraw him during the action to meet an attack advancing on the left of Colonel Bryant's brigade. But just when the two regiments of Colonel Woods seemed certain to be overwhelmed, for some unaccountable reason this force of the enemy retreated. Since the war I have made inquiry of Colonel Thomas P. Ochiltree, of Texas, — who was a staff-officer with this command, — why they went back. He could assign no reason for it, except that they were composed largely of Governor Brown's Georgia militia. It was certainly most fortunate for us. Colonel Bryant, who did such gallant service on the left in a little grove of pine-trees, was a very spare, bent, and elderly man, but of admirable quality. When he went into position he said, " Only give us ten minutes to cover ourselves, and no matter how many come." He needed the cover and made good his promise, as the dead in his ,ront showed. I have never seen him since that day.

This repulse decided Hood to evacuate Atlanta; and

about midnight we were awakened by remarkable explosions in the direction of the city. No one understood it. The succession of discharges was entirely novel, and different from anything we had ever heard. Soon after, it was found to have been the bursting of shells at Atlanta, where Hood was destroying his railroad train of ordnance stores.

The comparative importance of the work of my division here will be seen from the following extracts from official reports. General Harrow, commanding the adjoining division on my right, says : —

" The attack did not extend along our whole front, the heaviest part of the attack being on our right. The enemy was repulsed with ease. Killed of enemy in our front, twelve."

General Osterhaus, commanding the only other division engaged, reported a total loss in killed and wounded of but thirty-one; while the loss of the enemy in my front was two hundred and eleven that we buried, and one hundred and seventy-eight prisoners captured, with two stands of colors and one thousand stands of arms, which represents something under the probable number of wounded.

Of this battle the Rebel generals Hood and S. D. Lee report as follows : —

HEADQUARTERS NEAR LOVEJOY'S STATION, Sept. 3, 1864.
General B. BRAGG :

On the evening of the 30th of August the enemy made a lodgment across Flint River near Jonesboro'. We attacked them there on the evening of August 31 with two corps, but failed to dislodge them. This made it necessary to abandon Atlanta, which was done on the night of September 1.

On the evening of September 1 General Hardee's corps in position at Jonesboro' was assaulted by a superior force of the enemy [Jeff. C. Davis's corps], and being outflanked, was compelled to retire during the night to this point with the loss of eight guns.

J. B. HOOD, *General.*

COLUMBUS, MISS., Jan. 30, 1865.

COLONEL, — Owing to my temporary absence from the army
and to the movements of the troops, it will be impossible to make
a full report of the operations of my command. My corps did
not arrive at Jonesboro' till ten A. M. on the 31st of August, but
it reached there immediately in rear of Hardee's last division.
The enemy had during the previous evening and night effected a
crossing of and lodgment on the east bank of Flint River. The
preliminaries for the attack were arranged. My corps was formed
almost parallel to the railroad, and immediately to the right of
Jonesboro', connecting with Hardee's right, his line extending
towards Flint River and making a right angle with the railroad.
It was found that Hardee's corps did not cover as much ground
as was expected. I was instructed to move my troops so as to
fill up the interval, and my command was moved almost two
division fronts to the left.

Being satisfied that the battle had begun in earnest, I at once
gave orders for my corps to move against the enemy. The attack was not made by the troops with that spirit and inflexible
determination that would insure success. Several brigades behaved with great gallantry, and in each brigade many instances
of gallant conduct were exhibited by regiments and individuals;
but generally the troops halted in the charge when they were
much exposed, and within easy range of the enemy's musketry,
and where they could do but little damage to the enemy, instead
of moving forward against the temporary and informidable works
in their front. The attack was a failure, with a loss to my corps
of about thirteen hundred in killed and wounded. The enemy
being behind works, and apparently no impression having been
made upon them by the attack upon his left where his line was
supposed weakest, I was induced not to renew the attack. During the night of the 31st, about one A. M., I received orders from
General Hardee to march at once to Atlanta. My corps was
immediately put in motion, and was halted by Major-General
M. L. Smith, Chief Engineer of the Army, about six miles from
Atlanta, and then put in position to cover the evacuation of the
city.

I take pleasure in making special mention of the gallantry of Major-Generals Stevenson and Clayton during the battle of Jonesboro' on the 31st of August.

S. D. LEE, *Lieutenant-General.*

General Hood, in his official report of this battle, says : "Only fourteen hundred were killed and wounded out of the two corps." And General Hardee, in his official report, written from Smithfield, North Carolina, April 16, 1865, says of it: "This attack was made principally by Lee's corps, and the loss was chiefly in that corps."

The assault the next day by the Fourteenth Corps was upon Hardee's command, which had taken the place of S. D. Lee, whose corps was withdrawn the night before. This assault was made just in front of our position, which was on the hill, and where everybody could see it.

Although Davis was fairly successful, the failure to capture or completely destroy Hardee on this occasion was the finest opportunity lost by the Union forces, under my observation, during the war. While Davis was severely engaging Hardee at four P. M. September 1, and until he withdrew at ten P. M. that night, Hardee, with one corps, was the only Rebel force present, or within supporting distance. Hardee, in his Smithfield report, says of it :—

"On the morning of the 1st of September the situation was as follows : General Hood was at Atlanta with Stewart's corps of Georgia militia ; my corps was at Jonesboro', thirty miles distant [meaning twenty-one miles], and Lee's corps on the road from Jonesboro' to Atlanta, fifteen miles [meaning half-way from each place], and in supporting distance of neither. The Federal commander, on the other hand, had concentrated his whole army upon my corps at Jonesboro' except the one corps [Slocum's] left in front of Atlanta, and was now in position to crush in detail the scattered forces of his antagonist. My position at Jonesboro' had been taken up on the failure of the attack the day previous."

Hardee had in charge also the trains of the Rebel army. In addition to Davis's corps, the Fourth, Twenty-third, Fifteenth, and Seventeenth corps of our army were substantially present, and excepting Davis's were comparatively idle, and already enveloped two sides of Hardee. To close the other two also was perfectly feasible, and could have been done before night. Seeing this grand opportunity — such a one as is seldom seen in war, as it seemed to me — slipping away, on two occasions I was on the point of imploring to be sent (although a division commander with troops then confronting the enemy with my pickets sharply engaged) with positive instructions for the troops beyond Davis, the Fourth and Twenty-third corps, to close in and complete the investment; but on hearing the general in command say, " Commanders there already have their orders," I did not do it. But there are times when orders are not enough; when one should see them executed. The failure to do so here was most unfortunate ; and it requires but a glance at the map to recognize the gravity of our failure.

No one has yet written of it, but it is doubtful if any sufficient excuse can be given for not destroying the Rebel army here just as Bragg states we were in a position to do. When we consider the blood and treasure it would have saved at Franklin and Nashville, we can appreciate the gravity of the error. A map of the position of the troops at that important juncture is here given.

The battle of Jonesboro', and the skirmishing and pursuit to Lovejoy's, from which point we returned to Atlanta, may be properly considered a part of the Atlanta campaign. But the evacuation of that city began immediately after the Rebel failure at Jonesboro', on the 31st of August. Nothing could have been more admirable than the marching and fighting of the Second Division during the entire

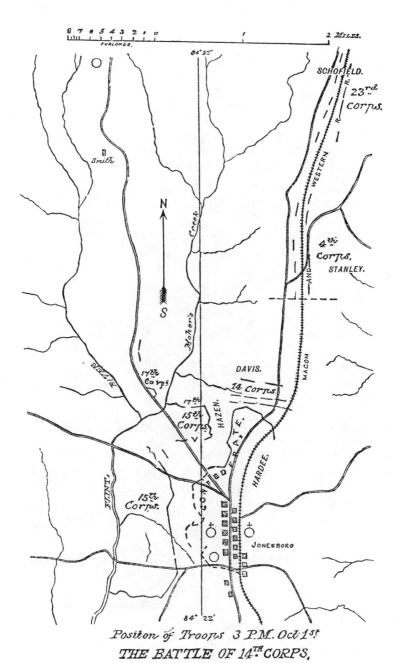

Position of Troops 3 P.M. Oct 1st

## THE BATTLE OF 14TH CORPS.

### JONESBORO.

The broken part of Confederate line [was held by a single broken line with intervals.

The 4th and 23rd Corps were from 2 to 4 miles away

LIEUTENANT COLONEL SAMUEL R. MOTT

(Fifty-seventh Ohio.)

movement. The whole Army of the Tennessee recognized it, and warmed toward me; and I found myself, from Jonesboro' on, standing solidly in my shoes.

There can be no impropriety in comparing the Army of the Cumberland with that of the Tennessee, as far as the differences seem to me most noticeable. As to the native character of the men and their excellence in battle there was no difference; they were alike, and both simply admirable. The general officers of the Army of the Tennessee were much younger in years and in commission, and were all acting under the spur of new zeal and in perfect harmony and good-will; while in the Army of the Cumberland the officers had been denied the rapid advancement to which their services in battle seemed to entitle them. Such recognition is indispensable in actual war. The result was that jealousies, dislikes, and dissensions were developing in the Army of the Cumberland, while they were nearly unknown in the Army of the Tennessee. As to discipline, instruction, and administration, the Army of the Cumberland was so far the superior as scarcely to admit of comparison. From some cause there had been in the Army of the Tennessee a singular omission in these particulars. Of the orders I found necessary to issue in this connection but a few have been given, yet enough to indicate the deficiencies which I found. The men had a most vicious and almost mutinous habit, if rations were late, of calling out, "Hard-tack" and "Sow-belly" to general officers who rode near them, or making catcalls and other disrespectful demonstrations; and while the officers would wince under it, no efficient effort was made to stop it. The following order was issued after the troops of General Osterhaus's division had behaved in this manner in my presence, as that officer was riding past them, and the shout had been taken up in a meaningless way by my troops.

EAST POINT, GEORGIA, Sept. 8. 1864.

I. Loud and boisterous shouting on frivolous occasions is prohibited in the division. The practice often noticed of calling out in a loud tone when general officers are passing, for the purpose of taking advantage of a crowd to cover certain expressions intended for his ear that soldiers would not make openly to their general, is one that it is hoped will not occur again in this division. It is of a class of acts that are done under cover, and are unmanly. The general commanding believes that on second thought no soldier of this division will repeat this conduct. He will at all times cheerfully listen and endeavor to correct any supposed wrong or hardship soldiers may see fit to call properly to his attention.

II. Lieutenant-Colonel Mott, Fifty-seventh Ohio Volunteer Infantry, now in arrest for taking no measure to check his men when calling out improperly, is hereby relieved from arrest and will return to duty.

III. Regimental commanders will be held strictly responsible for the proper observance by their commands of the first paragraph of this order.

This shouting was never made again and for my benefit but once, when passing through Warrenton, North Carolina in the spring of 1865, six months afterward. I at once arrested the colonel of the regiment, who for a week protested daily that he could not find out who did it; but on about the tenth day the offenders were brought to my headquarters and the colonel was released.

This was the first and last of this kind of insubordinate and disgraceful conduct after my order upon the subject. Many regiments in that army and some in the Second Division never learned their drill nor military etiquette, nor felt the proper deference that must be observed toward their officers by all good soldiers. Yet in battle no troops fought better. It may then be asked, Why make discipline so important? I would add, that all who were there fought well; but a thorough administration and discipline enables a government to put sixty per cent of the troops who are on the rolls and under pay in the front rank with muskets in their hands, — the prime object of every enlistment, — and it would have enabled us to do so, while in fact from lack of it we were able to put only about thirty per cent of the troops in line of battle. Besides, it would have been a saving of half the cost of the war. Living is better than dying, health better than sickness, thrift better than squalor. Therefore, order is better than disorder; for order is essential to all these things, and discipline alone makes order possible. Discipline, then, is indispensable to economy of life and money.

To illustrate: the beautiful and efficient working of a great steam-engine depends absolutely upon the perfect finishing, connection, and correlation of all its parts according to a prearranged plan. With these, a child's hand moves the ship. Without them, it is an inert, purposeless mass that a thousand strong men could not stir. This is true of an army, which becomes efficient in proportion to the perfection of all these relations of subordination and organization; and to become so, persistent, laborious toil for long periods of time by a strong and unswerving hand is necessary. Without these qualities an army is likewise inert and purposeless; and those who oppose discipline, oppose efficiency and economy of life and money. The simple purpose of both organization and discipline (nearly synonymous when applied to troops) is to give a government a cheap and efficient army; and cheapness and efficiency here are nearly related. "The more disciplined and regular the troops engaged in war, the less humanity suffers." And just in proportion as men oppose or officers fail to enforce organization and discipline, are they enemies to humanity.

## CHAPTER XX.

### PURSUIT OF HOOD.

THE army remained only from the 2d to the 7th of September at Lovejoy's, where there was no serious engagement, and then returned and took up a position looking southward, with Atlanta as a centre, covering itself with a simple line of earthworks except about the city, where a strong system of closed works was made. The flanks reached four or five miles each way to the east and west. We remained here till Hood passed our right flank and obliged us to move northward in pursuit.

During this period, up to the 13th of November, when the army set out for the sea, the division was either in active pursuit, destroying railroads, or under instruction and preparation for the remarkable campaign that followed. Our doings are accurately reported by my orders and official papers. From the 9th of September to the 4th of October we remained in the position taken up at East Point, and the following extracts from my order-book show how we were employed : —

EAST POINT, GEORGIA, Sept. 13, 1864.
Colonel Commanding each Brigade :

The general commanding the division directs that immediate steps be taken to improve as far as possible the proper officering of the troops in your command.

With a view to that end he suggests that an effort be made to secure at least one efficient field-officer to command each regiment, and a line-officer for each company. Although no one in the field is competent to appoint officers, yet much can be done by judicious administration to secure them.

Officers who fail to give the service the necessary assistance, either from prolonged absence or from inefficiency, should be made to give way to those who will. It is the duty of all commanding officers at once to give close attention to this matter, — even, if necessary, to advise retiring, — and to take steps for the removal of officers when they no longer render service commensurate with their positions.

The resignation of all officers will be recommended when their commanders, either by public indorsement or otherwise, advise that it would be for the good of the service.

EAST POINT, GEORGIA, Sept. 16, 1864.

I. Regimental commanders are directed to send at once, through the proper military channels, applications addressed to the adjutant-general of the army for assignment to their regiment of a sufficient number (stating it) of drafted men or substitutes to fill them to their maximum number.

II. The brigade of Colonel Oliver will be known as the Third Brigade of this division.

III. Drills will commence on Monday, the 19th, as follows: Company drills, from half-past seven to nine A. M., Sundays excepted, to be under the immediate supervision of the regimental commanders, or a field-officer from each regiment. Companies will be consolidated so as to have at least twenty files front. Battalion drill from half-past three to five P. M., Mondays, Wednesdays, and Fridays; and evolutions of the line at the same hours Tuesdays and Thursdays, in the First and Third brigades, — the Second having brigade drills on the days the others have battalion drills, and battalion drills when the others have brigade drills; the First and Second brigades for these exercises to be consolidated into three battalions each, and the Third into five; the battalions to be divided into eight equal companies.

IV. Brigade commanders will, in person or through a competent staff-officer, closely supervise all these drills; they will at once prepare suitable grounds where their entire brigade can be exercised under control of one person, and see that all the troops drill upon the ground specified. They will also cause the officer to be attended by a bugler, who will sound a rest of five minutes after each exercise of twenty minutes, when he will again sound the "Attention." No other rests will be permitted during the exercise. The calls for drill will be sounded at each brigade headquarters, and sufficiently before the hour for exercise to make all formations by that time. Drills will take place as near the camp as possible. Brigade commanders will see that the Tactics are not departed from in any particular, either in the order or manner of drills.

V. The chief of artillery will at once see to establishing drills for the batteries at such hours as he may prescribe, both in the school of the piece and battery; and the batteries may be manœuvred with limbers.

VI. At all drills, guard-mounting, parades, reviews, and all exercises of ceremony, officers will have their swords drawn, and both officers and men will have their coats buttoned.

No man will be permitted to appear in shirt-sleeves at any of these exercises, nor will any sentinel or guard under arms so appear.

EAST POINT, GEORGIA, Oct. 3, 1864.

In addition to the tools of the pioneer corps of this division there will be one wagon of tools, composed of one hundred axes, one hundred spades and shovels, and fifty pick-axes, attached to each brigade, to always follow it, and be under control of brigade commanders. Compartments will be made at one end of the wagon, so that the axes can be transported without spoiling them.

Quartermasters of brigades will at once procure the wagons and tools, receipting for the same. With the pioneer corps of the division, and with each brigade wagon, a suitable man will be detailed (he should be a mechanic) to take entire charge of all the tools, issue them, keep a strict account of all issued, and cause their proper return. He will also take proper steps to keep these tools at all times in proper trim. Weekly inspection will be made by division and brigade inspectors, to insure proper attention to this order.

IN THE FIELD NEAR KENESAW MT.,
GEORGIA, Oct. 9, 1864.

I. In obedience to orders from headquarters Military Division of the Missouri, the division will hold itself in readiness to march with the following allowance of transportation. For division headquarters, two wagons; for brigade headquarters, two wagons, one of which will be used exclusively to carry forage, and one for officers' messes at brigade headquarters, and one to each regiment.

The regimental wagons will carry a small quantity of medical supplies, the adjutant's desk properly supplied with blanks and stationery, two tent flies without poles, and the surplus ammunition.

The rations and blankets of officers must be carried by pack animals and servants, and axes must be carried in the hands of men. All other property must be shifted to the wagons to be left behind. Quartermasters must select their best teams to accompany the troops, and the division and brigade inspectors will personally see to the proper execution of this order.

II. While in the field the division will be ready to march at any time in ten minutes after the "general" is sounded.

III. This order will in no manner interfere with making camp at this point.

NEAR SUMMERVILLE, GEORGIA, Oct. 17, 1864.

While on the present campaign, foraging, in accordance with existing orders, will constitute one of the means of subsisting the command. Each brigade commander will appoint a suitable officer, who shall have control of all foraging for the brigade, who will be held responsible for the proper conduct of parties sent out with him. These parties shall be as numerous as the wants of the command require, shall be held under proper control, shall be in charge of an officer or non-commissioned officer, and shall carry their authority for foraging in writing. Unless engaged with the enemy, foragers will not discharge fire-arms. They will under no pretence pillage houses; but may take from them salt, flour, meal, and meat, if in so doing they do not leave the occupants destitute.

LITTLE RIVER, GEORGIA, Oct. 24, 1864.

I. A board of officers, to consist of Captain J. L. Pinkerton, Forty-seventh Ohio Volunteers, First Lieutenant Thaddeus Capron, Acting-Assistant Quartermaster First Brigade, and First Lieutenant Isaac N. Thomas, Thirtieth Ohio Volunteers, is hereby appointed to convene without delay at these headquarters, to appraise such public horses as may be presented for that purpose.

II. All officers required to be mounted, riding public horses, who are not entitled to the same, will, if they desire still to retain them, have them properly appraised by the board constituted by Paragraph I. of this order.

III. Hereafter all horses and mules procured in the country where the armies are serving will be reported to the immediate quartermaster, whose duty it shall be to take charge of the same, or cause them to be appraised and sold. Officers will bear in mind that all property taken in the country belongs to the Government.

CEDAR BLUFF, ALA., Oct. 29, 1864.

The quartermasters of brigades will at once take charge of all animals not owned by officers authorized to be mounted, found in and about their brigades, taking up the same on their returns of property, and branding them "U. S.," and will then assign riding animals to officers authorized to be mounted and desiring them, and pack animals to companies and regiments; no company to have more than one until all are supplied with that number.

Hereafter, on each Saturday quartermasters will take charge of and brand all animals that may have been secured during the week. The division quartermaster will see this order literally carried out, and will himself seize, brand, and take up all animals as above at division headquarters, with the trains of the division quartermaster, commissary, ordnance-officer, and pioneer corps.

DYKE'S STORE, Oct. 30, 1864.

The presence of the enemy's cavalry and guerillas upon the flanks of the army renders necessary the most stringent

observance of existing orders prohibiting straggling and the discharge of fire-arms.

Several men of the command are known to have been captured
and probably killed to-day while violating these orders. Soldiers,
excepting regular organized foraging parties under officers, must
not pass beyond the line of flankers. Any officer failing to exercise his whole authority to prevent these desertions is guilty
of a neglect amounting almost to a crime; and soldiers found
guilty of violating this circular, or recent orders upon this subject from corps headquarters, will be severely punished. This
applies to all servants and orderlies.

SMYRNA CAMP, Nov. 3, 1864.

Brigade commanders will detail a chaplain, or some worthy
officer (one whose term of service has expired), for the purpose of
conveying North moneys belonging to soldiers of this command.
They will report at once to these headquarters for instructions.

SMYRNA CAMP, Nov. 7, 1864.

Colonels Commanding each Brigade : —

On calling for a detailed report and explanation of the large
number appearing on the weekly report of your brigade as " present, ineffective," I find that all manner of inaccuracies and erroneous reporting exists, such as reporting commanding officers of
regiments, companies, musicians, and color-bearers as ineffective.
Also, unauthorized details still exist in disobedience to orders,
such as regimental blacksmiths, postmasters, and wagon-masters.
Also, six and eight teamsters are reported present with regiments. These inaccuracies show great carelessness upon the
part of adjutants.

I have marked on a report to be returned to your headquarters
the corrections to be made in each case; which, with the aid of
your inspector, be pleased to carry out literally before the next
report is due.

The campaign in pursuit of Hood, excepting the re-
nowned defence of Alatoona by the distinguished division
commander, General John M. Corse, was most uneventful.

I summarize from my journal the part taken by my command : —

*October* 4, 1864.   Marched at nine A. M., First Brigade in advance.   Crossed Chattahoochee River at Vining's Bridge at half-past three P. M.   Camped near Ruff's Station on the railroad at ten P. M., having marched nineteen miles.

*October* 5.   Marched at seven A. M. on Ruff's Mill road, four miles, then on Sandtown and Marietta road, three miles.   At three P. M. camped three miles and a half southwest of Marietta, taking position in old line of Rebel works, having marched seven miles and a half.

*October* 8.   Marched at six P. M. to Big Shanty, crossing Proctor's Creek and camping on Alatoona Creek, one mile south of Alatoona, at half-past eleven P. M., having marched twelve miles.

*October* 11.   Third Brigade took the cars for Rome.   Remainder of division marched at six A. M., passing Alatoona, crossing Etowah and through Castorville.   Rested at Etowah ; and after crossing Patias Creek, marched on the railroad track to Cassville Station, near which the Ohio troops voted.   Camped at four P. M. on Tursen Creek, near Kingston, having marched twenty-two miles.

*October* 12.   Marched at nine A. M.   Halted at Kingston until twelve M., then marched on river road, crossing Thomas Creek, Cedar Creek, and Dry Creek, camping at eight P. M. within four miles of Rome, having marched seventeen miles.

*October* 13.   Marched at 4.45 P. M.   Took the right, crossing Dry Creek.   Camped one mile south of McGuire's, having marched thirteen miles.

*October* 14.   Marched at seven A. M. to McGuire's Store, three miles and a half, then to Ostalooga Creek, within three quarters of a mile of Calhoun.   Camped at half-past seven P. M., having marched thirteen miles and a half.

*October* 15.   Marched at 4.45 A. M. through Calhoun to Resaca, five miles.   Crossed the Oostenaula at that place, then down through Sugar Valley, six miles, to mouth of Snake Creek Gap, where column was delayed three hours on account of Seventeenth Army Corps skirmishing with the enemy in our front ;

then through the gap, five miles, marching slowly on account of the obstructions the enemy had put in our way by felling trees across the road. Camped at half-past eight P. M. four miles from Villanow, having marched nineteen miles.

*October* 16. Marched at nine A. M., reaching Villanow at ten A. M. Crossed headwaters of Dry Creek and West Chickamauga, then through Drywood Valley, and camped at four P. M. in Ship's Gap, at Taylor's Ridge, having marched seven miles.

*October* 17. Marched at five P. M. from Ship's Gap to Lafayette, crossing the Chattooga near the town. Camped here at 9.45 P. M., having marched seven miles.

*October* 18. Marched at eight A. M., on Summerville road, seven miles to Cane Creek, then six miles and a half to Chattooga River, and on to within two miles and a half of Summerville. Camped at four P. M. in Chattooga valley, having marched fifteen miles.

*October* 19. Marched at eleven A. M. to Summerville. Sent back surplus wagons. Marched on the Alpine road and camped at eight P. M. on Mill Creek near Alpine, having marched nine miles.

*October* 20. Marched at 6.45 A. M. Camped near Gaylesville, Alabama, at half-past five P. M., having marched twenty-one miles.

*October* 21. Marched at nine A. M., First Division in advance. Took the Blue Pond road, crossing Chattooga River, and camping at two P. M. at Little River, having marched five miles.

*October* 22 and 23. Remained in camp.

*October* 24. At half-past one P. M. the Second Division and two brigades of First Division started on a reconnoissance in the direction of Gadsden ; passed Yellow Creek, marching eight miles, and camped at Leesburg.

*October* 25. Left Leesburg at daylight, First Division in advance. Passed King's Hill, and arriving at Blount's farm at half-past twelve P. M., rested one hour, then moved forward to First Division, which had found enemy's cavalry at Turkeytown, four miles distant, behind rail works. The Second Brigade, Colonel Wells S. Jones, formed and advanced on left flank of enemy, moving forward in good style, and driving the enemy easily from the position; the brigade lost four men wounded. The command returned to Blount's farm, seven miles from Turkeytown, where we camped for the night, having marched twenty-one miles.

*October* 29. Marched at 9 A. M. At 10.10 crossed the Chat- tooga, and at 10.45 A. M. reached Cedar Bluff. At 4.30 P. M. crossed the Cassa River and took the Jacksonville road. Camped at seven P. M., having marched nine miles.

*October* 30. Marched at nine A. M. in rear of army crossing Carvan's Creek, and after striking the old Alabama road, con- tinued on it in the direction of Rome. Camped at five P. M. at Dyke's Store, Georgia, a quarter of a mile from the Alabama line, having marched seventeen miles and a half.

*October* 31. Marched at six A. M., Second Division in advance. At eight A. M. reached Cave Springs, where we camped, having marched four miles and a half. Casualties during month, four enlisted men wounded. Number of miles marched, two hundred and seventy.

*November* 1. Marched at seven A. M., crossing Cedar Creek three miles and a half from Cave Springs, recrossing it again within a quarter of a mile, reaching Cedar Town at twelve M., where we camped. Marched twelve miles.

*November* 2. Marched at half-past nine A. M., following First Division. Roads heavy; country hilly. Rained during day. Camped on Nesbit's farm, six miles west of Van Wert. Marched twelve miles. One commissioned officer and seven men (Eighth Missouri), having left road, were captured to-day.

*November* 3. Marched at half-past six A. M. on Villa Rica road, First Division in advance. Roads rough and muddy on account of rain. Crossed Enhardee Creek and headwaters of Tallapoosa River. Country barren and wild ; pine timber. Camped at five P. M. thirteen miles from Powder Springs, having marched twenty miles.

*November* 4. Marched at seven A. M. in advance. Crossed Nosis Creek and headwaters of Sweetwater Creek. Camped at half-past one P. M. at Powder Springs, having marched fifteen miles.

*November* 5. Marched at seven A. M. in advance, passing Ruff's Mills on Nickajack Creek, southward to Smyrna Campground, where we camped at two P. M., having marched fifteen miles.

*November* 9, 10, *and* 11. In same position. Paymaster paying. Slowly making preparations for campaigning. Last mail went north on the 11th. The paymasters are under guard to hold them to their work, as they fear the train will leave them.

## CHAPTER XXI.

### MARCH TO THE SEA.

NOW came the question, What to do next? There were the usual two horns to this dilemma; and it is hardly too much to say that there was scarcely a soldier in the command who did not think of it by day and dream of it by night. We had to go on or go back. By going back we should give up the costly and valuable work of the preceding six months; and if Hood could be taken care of without it, then this sacrifice would be a crime that no commander would dare to commit. Nor is it too much to say that thousands of men, and of all grades, had solved the problem in their own minds precisely as did our commander, — that if Hood could be turned over to other troops or to our own, still leaving enough to hold what we had, then the problem was solved, and that to hold on was to move forward. So plain was this, that there is hardly a doubt that Generals Grant and Halleck, and others near the head of the army, had also written of it, and come to a similar solution. Thus have arisen many claims for the honor of originating this historic march. But the facts make plain and simple where the real honor lies. The plan was in the minds of thousands, but only one adopted and executed it; and to him — General W. T. Sherman — is the credit due. He saw that there were troops enough for both purposes, and disposed them for both. That he was right, the sequel proved. But there were honors for all who should heartily aid in the execution of these plans; and it is enough that all bore their part, from General Thomas to the most humble private soldier.

There is a singular rule of compensation that in all my experiences has never failed to manifest itself. Never has any great good fallen to my lot but some great sorrow has come with it. The greatest good fortune, as I estimate it, that ever came to me in the field was my going to the Army of the Tennessee as the commander of a veteran division of the force that marched to the sea But the hand that brought the order to march on the 12th of October brought also the tidings of the greatest sorrow I then could feel,— the death of my mother. During that march my staff never knew why I rode forward by myself, and wished to be alone; but it was to hide the tears that no one ought to see.

The march was little more than a grand picnic. The country was full of what were luxuries to us, and no army was ever stronger, in a sanitary sense, or lived better than we did. There were no strifes in this army, and all worked in harmony for the common end.

We moved to the right of Atlanta; and after passing beyond it and southward, the black column of smoke going up from the city told of what was happening there I have never seen the city since. General Logan did not go with the army; and the Fifteenth Corps was commanded by General Osterhaus, of whom I can speak only in terms of praise both as a soldier and man.

The following extracts from my journal and orders pertaining to the march will best illustrate its character : —

*Nov.* 13, 1864. Marched at seven A. M., taking road to Chattahoochee River. Passed Baker's, and moved down to Turner's Ferry. Crossed at nine A. M. Camped at White Hall, near the railroad, having marched fifteen miles.

WHITE HALL, GEORGIA, Nov. 14, 1864.

I. To carry out the directions of higher commanders, the supply, ordnance, and ambulance trains will be divided into three equal parts, and each assigned to the charge of a brigade quartermaster, who will assign one wagon of ammunition and one ambulance to each regiment of his brigade, and will march the remainder in the rear of the troops of the brigade. Regimental wagons will go in the rear of their respective regiments, and all other brigade wagons in rear of their respective brigades, and all division wagons not included in the above in the rear of the division.

II. Whenever a brigade performs the duty of advance-guard or rear-guard to the corps, its wagons will move in rear of the division.

III. Wagons and ambulances assigned to brigades will form permanent sections, and will be parked separately. Brigade commanders will furnish proper guards to them when marching and when in park. Quartermasters and wagon-masters will at all times on the march remain with their trains, and will at once turn out broken wagons or turn the column past them; will when locking on hills cause the wagons as they came up to double, so as to lose no time; will cause the trains to close up, pull out of the roads and into park whenever troops halt; and in every way exercise such authority and attention as will prevent any delay of the column in rear. . . .

*November* 14. In same place, preparing to march.

*November* 15. Marched at half-past eight A. M. down the railroad, passing Rough-and-Ready at 1.20 P. M. Took McDonough road when within six miles of Jonesboro'. Camped at five P. M. on Warel's farm, three miles from McDonough, having marched nineteen miles.

*November* 16. Marched at six A. M. in advance, reaching McDonough's at one P. M. After a short halt, crossed Calton River and moved on to Lemon's farm, four miles south from McDonough's, where camped at three P. M., having marched sixteen miles. Captured three Rebels to-day; also found abundance of water and forage.

*November* 17. Marched at half-past three P. M. in rear of corps. Moved wagons in two lines, and troops on side of road abreast, past Locust road, and camped at midnight on side of road at Thoxton's farm, seven miles northwest of Indian Springs, having marched sixteen miles, finding water and forage plentiful.

*November* 18. Marched at eight A. M. Camped at twelve M. at Indian Springs, having marched seven miles.

*November* 19. Marched at half-past three A. M. Reached Ruff's mills, on Ocmulgee River, at half-past six A. M. Crossed on pontoon bridge. Camped at one P. M. on Pye farm, on Hillsboro' road, having marched twelve miles.

*November* 20. Marched at 9.15 A. M., reaching Hillsboro' at two P. M. Roads bad; weather rainy. Captured two prisoners. Camped at half-past six P. M. on Dunderburg farm, having marched twelve miles.

*November* 21. Marched at six A. M., passing through Clinton at twelve M. Roads terrible. The Thirty-seventh Ohio and Fifteenth Michigan sent out on Macon road to protect passing trains attacked by cavalry, losing three men wounded. First Brigade was left at Clinton to fortify the town and await the arrival of Fourth Division. Camped at five P. M., having marched fourteen miles.

*November* 22. Marched at half-past seven A. M., crossing the Macon and Savannah Railroad at 9.45 A. M. Camped at half-past twelve P. M. on Dr. Gibson's farm, having marched nine miles. Fortified this position.

NEAR GORDON, GEORGIA, Nov. 23, 1864.

. . . In future the necessary guards for the various departments will be detailed for a period not exceeding ten days. Regimental commanders will report any failure to comply with the above order . . .

MRS. SHEPPARD'S, GEORGIA, Nov. 23, 1864.

Colonels Commanding each Brigade :

Having now given every opportunity for refitting the baggage-trains of regiments and brigades, it is necessary to refit the supply-train. The baggage-wagons will from this time forward be constantly with the troops, which will make pack-animals less necessary.

Be pleased to direct your quartermasters to collect all mules in your command suitable for the harness, and send them to me. Other animals in abundance will be left, suitable for pack animals. Receipts will be given when desired.

Be pleased to organize as well as you can the mounted foragers, so that when necessary they can be used as a mounted force.

Collect this evening all able unarmed men, giving them tools. Organize them into a brigade pioneer corps, to be put under a competent officer and marched at the head of your brigade. . . .

Mrs. Sheppard's, Georgia, Nov. 23, 1864.

Captain Voges, Quartermaster:

. . . I find the wagon-master's wagon loaded with the following articles: two mess-chests, two boxes of clothing, one wall-tent, one cot, and four rolls of bedding. This is half as much transportation as is used by the ten officers at my headquarters. The mess-chest and cot (articles I do not carry) must be thrown out, the blankets put on that part of the train to which their owners are assigned, and the wagon used for legitimate purposes, —that is, to lighten some wagons that may stop and detain the army.

Of what service is this wagon-master, that he should presume to have a wagon, and keep two servants and a private horse? Do you carry this horse on your papers? If not, take him up and issue him. In case the wagon-master has a *bona fide* claim to him, then pay him.

The sooner we dispose of all such abuses the sooner shall we have subordination in the various departments, — an element which does not now exist in its proper sense in some of them.

Be pleased to send, for Captain Earnest, the large chestnut horse I have frequently seen ridden by your orderly. I can find no other horse strong enough for him.

I shall soon be able to refit your train with mules. . . .

MRS. SHEPPARD'S, GEORGIA, Nov. 23, 1864.

The following are prescribed as duties of aides-de-camp, and will be performed by each on alternate days.

At tattoo they will report to the general commanding for instructions with reference to the march of the next day, and promulgate the orders then given, to brigade and battery commanders that night. They will see that reveille is held at these and at brigade headquarters at the prescribed hour, and will themselves rise and see by personal inspection that the same is observed in the entire command. After making the inspection they will again report for further instructions. They will cause the trains to be made ready and pulled out on or near the road at least ten minutes previous to the prescribed hour of starting, and the head of the leading brigade for the day must be there by the time of starting.

They will, after the "forward" is sounded, see all the troops and trains under motion, and superintend the same, seeing that each command falls in at its proper place. They will then ride along to the front, reporting to the general or his adjutant. They will afterward, each three hours during the day, halt, permitting the entire column to pass them, and coming forward, report its condition. When nearing camp they will ride to the front, learn the position to be occupied by the troops, and be ready to post them on their arrival.

Much address is required, in posting troops, to take proper advantage of the accidents of the ground for defensive purposes. Too much attention cannot be given to this subject. . . .

*November* 23. Marched at eight o'clock A. M. on the Irwinton road. Camped at Sheppard's farm, seven miles west of Irwinton, at one o'clock P. M., having marched nine miles. Fortified this position.

*November* 24. Marched at 11.15 A. M., following First Division. Reached Irwinton at four P. M. Camped outside the town, having marched eight miles. Roads bad. Country poor. Forage scarce. First Brigade reported to-night, having brought up pontoon train *via* Gordon.

*November* 25. Marched at seven A. M., and reached Poplar Spring Church at ten A. M., eight miles. Struck Leggett's Division, Seventeenth Army Corps, coming in from the left. Marched on to Oconee River, sixteen miles, finding enemy on opposite side at Ball's Ferry. Deployed Fifty-seventh Ohio and One Hundred and Sixteenth Illinois as skirmishers, who opened fire across the river. Two cannons opened at dusk on the enemy, who left at night.

*November* 26. Corps crossed Oconee River to-day on pontoons. This division commenced crossing at eight P. M., and finished at 10.15 P. M. Went into camp three miles from river, having marched five miles.

*November* 27. Marched at seven A. M. Reached Irwin's Cross-roads at half-past eight A. M., where took Settlement road to right; turned to left within half a mile, marching one mile and camping, having marched seven miles.

*November* 28. Marched at nine A. M. on Tarboro' road eastward two miles, crossed Clark's Creek, and during the day branches of Ohoopee River. Camped at five P. M. at Hesse's farm, having marched fourteen miles.

*November* 29. Marched at half-past seven A. M. through pine forests, on old Savannah road. Camped at six P. M., having marched sixteen miles.

*November* 30. Marched at five A. M. on the left of road, passing Third Division. Camped at four P. M. in Summertown, having marched twelve miles. Casualties during the month : captured, — commissioned officers, 1, enlisted men, 7 ; wounded, — enlisted men 3 : aggregate, 11. Number of enemy captured during the month, 5. The number of miles marched, 275.

*December* 1. Marched from Summertown at seven A. M. on old Savannah road. Camped at five P. M. on Johnson's farm, having marched fourteen miles.

*December* 2. Marched at seven A. M. Camped at half-past four P. M. on Scull's Creek, having marched ten miles through pine forest, and built three quarters of a mile of corduroy.

LOT'S CREEK, GEORGIA, Dec. 3, 1864.

Until further orders each brigade commander will detail a sufficient number of handy men, who will march at the head of the column to man the tools in the tool-wagons. They will assign to their command a good practical officer, a civil engineer preferred, who will march with them and superintend such work as may be assigned him. One wagon in addition to the tool-wagon will be used to carry the knapsacks of the detail, which will carry the tools they use.

This will not change the organization of the brigade pioneer parties.

The brigade leading the column will always take with it its unarmed pioneers, to clear the way for the infantry column and make crossings.

LOT'S CREEK, GEORGIA, Dec. 3, 1864.

. . . . . . . . . .

III. Each brigade commander may organize a mounted foraging party of sixty men and two officers.

IV. Each regiment may have thirteen pack animals, and if necessary one additional to carry medical stores. All persons in charge of these animals will be furnished a ticket signed by the brigade inspector.

V. Each brigade commander may mount one orderly, his sergeant-major, quartermaster, and commissary sergeant.

No other animals than above indicated, except those forming a part of the command, will be retained. All in addition will be turned over each evening at these headquarters. All horses used for packing or by foragers, suitable for artillery, will be turned over to De Gress's battery, and all mules used for like purposes, suitable for the harness, to the division quartermaster.

The foraging parties will be sent to these headquarters for inspection this evening, and receive tickets from the provost-marshal. Any person hereafter foraging without these tickets will be punished.

The attention of the entire command is called to the fact that all property taken in an enemy's country belongs to the Government; and any appropriation of it except by prescribed methods, or by trading and receiving pecuniary consideration for it, is an act of felony, and will be punished as such.

Quartermasters will this evening brand all public animals not now branded.

*December* 3. Marched at eight A. M. Had a long bridge to build over Lot's Creek. Camped at eleven A. M. on south side, having marched two miles. Enemy captured foraging party of one commissioned officer and eleven men, Fifty-seventh Ohio.

*December* 4. Marched at half-past seven A. M. At three P. M. the mounted foragers were attacked at Statesboro' by several hundred Rebel cavalry, and driven back to the main column, where a volley from the Seventieth Ohio scattered them. The enemy's loss was six killed, one wounded, and two captured. Our loss was eight wounded and twenty-seven captured.

*December* 5. Marched at ten A. M. in rear of Third Division. Crossed Black Creek at Brannon's Hill. Camped at half-past six P. M. on J. Proctor's farm, having marched sixteen miles.

*December* 6. Marched at half-past eight A. M., passing Briar Patch to Brannon's farm, where we camped at ten A. M. on the left of the Third Division, having marched a mile and a half. Third Brigade marched at five o'clock this morning to Jenk's Bridge, near Station 2.

*December* 7. Division marched at seven A. M., in advance of Third Division. Third Brigade marched from Jenk's Bridge to Black Creek. Crossed, and moved to Cannouchee River, where, after a skirmish with the enemy, we camped at Eden Court House. Division camped at three P. M. on Butler's farm, on Black Creek, having marched fifteen miles. Sent two regiments, Second Brigade, across creek to fortify.

IN THE FIELD, GEORGIA, Dec. 8, 1864.

I. The board of officers convened in General Orders No. 56, to appraise public animals, is hereby dissolved.

II. A board of officers, to consist of First Lieutenant Thaddeus Capron, Acting-Assistant Quartermaster First Brigade ; First Lieutenant John Doyle, Acting-Assistant Quartermaster Second

Brigade; and First Lieutenant John Stite, Adjutant One Hundred and Eleventh Illinois Volunteer Infantry, is hereby convened to meet at these headquarters December 11, 1864, at ten o'clock A. M.

III. All officers required to be mounted, riding public animals, and not entitled to the same, will, if they desire to retain them, present them to this board for appraisement. . . .

*December* 8. Marched at half-past eight A. M., crossing Black Creek, and reached Bryan Court House at half-past twelve A. M. Camped near Bryan Court House at three P. M., having marched twelve miles. Third Brigade rejoined the division to-day, and had some skirmishing with the enemy, who defended the crossing at Ball's Bridge over the Cannouchee with two pieces of artillery. Enemy retired after midnight.

*December* 9. Repaired bridge, and the Second and Third brigades having crossed on pontoons, marched at nine A. M. to the Gulf Railroad. Corse's division reached the railroad at two P. M., and tore up seven miles of track and burned the bridge over the Ogeechee, and several large trestle-works, capturing eleven of the enemy. First Brigade of this division camped at four P. M. near Ball's Bridge, having marched four miles.

*December* 10. Marched at half-past seven A. M., recrossing the Cannouchee and crossing the Ogeechee at Dillon's Ferry at nine A. M. Camped at six P. M. on Lloyd's plantation, nine miles from Savannah, and in support of Fourth Division, having marched fifteen miles.

*December* 11. Remained in the position occupied on the 10th.

*December* 12. Marched at four P. M., having received orders to cross the Ogeechee and take Fort McAllister. Camped at six P. M. near King's Bridge, having marched five miles. Were joined by section of De Gress's Battery and First Missouri Light Artillery (six guns).

*December* 13. Crossed the river on King's Bridge at seven A. M., reaching the vicinity of Fort McAllister at twelve M., having marched thirteen miles. Three regiments of the Second Brigade (Forty-seventh Ohio, Fifty-fourth Ohio, and One Hundred

and Eleventh Illinois), Colonel W. S. Jones commanding, were
sent cautiously forward and took up position on left of road, the
left resting on the river.  Three of the First Brigade (Thirtieth
Ohio, Sixth Missouri, and One Hundred and Sixteenth Illinois),
Colonel Theodore Jones commanding, were sent across the swamp
to the extreme right.  Three of the Third Brigade (Seventieth
Ohio, Forty-eighth Illinois, and Ninetieth Illinois), Colonel J. M.
Oliver commanding, occupied the centre.  The fort was invested
at half-past three P. M., our line being within six hundred yards
of the fort.  Up to this time but few casualties had occurred ;
but the command had sustained a serious loss in the death of Captain John H. Groce, Acting-Assistant Adjutant-General Second
Brigade, and also by Colonel W. S. Jones being wounded, which
placed the Second Brigade in command of Colonel J. S. Martin,
One Hundred and Eleventh Illinois.

The signal to assault was given at half-past four P. M., and all
moved gallantly forward ; and but a few moments elapsed until
the colors of the Thirtieth, Forty-seventh, and Seventieth Ohio
were planted on the enemy's works, followed in a moment by
the colors of the entire command.  The enemy made a stubborn
resistance ; but they could not withstand the impetuosity of the
assault, although in addition to the fire of sharpshooters and artillery the troops encountered, outside the abatis, an entire line
of torpedoes, which exploded with terrific effect.  Our loss was
as follows : killed, — commissioned officers 4, enlisted men 20,
total 24 ; wounded, — commissioned officers 7, enlisted men
103, total 110 : aggregate, 134.  The enemy's loss was as follows : killed, — commissioned officers 1, enlisted men 13, total
14 ; wounded, — enlisted men 21 ; captured, — commissioned
officers 17, enlisted men 178, total 195 : aggregate, 230.

We captured eleven siege-guns, one 10-inch mortar, and twelve
field-pieces, — in all, twenty-four ; also sixty tons of ammunition
and a large amount of commissary stores and liquors.  The following is a list of artillery captured : three 10-inch columbiads,
one 8-inch columbiad, one 42-pounder smooth-bore, two 32-
pounder smooth-bore, one 24-pounder howitzer, two 12-pounder
napoleons, three 32-pounder rifled sea-coast guns, two 12-pounder

### Captain Groce

Captain John H. Groce was born at Circleville, Ohio, and was twenty-four years of age when shot on the skirmish line at Fort McAllister, Georgia. He was educated under James A., afterwards President, Garfield, at Hiram, Ohio. He led the forlorn hope at the unsuccessful assault at Vicksburg, and was a dauntless and enterprising officer, having the admiration and respect of all.

Union Wagon Trains Parked at Fort McAllister.

field howitzers, two 12-pounder mounted howitzers, six 6-pounder guns (bronze), one 10-inch mortar, and one hundred stand of small arms.

In this action all officers and men behaved with the utmost bravery, and are alike deserving of commendation. The loss of Captain Groce is irreparable. He was one of the bravest, most accomplished, and most competent officers in the command, and was fast rising to distinguished honors, merited by a devoted attachment to the cause and a prompt and efficient discharge of duty, in various positions, ever since the commencement of the war. He was killed by a sharpshooter while advancing the skirmish line preparatory to the assault.

FORT MCALLISTER, GEORGIA, Dec. 14, 1864.

In consideration of the conspicuous part taken by the Seventieth Ohio in the assault of Fort McAllister yesterday, that regiment is detailed to garrison that place temporarily, and will make its camp near the fort with such force on duty in it as the colonel may deem requisite.

He will take immediate steps to put the fort in order, cleaning it, and adopting a proper system of police.

*December* 14. Went into camp on Middleton's plantation, near the fort. Established hospitals and made disposition of the captured property.

*December* 15. The Seventieth Ohio, Lieutenant-Colonel Phillips commanding, put in charge of the fort. Made landing for boats near the fort.

FORT MCALLISTER, GEORGIA, Dec. 16, 1864.

In compliance with special orders No. 199, from headquarters Fifteenth Army Corps, each brigade of this division, leaving one regiment in camp, will prepare to march without wagons to destroy the Gulf Railroad, as follows : the Second Brigade from Walthourville east to a point two miles east of McIntosh ; the Third Brigade from a point two miles east of McIntosh to the crossing of the railroad with the Midway or St. Catherine's River ; the First Brigade from the St. Catherine's to the Ogeechee.

It will be seen, from the order referred to from corps headquarters, that the work should be done in the most thorough manner, — every tie burned and every rail twisted.

*December* 16.   Engaged in cleaning up the fort and clearing away the debris surrounding it.

FORT MCALLISTER, GEORGIA, Dec. 20, 1864.

I have the honor to earnestly recommend and urge the appointment of Colonel Theodore Jones, Thirtieth Ohio Volunteer Infantry, as brigadier-general of volunteers.   This appointment is asked for the benefit of the service, and in consideration of the services rendered by Colonel Jones in the assault and capture of Fort McAllister, and at the battle of Jonesboro', Aug. 31, 1864.

To Brig.-Gen. L. THOMAS, Adj.-Gen. U. S. Army.

FORT MCALLISTER, GEORGIA, Dec. 23, 1864.

The general commanding the division is pleased to announce that official despatches have been received from Major-General Thomas, saying that he had attacked Hood in front of Nashville; had driven his left and left centre eight miles, capturing sixteen guns, a large number of prisoners, flags, earthworks, and trains; that night closed the battle, but he would fight or follow the next day, and expected to destroy the entire army.

Our own troops have done all they were asked to do, and all that could be expected.   The fall of Savannah, so soon following the splendid assault and capture of Fort McAllister, is deemed by the general commanding a fitting occasion to congratulate the division upon its uniform good and brave conduct since he has had the honor of commanding it, and upon the brilliant close of the late campaign, of which it can justly claim so important a part.

*December* 24.   The sick and wounded of the command, and those of the enemy in our hands, were sent away on hospital boat to-day.

*December* 25 *and* 26.   In same position, awaiting orders, and sending into the city large numbers of contrabands.

FORT McALLISTER, GEORGIA, Dec. 26, 1864.

No negroes, except division pioneers, authorized company cooks, and servants for officers entitled to them, will be permitted to remain with the division. All such will be furnished tickets by the division or brigade provost-marshals before the troops move from their present camp. All at that time without such tickets will be turned over for shipment.

FORT McALLISTER, GEORGIA, Dec. 26, 1864.

. . . Brigade adjutants will furnish tickets for the negroes of their respective brigades. They will be cautious, and not ticket more servants than officers are allowed by orders and army regulations.

*December* 27. Received orders to commence dismantling the fort preparatory to the abandonment of this side of the river.

*December* 28. Captain Pratt, depot ordnance-officer at Hilton Head, arrived with apparatus, and took charge of dismantling the fort and loading guns and ammunition on steamers for shipment.

FORT McALLISTER, GEORGIA, Dec. 31, 1864.

The troops being about to temporarily vacate the country west of the Ogeechee River, and the people south of the Gulf Railroad on what is known as Brian's Neck being destitute of provisions, Mr. Maxwell, Dr. Johnson, and Mr. Cranston, residents, are hereby appointed a committee to ascertain the number and wants of the people on said neck, both black and white; also to take possession of the rice now in the Middleton mills, guard the same, and supply from it the needs of said people. No more than two weeks' supply will be furnished any family at one time.

Frequent inspections by officers of the army appointed for that purpose will be made, to see that this order is complied with fairly and in good faith. . . .

*Jan.* 1, 1865. Marched from Fort McAllister at seven A. M. for Savannah, crossing King's Bridge at nine A. M. and Little

Ogeechee at three P. M., reaching Wood Lawn, four miles from Savannah, where we came up with the Second Brigade and camped for the night, having marched twenty-two miles.

*January 2.* Marched to the city, four miles, camping just outside.

The following extract is taken from my official report of the Georgia campaign : —

SAVANNAH, GEORGIA, Jan. 9, 1865.

. . . On the 15th of November, every preparation being complete, the division, with the army, broke camp at Atlanta, and set out on its march through Georgia. It then numbered an effective strength of four thousand four hundred and twenty-six officers and men, and was composed of seventeen regimental organizations, its three brigade commanders being Colonels John M. Oliver, Fifteenth Michigan; Wells S. Jones, Fifty-third Ohio; and Theodore Jones, Thirtieth Ohio.

The troops moved rapidly, passing through McDonough the 17th, Indian Springs the 18th ; crossing the Ocmulgee the 19th, at Reach's Mills ; reaching Hillsboro' the 20th and Clinton the 21st, where Colonel Theodore Jones's brigade was left to cover the Macon roads till the next division arrived. Some skirmishing took place here, with a few casualties.

On the 22d the Macon and Augusta Railroad was crossed and the march continued, passing Irwinton the 24th, and the Oconee River, at Ball's Ferry, the 25th. The enemy was found on the opposite bank, and two regiments were deployed to develop them. On the morning of the 26th they had left, and preparations were at once made to cross, which was commenced by eleven A. M. The march was resumed without loss of time, passing Irwinton's Cross-roads the 27th. We moved toward Summertown through continuous pine forests, crossing several low, marshy branches of the Ohoopee, and reached Summertown the 30th. . . .

On the 1st of December the march was resumed in the direction of Statesboro', along the right bank of the Ogeechee River. The remainder of the march was impeded by low, broad marshes, which it was invariably found necessary to corduroy.

From Summertown to the Cannouchee, which was reached the 7th, the Third Division (General John E. Smith), with my own, formed a separate column under my command, and was somewhat exposed to annoyance from the enemy — who had been stationed at Macon under Hardee — endeavoring to reach Savannah from the west before us. On the 3d the Fifty-third Ohio lost by capture a foraging party of one officer and eleven men.

On the 4th, near Statesboro', the foragers met a brigade of the enemy's cavalry endeavoring to join Wheeler, and were attacked by them, and driven to the main column, losing by capture twenty-seven, and by wounds eight. The enemy lost two killed and two captured.

The enemy defended the crossing of the Cannouchee with infantry and two pieces of artillery, having burned the bridge. During the night of the 8th he retired; and the bridge being repaired, at eleven A. M. on the 9th two brigades were crossed, — one pushed to King's Bridge, the other brigade to a point on the Gulf Railroad, about six miles from King's Bridge.

On the 10th the division recrossed the Cannouchee, moving to and crossing the Ogeechee at Dillon's Ferry, and proceeding to near the Anderson plantation, nine miles from Savannah. On the 12th the division moved back to King's Bridge, it having received orders to cross the Ogeechee there and move down its right bank to Fort McAllister and capture it.

The march to the sea was strategically a splendid movement, its true objective being Lee's army, with Savannah as a refitting station. Tactically it was little more than a plain march of several parallel columns of troops practically unopposed. It was novel in kind, and without much risk. Hood was too far away to interpose; and if Lee had left Richmond to meet us, the great purpose of the campaign would have been effected. The enemy hovered about us with some five thousand cavalry, picking up

stragglers and making a show of resistance at the crossings of rivers. Hardee was in Macon with eight thousand
men, and felt our right flank; then brushed past to reach
Savannah before us, which his lighter troops and smaller
numbers enabled him to do. As my command composed
the right flank of the army, his troops frequently came
in collision with my foragers; but only once — at Statesboro' — did he touch the main column.

Why an army corps was not thrown to the east of the
Savannah River, which seemed practicable, and Hardee
captured with the city, I never knew. The country we
passed through was in general a poor pine barren, — so
poor that one family was found who did not know there
was a war. Yet its products of food and forage were left
undisturbed for our use; and it was ample, and in many
camps there was at least a full day's rations for all hands
left behind.

We saw a great deal of the workings of slavery, and the
negroes everywhere appreciated the full meaning of our
presence. One young woman came to consult with me as
to what they ought to do, and told me she had been given
but a half-day from the harvest-field to give birth to her
baby. We could not take many negroes with us, and they
were told so, but directed to wait until their day should come.
Among those who sought refuge with my headquarters,
getting a ride now and then in my wagons, was an old
negro woman, — so old that she could scarcely speak aloud,
and knew but few words of English. But she kept along,
and never wanted for anything we could give her. She
seemed only to think of going "out to freedom." And she
was not long in finding it; for the day after we arrived at
McAllister my man Jess came to me with the message,
"The old auntie is free now" (she had no other name).
The relaxation after her toiling journey was more than her
little spark of life could bear, and her term of "freedom"

on earth was very short. We gave her a decent burial, and there were some tearful eyes at her funeral.

We found very few people friendly to us. An occasional Northern family, as mill-owners or railroad men, were about all. One of these — a Mr. Wadleigh, engaged in railroading, formerly from New Hampshire — accompanied us from somewhere in the middle of Georgia. We left him at Savannah; but he went back to his old place, and became one of the leading railroad men of his adopted State.

## CHAPTER XXII.

### FORT McALLISTER.

THE assault and capture of Fort McAllister was the only fight of the campaign beyond Atlanta. As a feat of arms it bore no comparison to the service of my command on several other fields; but its results were of vast importance, for it gave us connection with our depot, then afloat, and crowned the campaign with a striking success. The eyes of the world were turned to that point, looking for Sherman; and the affair came thus to have a celebrity which in a tactical sense it in no way deserved. It was the only fight of the war of which I had the exclusive management, and I will briefly describe it.

On the 12th of December I established the camp of my division at Lloyd's country house, about twelve miles from Savannah. It was a scene of tropical beauty; the lemon, orange, and other plants, known to us only as exotics, were growing freely in the open air, and loading it with their fragrance. Never before or since have I been quartered in such a paradise. After about one hour of this Arcadian existence I received an order to report to General Sherman at his headquarters, then at the Anderson plantation, a couple of miles away.

I found Generals Sherman and Howard at Anderson's, and they informed me of the work required, and gave me a little map of the country about the mouth of the Ogee-chee River. On the right bank, where this stream enters the sea-marsh, Fort McAllister was situated. The division

GENERAL WILLIAM T. SHERMAN

FORT McALLISTER (WATER SIDE).

From a Pencil Sketch.

was got under arms and marched that night to King's Bridge, on the Ogeechee. The bridge had been partly destroyed by General Corse's division, but by morning was repaired so that it could be used. The command was called, and breakfasted before day; and at light, on the 13th, we moved across the bridge, and advanced along about two miles of causeway, with rice-fields on either hand. Crowds of colored people came out to see the troops at every farm-house, all chattering at the top of their voices in a jargon like a mixture of French, English, and the clatter of blackbirds. They were the rice-field hands, and seemed to me a type of humanity as distinct as the gypsies.

The day was bright; and the march, after leaving the rice-farms, was along a lovely road of shells and white sand, under magnolias and wide-branching live-oaks draped in long hanging moss. About midway we passed the old McAllister mansion, called Strother Hall, whose inmates I had known before the war. There was their home, but they had gone. Kilpatrick's cavalry had been there before us, and the contents of the house were strewn upon the floors or scattered about the lawn. I saw a few familiar articles, and was recognized by an old auntie who had been with the family at the North. The negro servants showed no disposition to put things to rights again, thinking, perhaps, that it would only invite further mischief. After I had taken steps to prevent my command from adding to the disorder, we went on, and soon met Kilpatrick at the head of his men, returning from a reconnoissance of the fort. He gave me such information of it as he had gathered. So far as it referred to the armament and garrison, subsequent events proved it to be correct.

At about one mile from the fort we came upon the advanced picket, who, though mounted, was captured by a sudden dash of my topographical officer, Mr. Scupham, and my orderlies. This scout pointed out a line of torpedoes across the road; and while with his aid we carefully removed them, I withdrew the command a half-mile to the Middleton House, where dispositions were immediately made for the assault. I made no formal demand for surrender, believing that it would merely advertise our intentions, and be met with a boastful refusal. Three regiments from each of the three brigades, nine in all, were detailed as the assailing force, and posted in a thin line just beyond musket-range, and out of sight of the fort. They reached quite across from the Ogeechee on the left to the sea-marsh on the right. This left a reserve of nine regiments, — an overwhelming force for the work in hand.

Sharpshooters were then sent forward as near to the fort as cover could be found, and the garrison driven under shelter. Up to this time the enemy had used their artillery rather noisily, but with little effect. I used none, believing it of no practical advantage, although the artillery officer present was anxious for orders. The right brigade found itself behind a little stream, or sluice, and was a long time getting across and into position. This was especially annoying, as General Sherman's last injunction was, not to find myself behind any creek, so that we could not get forward. I waited till nearly sundown, and then, the right brigade still being reported not ready, determined to assault with the other six regiments. Each officer and man was instructed to advance rapidly, but in order, until the enemy opened, and then to charge with a rush, every man for himself. The "assembly" was then sounded by the bugle three successive times, followed by the "forward," and as with a single impulse the line advanced. To my great surprise and joy the right brigade, under Colonel Theodore Jones, moved out accurately at the same moment. It had crossed the stream and formed in line just in time to receive the order.

To make the chance of hits by the enemy as small as possible, the formation was in single rank, resembling a close line of skirmishers, and there were not more than half a dozen casualties before reaching the line of torpedoes, which was continuous around the fort and about one hundred yards in front of the entanglements. Beyond these was a palisade, and then the ditch and parapet. The two flanks of the fort were the weak points, — the one on the Ogeechee side presenting a broad gravelly shore left by the receding tide. Our charge, however, carried the whole front. Our losses, which numbered one hundred and thirty, were nearly all from torpedoes, and at close quarters. The garrison did not surrender; they fought within the works, and were overcome man by man.

As I leaped upon the parapet, the first man I saw was Captain Clinch, who commanded a light battery used for defence on the land side and temporarily thrown into the fort for that purpose. He was lying on his back, shot through the arm, with a bayonet-wound in his chest, and contused by the butt of a gun. He recognized and spoke to me. He was a brother-in-law of the Union General Robert Anderson, and I had known him before the war. Contrary to my expectation, he finally recovered. The garrison was composed of young gentlemen of Savannah, and was commanded by a son of the mayor of the city, Mr. Anderson, at whose country residence General Sherman was quartered.

The fight was watched by General Sherman from a rice-mill about three miles away. After the capture he came down in a small boat, arriving at about seven o'clock in the evening, while we were at dinner at the Middleton House, my headquarters. He sat down with us, and was greatly amused at a colloquy between Anderson, the captured commander of the fort, and one of his own family servants, who was waiting on our table. "Jim, what are you doing

here?"—"I'se workin' for Mr. Hazen now." After supper
General Sherman went down the Ogeechee in a small boat,
and met Admiral Dahlgren, the commander of the fleet.
He afterwards returned and shared my blankets, spread
upon the floor. The servants of the house hunted up
and unearthed many useful articles, and our table was
bountifully provided with fine stores, especially wines
taken at McAllister. There was a dinner-party at my
headquarters every day for a week, composed of the higher
officers of the army and navy.

The neighboring region, called Bryan's Neck, had been
the home of a wealthy and cultivated society. With a few
exceptions the houses had been left in charge of servants.
They were filled with rare books, bronzes, pictures, and
other surroundings of refined life. I tried to protect all
this, but soon found it hopeless. The houses were needed
for quarters, and were soon occupied. I doubt if they
contained much of value after we vacated them. We ate
up pretty nearly everything in Bryan County; but I left
an immense storehouse full of rice, appointing a committee
of citizens to see that it was fairly distributed. Moreover,
the coast, with its numerous bays, estuaries, and inlets,
was one continuous bed of oysters; so that come what
might, there was food for the hungry.

Our service on the Ogeechee was a holiday. There were
several fine packs of hounds, and, among the negroes, many
trained drivers of game. With hunting, boating, and a
perfect table, our three weeks at McAllister were keenly
enjoyed. We had a steamboat, and made excursions to
different points on that charming coast to gather supplies.
I once went with it through the Florida Channel, on a trip
to St. Catharine's Island, where we were told there was
a large quantity of corn. I found an old plantation, with
gardens, walks, and drives, and extensive buildings entirely
shut in by an orange grove. For several years it had been

FORT McALLISTER (LAND SIDE).

EDWIN M. STANTON

(U.S. Secretary of War.)

unoccupied, except by the negroes, and it was their little store that we had come to carry away. There were several hundred bushels of corn, a few hives of bees, and some bacon. The practical foragers rushed for it, careless that it was the main resource of the poor little colony. I interposed, and made my authority felt, though with difficulty. I never saw anything so beautiful as this island. It was a mile or two in extent, lay in an almost tropical sea, and was literally bounded by a bright reef of living oysters, whose white shells glittered in the sun. The island produced the best sea-island cotton, and the hedges and groves were golden with ripe fruit. The owner had been killed in the war, his family had left the island, and at the time of our visit the buildings were falling to decay, the grounds and walks were overgrown with rank weeds, the little wharf at the landing was rotting down, and the very negroes seemed sinking into decay also. Their silent tears, when they feared for their scanty stores, would have moved a heart of stone.

Soon after New-year's Day we went to Savannah. I was quartered with Mr. Octavus Cohen, an old acquaintance, whose interesting and estimable family I had also known. Mr. Stanton met us here. It was my first introduction to him. He came down, bringing the congratulations of the President, and to do what might be in his power to further our work.. He had in his portfolio but one gift of the magnitude of a major-general's commission, and, greatly to my surprise, it fell to me. I was told that the general officers of the Army of the Tennessee asked it for me; but this I never positively knew.

The people of Savannah displayed great good sense in their reception and treatment of our army. And they in turn, and their parks, trees, and property generally, received that care and protection which robs war of half its asperity.

# CHAPTER XXIII.

## SOUTH CAROLINA CAMPAIGN.

AFTER resting and refitting, we marched on the 14th of January, 1865, to Thunderbolt Bay, to embark for Beaufort, South Carolina, where we arrived on the following day, after a rough and in every way uncomfortable passage. On marching from Savannah to the place of embarkation we passed the residence of the Rebel Commodore, Tatnall, where the colored division of General Cuvier Grover had just arrived, and were busy tearing down the house, — a large wooden one, — to get material for their bivouac. At Beaufort we found General Rufus Saxton, who was on duty there organizing colored troops. We remained for several days at a point a few miles north of Beaufort, repairing the roads to Port Royal Ferry, in the direction of Pocotaligo. The weather became very cold while we were here. The wind was filled with sand and dust, and blew severely, making our stay uncomfortable. The military occupancy of Beaufort had prevented the abuse of private property at that place; but no sooner had we passed Pocotaligo than the demon of destruction seized possession of everybody. South Carolina had fired the first gun, and even the smallest drummer-boy seemed determined to get even. This feeling was not confined to the army, nor even to the North. Often have I heard Georgians say: "Why don't you go over to South Carolina, and serve them this way? They started it."

We were not out of sight of Port Royal Ferry when the black columns of smoke began to ascend. Within half a mile of Pocotaligo we halted near a large farm-house while the head of the column was skirmishing. As we waited here, I was requested by a staff-officer to send and burn the house. I did give the order, but quickly withdrew it, and sent my men away. This did not save the house, which was soon in flames. Here began a carnival of destruction that ended with the burning of Columbia, in which the frenzy seemed to exhaust itself. There was scarcely a building far or near on the line of that march that was not burned. Often have I seen this work going on in the presence of the highest officers, with no word of disapproval. I never could bring myself to aid in the destruction of private property, and always did all I could to prevent it. I called one day at a large, handsome house, and found a beautiful and refined lady in charge of it. She proved to be a relative of Dr. Brodie, of Charleston, formerly of the army, a very dear friend of mine, who had tended me in Texas, before the war, during a long sickness from wounds received in Indian warfare. Her house was such a home as only a cultivated woman can make. She expected to be told at any moment that it was on fire, but never lost her perfect composure, though the effort at self-control showed itself in a slight quivering of the lip. No like episode of the war impressed me so much. I called a trusty staff-officer, and directed him to remain with two orderlies until the army and stragglers had passed, and see that no harm came to anything. The gratitude of the lady was unbounded. I was very happy, and rode on, feeling that I had done a good act. But at night my officer reported that, supposing he had fully executed his orders, he came forward, and was not out of sight of the house when it was in flames. Stragglers loitering behind had no doubt fired it.

A day or so after this I entered a fine residence, and found it occupied by an old lady and her two daughters. They were seated in a plain room in the rear of the house, and were all knitting. They received my inquiries with a sullen and stolid manner, and showed no concern or interest in what was passing. I tried to save the place, and called my staff and orderlies to aid me; but the out-buildings were soon in flames. We then devoted our efforts entirely to the dwelling-house; but to no purpose, for it took fire in two or three places, and was consumed. The occupants quietly walked out, without acknowledging my efforts in their behalf, and with apparent indifference to the ruin of their home. Thus we soldiered in South Carolina. An order prohibiting the destruction of property in any particular case was of no effect beyond one's immediate presence and power to enforce it.

In Georgia, and especially in South Carolina, a great deal of road-making was necessary. Long stretches of marsh and quicksand required corduroying, and my command became very expert at it. The amount of work of which a large body of troops is capable is almost incredible. When the will is right, the question is one merely of organization. The entire army felt a joyous enthusiasm in the realization of the vast effect our campaign was having upon the war. The men had only to be shown what was wanted, and it was soon done. The rapidity of the road-making was remarkable, and our march was scarcely impeded by obstacles thought by the enemy to be insurmountable. A river with well-defined banks is easily crossed by a well-appointed army; but when flanked by broad marshes, especially in high stages of water, it becomes more difficult.

I quote from my diary : —

*January* 14. Command marched at six A. M. for Thunder-bolt Bay, which we reached, and camped at nine A. M., and prepared to embark for Beaufort as rapidly as possible. One regiment, the Fifteenth Michigan, embarked at five P. M. on steamer "Louise."

*January* 15. The remainder of the Third Brigade embarked to-day for and arrived at Beaufort, South Carolina. Distance, sixty miles.

*January* 16. The remainder of the command, except the supply train and two regiments, having arrived from Thunderbolt, camp was established two miles from the city (Beaufort).

*January* 19–24. Remained in same camp, during which time the troops were exercised in company and battalion drills and evolutions of the line.

*January* 24. To-day nine regiments, three from each brigade, were distributed along the shell road to Port Royal Ferry for the purpose of repairing the road, and commenced the work.

The following orders were issued : —

BEAUFORT, S. C., Jan. 20, 1865.

General orders first published on assuming command of the division, requiring the hair to be kept short, having been in many cases disregarded, hereafter any enlisted man of the command seen with long, slovenly locks will be arrested and put at hard labor.

Officers are reminded that they have been no less derelict with regard to themselves than with their men.

The practice in many commands of allowing soldiers to wear officers' badges, and those of other arms of the service, is not only prohibited by all the rules of the service, but by this order.

It is difficult to account for the laxity of commanding officers in such matters, and their attention is urged to a more clear regard for duty.

BEAUFORT, S. C., Jan. 20, 1865.

Commanding officers are directed to make all necessary preparations for an immediate campaign. The division will remain at or near its present position until the army moves, which will not be for several days.

The same allowance of transportation as on the last campaign, namely, one wagon per regiment, two per brigade, and three per division, will probably be given.

No negro women or children will be permitted to leave this point with the troops. Commanders will see that on leaving here each of their enlisted men carries one shelter-tent. While lying at this point, the weather permitting, each regiment will be exercised in the drill of the battalion from twenty minutes past nine to eleven A. M. each day, and in evolutions of the line from half past-two to four P. M. each day.

POCOTALIGO, S. C., Jan. 31, 1865.

In compliance with orders from superior headquarters, General Orders No. 55, of date Oct. 17, 1864, is republished.

While on the present campaign, foraging, in accordance with existing orders, will constitute one of the means of subsisting the command. Each brigade commander will appoint a suitable officer, who shall have control of all foraging for the brigade, and will be held responsible for the proper conduct of parties sent out with him. These parties shall be as numerous as the wants of the command may require, shall always be held under proper control, shall be in charge of an officer or non-commissioned officer, and shall carry their authority for foraging in writing. Foragers have no authority to discharge fire-arms, except at the enemy. They will under no pretence pillage houses, but may take from them salt, flour, meal, and meat, if by so doing they do not leave the occupants destitute. . . .

OSWALL'S CROSS-ROADS, S. C., Feb. 4, 1865.

Brigade commanders are directed to organize into pioneer corps for labor on roads and other purposes all unarmed men and superfluous servants now or that may hereafter be in their commands. They are also directed to gather up able-bodied negroes for this service. They will be borne on the rolls of the brigade quartermasters as pioneer laborers, and will receive ten dollars per month, with rations. No clothing will be issued them beyond the amount due for labor, which will be charged against their pay. . .

ANGLESEY'S POST-OFFICE, S. C., Feb. 4, 1865.

This campaign will bring the troops of the army into constant proximity with the light troops of the enemy, and the utmost caution is enjoined upon the command at all times. Whenever any party of any size, on or off duty, goes beyond the line of pickets, the utmost precaution should be observed, and arms ready for use will always be carried ; and to this end the riding in vehicles, excepting by the sick, is prohibited.

A strict observance of the above by every officer and soldier of the command will save to the division many valuable men. . . .

NEAR LIBERTY HILL, S. C., Feb. 22, 1865.

Major MAX WOODHULL, Assist. Adj.-Gen. 15th Army Corps :

I have the honor to state that until the reception of Special Orders No. 55 of this date from headquarters Fifteenth Army Corps, I had supposed the mounting of foragers authorized, if not in orders, at least from custom and necessity. Upon this supposition I had directed my brigade commanders to mount about five per centum of their commands for the purpose of gathering food.

They had done this at no little trouble, and had just reported that they could subsist their brigades with but little assistance from the Commissary Department. This cannot be done without mounting the foragers ; and as our main supplies must be derived in this way, I would most respectfully call especial attention to the subject.

Late orders regulating issues from the wagons make it necessary for each division of the army to procure from the country about seven thousand pounds of food daily, which amounts do not exist along the immediate line of march, but must be procured from points more or less remote along the flanks. It is as much as footmen can do to make long marches along the straight line of the road.

Since foraging was adopted as one of the means of subsisting the army, I have given the subject the closest attention, and have at no time permitted more men to be mounted than the minimum number necessary to perform the duty ; and unless they are so authorized, or mount themselves without authority, this command cannot be properly fed. This is corroborated by all my brigade commanders, who with myself desire only the best interests of the service.

On the late campaign in Georgia I found no difficulty in supplying my command, and furnished twenty-two thousand rations to needy troops when the campaign closed, and at no time had more than five per cent of my men mounted, and never had them dismounted. Should this arrangement be broken up, my supplies will fall short of what is absolutely required.[1]

The journal now completes the narrative.

*January* 25. In compliance with orders, Captain De Gress, commanding Battery H, First Illinois Light Artillery, reported to this command for duty.

*January* 26. To-day the command moved out to Gray's Hill, seven miles from the city of Beaufort, where it camped, having marched five miles.

*January* 27. Finished repairing the road to-day, having built, since the 24th, three thousand six hundred and seventy yards of corduroy.

*January* 28. In the same place, preparing for the campaign.

*January* 29. The supply-train and remainder of troops having arrived by water, arrangements for marching were made by drawing supplies, etc. The command was reviewed this afternoon by General Hazen.

*January* 30. Marched this morning at seven o'clock, crossing the Coosaw River at Port Royal Ferry, and taking the Pocotaligo road, which point we reached at two P. M., then moved on to Pocotaligo Station, on the Charleston and Savannah Railroad, where we camped at half-past three P. M., having marched seventeen miles. We found in command here General Van Wyck, of New York.[2]

---

[1] This correspondence concerned an order issued by General Logan, who, not having been on the Georgia campaign, was unacquainted with the system of foraging, which he prohibited, but afterward found necessary to recognize.

[2] General Van Wyck is now United States Senator from Nebraska.

*February* 1. Marched at seven A. M., reaching McPherson-ville, five miles, at 8.45 A. M., where we halted one hour, then moved on through Brailfordsville to Sand Hill Church, near Alligator Creek, where we camped, having marched thirteen miles.

*February* 2. Marched at half-past six A. M., crossing Alligator Creek, and during the day many swamps, on account of which the march was very severe, the infantry marching on the right of the road and crossing all the swamps on felled trees. The enemy was encountered a few miles from Loper's Cross-Roads, but driven without difficulty beyond that point by two regiments of the First Brigade. Two of the enemy were killed, and five of our own men wounded. Camped at this point, having marched seventeen miles.

*February* 3. Remained in same position during the day. The Third Brigade effected a crossing of Duck Creek this morning. One gun of De Gress's Battery was engaged. The enemy was driven three miles beyond the creek. Our casualties were one man killed and one officer wounded. Captured one prisoner.

*February* 4. This morning thirty wagons from the supply-train were sent back for additional supplies. Several men who had the small-pox were sent also. The command marched at twelve M. on the road to Anglesey's Post-Office, which was reached at five P. M., distance eight miles. The road was corduroyed nearly all the way by three regiments sent ahead of the column. Had a slight skirmish with the enemy this evening, who captured two horses and wounded two men. One Rebel was killed.

*February* 5. Marched at nine A. M., crossing the Great Salke-hatchie on Buford Bridge, six miles and a half from Anglesey's, at twelve M. Marched one mile after crossing on Barnwell road, where we camped at three P. M., having marched eight miles.

*February* 6. Marched at twelve M. on Orangeburg road in rear of column, crossing Little Salkehatchie at dark, and camped at Springtown Church, one mile from the river, at half-past eight P. M., having marched eight miles. Rained all night. The thirty wagons sent from Loper's Cross-Roads joined the column, not having any supplies, as they had been turned back at Hickory Hill. Captured one prisoner to-day.

*February* 7.   Cold and rainy.   Marched at daylight in rear of First Division, and on the Orangeburg road, reaching the Charleston and Augusta Railroad at Bambery Station at eleven A. M., and camped one mile west, having marched eight miles.   The Third Brigade destroyed one mile of the railroad toward Midway.

*February* 8.   Remained in same position to-day.   The First Brigade destroyed one-half mile of railroad toward Midway.   The Second Brigade made a reconnoissance to Cannon's Bridge over the Edisto River, finding the bridge burned and enemy intrenched on opposite side, and returned to camp.

*February* 9.   Marched at daylight on Charleston and Augusta road, passing Binnaker's Bridge road, crossing Byer's and Syke's creeks, and taking road to Holman's Bridge, where, finding enemy on opposite side, went into position, having marched eleven miles.   The First Brigade was sent forward to reconnoitre and effect a crossing.   One battalion crossed on fallen trees three fourths of a mile above the bridge, advanced into the swamp beyond, and night coming on, were unable to accomplish anything. Casualties, two men wounded.   To-night the enemy retired on the road to Columbia.

*February* 10.   The First Brigade crossed at nine A. M., and went into position at Forks of Orangeburg and Columbia roads. Three fourths of a mile of corduroy had to be made beyond the bridge for the infantry to cross the swamp.   The remainder of the division crossed at four P. M. and moved out a mile and a half on Columbia road, where it camped, and intrenched the position, having marched two miles and a half.

*February* 11.   Marched at daylight on Orangeburg road in advance, crossing several small streams and arriving at Poplar Springs at four P. M. where we camped, having marched fifteen miles.   Intrenched this position.

*February* 12.   Marched at seven A. M. in advance, reaching Shilling's Bridge (four miles) at nine A. M., finding the bridge burned and enemy intrenched on the opposite side.   The Second Brigade was sent forward to cross, the enemy engaging them sharply.   At eleven A. M. a crossing of one brigade was effected on fallen trees and rafts at two different points above the bridge. At the same time the First and Third brigades crossed two miles below. In crossing, a swamp three fourths of a mile in width and waist-deep was encountered, which all the officers and men, including the general commanding and staff, waded with cheerfulness and enthusiasm. The Second Brigade drove the enemy from his works, killing two and capturing fifty-seven. Our casualties were five men wounded.

The First and Third brigades, under the immediate command of General Hazen, having crossed below, moved forward and struck the Orangeburg road four miles from that point, where they camped. The Second Brigade joined them at eleven P. M. The trains were also brought forward. Distance marched, seven miles.

*February* 13. Marched at eight A. M. in rear of Third Division, crossing Can-Can Swamp, then taking a neighboring road across to the Columbia road, on which we crossed Saddler's and Little Crotchpen swamps, camping on south side of Big Crotchpen Swamp, having marched thirteen miles. Captured one prisoner.

*February* 14. Marched at half-past six A. M. in advance and on Columbia road, crossing Big Beaver Creek at ten A. M. Arrived at Sandy Run Post-Office at one P. M., and crossed Sandy Run, and moved forward three miles and a half to Thomas Creek, in support of First Division, where we camped, having marched seventeen miles. Captured seven prisoners.

*February* 15. Marched at seven A. M. on old State road, in rear of First Division, which encountered the enemy at Congaree Creek, where one gun of De Gress's Battery was engaged. As soon as the First Division had crossed, the Second followed, taking up a position on the right of First Division, the right resting near the Congaree River, and in front of the enemy's line. This position was intrenched. Marched nine miles. At night the enemy opened a battery from the opposite bank of the Congaree, on our right flank, which had come out of Columbia for that purpose, enfilading and shelling our line most severely. One officer and two men were wounded.

*February* 16. The skirmish line was thrown forward this morning on the Columbia road, reaching the Congaree Bridge, in front of Columbia, four miles, at daylight. The bridge had been destroyed, the enemy having retired across it during the night. The column moved forward at eight A. M., the enemy firing from the opposite bank and wounding two men severely. One section of De Gress's Battery and a regiment of sharpshooters engaged the battery on the opposite bank, and succeeded in silencing it for the time. One section was brought forward, and was engaged in shelling the city. It being deemed impracticable to attempt a crossing at the Congaree Bridge, the command moved at eleven A. M. two miles up the river to the Saluda Bridge, which having been burned, two regiments of the First Brigade were crossed on pontoon boats and pushed forward, driving the enemy from the opposite bank. The remainder of this brigade, supported by the rest of the command, followed as soon as the pontoon bridge was laid, driving the enemy rapidly across the creek to, and over, the Broad River Bridge, but did not succeed in saving it from being fired and burned by the enemy. The command camped at this point at half-past five P. M., having marched eight miles. Casualties, one officer and two men wounded. Captured eight prisoners.

*February* 17. The command moved at about mid-day in rear of the corps, leaving the trains behind, and crossing Broad River on the pontoon bridge. Marched through the city of Columbia at half-past five P. M., and took position one mile beyond, on the Columbia and South Carolina Railroad, having marched five miles.

*February* 18. The Third Brigade was sent through the city at three A. M., to clear it and prevent the further destruction of property. The division was employed during the day in destroying the railroad.

*February* 19. The command finished destroying the portion of railroad assigned to it and the Fourth Division (seven miles and a half) ; and in addition three 10-pounder Parrott guns, a large amount of machinery for rolling-mills and foundry, and six stationary engines were destroyed. Captured seven prisoners.

# CHAPTER XXIV.

## THE BURNING OF COLUMBIA.

A S we were approaching Columbia on the 15th of February there was sharp skirmishing on the west side of the Congaree, at a point about twelve miles distant from the city. A small stream, Congaree Creek, puts in here, and the enemy from behind this stream, which was parallel to our front, offered considerable resistance, and endeavored to detain us. They were driven off, and toward evening Woods's division, followed by my own, crossed, and both then moved forward in line to within three miles of Columbia. I was on the right, with my right flank about one half-mile from the Congaree, and nearly at right angles to it. As our line could be enfiladed from across the river, a good infantry work was thrown up, and a number of traverses constructed. At about midnight the Rebels brought down a light battery from Columbia, stationed it on their side of the river, and kept up a desultory fire until nearly morning. My loss was one officer and three men. The damage was small, but the annoyance great. We were all driven to dig holes in the ground to lie in, and the shrieking of shot in the darkness just over us was unpleasant beyond expression. They withdrew, and at daylight I pushed on to the little clump of houses on the bank of the Congaree, opposite Columbia, at the end of the long bridge, which had been burned in the night. The town was already up, and in great alarm. The main street leading down to the bridge was filled with citizens and a sprinkling of cavalry, all rushing about in evident excitement. Just across the river, at easy musket-range, were the cadets from the citadel working away like ants, with pick and spade, at a flank defence for the piers, to be used in case we should try to relay the bridge. They were such young things, — mere boys, — that I prohibited any firing upon them. I then directed a few shots from a 6-pound battery up the street at some cavalrymen. This had a magical effect in clearing the street.

General Sherman came up at this moment, and called my attention to the railroad station, round which a great crowd had collected. He said that it was full of corn and flour, which we must have; and that the crowd were carrying the provisions away. A few well-aimed shots at the building — not at the people — put a stop to this. He then directed me to turn the guns and fire six shots at the new, unfinished State House. Captain De Gress, of the famous De Gress's Battery, delivered the shots, the marks of which will be pointed out for generations to come. I then sent one brigade up to Saluda Factory, on the Saluda River, three or four miles above the city, and about two miles above where the Saluda and Broad unite to form the Congaree. The bridge here had been burned. We found some small boats, and one large enough to cross horses; and getting a regiment over with a few horsemen, we drove the enemy's pickets rapidly across the tongue of land between the two streams, and tried by a sudden dash to save the bridge over the Broad. I was with this party, but we failed; for it had been prepared with tinder, which the retiring guard set on fire, and the fine covered bridge was soon in flames throughout its entire length. We at once laid a pontoon bridge over the Saluda, and my division was marched across that night. Details from it were directed to lay the pontoons across the Broad, and this work was finished at daylight on the 17th.

*Francis De Gress*

Captain Francis De Gress was a mere youth, but the best artillerist in the
Western armies. He was born February 4, 1841, at Cologne, Prussia, and
when nine years old entered the Royal Military Academy at Bensburg,
Prussia, where he remained until 1854. During that year he left the Academy
and joined his father in New York. In 1856 he moved to Cape Girardeau, Mo.
After the war he was engaged in business in Mexico, and died in 1884.

GENERAL CHARLES R. WOODS

A small detachment of cavalry was at once sent over, and soon met a deputation coming out from Columbia to surrender the city.  General Logan, the corps commander, told me that my division was entitled to enter the city first; but as we were worn out by two sleepless nights, I waived the privilege.  I have always regretted this decision.  General Charles R. Woods's division was at once sent across and took possession.  At about mid-day my command followed, headed by General Logan and myself. We advanced along the main street, on which General Woods's division was standing at rest, with arms stacked, with but few officers present.  In this street cotton-bales were piled in long lines, and it had been fired by the departing enemy.  The engines were on the street, and had evidently been at work putting out the fire in the cotton, which still smoked in a few places.  The fire was completely under control, and was nowhere blazing.  A dozen men with tin cups could have managed it.  I saw no officers of rank with the troops.  A great many men had left their places, and were straggling about the city.  Many of the people were fraternizing with the soldiers, and even treating them, very unwisely, to wines and liquors, which were passed along the line in buckets and tin pans, and in one instance in a large tin boiler such as is used on kitchen stoves.  Many men in the ranks were already drunk.  All this I noticed as we marched by.  I passed through the city, and posted my division about a half-mile to the south of it.  The men were still too sleepy to care much about sight-seeing, and few of them left camp that evening.

I observed, as I passed along the street, that many shops had been gutted, and that paper, rags, and litter of all kinds lay scattered on the floors, in the open doorways, and on the ground outside.  I was told on good authority that this had been done by the Confederate troops before our arrival. It was a windy day, and a great deal of loose cotton had been blown about and caught on the fences and in the branches of the shade trees along the street. It has been said that this had something to do with spreading the fire which afterward took place. I think this very doubtful.

There were in the city a large number of Union officers — probably from one to two hundred — who were prisoners of war, properly belonging to a prison camp over the river, but permitted to live in the city, who were liberated by our arrival. They had suffered great hardships, and were in a wretched condition, — dressed for the most part in shirts and pantaloons, without hats or shoes. They were overjoyed at their deliverance, and justly indignant at their treatment. They spoke, however, with warm gratitude of the kindness of the ladies of Columbia.

I spent the afternoon in riding about, and at sundown went again from my quarters to the city just as a fire broke out in several places in a clump of isolated wooden buildings a little to the north of the principal hotel. A few men could easily have torn these buildings away and prevented the fire from extending.

I met Colonel W. B. Woods, who commanded a brigade in the division of his brother, General Charles R. Woods, and was provost-marshal of the city, and suggested that he take his guard and pull the buildings down. He told me that he could not get men enough together to do any good. This seemed to annoy him very much. I then rode to General Sherman's headquarters in the eastern suburb of the city, and took supper with him. On finishing our meal we went into the yard, and saw the darkness lit up with the lurid hue of a conflagration. He remarked regretfully, "They have brought it on themselves." I mounted my horse and hurried to the city. The houses on the main street were now burning in many places along nearly its whole length. The fire could not have been communicated from the clump of houses I first saw burning. It was evident that incendiaries had been actively at work. The buildings were mainly of wood, and the wind was carrying large sheets of blazing siding and shingles high into the air, and landing them hundreds of yards away, on the roofs of buildings, all over the eastern part of the city. The wind now set in with great force, much increased by the fire itself. Any general effort to stop the conflagration would have been entirely useless.

I sent for my staff and orderlies, and went to the residence of a gentleman in the eastern part of the town, where I had casually stopped in the afternoon and been treated with marked courtesy. Hoping to save his house, I at first posted my party on all the outbuildings, but soon found that my men were too much dispersed, and pressed some passing soldiers of General Woods's divison to aid us. They obeyed readily, but went off as soon as my back was turned. As fast as I could get others they also slipped away. The outbuildings were soon on fire, and we turned all our efforts to saving the dwelling. A deep well contained our only supply of water. A line of men passed buckets from the well to the roof, which was kept wet, while others with brooms and boards swept off the fast-falling flakes of fire. By these means, and in a perpetual blast of almost red-hot air, we kept down the fire until all the buildings in the vicinity were entirely consumed, excepting one just across the street to the north. The house now seemed safe; and as it was past midnight and I was nearly exhausted, — it being my third sleepless night, — I posted a few men on the roof, out of abundant caution, and started for the burnt district, intending soon to go to bed. I had not ridden two squares, when on looking back at the house I saw that there was not a man on it, and that a little flame was going up from the end of the roof nearest to the blazing building across the street. All my three hours of effort had gone for nothing.[1]

I rode on to the heart of the city, and stopped at the residence of a gentleman I had met during the day, whose name, I think, was Mordecai. His house was of brick; but every one said that it could not be saved, and he had given it up. I found there a number of staff-officers. We were agreeably entertained by the host and his accomplished daughter, who played the piano delightfully, while her father passed us sherry in delicate glasses. They made no attempt to save anything, and nothing in their manner indicated anything unusual. At last our host said, " My daughter, it is time to go ! " We all walked out, chatting pleasantly together. I noticed that the shutters were already on fire. I saw no more of the family, but was much gratified the next day to see that the house had not burned. This incident impressed me deeply. It was a striking instance of a quiet, well-bred stoicism, which was a noticeable trait of the better people of South Carolina. I have never quite known how to understand it.

I now went to my camp, and had just closed my eyes, when I was awakened by an orderly from corps headquarters with an order from General Logan to patrol the city, and arrest all soldiers and disorderly persons.[2] I detailed for patrol duty General John M. Oliver and his brigade. They marched to the north end of the city, and deploying, moved through the town like a drag-net. The

---

[1] I may mention here, that I was once called off from my fireman's work by a message from a house some distance to the south, to the effect that a party of men were endeavoring to fire it. When I arrived in answer to the message the party had gone.

[2] I may say, in passing, that General Logan's headquarters were at the fine residence of Mr. Preston, the father-in-law of General Wade Hampton, in the northern part of the city. The house was filled with rare works of art, and received excellent care at the hands of General Logan.

haul was by no means a light one. About twenty-five hundred citizens and soldiers, including officers of nearly every grade, were turned over to the provost-marshal.

The sight when day opened was most saddening. An oppressive stillness prevailed. The solid portion of the city was in ashes. In the vicinity of the unfinished capitol there was a bed of quick-lime where the day before, stored in wooden sheds, had been acres of beautiful marble capitals, cornices, pilasters, columns, and mouldings. Crowds of homeless women and children were gathered in the public squares.

The citadel at Columbia was blown up at ten o'clock on the morning of the 19th. It was a grand sight. While our men were removing the fixed ammunition to the river, a pile of shells exploded on the bank and killed and burned many people. These, with the loss of one man at the fire, were our only casualties at Columbia.

Thus the city where secession was first proclaimed was turned to ashes. I have never doubted that Columbia was deliberately set on fire in more than a hundred places. No one ordered it, and no one could stop it. The officers of high rank would have saved the city if possible; but the army was deeply imbued with the feeling that as South Carolina had begun the war she must suffer a stern retribution. The idea that South Carolina was in a special and peculiar sense the originator of rebellion is a very common, but in my opinion a superficial and mistaken notion. It matters little where the first overt act was committed. The egg was laid by the importation of slavery. The incubation had been going on ever since. The age doomed slavery, and war was inevitable. The issue involved, for those who owned slaves, the loss of property worth thousands of millions of dollars. No such sum was ever surrendered without bloodshed, and it was absurd to expect it.

We saw very little of the citizens of South Carolina. They impressed me as a highly cultured people. The farming and roads were the best I had seen in the Southern States. The maps of the country were accurate, and were the only ones of any value we found in the South.

# CHAPTER XXV.

## CAMPAIGN IN NORTH CAROLINA.

ON the 20th of February we left Columbia and moved on toward Cheraw. We were accompanied by a multitude of fugitives, both white and black. They formed in my division a separate column, under the direction of two rescued Union officers, — Captain Burbank and Lieutenant Mitchell, of the Thirty-second Maine Infantry. This column had its own camps and its own foraging parties, and also looked after its transportation. The fugitives gave very little trouble. There were several families of high respectability among them. As we advanced, the negroes along the route joined us in great numbers, many of them clad in garments strangely and wonderfully made of an infinity of old patches. On the 24th we passed Camden, that old landmark of Revolutionary fame. Here was a mounted home-guard on duty for some inscrutable purpose. Among our captures was a clergyman, with his horse and shot-gun. He was a man of Jacksonian type, and not at all unsocial, but never would give much account of himself. After keeping him a couple of days, I restored all his property and released him. For several days I had two divisions in my column. One of the sub-columns captured a platoon of venerable home-guards, with their arms and ammunition carefully packed away in a wagon. I did not turn these old gentlemen over to the provost-guard, but gave them some tents near my headquarters. In the evening they all came over to my camp-fire, and

entertained me with an account of their novel war experiences.    Each man had some peculiar and personal
malady, an account of which figured largely in the conversation.    In the morning I had a handsome walking-
stick cut for each, gave them a good breakfast, and let
them go.    They thanked me pleasantly for their enter-
tainment, liked the walking-sticks, and did not see the
joke.

We captured besides several staff-officers, and let most
of them go, as they were non-combatants.    They were an
agreeable, gentlemanly set of men.    One of them — Captain
Devoreau, a commissary — had ridden out of Camden on a
by-road to avoid us, but on turning a corner found himself
not more than ten paces away from the head of my column.
He wore a new uniform and tight boots.    At the first opportunity I sent him to corps headquarters, where he was
turned in with the common crowd of prisoners.    It had
been raining for a week, and the roads were wretched.
Two days later, who should appear at my quarters, an hour
or so behind the column, but Captain Devoreau in charge
of a guard ?    He was a sad sight, and sank down before
me with an inimitable expression of misery, humor, and
supplication.    He joined in the laugh at his own expense.
He had never marched before, and was completely used up,
and told his guard that he might shoot him, or do anything he pleased with him ; whereupon I wrote a receipt,
and the guard went away.    We gave him a seat at table
and a horse to ride, and he remained with us until the
final peace.    Two days later we captured a bank *in tran-
situ*, and I turned over to him a large sum of Confederate
money, worthless to us, but which he sent back to his wife
at Camden, to keep her, as he said, from starvation.    Before he got his horse he rode in an ambulance with our
cook, who was very black.    One day a soldier, thinking
that he would take a short ride unobserved, was climbing

into the ambulance, when he caught sight of the occupants, and cried out, " Good God, boys! a Johnny and a nigger!" and declined their company.   Captain Devoreau after that avoided the ambulance.

On the 26th we reached Lynch's Creek, — at ordinary times an inconsiderable stream crossed by a two-span bridge.   We found it a seething torrent half a mile wide, and for the greater part of the distance about four feet deep.   We waited until the 28th for it to subside, when, as it was still slowly rising, I set to work to build a bridge; and in just twenty hours, with only the men and tools of my command, actually built a bridge nineteen hundred feet long on ninety trestles, over which an army corps passed in safety.   This was the exact spot occupied by Gates, De Kalb, and Lord Rawdon just before the battle of Camden.

We then passed on through constant rains to Cheraw, where we arrived on the 4th of March.   We were detained two or three days on the way in corduroying the roads and assisting the trains.   The Seventeenth Corps had reached the town about two days before us; and its commander, General Blair, and nearly all the officers of high rank were already settled in comfortable quarters.   General Blair had found at the house which he occupied a large cellar of fine sherry, which he distributed to the several corps and division commanders with impartial liberality.   It lasted us through the campaign.   The wine had probably been sent up from Charleston for safe keeping.

My own quarters at Cheraw were at the residence of a most amiable and respectable citizen, who was judge of one of the courts.   He assigned to me, with my approval, one half of his house, including a very good library, on which he claimed to set great store.   He proposed to remove the books; but I assured him that there was no occasion for doing so, as no one at my headquarters ever disturbed property in the houses we occupied, and that books especially would be held sacred. He was perfectly satisfied, and went away. A few minutes after, General Sherman came in. He is a rapid and constant reader, and his eyes at once fell upon the library. He examined it closely, and ended by appropriating such volumes of Scott's novels as he just then happened to want. He was taking a course of Scott at the time, and read the full series during that campaign. I expostulated, and he remarked in a pleasant way that it made no difference, as he would leave as many more in town. I was annoyed, and was on my way to account to my host for the books as best I could, when, with a great racket, my chief orderly came down-stairs collaring a fine-looking, well-dressed young man whom he had captured in the garret. On my first taking possession of the house the judge had requested me to make no search of the premises, assuring me that there was nothing concealed. On this assurance I had given directions in accordance with my host's wishes. My orderly, however, had become suspicious, and instituted a search on his own responsibility. The appearance of the prisoner, who was the judge's son, and a Rebel customs-officer from Charleston, and was hidden away with the knowledge of his father, completely nonplussed the latter; so that when I told him about the books and proposed that we should call it even, he felt perfectly satisfied. No man ever lived who was more thoroughly free from venal taint than General Sherman; but he claimed, and perhaps rightly, that reading-matter was necessary food, and that we had a right to forage for it.

On the day following our arrival at Cheraw we moved toward Fayetteville, and reached that place on the 12th. We crossed Cape Fear River about six miles below the city, and here I was assigned the duty of detaining the refugees who accompanied us, preparatory to sending them by boat to Wilmington, North Carolina. As we crossed, a guard on the other side turned these people away from the column into a great field, which they seemed nearly to fill. I then issued rations for their immediate use, and detailed Colonel John Windsor of an Illinois regiment, with two companies of troops as an escort. I attended in person when the rations were issued. A drizzling rain was falling, and it was a singular and pathetic sight, as the refugees, without shelter from the weather, of all ages and both sexes, with skins from the fairest Saxon to the blackest Ethiopian, some with delicate patrician features, and some of the most grotesque negro type, came forward in turn, and held out their hats, bonnets, handkerchiefs, aprons, and their skirts, — some of silk and others of the coarsest tow, — to receive the army bounty. We made them as comfortable as our facilities permitted, and sent them off. What became of them at Wilmington I never knew.

We remained at Fayetteville two days, destroyed the arsenal and public buildings, and then moved on toward Goldsboro'. On the 19th we reached the vicinity of Bentonville. During the afternoon the sound of distant artillery and the appearance of an occasional straggler told that an engagement was going on. I could not start until three P. M. on that day, and at dark had just reached a remarkable swale, or swamp, about five miles across, traversed by the worst road of the whole campaign. Our camp was on the other side. I reached camp at 11 P. M., and disposed my men for the night, when I was ordered to retrace my steps and report to General Slocum, who had been seriously engaged. We marched back across the swale to our last camp, then turned north, and reached Slocum's command at Harper's house at daylight on the 20th. My force was at once posted on the right flank, and in the afternoon was slightly engaged, losing three officers and twenty-six men. Later in the day Major-General Mower carried our attack quite around the right flank of the enemy, which induced him to retire that night; and soon after we moved over to Goldsboro', where we arrived on the 24th. Here we were reinforced by General Schofield with the Army of the Ohio, and by a corps under General Terry; and the war seemed unmistakably drawing to a close.

This was a point of general refitting, and our lines and camps were posted with a deliberation and accuracy we had not seen since commencing the Atlanta campaign. My own front, with its works, palisading, approach, and picket line, was the finest I ever saw in the war; and an attack upon it would have given me no more anxiety than a parade for muster. The patrolling parties of the enemy were very active, and captured some of our foragers, with their stores; but our losses here and at Bentonville were trifling. Drills were resumed; and when, on the 10th of April, the Army of the Tennessee set out for Raleigh, it was in better condition than I had ever seen it. It was, in fact, with certain exceptions, as nearly perfect, in instruction, equipment, and general efficiency, as volunteer troops can be made while in the field.

We reached Raleigh on the 14th, after an easy and uneventful march, and went into camp four miles beyond the city. The next morning we heard of General Johnson's proposition to surrender his forces. The news of Lee's surrender reached us about the same time. Then came a delightful sense of perfect rest after the accomplishment of a long and toilsome work, — a sudden relief from tension, and from the half apprehension, present in the mind for years, that the next moment might bring the fatal bullet. As the day broke next morning, the band, without direction, burst out in that soul-stirring air, "The Star-Spangled Banner." The effect was electrical; and a spontaneous shout went up from near and far, that beat the Rebel cheer at Chickamauga out of sight. It seemed as if no such music was ever heard before. It was one of those supreme moments, a few of which occur in every lifetime, which we would not miss for a year of ordinary existence.

We moved back near the city, and there enjoyed a few weeks of delightful rest, with just enough of duty to give it a relish. It was here that we learned of the death of Mr. Lincoln, and the final peace; and from this point we set out for our homes.

The journal shows our daily work.

*Feb.* 20, 1865. Marched on Camden road in rear of Third Division eleven miles and a half; then taking road to Muddy Springs, marched nine miles and a half, when we camped at half-past six P. M., having marched twenty-one miles. The One Hundred and Twenty-seventh Illinois reported back to the division for duty, having been relieved from special service at department headquarters.

NEAR POPLAR SPRINGS, S. C., Feb. 21, 1865.

.    .    .    .    .    .    .    .    .

II. Captain A. H. Heath, Ninety-ninth Indiana Volunteer Infantry, is hereby appointed commanding officer of the division pioneer corps, and will report accordingly, receipting to Captain Doty for the property belonging to the corps.

III. Lieutenant John McAssay, Ninetieth Illinois Volunteers, First Lieutenant J. B. Myers, Ninety-ninth Indiana Volunteers, Sergeants A. J. Stanley, Company A, Fifty-third Ohio Volunteers, and George Wisby, Company A, Forty-seventh Ohio Volunteers, are hereby detailed for duty in the division pioneer corps, and will report accordingly.

IV. Brigade commanders will cause all the unarmed men and negroes in their respective pioneer corps to report at once to the commanding officer of the division pioneer corps for duty.

V. Captain Heath will at once organize the corps into four companies, with an equal number of white men in each, to be commanded by the four commissioned and non-commissioned officers above named, equalizing the mechanics and negroes. These companies will always be kept distinct, both while marching and working, will be divided into two equal platoons, and will be governed in a strictly military manner, each having two armed men in rear, keeping up stragglers, and preventing men from running in the way of the work. Roll-calls will be held at reveille and tattoo, and absentees severely punished.

VI. Captain H. H. Burbank and Second Lieutenant H. G. Mitchell, Thirty-second Maine Infantry, and Private Melville Rigby, Second Wisconsin Cavalry, escaped prisoners, are hereby detailed to take charge of the refugees moving with this division, and will report to these headquarters without delay for instructions. They will subsist the people and teams in their charge from the country, and will also procure from it what further transportation may be required.

*February* 21. Marched at eight A. M. in rear of Fourth Division. Roads hilly. Mud and quicksands delaying the march greatly. Arrived at and crossed Dutchman's Creek at eight P. M., where we camped, having marched twenty-two miles.

*February* 22.   Marched at six A. M., passing Poplar Springs at eight A. M., and moving to Peay's Ferry on the Wateree River, where we halted until pontoon bridge was laid.   Crossed at three P. M., and moved forward to Shingleton's Creek, where we camped at seven P. M., having marched eleven miles.

*February* 23.  Marched at one P. M. in rear of Third and First divisions, passing Liberty Hill and marching on Camden road six miles, then on Settlement road across to Lancaster and Camden road on White Oak Creek, five miles from Flat Rock, one mile south of Red Hill Post-Office, where we camped at five P. M., having marched twelve miles.

*February* 24.   Marched at nine A. M., in rear of Fourth Division, on Camden road.   After passing Sander's Creek, six miles from Camden, turned to the left, crossing the Camden and Lancaster road at Cold Spring, leaving Kirkwood on the right, striking the Cheraw and Camden road two miles from Camden.

Camped at Marengo Mills, six miles northeast of Camden, at nine P. M., having marched twenty miles. The day was rainy and the roads heavy, especially near camp. Foragers killed one Rebel in skirmish at Cold Spring.

*February* 25. Marched at eight A. M. on Cheraw road in advance. Roads good; timber pine. Camped at one P. M. at Sandy Grove Church, having marched eight miles. The First Brigade went forward to Tiller's and Kelly's bridges, on Lynch's Creek, eight miles, securing both, and camping at those points.

*February* 26. Marched at eight A. M. on Darlington road, reaching Kelly's Bridge at eleven A. M., eight miles. Roads good. We found the water very high, extending nearly a mile in width, and a crossing of trains was deemed impracticable. The Second and Third brigades and the battery were pushed across; with so much difficulty, however, that with the continued rise of the water further crossing was abandoned. The Second and Third brigades and battery, under command of General Oliver, took up a defensive position one mile from the bridge.

*February* 27. Remained in same position to-day. At one P. M. the water ceased to rise. Enemy's cavalry made their appearance in small parties on east side of the river.[1] Captured one prisoner.

*February* 28. In same position, the water falling slowly. Commenced building a bridge across the creek. General Oliver pushed forward a reconnoissance five miles on the Darlington road, not finding any force of the enemy. Captured one prisoner. Number of miles marched during the month, 253½. Number of casualties during the month : killed, — enlisted men 1 ; wounded, — commissioned officers 3, enlisted men 18 : total, 22. Number of enemy killed, 6 ; captured, 84.

*March* 1. The Second and Third brigades, under command of Brigadier-General Oliver, moved forward to Kellytown, six miles and a half. The bridge across Lynch's Creek was relaid on the ground. The First Brigade crossed at six P. M. Captured sixteen prisoners.

---

[1] This is the exact position where Gates and De Kalb met Lord Rawdon, with the same stream between them ; and they remained here three days just before the battle of Camden.

*March* 2.   The trains of the division finished crossing at
1.15 P. M.   The First Brigade, with trains, moved forward to
Kellytown, arriving at four P. M.   The whole command then
moved on to Black Creek, where it arrived at half-past six P. M.,
and camped, having marched eleven miles.

*March* 3.   Command crossed Black Creek at half-past six A. M.
Roads to-day were good.   Crossed Juniper Creek at half-past
six P. M., and camped, having marched eighteen miles.   Captured
two prisoners.

*March* 4.   Marched at daylight, coming upon the First Division near Thompson's Creek, five miles, where we halted till
two P. M; then moved on to Cheraw, six miles, where we camped,
having marched eleven miles.   One man was wounded.

*March* 5.   Marched at four P. M. to pontoon bridge across the
Great Peedee, one mile, and pushed forward on Fayetteville road
to Harrington's plantation, four miles, where we camped, having
marched five miles.   Captured eight prisoners.

*March* 7.   Marched at twelve M. on Fayetteville road in rear
of Third Division, crossing Society Hill and Rockingham road,
fifteen miles and a half, and Phill's and Heel's creeks, and
camping on east side of Crooked Creek, having marched eleven
miles.   Captured two prisoners.

*March* 8.   Marched at half-past six A. M. on Telegraph road
to Fayetteville.   Crossed State line one mile from camp, and,
during the day, Little Peedee River and Joe's Creek, reaching
Laurel Hill at twelve M.   Moved across Jordan's Creek, and
camped, having marched fifteen miles.   Captured three prisoners.
Two regiments of Second Brigade were sent forward to Lumber
River, seven miles and a half.

*March* 9.   Marched at half-past six A. M. on the Fayetteville
road, crossing Shoe-heel Creek, and reaching Lumber River at
Gilchrist's Bridge at half-past eleven A. M., where we halted half
an hour, then crossed on pontoon bridge, and moved forward
to Bethel Church, where we camped, having marched fourteen
miles.   The roads were impassable on account of rain, and trains
did not come up.   One regiment of Second Brigade was sent to
the right with department headquarters.

*March* 10. Spent to-day in corduroying roads. Moved across Raft Swamp at two o'clock P. M., two miles, sending the advance forward six miles, and bringing up the trains to Bethel Church.

*March* 11. Marched at seven A. M. Crossed Duke's Branch and Rockfish Creek, thirteen miles, and moved on toward Fayetteville to Little Rockfish Creek, seven miles. Casualties: one man killed and two missing.

*March* 12. Marched at seven A. M. on Fayetteville road. Crossed Little Rockfish Creek near camp, and camped one mile nearly south of the city, having marched six miles. Casualties: one officer and seven men captured; one man killed.

*March* 13. Remained in camp at Fayetteville.

*March* 14. Marched at three P. M. Arrived at pontoon bridge, one mile below the city, two miles from camp. Halted one hour and a half to get the bridge finished. Crossed at half-past eight P. M. and moved out to Warsaw road, where we camped, having marched three miles and a half. Left refugees and surplus negroes at this point, also the ordnance and supply trains.

WARSAW ROAD, NORTH CAROLINA, March 15, 1865.

. . . . . .

III. Captain William M. Fisk, Company E, Seventy-third New York Volunteers, is hereby detailed to take charge of the refugees travelling with this division, and will proceed with them to Wilmington.

*March* 15. Marched at eleven A. M. on Goldsboro' road. Camped at half-past six P. M. in rear of Fourth Division and a mile and a half from Maxwell's Bridge on South River at Bethany Church, having marched ten miles.

*March* 16. Marched, half-past seven A. M., to Maxwell's Bridge across South River, a mile and a half. Then on Fayetteville and Beaman's Cross-Roads, four miles and a half; then up the river, crossing Jones's Swamp to Wesley Church, three miles, where we camped, having marched nine miles. Captured five prisoners.

*March* 17. Marched at nine A. M. to the intersection of Bentonville road, crossing Taylor's Swamp and camping at Robert's Cross-Roads, having marched six miles. Captured two officers and three men. One man was wounded.

*March* 18. Marched at six A. M. in advance, crossing Little Cohera, Seven-Mile, and Great Cohera creeks, taking the shortest routes toward Everettsville, and camping east of Newton Grove Cross-Roads, having marched eleven miles.

*March* 19. Marched at twelve M. in rear of corps, halting at Pleasant Union and Canaan churches, one mile, until four P. M.; then moved on toward Cox's Bridge over Neuse River, corduroying much of the road, which was found next to impassable. Crossed a branch of Falling Creek and arrived at King's plantation at midnight, having marched seven miles.

*March* 20. Marched at near one o'clock A. M. back on road we had come, having received orders to report to Major-General Slocum, commanding left wing of the army. Passed camp of previous night and Benton's plantation, eight miles, and arrived at Harper's house, in rear of left wing, and reported to General Slocum at half-past six A. M., having marched fourteen miles. Moved forward at twelve M. to rear of Fourteenth Corps, two miles, where we camped. Two regiments of the First Brigade were pushed forward two miles farther, to develop the left flank of the enemy. At about half-past two P. M. these regiments formed on the right of the Fourteenth Corps, three miles from Bentonville, joining at the same time with the left of the First Division, Fifteenth Corps; shortly after which the line moved forward, driving the enemy's skirmishers and developing his main line, which position they held until the remainder of this brigade moved to their support and threw up temporary works. The command reported back to Major-General Logan, commanding Fifteenth Corps. Our casualties were, — officers wounded, 4; men killed, 3; wounded, 7: total, 14.

*March* 21. The Second and Third brigades, after corduroying a road through the swamp to rear of First Brigade, went into position on same line, and threw up works, having marched three miles. Casualties to-day: killed, 1 officer and 2 men; wounded, 1 officer and 15 men: total, 19.

*March* 22. The enemy having retreated during the night, the skirmishers pushed forward at daylight, capturing four prisoners. The command marched at twelve M. on Goldsboro' road, corduroying it as far as Grantham's house, where it camped, having marched nine miles.

*March* 23. Marched at seven A. M. on Lower Goldsboro' road half a mile, then on Everettsville road, crossing Falling Creek, and camping at half-past nine A. M. at Hall's plantation, having marched six miles and a half.

*March* 24. Marched at seven A. M., crossing the Neuse River near Wilmington Railroad bridge, four miles and a half, at nine A. M., and moved through Goldsboro', three miles, at twelve M. ; then moved out two miles on Newbern road, where we went into position on right of road and Seventeenth Corps, facing eastward. The First and Third brigades in front line intrenched, Second Brigade in rear. Distance marched, nine miles and a half.

*March* 25. Received in camp, belonging to our regiments, quite a number of officers, and about three hundred and fifty men (recruits and convalescents), who came to Goldsboro' with the Twenty-third Corps, and joined the command to-day.

GOLDSBORO', NORTH CAROLINA, March 28, 1865.

. . . No praise can ever reach the full measure due the soldiers of this command, who without a murmur have waded rivers and swamps in the most inclement weather, crowding their enemy from every stronghold he chose to occupy, permitting no obstacle, natural or artificial, to check their progress, and gathering for themselves the food that could not be furnished in any other way. Without this method the campaign could not have been made.

In all this the soldiers of this army, passing through a country traditional for its efforts to destroy the Government, and often from the nature of their duties beyond the control of officers, have shown a humane forbearance such as was never before seen in any war. A few acts of atrocity by straggling vagabonds that encumber all armies have from time to time been committed ; and often the good soldiers of the army, who gathered its necessary food, and to whom the country owes the success of the campaign, have borne the odium of such conduct. But by proper attention to this duty (foraging), which may at any time become the most important in an army, there is no reason why its dignity should be less conspicuous than its importance.

GOLDSBORO', NORTH CAROLINA, April 1, 1865.

I. The commanders of the corps and army to which this division belongs, having issued orders prohibiting foraging in the country and the use of unauthorized animals and vehicles, which orders are not in all cases obeyed, the use or possession of any such unauthorized property will subject the implicated party to arrest, and in case of enlisted men to hard labor under guard. Brigade commanders are requested to assist in the full execution of this order, and the provost-marshal of the division will keep a sufficient force on duty to insure its implicit observance.

II. The weather permitting, the division will be reviewed and inspected at three P. M. to-morrow, on the grounds near the picket lines, in front of the troops. All enlisted men at these headquarters will be inspected at ten A. M. Brigade commanders are directed to hold similar inspections at the same hour.

III. While at this camp brigade commanders will establish a sufficient camp-guard to preserve the purity of their camps and keep men from climbing over the works.

IV. The picket line will be kept a closed line, and no one, except with an organized regiment, will be permitted to pass out.

*April* 1. In compliance with orders, all foraging was suspended, and all surplus vehicles and animals were turned over to the quartermaster department. The day was spent in working on the defences of the position and completing camps.

*April* 7. Spent in drilling. The commanding general exercised the division in evolutions of the line at half-past three.

*April* 8. Division drill at half-past three.

*April* 9. The commanding general inspected the transportation of the division. The trains were loaded for marching.

IN THE FIELD, NORTH CAROLINA, April 10, 1865.

Foraging, except by organizations of regiments or brigades, or along the line of march under an officer, having been prohibited from department headquarters, all commanding officers are directed to obey this order implicitly.

General orders published at Goldsboro', prescribing punishment to all soldiers having in possession horses or mules not authorized, will remain in force until rescinded.

Straggling from any cause is prohibited.  Servants and camp-followers must be kept in their places.  An officer with a detail of men will be placed on duty each day to enforce this order.

*April* 10.  Marched at seven A. M. on Snowhill road five miles; then across to Pikeville on the Weldon Railroad eight miles; then on Whitley's Mill road four and a half miles, camping on Pike's plantation at dark, having marched seventeen miles and a half.

*April* 11.  Marched at half-past eight A. M. on Whitley's Mill road six miles; then to Lowell Factory, on Little River (seven miles), where we crossed, and marched out one mile to Tulghem's place, where we camped at dark, having marched fourteen miles on very bad roads, which required much corduroying to be made passable.  Received seven deserters from the Rebel army.

*April* 12.  Marched at nine A. M. on the direct road to Pineville, finding the road comparatively good.  Crossed the St. Charles road (eight miles) at three P. M., reaching Pineville at six P. M., where we camped, having marched fourteen miles. Received two Rebel deserters.

*April* 13.  Marched at eleven A. M. on Louisburg road to the intersection of the Erpsboro' and Raleigh road (nine miles); and thence on Raleigh road, passing Eagle Rock, and camping at dark on Clay Hill Plantation, one mile from Hinton's Bridge, across Neuse River, having marched sixteen miles.  Received three Rebel deserters.  Loss, eleven men captured.

*April* 14.  Marched at six A. M., crossing Hinton's Bridge, and massing the division, in rear of the First Division, until half-past eleven A. M., when we moved on to and through Raleigh, being reviewed by General Sherman while passing the capitol. Marched four miles northwest of the city to Crab-tree Creek, where we camped at half-past three P. M., having marched eleven miles.  Roads good.  One man was captured.

*April* 15.  Remained in same position, orders for marching having been countermanded.  Received one deserter from the enemy.  Two men were captured.

RALEIGH, NORTH CAROLINA, April 19, 1865.

I.  While at this point every effort will be made to give the troops a soldierly bearing.  Brigade commanders will cause a short drill, preceded by an inspection, to be held each morning and evening; also guard-mounting and dress-parade as prescribed by Army Regulations.

II.  A strong guard will be established around the entire camp, and the duties of sentinels thoroughly taught.  Each brigade and regiment will have an officer of the day, who will look carefully to the above; and an officer from division staff will be constantly on the lines or about the camps.  Sentinels on post must be clean in person and dress, must be properly and neatly dressed, and must walk their post in a soldierly manner.  Any sentinel seen sitting down, with his gun at an order, standing, smoking, or improperly dressed on post, or in any way failing to properly perform his duty, will be relieved, and sent to these headquarters for punishment.

III.  No soldier will be permitted to pass the chain of sentinels without a written pass from a brigade commander, and if to go to town, he must be cleanly and properly clad.

RALEIGH, NORTH CAROLINA, April 22, 1865.

In view of the probable speedy disbanding of the army, brigade commanders are directed to cause applications for the release and restoration to duty, and will see that such action is properly noted on the company rolls, of all men in their commands under charges, or who have been reported for desertion or other offences requiring the action of a division commander.

Before forwarding them, they will be pleased to see that the statement and application are full and explicit, adding their own recommendations in each case.  This is of vital importance, as it will affect the future history of these men.

# CHAPTER XXVI.

## HOMEWARD.

O N the 28th of April we set our faces homeward, with feelings of thankfulness and joy no language can express. These feelings were not unmixed with sadness, however; for many of those who had set out with us four years before, indulging the same hope of safe return, now filled soldiers' graves. The following order was now published to my division : —

RALEIGH, NORTH CAROLINA, April 28, 1865.

In setting our faces homeward with the certainty of speedy and permanent peace, the soldiers of this division should require no special charge to perform their full duty as good soldiers, and not tarnish their bright record by acts of pillage and wantonness.

All officers and men are enjoined to preserve the most rigid good order on the coming march. All straggling or other disorderly acts, of whatever character, will be punished in the severest manner.

Orders heretofore issued prohibiting foraging, the use of animals and vehicles, are still in full force.

The marching was so eagerly done that it was difficult to regulate and hold it back ; so that many of the weaker men were very much worn by it.

*April* 29, 1865. Marched at nine A. M., reaching the Neuse River at Rodger's Bridge at four P. M., and camped two miles beyond at five P. M., having marched eleven miles.

*April* 30. Remained in same position, and made bi-monthly muster. Recapitulation : Number of miles marched during the month, eighty-seven ; number of men lost by capture during the month, fourteen ; number of enemy captured during the month, fifteen.

*May* 1. Moved at six A.M. on the Louisburg road, passing through Rolesville, three miles, at seven A. M., at which point the trains of the division were inspected by the inspector of the corps. Crossed Little River (seven miles), Crooked Creek (twelve miles), Cedar Creek (sixteen miles), and camped at two P. M. at Tar River, opposite Louisburg, having marched eighteen miles.

*May* 2. Marched at eight A. M. on Shady Grove road. Crossed Tar River, and passed through Louisburg at half-past eight A. M. ; crossed also Sandy Creek (ten miles), Little Shocco Creek (fifteen miles), Big Shocco (seventeen miles), camping near Shady Grove, on Williams's plantation, having marched eighteen miles.

*May* 3. Marched at six A. M. on Warrenton road ; crossing Rich Neck and Fishing creeks, and passing through Warrenton, ten miles, at ten A. M. ; crossed the Raleigh and Gaston Railroad, near Macon Station, fifteen miles, at one P. M. Camped on Roanoke River at five P. M., having marched twenty-four miles.

*May* 4. Marched at twelve M. Crossed the Roanoke River at Robinson's Ferry on pontoon bridge, and in rear of Fourth Division, crossing State line and into Virginia, two miles, at half-past one P. M. Camped at eight P. M. on the Meherrin River, having marched seventeen miles.

*May* 5. Marched at half-past five A. M. on Lawrenceville road. Crossed the Meherrin River at Pendleton's Bridge, one mile ; also Toter's and Great creeks, reaching Lawrenceville, eight miles, at nine A. M. Crossed Rose Creek (near town), Reedy Creek (fourteen miles), Sturgeon Creek (sixteen miles), Wagna Creek (twenty miles), and Nottaway River (twenty-six miles), near the junction of the Petersburg road and Boydton Plank road. Camped two miles from river and two miles on right of road near Supony Church, at five P. M., having marched thirty miles.

*May* 6. Marched at half-past five A. M. in advance. Crossed Stony Creek, eight miles, and passed Dinwiddie Court House, nine miles, at ten A. M. Crossed Gravelly Run, thirteen miles, and camped on Hatcher's Run at three P. M., having marched nineteen miles.

*May* 7. The division moved forward to within one mile of Petersburg, where it camped, having marched five miles.

*May* 8. Remained in same position as on the 7th.

*May* 9. Marched at nine A. M. in rear of corps on the Petersburg and Richmond pike, passing through Petersburg, and being reviewed by Major-General Howard. Crossed the Appomattox River (near town), Old Town Creek (one mile), Swift Creek (three miles and a half), Tinsberry Creek (five miles), and camped near Proctor's Creek and Perdue's plantation at three P. M., having marched ten miles.

*May* 10. Marched at nine A. M. in double column. Crossed Proctor's Creek, and camped at one P. M. two miles south of Manchester, having marched nine miles.

*May* 13. Marched at eight A. M. Passed through Manchester, crossed the James River on pontoon bridge, and marched through Richmond, the column being formed in eight ranks. Took Brooke's Turnpike, crossing Brooke's Creek (seven miles), Chickahominy River (twelve miles), camping at five P. M. on the east side of Stony Creek, having marched fourteen miles.

*May* 14. Marched at five A. M., taking Fredericksburg road, crossing Machusep Creek, and camping near Hanover Court House at nine A. M., having marched nine miles.

*May* 15. Marched at five A. M. Crossed the Pamunkey River (one mile and three quarters), Reedy Swamp (ten miles), Mattapony River (fourteen miles), camping at half-past three P. M. on De Jarnett's plantation, having marched twenty miles.

*May* 16. Moved at seven A. M., in rear of First Division, through Bowling Green, passed Hickory Hill, and camped at six P. M. on Massaponax Creek, six miles south of Fredericksburg, having marched twenty-two miles.

*May* 17. Moved at five A. M. in advance. Passed through Fredericksburg, six miles, at eight A. M., crossing the Rappahannock River at the city on pontoon bridge, and passing Stafford Court House (sixteen miles), Thomas Creek (eighteen miles), and camping on Aquia Creek at half-past five P. M., having marched twenty-one miles.

*May* 18.   Moved at seven A. M. in rear of First Division. Passed through Dumfries, where we halted one hour; crossed several small streams; and camped at six P. M. two miles south of Occoquan, having marched sixteen miles.

*May* 19.   Moved at six A. M., crossing the Occoquan River at Occoquan on pontoon bridge.   Crossed Pohick Creek and passed Pohick Church at eleven A. M. on Alexandria road.   Crossed Occutuck Creek, and camped on Grant road at three P. M., four miles south of Alexandria, having marched seventeen miles.

*May* 20.   Remained in camp in same position.

*May* 21.   Moved at eight A. M. to Fairfax Seminary, near Alexandria, where we camped at 12 M., having marched six miles.

*May* 22.   Remained in same position, preparing for the review of Sherman's army, to take place in Washington City, D. C., on the 24th instant.

*May* 23.   Moved at ten A. M. to south end of Long Bridge, where we bivouacked for the night, having marched five miles.

The Army of the Potomac was reviewed to-day by the President and Lieutenant-General Grant.   The First Division crossed the Potomac and bivouacked on Virginia Avenue, near the Capitol.

NEAR WASHINGTON, D. C., May 22, 1865.

To preserve uniformity in the coming review, it will be necessary to equalize companies, consolidating them to not less than twenty files front.   Small battalions should be consolidated two in one.   A careful inspection should be made, and no clothing out of uniform allowed.   The hair must be cropped and the beard neatly trimmed.   Whenever the haversack is not new it should be cleanly washed.   Canteens should also be taken.

The troops will appear with bayonets unfixed.   Only commanding officers of brigades and regiments, with such staff-officers as are with them, should salute.

GENERAL HAZEN (LEFT REAR)
WITH GENERALS LOGAN, SHERMAN, DAVIS (STANDING) AND SLOCUM.

FLAG PRESENTED BY GENERAL HAZEN TO THE FORTY-FIRST OHIO.

Instruct the regiments joined from the Third Division with especial care.

All, including soldiers, should cast their eyes toward the reviewing personage while passing, and without turning the head. When nearing the reviewing-stand, commanding officers will require steps to be shortened, even at the shortening of distance; and after passing will not allow any company to halt or mark time, even at a loss of intervals.

Be pleased to give close attention to all the above.

*May* 24. By command of the President, Major-General Hazen assumed command of the Fifteenth Corps; Major-General Logan succeeding Major-General Howard in the command of the Army of the Tennessee. Brigadier-General Oliver succeeded to the command of the Second Division.

At eight A. M., the remainder of the corps having crossed the Potomac on the Long Bridge, the command was massed north and east of the Capitol, on Maryland Avenue and adjacent streets, the head of the column resting on North Capitol Street. At nine A. M. a signal-gun was fired; and the corps, preceded by Major-General Sherman (commanding the armies) and staff and Major-General Logan (commanding Army of the Tennessee) and staff, moved forward on Pennsylvania Avenue, marching in column and in the following order: Major-General W. B. Hazen (commanding Fifteenth Army Corps) and staff; the First Division, Brevet Major-General C. R. Woods commanding; the Second Division, Brigadier-General J. M. Oliver commanding; the Fourth Division, Brevet Major-General J. M. Corse commanding; the Artillery Brigade, Lieutenant-Colonel W. H. Ross, chief of artillery, commanding.

After passing the reviewing-stand (in front of the White House), occupied by the President of the United States and Lieutenant-General U. S. Grant (attended by many civil and military officers of distinction), the division moved out four miles on Seventh and Fourteenth streets, between which they camped, having marched eight miles.

The review of the troops was most satisfactory. The city

was thronged with neatly clad men and women, representatives from all parts of the Union, and the most gratifying acknowledgments were everywhere showered upon the officers and men of the command. The corps was followed in review by the Seventeenth, Twentieth, and Fourteenth corps.

WASHINGTON, D. C., May 26, 1865.

I. Division commanders will at once establish strong guards about their encampments, and take such measures as a proper control of their commands requires. A limited number of men and officers can receive passes from division commanders to visit Washington each day. Guard headquarters should be established on the roads leading to the city ; and officers of guards, who will not leave their posts of duty during their tours, will inspect passes, and require that all men passed shall be neatly and cleanly clad. Division commanders will cause these guards to be posted as required by the Army Regulations, and will endeavor in every way to perfect the performance of guard duty.

II. The custom prevailing with sentinels in some commands, of halting at the end of their beat and coming to an " about face " while halting, is neither graceful nor the established custom of the service, and officers of the guard should be instructed to cause it to be discontinued.

There was nothing more remarkable in this campaign than the entire change in the treatment of private property after we entered North Carolina. The men all knew where the State line was, and their voluntary conduct in this regard was of itself evidence as to how the burning of Columbia came about. There were lawless men in the army, and great care was taken to hold them in check, and enforce respect for private rights. The provost-marshal commanded a large guard, and had instructions to leave trusty men in charge of all houses until the troops had passed, and to arrest all men and officers found away from their commands.

We were, of course, compelled to use fuel and material for pitching our camp, as the men carried no rods for their shelter-tents. At night a large draft was made on young saplings, rails, and old lumber, to furnish from eight to ten thousand of these small rods. But no trouble came of this necessity until we reached the heights opposite Washington, beyond the Long Bridge. My division camped there; and the only material for rods was an old rail-fence, along one side of a field, the fence on the other three sides having been already used. I gave the necessary authority for the use of this fence. Very soon after, the negroes belonging to the place came and reported that their former master, the owner of the fence, had sent three sons to the Rebel army, and was a Rebel himself. To this I paid no attention. Soon after, the proprietor himself appeared in a high passion, and demanded by what authority I had used his fence. When I replied, "By the authority of the United States," his rage knew no bounds, and he said that he would see General Augur at once. General Augur had been for about two years in command of the Department of Washington, and the man's manner led me to believe that he had reasonable grounds for expecting favor in that direction. As his errand could end in no good, and might perhaps lead to annoyance, I waited until he had saddled his horse, and then quietly arrested him, and left him under guard, with directions to hold him till further orders. I never heard of him afterward.

While we were about Washington, it was difficult to keep down the spirit of reckless appropriation of other people's property. Many scenes more ludicrous than evil were constantly occurring, and the robbery of a hen-roost, or the use of a few panels of fence, was sure to be reported directly to the War Department, and an amount of investigation and police-court work was done daily which very soon made it necessary to send the Army of the Tennessee away; so that our expected long rest at Washington was reduced to a few days.

Among the disorderly acts of my men was the "capture," as they facetiously called it, of the Fourteenth Street Railroad, which they reported to General Sherman as a good joke. The Corps was camped on the heights just beyond, and the men ran the road for their own convenience. They also appropriated the horse and buggy used by the captain of the Capitol police. These are only examples of their daily mischief. Finally, General Sherman received an order to get his army away from Washington as quickly as possible.

We went to Louisville, and after sending one division to Arkansas, were soon mustered out of service.

I attended the general review at Washington on both days, and watched everything very closely. Our long practice in marching, which was in one sense a drill, told greatly in our favor; while frequent reviews, and the presence of distinguished personages, had bred some evil habits in the Eastern army. In passing the reviewing-stand, a very large proportion of their regiments cheered, many men swinging their hats, and so losing their cadence and military bearing. In the Army of the Tennessee, with perhaps rare exceptions, the sense of military exactness was not offended by such demonstrations, and the cadence was perfect; while the robustness of the men and their even, swinging gait were very striking.

The Army of the Potomac which marched in review that day must have been a very different one, so far as military appearance went, from the boasted army of McClellan. Of all the armies that I saw in the war, none equalled that of Buell in the traits that are generally thought to be characteristic of fine soldiers.

The mounts of our army, when we reached Washington, were magnificent, owing to our frequent opportunities for capture. It was much regretted that our trains could not have been displayed at the review. They were the finest that can be imagined. We had gleaned the best mules from a large portion of the South, and had changed off and left behind at least three mules for every one we brought along, till there was no bettering them by exchange. Many of these teams were sent to Leavenworth, and furnished the splendid trains of that department.

The muster-out of the Fifteenth Corps took place at Louisville, and was done quietly, the men going to their homes, and taking up their various occupations, as if they had never left them. The chief quartermaster of that corps, Colonel Fort, is now dead, but recently was a distinguished member of Congress from Illinois. Another member of my staff, Colonel C. C. Carpenter, has been one of the auditors of the Treasury, Governor of the State of Iowa, and a member of Congress. Another of my staff-officers, Colonel C. C. Parsons of the regular army, left the service soon after the war and entered the ministry. He died at his post during the yellow-fever season at Memphis, displaying the same spirit of self-sacrifice and devotion to duty that always distinguished him as a soldier. I never knew better men.

## CHAPTER XXVII.

### LESSONS OF THE WAR.

SO great a war as that of the Rebellion could not fail to be rich in valuable lessons, which, if not new, had been forgotten until recalled to mind by a fresh demonstration. I have always thought it a duty incumbent upon officers of large experience to give some formal expression to their views as to the military teachings of the war; and I regard this as specially important, because, in time of peace, much of our military control and administration is in the hands of men who do not take the field, and who are consequently lost sight of in war, to come again to the front when war ceases. This is a bar to the prompt recognition and adoption, when war begins, of many things the value of which has been tested and proved in actual service. Our written rules change very slowly. Thus the light equipment and simple belt for ammunition were not formally adopted until they had been in general use for nearly ten years. So also the necessity of teaching our troops the full use of the rifle seems to have been first perceived by persons outside of official circles.

In all actual affairs it is as important to know what to avoid as what to adopt. I early learned to take account of the feelings, preferences, and prejudices of civilians, and to forego sometimes, out of deference to their opinions, things that I believed were proper and needful. Too absolute and abrupt an enforcement of discipline once nearly cost me my volunteer commission, and with it my opportunity for usefulness in the field.

This chapter records, under appropriate heads, some of the results of my own practical observation and reflections. The theoretical composition, organization, control, and discipline of armies has been treated at length in my book entitled "The School and the Army in Germany and France."

### Defensive Works for Infantry.

During the first year of the war the importance of a cover for infantry while under fire was not understood. This is to be accounted for by our general apathy as to all military matters, and by the fact that in the days of the old musket, then just disused, such defensive lines were not thought to be of much consequence. But they were necessary, even then, and are now indispensable. If such a line, which could have been easily constructed, had been made on our right at Stone River, and held by troops properly posted, the result of that battle must have been very different. At Chickamauga the work of logs, begun after daylight at the suggestion of Colonel Suman, and at first objected to by Johnson, the officer who suffered most at Stone River from the want of such a defence, had a most important bearing upon the fortunes of that day.[1] The little damage done by Polk's corps proves this. With more effective fighting than the day before, I lost only thirteen men, against more than four hundred the previous day.

Such remarkable results led me, after Jonesboro', to call attention to the subject in the following report : —

[1] At the reunion of the soldiers of both armies at Chattanooga on the 19th of September, 1881, General Cheatham, when visiting the battlefield, and speaking of this old crumbling line, said, " Only for this little work, we should have swept you from the field before noon." And I do not doubt it.

EAST POINT, GEORGIA, Sept. 10, 1864.

Lieut.-Colonel R. R. TOWNS, Assist. Adj.-Gen. Fifteenth Army Corps:

.     .     .     .     .     .     .     .

I must also ask the indulgence of my commander for calling attention in this report to the subject of attacks on the front of an enemy in position. I cite, as an evidence of the disproportion of advantage in these contests in favor of the assailed, the battle of the 28th of July, when the enemy left in front of this division three hundred and twenty of his dead, while the killed of this command on the same front were but twelve; and the battle of the 31st of August, when he left over two hundred dead, and killed but eleven.

Since the accurate-shooting rifle has replaced the random-firing musket, since troops now, when in position, protect their persons by shelter, and since they can no longer be scared away from the line, but see safety in maintaining it, this remarkable result has followed.

The methods of construction and dimensions of these covers were formulated in the following order : —

NEAR JONESBORO', GEORGIA, Sept. 4, 1864.

Hereafter when this command constructs breastworks the following specifications will be observed : —

A revetement along the line determined upon, either of logs notched into each other, or of rails placed between strong stakes, or of stone, or sods, or any material that may be convenient, will be placed $2\frac{1}{2}$ feet high; then, on the rear side of the works, an excavation will be made $2\frac{1}{2}$ feet deep, a step being left on the front side $1\frac{1}{4}$ feet high. No earth to be broken in front of the works.

This excavating must be wide enough to furnish all the earth required in front. Head-logs will be added, if needed.

This construction gave a quick and excellent cover against infantry and field artillery. The rapidity with which such lines were made, when the working parties knew precisely what to do, was astonishing. Almost any

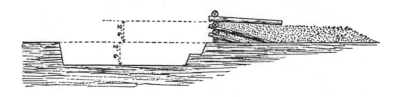

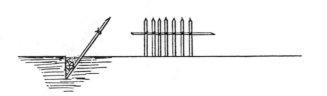

FIELD - WORKS.

material makes a sufficiently firm revetement of two and a half feet, and the step permits volley-firing by rank over the head-log.

Security of person gives the soldier composure and deliberation. He aims carefully, and fires at his mark; while without cover he is excited, seldom aims at all, and often fires high in the air. The great improvements that have taken place since the close of our war in the range, accuracy, and rapidity of fire of small arms have increased the importance of this defence. The Turks, depending upon long range and rapidity rather than accuracy of fire, succeeded so long as they could induce their enemy to attack in front. In future this sort of attack must generally be avoided.

A row of stakes, six feet long, strong enough not to be broken by the hand, and so constructed that an advancing line cannot pull them out nor overturn them, will stop any advance of an enemy if placed at point-blank range. Such a line is constructed by cutting a triangular trench two feet in depth, with the side next the works vertical, and the other at an angle of forty-five degrees. Stakes are placed six inches apart, sloping with the angle of the trench. A long piece of round timber is then placed in the trench, on the ends of the stakes, which are bound to it by telegraph-wire. The trench should be partially filled before the timber is placed in position, and should afterward be filled up and strongly rammed. Then near the top of the stakes a strong withe is woven in and out, and wired. The ordinary row of stakes is a very slight impediment; but such a construction as I have above described will check any attack long enough to enable the force assailed to break up and destroy the assaulting troops. The stakes cannot be pulled out singly, nor can the row be overturned bodily; and it affords no cover to the enemy, which is an objection to ordinary entanglements of brush and trees. The fastenings that join chevaux-de-frise can be parted with a single blow of a hatchet, and the work then removed. These defences here described admitted of variation, according to time and material at hand ; but the prescribed dimensions were observed, and as every one knew just what to do, the lines were constructed with great rapidity.

## The Officering of Troops.

So much of the efficiency of troops depends upon the character of those who command them, that it behooves a government to take every means to secure the best officers possible. That we failed, in many cases, to do this, was evident from the beginning. We followed too much the rule that an officer should be commissioned to a rank determined by the number of men he had brought into service. This is perhaps a good working plan in a purely volunteer system, for the purpose merely of fixing the initial rank. But a government that should insure officers their positions without regard to their capacity, would be inexcusably neglectful of an important duty.

This duty of wise selection became incumbent on the Government as soon as a regiment was received into service. A neglect of this duty greatly impaired the efficiency of the army. There was scarcely a regiment in the service that did not possess the very best material for officers. Unfortunately, by a simple order of two lines the War Department conferred upon governors of States, without rule or system, the arbitrary power to appoint and promote. Some governors, no doubt, acted wisely ; but in many cases all checks and tests, especially the supreme one of conduct in battle, were entirely ignored, and promotions were made by the blind rule of seniority, — a rule which in a regular army, in time of peace, has much merit, but is vicious in war, with new troops. I quote the following communications, which were called out from time to time upon this subject.

CAMP WICKLIFFE, KENTUCKY, Jan. 18, 1862.

C. P. BUCKINGHAM, Adjutant-General of Ohio:

I notice by a newspaper received this evening that certain promotions have been made in the Forty-first Ohio Volunteer Infantry.

Whenever vacancies have occurred in the regiment I have always followed the orders from the War Department, and recommended some member of the regiment as successor, always taking some one from the grade next below. The regiment has been taught to believe itself entitled to whatever promotions might occur in it (as I certainly think it is). This has been a great incentive to study, and all the officers and the better class of non-commissioned officers have learned and recited one lesson each day since I joined the regiment, and by unceasing labor I have thoroughly educated several in each grade for the duties of officers in grades above them.

I notice that First Lieutenant —— is promoted to be captain. He is not competent, has never been recommended, and if he accepts, I shall be obliged to call a board to decide upon his case. He performs his duty as lieutenant indifferently, and might maintain his position; but to place him in a higher one which he could not fill creditably would be equivalent to dismissing him from the service.

I notice also the appointment of a Mr. ——, a citizen entirely outside of the regiment. In regard to this I would most respectfully say that there are several sergeants in the regiment, as bright and deserving young men as are to be found in Ohio, who have studied early and late, and have not failed to have a perfect recitation for three months, under the promise of, and in view of a supposed right to, these places as they may become vacant. Half the success of the regiment has been due to this. I can but say that outside appointments to the regiment will destroy the spirit which now exists in it, besides placing inefficient men in places that men already in the regiment have been thoroughly educated to fill.

CAMP WICKLIFFE, KENTUCKY, Jan. 30, 1862.

Captain JAMES B. FREY, Chief-of-Staff, Headquarters Department of the Ohio, Louisville, Kentucky:

The present method of filling vacancies in volunteer regiments is by arbitrary appointment by governors of States that furnished the regiments. This absolute and unconditional power is liable to great abuse, greatly to the prejudice of the claims of meritorious men, and of the service. All volunteer regiments were originally organized upon the elective system. Many non-commissioned officers were as effective in recruiting companies as the officers. All could not be elected; and the non-commissioned officers go in the ranks with the full assurance, and if they prove good soldiers it appears with the right, of promotion when the other officers go out.

The hope of promotion is a great stimulus to the soldier. In my own regiment I organized classes of non-commissioned officers three months ago as candidates for promotion. They have recited daily since, and many of them would do credit to a first section of cadets. They are thoroughly instructed, even better than many of the commissioned officers, have been promised promotion, are entitled to it, are highly deserving of it, and have been educated expressly to fill vacancies that may occur.

The Executive of Ohio has seen fit to appoint a Mr. —— to one of these vacancies, a person entirely ignorant of the duties of a soldier, who resides three hundred miles from where the regiment was raised, and who had not the shadow of a claim upon the regiment, or any person in it. He knows less of his duties than any corporal in the regiment. Another appointment has been made, and although from the regiment, the person has not been recommended, should not have been promoted at this time, and was so promoted from personal motives of some one near the Executive.

These appointments have a depressing and demoralizing effect upon the enlisted men of the regiment, and upon the service, and I cannot witness their repetition without urging the promotion of those who deserve it; and would most respectfully ask if an arrangement cannot be made by the Department of War with the governors of States to insure their co-operation hereafter in filling vacancies that may occur among the commissioned officers of volunteer regiments.

NEAR ATLANTA, GEORGIA, July 31, 1864.

Hon. JOHN BROUGH, Governor of Ohio:

I trust not to be considered obtrusive in offering one word for the old officers and veteran organizations, in connection with the new forces to come from Ohio.

In many cases the re-enlistment of veteran regiments is due entirely to the individual efforts of the commanders of those regiments. It is questionable if there were any regiments from Ohio but could have been retained in the service had the proper steps been taken by their commanders. This of course presupposes that their commanders had previously brought up their regiments under a judicious military guidance, and that they were themselves inspired with an unselfish patriotism which always gives great weight to the wishes of a commander. With a full appreciation of the obligations due these true officers, who have retained the services of veteran regiments, I would respectfully express a hope that the first effort of the State will be, whenever it becomes necessary to resort to draft, to fill up these veteran and war-tried organizations before any drafted men are put in new regiments. I would also respectfully call attention to claims for promotion to the new regiments of those officers who have served through all the war so far, who have never been found wanting in any of the battles, who have proved fitness for command by the highest test, and are still fighting at the front.

These officers deserve a word spoken for them, as they are not at home to speak for themselves. But there are many men at home in Ohio who have held not less than three or four commissions in as many different regiments since the war commenced. These men do no service to the country; but when any of the thousand vexations of the service makes it distasteful to them, resign, usually leaving the seeds of discontent and insubordination behind them. These men seek new and higher grades in the new organizations, and usually get them. There is no limit to the difference in true value of regiments, due entirely to the character of their commanders ; and these officers who fight with their men in battle have a just and real claim to the promotion the new organizations will give.

BEAUFORT, S. C., Jan. 29, 1865.

Assistant Adjutant-General of Ohio, Columbus :

I would respectfully recommend that Captain C. A. Earnest, Thirtieth Ohio, be appointed lieutenant-colonel of that regiment.

You will pardon me for occupying your attention for a moment upon the subject of promotion. I give as my reason a wish to advance the interests of the service.

I was shown to-day your reply to a respectful and earnest request for a like promotion of this officer, made some time ago, saying that three officers of the regiment ranked him, and he was not, therefore, entitled to promotion.

These three officers were not in the battles, were eminently unfit for promotion, and were therefore not recommended. The mere fact of seniority in active service is not a just or solid reason for promotion. The fact that one officer is senior to another in the volunteer service usually comes purely from accident, and the true merits of officers in regiments is not infrequently nearly in the inverse order of rank. I have served at the front nearly every day of the war, and have seen all kinds of men in the most difficult and trying situations, and I find that they differ in character, ability, merit, and in everything, more than pebbles upon the sea-shore. There is nothing so practically useful to the service as the ability to choose the good and competent men to guide and control the great responsibilities of service. The present system of appointing by seniority destroys or ignores that benefit, and is driving out of service the men of usefulness, and is very harmful to our service.

An officer once appointed, is to all intents a fixture. The activity of our movements prevents any action of boards to dispose of incompetent officers ; or if a board be instituted it may find the incumbent indifferently good, or a personal friend, and keep him in the service.

There are no men who can feel the deep interest in the well-being of troops that their service-commanders do. This, and the constant observation of the performance of duty, affords a criterion for promotion that has a real, solid, and meritorious basis, which, if followed, gives results in every way the most useful to the service and encouraging to the real heroes of the army.

I have tried this plan in a regiment I once had the honor to command, and have observed its workings so closely that I feel it my duty to call your attention to this subject. The command of a regiment is a first-class responsibility, and out of the officers of a regiment but few are competent to direct and control it. The duties of all commissioned officers are highly responsible; so much so that but few of those appointed by the present system perform them with any degree of correctness or efficiency.

The commanders of our troops are honest and high-toned, — men who would not recommend what they did not feel sure was for the good of the service; and I respectfully contend that these war-scarred veterans are too little considered, and their recommendations too lightly regarded.

As a division commander, I command the Thirtieth Ohio, and have done so in many severe battles; and I contend that its usefulness in battle under Captain Earnest would be greater by twenty per cent than under either of the other men you would promote in preference to him; besides, the three or four hundred men he would then command would be better clothed, better fed, and better cared for in every way. I mention this only as an example of the workings of this system of promotion by seniority. It will ruin any body of troops in active service if persisted in. It is unjust to the men commanded and unjust to the Government, to permit the command of these brave men to be regulated by accident; for such it is when seniority is the only rule. I have just reviewed my division, and the sad want of this discrimination was deplorably apparent. The good men are all mustering out, from the causes herein mentioned. We must have the power to use our best men, and the present system deprives us of that power, and drives them out of the service. The fact of seniority in a service, when perhaps the officers drew straws at first to decide it, carries with it a very weak claim for promotion.

It is hoped that in case of another war this subject will not be ignored by the General Government.

There is no greater misapprehension than a very commonly entertained opinion, that to be a good officer, one must have a special natural gift peculiarly adapting him to the military profession. To be a good officer, one must first be a good man ; and the same qualities that fit one for other active vocations, such as intelligence, culture, mathematical training, and an acquaintance with affairs, make the good officer. The old militia or parade officers, soldiers of the Mexican War, and show-brigadiers, so much sought for at first, were as a rule utter failures, while the young men of mark in all departments of civil life nearly always succeeded as officers. Men accustomed to the exactness of the counting-room, and used to dealings with men in large concerns, like railroads, rolling-mills, and manufactories, could be counted on with most certainty. In short, the good efficient man made a valuable and successful officer.

The first quality of a good soldier is obedience and discipline. The first quality of a good officer is a sense of the indispensable need of order, and of discipline as the condition of order.

When officers are at last obtained, a just bestowal of rewards and punishments is a vital element of success. This cannot be neglected, except at great risk of life and treasure. The government that does not reward and punish with promptness and impartiality sacrifices a powerful weapon in war.

## Equipment of Troops.

The use of the rifle, which has effected such a revolution in tactics, has made it of the first importance to lighten in every possible way the weight that the soldier carries. The plan of carrying all the cartridges in a box suspended from the shoulder, and all on one side, had three serious defects. By suspending the weight from a point two feet away from the centre of gravity of the person, it created a leverage to be overcome and kept in adjustment; it produced curvature of the person; and by the pressure of the shoulder-belt it prevented free evaporation from the surface of the body. The soldier readily overcame the first and third of these evils by throwing away the shoulder-belt altogether, and carrying his cartridge-box on his waist-belt; and the second he overcame, when permitted, by using two boxes, one on each side. This proved the easiest way to carry ammunition. The knapsack, with all its gearing, was also thrown away for like reasons. On our arrival at Savannah there were whole regiments without a knapsack, and the cartridge-box was almost invariably slung to the waist-belt. The canteen, haversack, and a tin cup are indispensable. The necessary things usually carried in the haversack — like combs and brushes — were rolled in the blanket with the poncho, which was thrown in a coil over the shoulder, with the two ends tied on the opposite side. The rigidity of the roll prevents it from pressing upon the chest. The men on the march worked out the problem for themselves by experience, which combines experiment and proof, and almost universally reached this result.

But instead of accepting these lessons, we have nearly ever since been experimenting on all kinds of complex harness for knapsacks, bags, satchels, and shoulder-belts for the cartridge-box, when the simple device learned in the war was all that was necessary. Large sums of money have been spent uselessly on these articles. As soon as the metallic cartridge was invented, the problem of carrying it was at once solved by the frontiersmen of the West. In 1867 I had a few simple looped belts made by the Ordnance Department at the St. Louis Arsenal, copied from those worn by frontiersmen, and used them with my regiment (the Thirty-eighth Infantry) with such admirable results as to satisfy me that they must eventually come into general use in the army. I reported the subject fully to the Government, and received back four solid foolscap pages of objections. But these belts were soon very generally tried. No other is ever now seen in actual service. The same true guide, the experience of the war, would quickly settle all questions as to other equipments.

New regiments suffered most from the old gear. I have elsewhere described the experience of the One Hundred and Tenth Illinois, assigned to my command at Louisville in September, 1862. This regiment, in just three weeks, without being in battle, lost six hundred men, mainly from being put upon the march weighted with an equipment which they could not carry in the manner required of them.

I am clearly of the opinion that the bayonet should be relegated to the shelves of the antiquary, with the flintlock, the knapsack, and the old cartridge-box. So useless was this arm that during the last year of the war those lost in battle in my command were not replaced. At the grand review at Washington I ordered that they be not fixed. When the column filed round the corner of the Treasury building, General Sherman sent an order from the President's stand that they be fixed as the men marched, which was done.

The use of tents with marching columns need not be discussed, as it is hardly possible that they will ever again be seriously advocated for that purpose.

The overcoat or blanket and waterproof poncho ought to be all the covering that is carried in addition to the ordinary dress.

The following is my personal report upon the subject of equipment, called for by the War Department, ten years ago:

HEADQUARTERS SIXTH INFANTRY,
FORT BUFORD, DAKOTA, Aug. 14, 1874.

Captain MAY H. STACEY, 12th Infantry, Recorder of Board on Infantry Accoutrements, Fort Leavenworth, Kansas:

SIR, — Your circular letter of July 9 has just reached me. Scott gives the definition of " equipments " to be " the complete dress of a soldier, including arms and accoutrements." As to arms, it is understood that the best patterns, determined by competent boards appointed for that purpose, will control; and for uniform, it is believed that for real service this is a matter of minor moment, provided the dress be of good material, well made, graceful, and simple. This matter is fixed by boards appointed for that purpose; so it seems that what is desired is, how best to accoutre the infantry soldier. This, next to the arming and feeding, is the most vital matter pertaining to the soldier, the weight and adjustment acting directly upon and consuming a part of his physical energy, which must be subtracted from what is available for him as a fighter.

My opinions upon these subjects are so radical that I doubt their practical value before a board; but I give them, fully convinced of their correctness, having so repeatedly seen them voluntarily adopted by the men who apply them to use under circumstances the most perfectly calculated to bring out the strongest possible expression of their own natural solution of all these questions.

So very important is this subject, that I will give an example of its effects on troops. When, in September, 1862, the Army of the Ohio was at Louisville, Kentucky, reorganizing for the pursuit of Bragg's army, an Illinois regiment, eleven hundred strong, was assigned to my brigade. They were strong men, had just taken the field, and were fully equipped, each man having everything the United States had prescribed for him;

but this "everything" meant a great deal more than many men
not accustomed to marching could well carry. As we moved
slowly toward Perryville, these men, overcome by the immense
loads, fell by the wayside at the rate of fifty a day, until
they finally went into the battle at Murfreesboro', three months
afterward, four hundred strong. But few of the remainder
ever rejoined their colors. If the true cause of the majority of
these casualties was ever reported, it must have been, "inca-
pacitated by United States equipments."

There is no truer military principle than that in peace an
army should be accurately prepared for war, so that when war
comes we need not lose valuable time in unlearning errors perpetuated in peace. This makes the double plan recommended
by some, — one for peace and one for war, — a grave mistake;
for in peace we forget the war plan.

The long War of the Rebellion was full of instruction in all
matters of equipment; and I think we cannot afford to lose its
very valuable lessons, as we are likely to, since the men who
control in details were not in the field, and naturally cling
more to theory than to examples that they did not see.

*The Knapsack.* If the war taught anything, it was that the
knapsack was distasteful to the American soldier, and that he
would not wear it; that he would throw it away, and prefer
putting the few necessary articles required in a roll he made of
his blanket, or poncho, or both, which he then slung over his
shoulder. This relieved him of some weight, but particularly of
the leverage a knapsack always exerts by being all on one side
of the axis of motion, and more especially of the binding
of the respiratory and other muscles upon which the straps
always press. It is true that in European armies, where there
is a more absolute respect for arbitrary rule, and officers are
trained to unquestioning obedience, the men cling to their
knapsacks; but in the American army I believe the attempted
use of the knapsack a mistake, — that the soldier will always
cast it aside, as he did in the war, and that it should form no
part of the equipment. In garrison, each man should have a
small wooden locker as a fixture to the barracks.

*Haversacks.* As now in use, to be made only of the best cotton duck. This is impervious to water, while the threads of linen shrink when wet, and become pervious. No paint of any kind should be applied, and the haversacks should be often washed. These were the best used in the war, and were entirely satisfactory.

*Canteens.* Of tin, the same as now in use, which, with good flannel covering, I believe are the best used in any army.

*Cup and Griddle.* A light griddle weighing but a few ounces, to slide into the haversack, and tin cup of like weight. These latter the soldier will eventually provide for himself, but he is often at considerable trouble in doing so. The cup he slings upon his belt.

*Poncho and Blanket.* Each soldier should have an india-rubber poncho, to be used as a shelter-tent if he wishes, and a blanket or overcoat, but not both, to be worn, when marching, in one roll.

I am not prepared to say that a soldier should have both poncho and tent-d'abri. The best examples of soldiering, on both sides, in our own war, were without either. The tent forms no part of the soldier's equipage in the best foreign armies. Should the tent-d'abri be issued, the poles for it (like broomsticks), still furnished troops, but never used, should be discontinued. This is at present waste, as the men will not carry them, but provide substitutes at each camp.

*Bayonets.* The bayonet should be discontinued, as it is rendered useless by the increased accuracy and rapidity of fire.

*Intrenching Spade.* This instrument should be light and strongly made, to be slung to the belt with the canteen, opposite the haversack, by a spring-hook at the handle, to be finished on one edge as a cutting-tool, and on the other for driving. This should have no relation to the gun.

*Cartridge Belt and Holder.* There should be as little to interfere with the muscles of the shoulder and of respiration as possible. Nothing more than the haversacks, canteen, and spade should be put upon them, except the blanket-roll, which is frequently shifted. I believe that cartridges when suspended from the shoulder are carried in the worst possible way. Mechanically, the man is all day balancing their weight upon an upright lever, the length of which is the distance from his centre of gravity to the point of his shoulders, and the point of suspension is half the breadth of the shoulders, or one side of the axis of the man. This fatigues him unduly. The belt also compresses and binds his clothing close upon the muscles of respiration, greatly to his discomfort. The result in the war was, that he would first unbuckle this belt, leaving the ends hanging, the box being suspended by the waist-belt, and finally would throw them away, wearing his cartridges on the waist-belt. This weight, being all on one side, caused a curvature of the body, which is always a condition of weakness.

Although in the war we never heard of hernia arising from carrying the cartridges about the waist, after it was over, the surgeon-general discovered that it was so produced, and upon his representation an order was issued requiring the use of shoulder-belts. But so repugnant is this belt to the soldier, that the only practical effect of the order has been to cause the expenditure of about $80,000 to furnish them, and they are quickly converted into the looped waist-belt.

In the summer of 1866, in crossing the country, my attention was called to the way in which the mountain men carry the new metallic cartridge in a looped belt. This carries forty rounds easily in the circumference of a man, and in battle another belt of equal capacity can be swung below it. I got authority from the chief of ordnance to have a number made at the St. Louis Arsenal for trial. I used them in marching my regiment from Missouri to New Mexico, and with surprising results. The men that used them came in fresh after marching all day, while their companions were much fatigued. They never seemed to be aware that they were wearing their ammunition, while their comrades would at once, on reaching camp, remove their cartridge-boxes, as if they were being relieved of a great incumbrance. So much in quest were these belts, that the members of the guard would dress for them as if competing for orderly. On making my report, the Ordnance Department made very many objections to the belt.

The facts in the case are, however, that in all parts of the army they are kept on hand for detached service, and officers permit them to be worn. I saw the Yellowstone Expedition return in 1872, and I think every man wore one. When three companies of my garrison were detailed this season as escort to the boundary commission, every man at once made for himself, without direction, one of these belts, which he wore away.

Should there be war, in less than thirty days I believe every man in the army would wear one of these belts. Their advantages are, that since the weight of the cartridges is equally distributed about the centre of gravity of the man, and on the same level with that centre, it is in the best possible position, as there is the least leverage to overcome, and the body is not drawn out of its perpendicular by the weight being all on one side.

The objection to the boxes is, that the weight is carried farther away from the centre of gravity in boxes than in belts, and the leverage becomes greater; and although being on opposite sides, yet, since the centre of gravity continuously shifts from side to side as men step, the farther removed from it these weights are, the more effort a man must make to correct the oscillations.

I believe this subject to be worthy of the fullest consideration; for all that can be saved of the energy of the soldier for the emergency of battle should be husbanded for that purpose. This is the prime object in the management of troops.

I am, respectfully, your obedient servant,

W. B. HAZEN,

*Colonel 6th Infantry, Brevet Major-General Commanding.*

### Ammunition in Battle.

The firing-line in battle must be kept supplied with cartridges. This matter, always important and much neglected, and becoming more serious as improvements in small arms increase the rate of fire, calls for immediate attention. The complaint, "out of ammunition," used to be heard from regimental commanders fifty times during a

great battle. This was often due to want of control over
the fire from poor drill; but the methods in use for bringing the ammunition forward from the wagons were inade-
quate and uncertain. The boxes of cartridges were usually
brought up on the shoulders of men, and the packages
were sometimes carried in old gunny-sacks by mounted
orderlies. The Turks, and sometimes the Russians, in their
late war, used pack-mules; but this was merely a temporary expedient, and the subject has yet to be considered.
Whatever plan be adopted, a colonel must have absolute
control of the fire of his regiment. With proper drill and
discipline this can certainly be secured. I found no difficulty on this point, and toward the close of the battle of
Chickamauga, after the splendid repulse of the enemy on
the left, in which my command had a full share, was able
to go over and aid in the repulse of Hood on the right,
with forty rounds to the man.

### Special Details.

The custom of detailing fighting men for non-com-
bative duties is the worst feature of our defective system.
The infantry is the army. All else is subsidiary. It is
the trunk; and unless it be strong and vigorous the
whole tree withers. In other armies the collateral services are specially provided for. But with us they were
manned by details from the best men in the fighting force.
It is costly and wasteful to teach a man to be a soldier
and then put him on unsoldierly duty. It would be much
better to enlist him at first for this subsidiary service.
The effect is to weaken the army. There must be orderlies, clerks, headquarter guards, officers' servants, teamsters,
laborers, hospital attendants, and hostlers. The quartermaster's and commissary departments, the ambulance corps
and ordnance trains, are indispensable. There was nothing
to do but to make details from the front rank.

I reported as follows upon the subject of the ambulance corps : —

IN CAMP, GEORGIA, June 7, 1864.

General WILLIAM D. WHIPPLE, Assist. Adj.-Gen., etc. :

Immediately before the opening of this campaign an organization called "an ambulance corps" was made, taking from this brigade thirty-seven enlisted men and one commissioned officer, and being under control of officers outside the authority of brigade commander. This organization having control of all ambulances and stretchers, I would respectfully report that at Resaca, where the brigade lost two hundred and fifty men, there were but few if any stretcher-bearers upon the field, and the wounded were removed by details from the efficient fighting command. Also that at the affair of the 27th of May, where my brigade lost over six hundred men, there was but one stretcher to be found anywhere about the field, and that far to the rear. The men who were carried off the field at all were carried by the members of the command, on guns, poles, and in blankets, and seventeen of the wounded are known to have fallen into the hands of the enemy from this neglect ; and I have to ask that the person from whose neglect this occurred be brought to punishment.

I would respectfully state that there are in my command a sufficient number of unarmed musicians to carry all of the stretchers furnished for the troops ; that before the organization of this expensive corps these musicians were well drilled in the use of stretchers ; that in the many engagements the command has been in, the musicians have speedily removed all the wounded under direction of a staff-officer sent out by myself ; and that in my opinion they can perform this duty satisfactorily in future. Had the stretcher-bearers been under my control, or with the troops, none of the wounded would have fallen into the hands of the enemy on the 27th ; and in view of these facts I would respectfully ask that the stretchers be returned to me, to be carried by musicians, and that the strong men now supposed to be carrying them be returned to the ranks with muskets in their hands.

HEADQUARTERS 2D BRIGADE, 3D DIVISION,
4TH ARMY CORPS, June 28, 1864.

Lieut.-Colonel J. S. FULLERTON, Assist. Adj.-Gen. :

In addition to the thirty men previously furnished for the ambulance corps, I to-day filled a detail of twenty men, making about four per cent of my fighting force, to perform a duty that can be, and in this command always has been, better performed without taking any fighting men. These men, after reporting as ordered, were sent back to their regiments without any stretchers, for the reason that there were none for them, and without even any of the instructions necessary for their duties. The entire detail of stretcher-bearers are with their regiments doing no duty, having been disarmed ; while there are not half enough stretchers for the musicians, who can amply and properly perform this duty, as they always have done until the innovation of this corps.

I have respectfully to ask authority to arm these men and put them in the ranks. While the fighting force is being fast depleted in battle, so that but about twenty per cent of the maximum organizations remains, the maximum of these details are kept up as if the regiments were full; and I can say no less than that the effect upon regimental and other commanders, who have the good of the service at heart and strive honestly to keep a few men still in their ranks, is exceedingly discouraging. This is especially so when men, as to-day, are detailed from them in large numbers only to be returned disarmed and without the shadow of employment.

This hospital corps will accept none but the strongest and most able men, when there are numbers with perhaps a maimed hand who can, and have previously driven all the ambulances. The musicians have been thoroughly trained to carry away the wounded ; and at the skirmish of a few evenings since they went forward quite to the front, where the members of the *ambulance corps* cannot be made to go. I am anxious to hold to the fighting force of my command, and can do so in no way, in my opinion, so properly and judiciously for the interests of the service as to arm these stretcher-bearers who have no stretchers ;

and if they had, I have other men, who cannot carry arms, to do this work.

EAST POINT, GEORGIA, Sept. 16, 1864.

Lieut.-Colonel R. R. TOWNS, Assist. Adj.-Gen. 15th Army Corps :

I have the honor to make inquiries based upon the following facts relative to the organization of an ambulance corps just ordered.

The acts of Congress, it is presumed, contemplate an ambulance organization ample for full regiments, or in this division for seventeen thousand men, which would be the organization were the regiments full.

The order just received requires the same number to be detailed for the reduced regiments, that is, for four thousand men, making a detail of over two hundred and twenty men from the effective strength of the division.

Having served during the campaign, till coming to this division, near the ambulance corps, and invariably observing less prompt and effective service by it than when these duties were performed by the musicians of the regiments, and it being a heavy and constantly repeated tax upon the men for duty, I would respectfully ask, if in addition to keeping up the service of the field music for stretcher-bearers, it would not be sufficient to make an organization proportionate in size to the depleted condition of the command.

Considerable further correspondence grew out of this organization. Its purpose was excellent. If organized at the outset on an independent basis, it would have been most beneficent; but under the circumstances the cost was greater than the advantage. At last, men who could not use a gun were allowed to exchange into this corps for men who could; but the deduction from the infantry was kept up to the end of the war.

It even became a custom to detail infantry men to batteries. When the surplus artillery was sent to the rear just before the advance from Atlanta, the horses and men thus liberated were not detailed, as they should have been, to fill up the organizations that were to go forward. Soon after, orders were sent out to dismount nearly all who rode horses, for the use of the artillery. An effort was even made to dismount field-officers, and details from infantry were ordered for cannoneers. My views were expressed in the following terms : —

Indorsement on communication of Captain De Gress, commanding Battery H, First Illinois Heavy Artillery, requesting to have twenty-one men detailed to serve in his battery.

SMYRNA CAMP, GEORGIA, Nov. 10, 1864.

Respectfully returned, disapproved. When this battery formed a part of my division, from personal regard I gave Captain De Gress assurance of this detail ; but since the present arrangement has taken place he no longer belongs to my command, and I do not consider the arrangement longer incumbent upon me.

From my observation, which has been close and extensive, I have come to the belief that this number of good men armed as infantry is of more value to the service than a full active battery of artillery, even with the old system, when the artillery formed a part of the army.

I now consider the men, if so detailed, since the artillery is detached and under separate control, an actual deduction from the serviceable fighting force of the army.

I am at this moment making a detail of twenty-three enlisted infantry men to guard the little artillery now present; and should these other men be detailed and disarmed, an additional guard of effective men might be required to take care of them.

I am surprised that the batteries that remained in front were not recruited by details from those in that arm of the service who went to the rear.

Besides furnishing the artillery one hundred and seventy of the best mules of the division, which they did not keep, nor take any proper steps, when they went to the rear, to return to the division ; besides having a field-officer and his orderly summarily dismounted by the artillery upon the pretext of the needs of that arm of service, upon which horses were mounted a sergeant and private ; besides attempting to deprive field-officers of infantry generally of their horses, and the laboriously tasked foot-officers of the pack-animals that carry their humble blankets and rations, the duty of guarding the artillery is now imposed on the infantry. To call upon the infantry for men to make artillery soldiers of, is a proposition that will find no favor at these head-quarters.

This custom of making details was very annoying and disorganizing, and detrimental to the service. It was usual to make them by name, after means had been taken to find out the best men, and often without the knowledge of immediate commanders, who then lost sight of the men forever.

The following is a case in point : —

BEAUFORT, SOUTH CAROLINA, Jan. 23, 1865.

Capt. Samuel L. Taggart, A. A. G. Army of the Tennessee :

I have the honor to request that the following communication be laid before the Major-General commanding the army.

In September last, an officer of my division staff, Lieutenant ——, Thirtieth Ohio, Acting Assistant Quartermaster of the ordnance train of the division, was detailed away by a special order from the headquarters of the army. I was not notified of the intention to make the detail, nor of the detail itself, and only by accident came to the knowledge of it at all, about two weeks afterward.

The result of the detail, which I claim was irregular, was, that the ordnance train left East Point in an unserviceable condition, and about two hundred thousand rounds of ammunition were in consequence lost to the Government. Lieutenant —— took with him, without any authority, or my knowledge, a private soldier of his regiment, Josiah Ranig, of Company B. Ranig was next heard from, acting as servant to Mrs. Colonel ——, wife of the Chief Commissary of Subsistence, Fifteenth Corps, at Huntsville, Alabama.

On arriving at this point, Ranig was found acting as clerk at a news store, and was taken to his regiment under arrest. About two hours afterward a special order, No. 20, January 18, was received from headquarters Department of the Tennessee, detailing him as clerk in the commissary department of the First Division, Fifteenth Army Corps.

When near Gordon, Georgia, in November, a special order from headquarters Department of the Tennessee was received detailing Private T. R. Rhodes, Company I, Thirtieth Ohio, on duty in the commissary department, with orders to report to Lieutenant ——, it being notorious in the regiment that Rhodes was a good servant and cook ; and —— procured him without the knowledge of any of his commanders, by an order from the headquarters of a department, to serve him solely as a private servant. This officer has since been mustered out of service, but he did not return Rhodes to his command.

None of these details have been made with the advice or knowledge of the commanders of these men, who are responsible for them.

I will further respectfully add, that these are only instances of frequent details of this character, and it is claimed that they are made for individual convenience. I believe they are made without a full knowledge of all the facts, and that these facts ought to be known by the general upon whose authority these orders are predicated. These details are disorganizing, and fruitful sources of decimation in our armies, as the rolls of every company will show.

Could these necessary organizations be at once provided for in case of war, as distinct bodies, as they are in other armies, and as they will have to be eventually in our own army, the detailing of men from the ranks prohibited, and the infantry placed at the head of all, in theory as it is in fact, a great step would be accomplished in improving our service and reducing its cost. The continual hewing away at the trunk to strengthen the branches weakens the former, and at last destroys both.

## Pioneer Corps.

Soon after General Rosecrans took command of the army he directed each regimental commander to select two of the best artisans and mechanics from each company, and place the twenty under an officer.— a civil engineer preferred — as pioneers.

This order was gladly obeyed, and twenty of the very best men in each regiment were so selected. They were then consolidated at brigade headquarters, and soon ordered to the headquarters of the army and formed into the famous Pioneer Corps. This was afterward organized into regiments, and brigaded under an officer of the regular engineer establishment. It finally formed the Veteran Engineer Regiment, with William E. Merrill of the army as colonel. These men were of course very useful, and served faithfully, but were permanently lost to their regiments. The transaction was vicious, and a positive injury to the army, and, in the result, was a surprise. The order, at first, led every one to suppose that the pioneers were to remain with their regiments ; and men were often chosen who were almost indispensable there, and would not have been selected had it been known that they were to be taken away.

All bodies of men, and none more than troops, have their own leaders, who give character to and shape the acts of those immediately about them. These men are a sort of leaven. Remove them from the general body, and you weaken the collective power and character. This was exactly the result of the course pursued by General Rosecrans.

This corps, as large as a brigade, was at the battle of Stone River, and was partially engaged. Its casualties were forty-eight, — about ten per cent of what they were in my brigade. The commanders of regiments were afterward requested to give a share of promotions to men in this pioneer corps. To this I replied as follows : —

READYVILLE, TENN., Jan. 16, 1863.

Major C. GODDARD, Assistant Adjutant-General:

In relation to the circular this day received from headquarters Fourteenth Army Corps, requesting regimental commanders to give a fair share of promotion to officers on duty with the Pioneer Corps, I have the honor to submit the following statement and request. In my command it is a custom to recommend for promotion those officers who have shown the greatest efficiency in active service. The officers of my brigade who have successfully undergone the recent fearful test, "the battle of Stone River," who led their men unflinchingly through the eight hours of desperate conflict on the 31st of December, 1862, while nearly one third of their number were stricken down ; who led them just as gallantly on Friday evening to repel the onslaught upon the left, — these officers have claims which the General commanding the army will not be slow to recognize. With the services of the officers on duty with the Pioneer Corps I have no means of becoming acquainted. That the General's request may be intelligently complied with, I respectfully ask for such information in regard to the services of the pioneer officers in the late battles as will enable their regimental commanders to judge justly between them and those who have certainly proved their valor, fidelity, and capacity upon the field of Stone River, under the eyes of their colonels.

These men with their regiments were each worth as much as a half-dozen other men, while in their new corps they only counted as so many men. This was in the aggregate a great waste, besides being unfair to the regiments. Afterward, while on the march, feeling the need of these men more and more every day, and seeing their usefulness going to waste, I informally applied for them in the following letter : —

MANCHESTER, TENN., July 22, 1863.

MY DEAR GARFIELD, — Have you time for a word about pioneers? Like every commander, I want, if possible, my craftsmen. When the pioneer detail was made, it was supposed that they were to be with their regiments, or at most with brigades, to always remain with their proper command, unless detailed for a special duty, and then to be returned. Under this impression I caused the good and useful tradesmen to be detailed, it taking nearly all I had from the brigade. These parties were afterward permanently detached, and we are left with scarcely any one to do the thousand and one things required about a brigade. Without exaggerating, the loss of these men is almost a hardship. It is a constant detail of a hundred good men from a small command. And now a word about their utility. For building bridges, forts, and special work, I cannot question their use. I have, however, been thrown with a battalion of them on the march, and in camp, since leaving Readyville, and have no hesitation in pronouncing them a failure. They were straggling along, no one having any particular charge of them, their tools never being unpacked, and whenever any work was to be done, a detail was always made from regiments to do it. They did no good, but got much blame.

You may ask, "Could they not have been used if called upon?" It is only necessary to reply that the fact of the organization having cost every colonel twenty-five or thirty of his best men, and every brigade and division commander a proportional number, has made the whole pioneer concern a stench in everybody's nostrils, and no one seems disposed to use them.

If each brigade had had with it its little party of one hundred men, with tools and training, the latter would have been ten times as useful, and after the march could have answered any requisition for other work. As it is now, the pioneers get no drill, very little control, no sympathy, but the contempt of everybody. All this would be set right were they with their proper commands except when needed elsewhere.

The matter has been talked up until it sometimes expends itself upon the head of poor Morton himself, as at this place one

evening. The fellow is not in fault. An active engineer has
no time to discipline troops. Think of all this, and talk with
the General about it. I want and need my craftsmen very
much, as I know every one else does. We can both have them,—
you, when you need them ; and we, when you don't."

The "Morton" referred to in this letter was General
St. Clair Morton, a captain of the Engineer Corps, and
Chief Engineer of the Army of the Cumberland, a most
worthy and promising young officer, who was brigade commander of the pioneers, and, upon the request of General
Rosecrans, was appointed a brigadier-general. So obnox-
ious had this corps become, for the reasons I have stated,
that General Rosecrans, blind to the real cause, one
evening, at his headquarters at Manchester, Tenn., after
listening to a complaint from General McCook that the
pioneers cumbered the way, and gave no help when
needed, sent for Morton, and abused him in a rough and
violent tirade. The scene was humiliating. I have never
been able to rid myself of the impression left upon me by
the coarse and unjust language of General Rosecrans.
Morton at once sought and obtained service in the Army
of the Potomac, and soon fell while gallantly leading his
men. It was believed that, still smarting under the sting
of such a lash, he had felt called upon to act with rash
bravery, which led to his death.

I again asked for these men in the following terms, but
never got them : —

CHATTANOOGA, TENN., Nov. 23, 1863.

Brig.-Gen. WM. D. WHIPPLE, A. A. G. Dep't of the Cumberland:

I have the honor to forward applications for the return to
their proper regiments of the officers and men of my brigade
known as pioneers. There are now absent under that pretext over
two hundred men, or more than ten per cent of the fighting force.
The detail for this service was made about one year ago, with

the understanding that they were to be organized and attached to their proper brigade, being subject only to such details as the Engineer Department might from time to time think proper. The effect was that the most valuable men of each regiment were detailed; such men in fact as could ill be spared, and the lack of whom, in many cases, has been grievously felt. No sooner was the detail effected than these men were permanently detached and organized into a separate command, and are yet so organized, or are purported to be.

Having had proper opportunities of observing the service of this organization, I would respectfully state that they have lost very much in discipline by the separation from their command; and whenever I have served near them, one half their number taken from the brigade, and held and worked under proper control, would have performed double the service, besides being ready for the fight.

In view of the facts above stated, and that their return would increase the fighting force of this command over ten per cent, I have respectfully to ask that they be ordered to report to the colonels of their regiments.

Pioneers should consist of regular organizations formed and maintained for pioneer service. If the Government neglect to make such a special provision, such a force may consist of companies or regiments detailed entire; but the plan adopted by General Rosecrans was like dragging a magnet, that attracts and then removes the richest metal. The French Government, under Napoleon III., selected recruits for the special corps in the same way, and with disastrous results.

### Artillery.

The advantage of using light artillery, to the extent it was provided at the beginning of the war, came to be seriously questioned before its close. As guns are not reduced in number by the wear and tear of service so rapidly as men, this arm tends to preponderate. But even when kept down to its regular proportion it is difficult to see that it secures advantages at all commensurate with its cost in money and men. Casualties seldom occur from its use, and it has little effect on the result of a battle. When used, as was customary, to fire over the heads of troops, it is a positive evil. We usually followed the old custom of advertising our intentions by a cannonade. I departed from this course at Fort McAllister, the only occasion when I had authority in the matter.

Since the war the range of small arms has increased, and places light artillery at a still greater disadvantage. The time is not distant when we must review the subject of the proportionate value of artillery. Its relative value has grown less and less in all successive modern wars. Lieutenant Greene says of it, in his "Russian Campaigns in Turkey," after noticing its service at Telis, Lovtcha, and Aladja Dagh : —

"With these few exceptions, it contributed to no victory and averted no defeat. It consumed several thousand tons of ammunition, transported with enormous difficulty and expense; it hammered away at earthworks for weeks at a time without producing any substantial result; and the total losses inflicted by it were probably not over one per cent of those inflicted by infantry, and these were nearly all by shrapnel. The breech-loading musket keeps the artilleryman at a distance of not less than one thousand yards, otherwise his horses will all be picked off. At this or greater distances the angle of fall of the projectile is so great (with the guns in use by the Russians during the war) that it buries itself in the ground before exploding, and often expends its whole force in throwing up a cloud of dirt, while the pieces of the projectile remain in the crater.

"With the new form of double-walled shells, and a flat trajectory, different results may be obtained.

"The damage which shells can produce against earthworks

is now well acknowledged to be very slight; and as the infantry fights in open order, shells can evidently do but little against it."

In fact, a solid shot at short range can only cut through its breadth, and a musket-ball does the same. No careful commander will expose his masses to either.

The foregoing expressions of Lieutenant Greene do not differ in any material way from the opinions of those persons whose opportunities and observation in other modern wars entitle them to the fullest consideration. In the Franco-Prussian war, where the artillery arm was certainly most admirably handled by the invaders, and where it seemed to take so important a share in nearly all engagements, the records show that the real effect was scarcely appreciable. Should this proportion of effect as compared with that of infantry be calculated relatively to their cost in men and money, artillery for field operations must of necessity in future wars hold a still smaller relative place in the formation of armies.

### Hospitals.

The subject of hospitals in war is of great importance. Field hospitals only should be used. Diseases infect permanent buildings. At Chattanooga the Army of the Cumberland used permanent hospitals in the town, which took six weeks to prepare, while the Army of the Tennessee used tents and open buildings in the country. The per cent of recoveries was greatly in favor of the latter army. When Colonel Wiley, of the Forty-first Ohio, lost a leg at Mission Ridge, I forbade his being taken to any of the hospitals, and caused a hut to be built for him on the field. His recovery was remarkably rapid; while other officers, with slight flesh-wounds, were taken to the hospital, and died of hospital diseases.

I introduce here an expression of my views on this subject, which has appeared elsewhere : —

" It is unaccountable that scientific and practical medical men
do not appreciate and advocate the advantages of outdoor over
indoor hospitals.

" It is a matter of the gravest importance, and the humane
societies of Christendom can in no way do more good than by
thoroughly investigating and making generally known the facts
relating to permanent hospitals in time of war.   The seeds of
disease seem to cling to the walls, ceilings, and floors, and the
death-rate of the wounded is often greatly increased by putting
them in these places.   So strongly was I impressed with this in
our war, that as far as was in my power I kept my wounded out
of them.

" Among the many casualties in my command was that of
Major S. B. Eaton, of my staff, at Peach-Tree Creek.   He was
wounded while we were repairing the bridge, the ball striking
his belt, and, without perforating it, driving the belt into the
abdomen, so that on withdrawing it, a very ugly and dangerous
wound was left.   He was a man of culture and great worth, and
I desired, if possible, to save him from exposure to hospital
diseases.   I therefore sent him privately at night in an ambulance
to the railroad, some distance to the rear, with orders to get on
the train and make his way north as quickly as possible, exercising his own wits to avoid the doctors and hospitals.   He got
on well enough till he reached Nashville, but was intercepted
there and taken to the hospital, where he at once became inocu-
lated, and came near death's door with gangrene.   Luckily, his
perfect health and constitution saved him.   I trust in the cause
of humanity there will never again be known in any war such a
thing as a permanent hospital ; and that they should have been
continued through our war is to me an unaccountable anomaly,
in consideration of the high character and attainments, unequalled
in any war, of our medical corps.   It is the only blot on their
great and well-earned fame.

### The Whiskey Ration.

During a portion of the war whiskey was issued to the troops as a part of the ration. In my opinion the custom is at all times vicious. The use of liquor by officers, particularly upon the field of battle, cannot but be harmful. Except when prescribed medicinally, I doubt whether any good ever resulted from it in war. Who in the service does not know that three fourths of the trouble in it arises from the use of liquor? And who does not remember some peculiarly happy period, when he was stationed where no whiskey could be got? It is true that many good men used it, and favored its use, and that their services were of great value in spite of it; but I know that it did a great deal of positive harm. Lord Wolseley unqualifiedly condemns it.

The following is my protest against it being furnished to my command : —

MANCHESTER, TENN., Aug. 11, 1863.

Captain J. R. MUHLEMAN, A. A. G., 2d Division, 21st A. C. :

I have respecfully to request that no more whiskey be issued to the commissary of this brigade as a ration for troops unless on special requisition. Its indiscriminate issue on ordinary occasions has produced much mischief, and, in my opinion, no good.

Intemperance is unquestionably the greatest evil that besets mankind.

Charles Buxton says : " Add all the miseries of war, famine, and pestilence, the three great scourges of mankind, and they do not exceed those that spring from this one calamity."

The " London Times " has said : " The use of strong drink produces more idleness, crime, want, and misery than all other causes put together."

Governor Gaston, of Massachusetts, in a message, has

said: "Intemperance has been the most prolific source of poverty, wretchedness, and crime; it has filled the State and the country with its destructive influences; and its progress everywhere begets only misery, misfortune, and degradation."

There is no form of misery and vice it does not nurture, and there is no stage of drinking which is not in some degree intemperance. Who of us, in the retrospect of our lives, do not count the numbers of noble fellows who have fallen in the mid-day of life from this scourge? We may call the cause by many names, when the real one is a weakened condition of the vital forces from excess at some time, that renders them incapable of rallying from disease that otherwise would not be dangerous.

Why we should scatter this scourge in armies, as a ration, is beyond answer.

The annual cost of this evil in money in this country is over six hundred million dollars, in industries as much more; while the cost in misery is beyond words.

### Foragers.

The existence of an army in an enemy's country when regular supplies are interrupted, depends upon the foraging service. This important branch of military duty must, therefore, be carefully organized, so as to secure efficient action, with a minimum of inconvenience to the non-military community. The character of this service must be raised as high as possible, by impressing at all times upon those who engage in it the fact that their duties are legitimate, necessary, and honorable. It was, unfortunately, common to call foragers by the opprobrious name "bummers," and this has left an unjust and erroneous impression. It is true that there were many bad characters with the army; but the foragers were selected carefully, and as a general thing were the bravest, most trustworthy, and best of men. The orders organizing this service have already been given.

The quantity of good food furnished daily by these foraging parties was very great. The stores were brought to the road along which the column would pass, and left under guard, to be taken up by spare wagons. If teams were found, they were loaded, and brought daily to camp at the end of the march. There was no way of exactly gauging the quantity needed, and a large amount was often left in camp. So well did my foragers do their duty, that after arriving near Savannah I was able to distribute to the needy in other commands twenty-two thousand rations of hard bread carried from Atlanta. The foragers performed also a most necessary and excellent service as patrols and advanced guards.

General Howard at one time published an order, not only prohibiting men from leaving the ranks, but directing that any soldier found robbing should be tried by a drumhead court-martial, and shot if convicted. But the sense of the army did not go as far as this. A case was brought to my notice coming directly under this order. The testimony was positive. I called a court, and the following was the result.

FORT McALLISTER, GEORGIA, Dec. 22, 1864.

Before a drumhead court-martial which convened at Statesboro', Georgia, Dec. 5, 1864, pursuant to Special Orders No. 188, Headquarters Second Division Fifteenth Army Corps, of date Dec. 5, 1864, and of which Colonel James S. Martin, One Hundred and Eleventh Illinois Volunteer Infantry, is president, was arraigned and tried, Private ―― ――, Company F, Forty-Seventh Ohio Veteran Volunteer Infantry.

*Charge.* — Pillaging a house.

*Specification.* — In this, that the said ―― ――, private of Company F., Forty-Seventh Ohio Veteran Volunteer Infantry, did on the fourth day of December, in the year of our

Lord one thousand eight hundred and sixty-four, unlawfully enter the dwelling-house of Louisa Alderman, then and there situated in the county of Bullock, State of Georgia, and did then and there unlawfully and feloniously open one trunk, take therefrom, steal, and carry away one watch, then and there being the property of Louisa Alderman, contrary to orders in such cases made and provided. This at the county of Bullock and State of Georgia, this fourth day of December, in the year of our Lord one thousand eight hundred and sixty-four.

*Findings.* — Of the specifications to the charge "Guilty," except the words "unlawfully enter and take therefrom."

Of the charge, "Not guilty."

*Sentence.* — And the court do therefore sentence him, the said ———— ————, of Company F, Forty-Seventh Ohio Veteran Volunteer Infantry, *to forfeit six months' pay.*

Examined, and proceedings, findings, and sentence approved and stoppages ordered.

As will be seen, the court, although finding the truth of the facts charged, did not find the act of robbery to have been wrongful or wilful. This was an anomalous conclusion, but necessary to save the man's life. Considering the great number of vicious men there must have been in an army seventy thousand strong, the amount of actual lawlessness was exceedingly small, and no well-authenticated case of the violation of women ever came to my knowledge.

### Disabling Railroads.

The disabling of an enemy's railroad, though it interrupts rather than breaks his line of communication, may be very embarrassing to him. Where large bridges or extensive trestle-work are destroyed the damage is most serious. But it is often desirable to break a road at points where such structures do not exist. If done superficially, it results only in a slight interruption. The mere displacement of the track and bending of rails is not of enough importance for the risk involved and time employed. Until near the close of the war the breaking of railroads by raids of cavalry was a mere farce. There is not time to destroy embankments or fill cuts. Ties are quickly replaced, and rails, no matter how badly bent, are readily straightened on any log by the roadside with a sledge-hammer, usually found at the nearest station. We finally learned how to twist the rails, which makes them permanently useless. Before this they were sometimes heated and coiled round trees. This was laborious, and the rail could not be heated along a sufficient length without making it too hot to be handled.

The plan prescribed in my command was first to line the track with men, and then by a simultaneous lift overturn it. The ties and rails were easily knocked apart with bars and sledges, usually found about station-houses. The ties were then piled crosswise at intervals of from five to ten rods along the track, in square forms some two or three feet high. Other ties were then laid in parallel layers with dry wood, on top of these forms and on top of all the rails. Then the whole was fired. The fires were found to burn better when the upper layers were parallel than when they were crossed. As the form of ties under the rails was laid crosswise, and not close, it gave a good draught to the fire above, and did not readily burn down, but supported the rails until for six or seven feet of their length they had come to a white heat.

The iron chairs, into which the ends of the rails fit, were lashed with telegraph wire to wooden bars about four feet long. Two men at the ends of a rail would slide the chairs on the rail, and then turn the bars in opposite directions. This would convert the heated part of the iron into a corkscrew which nothing short of a rolling-mill could straighten out.

A regiment can thus thoroughly disable two miles of

road in a day. A brigade of four regiments can destroy eight or ten miles of road in the same time. There is no heated iron to handle, and as the work admits of regular organization it is not very laborious. We served in this way a road between the Ogeechee and Appalachee rivers in Georgia, and it was a long time before it was again put in running order. Finally, the short untwisted pieces of rail were laboriously cut off with a cold chisel, and so a part of the rails was utilized. The entire rail might be twisted by heating the ends also.

### Movement by Wings of Regiments.

In actual war it is necessary to simplify the movement of troops as much as possible. I know of nothing so good as the movement by wings of regiments, particularly where regiments are small, as ours became after some service. It gives facility and quickness, and shortens the column by one half when marching by the flank, as we generally did. The movement is little more than the folding of the two wings, as if by a hinge in the centre; the color-guard, which remains faced to the front, being the hinge. By this movement my command with ease and rapidity formed line of battle, moved into column, and disposed itself in camp after the day's march. The regiment can be formed for action in any direction by a single command. The movement was formulated in the following circular. Towards the close of the war I always employed this method, with a saving of at least half the time ordinarily required for such movements.

JUNIPER CREEK, S. C., March 14, 1865.

I desire the regiments of this division to be exercised in "movements in eight ranks." These movements have the great advantage of simplicity and quickness. They are also adapted to all grounds, and are especially advantageous to pass defiles, when moving in line to the front, and when driving an enemy along a road. A regiment being in line, faced to the front to move forward in eight ranks : the color-guard stands fast, the two wings are faced towards it, and at the command "March," the guard moves to the front, the two wings filing to the right and left following it. When reaching a given point, if it is desired to form line facing to the front, at the command, " Forward into line, march " the guard halts or keeps moving as indicated, and the wings form forward on the right and left at the required speed. If, when moving, it is desired to form line facing the right, the right wing halts and faces, and the left forms " on the right by file into line." If it is desired to form line facing the left, the left wing is halted and faced, and the right wing forms " on the left by file into line."

At the command "movement in eight ranks," the wings should at once face inwards. The foregoing is all that is necessary to make any formation that is required in actual service ; and as the movement can be executed at any speed with the aid of a good staff, a brigade can be manœuvred in one third the time required by the usual method.

In changing directions of long lines, a staff-officer should be sent to direct the head of each regiment, and coming on the new line each deploys independently.

I desire the command familiarized with the foregoing movements, and to always use it when it is wished to move doubled, and in going into camp.

### Long-range Fire.

My brigade took up its last position in front of Atlanta on the 22d of July, 1864. From this date until the 17th of August, when I joined the Army of the Tennessee, a clear open space about twelve hundred yards across separated us from the enemy. We had lost several men in camp from bullets coming from unknown places, and the opportunity to practise regularly the same tactics was now presented. The picket line was directed to keep up a slow but regular fire, with pieces so elevated as to carry into the camp of the enemy. Colonel Kimberly, an officer of rank and experience, was placed in direction. There was a peach orchard just in front of the picket line, and the men first of all cut this cover away with their shots. Then the steady dropping of bullets into the hostile camp, sometimes as many as five thousand in a day, was begun, and kept up for three weeks. After the war I took pains to learn the effect, and found that during this time from three to five men in each of the regiments in our front were put *hors de combat* in each day. About one shot in five hundred took effect. It is easy to see that a regiment would soon be depleted by such a fire. It is said that the waste of ammunition makes this long-range firing objectionable. This is the argument of a mere obstructionist. It costs in ordinary wars from one to many thousand dollars to kill or disable one of the enemy. The army being already on the spot, the object must be to put as many of the enemy out of the fight as possible; and in this case the cost per man was only the value of five hundred cartridges, or about twenty-five dollars. This is an element in war of recent date, and calls for careful attention.

## War Correspondents.

In future wars the newspaper press must be recognized, and the correspondent given a place with the troops. With a few exceptions, it was our custom to ignore the press, with the ruling notion that nothing unofficial ought to be published with official sanction concerning military operations. This, however, had very little effect. Correspondents were present and wrote what they thought fit. The only result of our policy was that facts were often misstated, and general officers maligned for real or supposed errors, while those who chose to do so could give color to accounts of battles favorable to themselves.

It will be the wisest course to admit properly accredited members of the press, and attach them to the several headquarters under proper regulations. The people have a right to know what is going on ; and it will be wise to recognize the fact, placing correspondents under proper restrictions at the outset, in order that only truth shall be told.

The want of regulation sometimes did harm. The message announcing the death of General Polk was read easily by our signal-service men. The newspapers published the fact, and thus disclosed to the enemy that we knew their code. They accordingly adopted a new one.

The correspondents were usually good and well-intentioned men, and were often of a high order of ability. Their energy and enterprise were remarkable, and would have done credit to professional soldiers.

I gave the cold shoulder to all correspondents until late in the war. As we set out from Atlanta for the sea I attached to my headquarters, upon urgent request, a Mr. Hayes, of the " New York Tribune." He was a gentleman, and my views as to correspondents underwent a change. On reaching Savannah, Hayes, against advice, bought out a newspaper and started it as a sheet of strong Republican principles. We left him behind with regret and apprehension. He made many friends, but was not quite calculated to bear up against the rough treatment a disciple of Horace Greeley was likely to receive in the city of Savannah in the year 1865. He became engaged in bitter controversies, and died, after about a year, from personal injuries received in some affray.

A service embracing such men as Whitelaw Reid, Murat Halstead, J. A. McGahan, and Archibald Forbes is worthy of respect, and will submit to wholesome discipline.

## CHAPTER XXVIII.

### GENERAL STAFF AND WAR SCHOOL.

ONE of the first great needs of all armies is a general staff in the true sense, — such as every good army in Christendom has save our own. Such a staff is a body of military men, who are technically soldiers, with duties essentially military, and who serve by turn with troops at the several subordinate military headquarters and at the central office, their interest and view thus comprehending the whole of the army in all its relations. They perform duties of inspectors, adjutants-general, chiefs-of-staff, have control of the military archives, prepare plans for military operations, are acquainted with all military affairs, and are conservators of the whole.

Such a body of men is indispensable to the efficient administration of an army ; and until established for our own, we shall be behind other nations in a prime element of efficiency, and shall be subject to certain serious evils that beset us in the late war, which are recognizable by all good soldiers.

Want of success in our war was due largely on many occasions to the lack of such a staff. Its place is tardily supplied, when war begins, with men from civil life, who, however bright and good they may be, are necessarily without experience. This is a high branch of an army, because its duties are wholly military, and worthy to be made the lifework of the best men in any land, and without it our army may soon be unable to get them.

A spectacle more pitiable than a commander of an active army without a suitable military staff can scarcely be imagined. The want of it renders him timid and irresolute, because he is not in possession of the means to gain accurate and speedy knowledge of all parts of the field; nor can he with confidence and discretion devolve upon his staff the authority in the carrying out of orders so essential to success, when much depends upon conditions known only after the staff-officer has become separated from his chief. The chief may even be led, from want of information, to do nothing, when with it success would be within reach.

There was a singular lack of tactical manœuvring in our war. Many battles were little more than the posting of lines to give or receive the attack. The men then fought the matter out in their tracks, and the affair ended with a disorderly retreat or a broken and ineffective pursuit. This was in part due to the too loose moulding of regiments by drill and discipline to enable them to be properly manœuvred in the presence of the enemy, but very largely to the lack of a staff fully imbued with the military character, and clearly comprehending the situation and the needs of the moment.

With a proper general staff the disasters at Chancellorsville, Chickamauga, and Red River, with all their untold cost in life and treasure, and the attendant bitter humiliation, could hardly have been possible. When a commander is his own chief-of-staff, and is lost in battle, from whatever cause, all is lost. I have never had a doubt that if, at the second Bull Run, Pope's staff had been what it should have been, like the Prussian staff,— a staff that would have kept him accurately informed of the movements both of his own and of the enemy's troops, — the results of that field would have been very different.

A staff school of the right sort would go nearly as far to

put our country on a good military basis as all our present army. Young officers who had gone through a few years' service with their regiments by way of practical test, should be selected by a board constituted by law, and acting without personal favor, for this special training in staff duty. There were no better, more patriotic, or more enterprising men than those who in our war formed the military families of our commanders; but, with the best of motive and energy, they were without experience and military training. Young lawyers, bank clerks, railroad engineers, and merchants form the material out of which excellent soldiers can be made; but we made them staff-officers, and even chiefs-of-staff, before we made them soldiers.

A war school, and the creation by this means of a general staff, the chief of which shall command the army, is the great need of our service; and with it we would take a long and useful step forward, and harmonize the duties of the army commander and Secretary of War. Such a school in Prussia — from which comes the staff of their army, to which Von Moltke and Von Blumenthal belong — has given the best results of any plan ever tried, and is an example that should be followed. Its pupils must have served with their regiments three years or more, and are those who within that time have shown the best soldierly qualities and the greatest promise for the future. They must have a perfect acquaintance with regimental duty; practical ability, and taste for high scientific attainments; a physique promising long life; freedom from debt; and an untainted moral character. Professional zeal and distinguished field-service count largely in making selections. The course is three years, and covers a broad range of studies. Its diploma carries with it no certain advancement; but from these students, under certain fixed rules of selection, comes the best military staff in the world.

There can be no doubt of the very great advantage of such a school. West Point, although admirable in its place, having no equal of its kind anywhere, cannot come up to this standard nor supply this want. It has no tests of the practical work in real life to guide selections, for its pupils have given no real sign of what they will do with themselves, and the art of war may have progressed beyond its curriculum. No army in the world is recruited from a better class of young officers than ours from West Point. But many of these are lost to the country by sheer inanition, there being nothing better to do than join one of the supply branches, or suffer the inevitable corrosion of perpetual service at a remote post.

These supply branches have in a measure taken the place of a general military staff in the public estimate, when in fact they have scarcely any resemblance to it. They are manned by worthy, good men; but their duties, while high and honorable, are not military, and it is a misfortune that there should be no place of a higher military character than they offer for young and aspiring officers of the army.

The duties of these corps are now only correlated in the person of the secretary of war, — a civil minister, and not technically a military officer. These semi-civil branches, from their social and other advantages, are the loadstones which draw away from the army the best young officers in it, who ought to find place for their ambition in a military staff, but are now lost to the army as soldiers because there is no higher place where rank and exemption from the petrifaction of frontier inactivity can be given them. The advantages to a country that does not maintain a standing army, of a full military staff, to be composed of men thoroughly versed in great military operations as well as small, who shall comprehend the movements of an army as well as of a company, would be in case of war beneficial beyond comprehension. A nation without a class of men so trained may find the want of them, when war comes, exceedingly embarrassing. West Point does not fully furnish them, nor are they now furnished in our country anywhere; and since it is not the policy of the country to keep standing armies in time of peace, a large and highly trained general staff of sober, earnest men, which a war academy alone can supply, would go far, without great cost, in placing the country upon a good military footing. Some of these men should be attached to every active foreign army, and to every great military encampment and manœuvre.

## Signal Service.

As a new feature in war, there was nothing that attracted more attention, or was more efficient and commended, than the new method of sending messages by flag and torch. It was the invention of a young surgeon of the army, Dr. Albert J. Myer, afterward General Myer.

The system was not a difficult one to master; and an officer charged with this duty, with a few trained men, was attached to each division, and at the close of the war every general officer of experience was explicit in praises of this service. These parties in a short time would establish stations on the commanding points, so as practically to put the general in speaking communication with every place where it was actually necessary.

These young officers, always at the front, soon became most enterprising as scouts and topographers ; and it was from their first sketches that we marched, found, and fought the enemy. They became very alert, having a complete knowledge of the enemy, of their position, strength, and intentions, and in many ways were most valuable.

No army in the future will be without a fully organized Signal Corps, equipped for communicating by flag and torch, and by heliostat, or sun-flashes, and prepared with field telegraph trains for connecting the various head-quarters with each other, and with the commercial lines of the country.

While in front of Atlanta, on establishing camp I caused to be selected some large tree well situated, and by boring and driving pins in it, a ladder was made. By mounting these elevated stations, on a still day, particularly at early morning, the positions of the enemy, with all their detachments and outposts, were as readily determined, from the smoke and dust, as if their camps were actually in sight. These little observatories never attracted the attention of the enemy; and in future this advantage, which at times may become most important, can be realized by the use of small captive balloons. From them, marching detachments and flanking movements can be readily detected, and a sagacious officer can find out much that cannot fail to be valuable.

# APPENDIX.

## SERVICE IN INDIAN WARFARE.

A FTER graduating at the Military Academy, I served two years on the Pacific coast. The following official documents relate to this part of my early service.

FORT LANE, OREGON, Jan. 8, 1856.

CAPTAIN, — In compliance with Post Order No 1, dated Jan. 1, 1856, I left this post on the 2d instant, with thirty-five men of Company D, Fourth Infantry, in charge of the mountain howitzer, and proceeded to a point near Star Gulch on Applegate Creek, where the Indians were reported to be strongly fortified. After a difficult march (losing the ammunition I had taken with me for the howitzer, and the mule on which it was packed, by falling over the side of a mountain), I reached my destination about two o'clock on the 4th instant. Immediately afterward Lieutenant Switzer arrived with the second supply of ammunition, for which I had sent an express back to you.

I found the Indians occupying three heavy log-houses and apparently secure in their position. A force of about two hundred volunteers was encamped near by.

After having selected a position for the howitzer, I put it in charge of Lieutenant Hazen, who immediately opened a fire and succeeded in throwing two shells through the roof of one of the houses. Our exposed position was soon discovered by the Indians, and all their rifles were brought to bear upon us ; a constant firing was kept up by them while the howitzer remained on the hill.

About sundown I ordered the gun to be withdrawn.

Very respectfully, your obedient servant,

ED. UNDERWOOD,
*First Lieutenant Fourth Infantry.*

To Captain A. J. SMITH, Commanding Fort Lane, Oregon.

FORT YAMHILL, O. T., Oct. 30, 1856.

MAJOR, — I am happy to report, for the information of the commanding general, that through the energy of the acting-assistant quartermaster at this post, Lieutenant Hazen, the officers and men of this command are all in quarters so far completed as to be very comfortable for the winter.

Very respectfully, your obedient servant,

A. J. SMITH,

*Captain First Dragoons, Commanding.*

Major W. W. MACKALL, Assist. Adjutant-General, Benicia, Cal.

HEADQUARTERS DEPARTMENT OF THE PACIFIC,

BENICIA, CAL., Dec. 3, 1856.

SIR, — Your letter of the 30th of October, received on the 1st of December, has been submitted to Major-General Wool. He directs me to express his gratification that you have been so soon able to secure the comfort of your command ; the energy of Lieutenant Hazen receives, as it deserves, his commendation. . . .

Very respectfully, your obedient servant,

W. W. MACKALL.

*Acting-Assistant Adjutant-General.*

Captain A. J. SMITH, First Dragoons, Commanding Fort Yamhill.

Promotion carried me from Oregon to Texas, where I was engaged in active service until disabled by wounds received on Nov. 3, 1859.

The following official documents refer to the principal events of this period : —

HEADQUARTERS OF THE ARMY, NEW YORK, Nov. 10, 1859.

*General Orders,* No. 5.

I. The combats between United States troops and hostile Indians, mentioned below in the order of date, with conjoined gallant acts and soldier-like endurance of hardships highly creditable to the troops, have been brought to the notice of the general-in-chief since the publication of General Orders No. 22, of 1858 ; namely : —

II. *June* 14, 1858. Second Lieutenant William B. Hazen, Eighth Infantry, with a command of two non-commissioned officers and twenty-eight privates of the Eighth Infantry, after following for two hundred and twenty miles a party of Apache Indians that

had driven off animals from Fort Davis, Texas, came upon a ranch
of fifteen lodges, killed one Indian, captured another and also thirty
horses and mules and much other valuable property, and destroyed
their lodges and entire possessions, among which were several thousand pounds of prepared food. Much of this march was over a
country destitute of water and grass.

. . . . . . . . . . .

XV. *May* 16, 1859. Second Lieutenant William B. Hazen, Eighth
Infantry, with one non-commissioned officer and nine privates of
Company F, Eighth Infantry, accompanied by a guide and four
citizens of Uvalde, Texas, all well mounted, left Fort Inge in pursuit
of a party of Indians (ascertained afterward to be Kickapoos), who
had stolen horses from the vicinity of the Nueces crossing. The trail
was followed over barren and difficult mountains; and on the evening of the fourth day Lieutenant Hazen came up with and attacked
a party of eight or ten Indians, killing four, severely wounding the
others, and capturing their property, including seven horses. Messrs.
Adams and Hale are highly commended by Lieutenant Hazen for
their valuable services. By command of
Brevet Lieutenant-General Scott.
H. L. Scott,<br>
*Lieutenant-Colonel and Aide-de-Camp.*

Fort Inge, Texas, Oct. 7, 1859.

Sir, — Information having reached this post at "retreat" on
Wednesday evening, the 29th ult., that Indians had killed or carried
away two negro boys, and driven off a large caballado belonging to
Mr. H. Ragsdale, from the Frio near its junction with the Sabinal,
and had passed to the west of this post, I made ready, agreeable to
your directions, and left the same evening at about "tattoo," with
two non-commissioned officers and eight privates of Company F,
Eighth Infantry, and three citizens, all well mounted, and proceeded
on the Eagle Pass Road to a point where they probably crossed it,
and then encamped for the night. A slight rain set in about midnight, and continued till morning. We were under way at dawn,
and had proceeded only a few hundred yards, when we came upon
the trail, which was as plain as a wagon-road. A heavy rain now
commenced, and continued until about ten A. M., entirely obliterating
all signs of the trail; but we continued on our course about twelve
miles, crossing the El Paso Road near its junction with the Nueces
River. We passed beyond the effects of the rain, and again came

upon the trail, and followed it till night, camping about eight miles in rear of the Indians.

The next day we passed on with all possible speed, and about eight A. M. came upon one of the negro boys, who had made his escape from them early that morning while they were catching horses. After losing this boy they greatly increased their speed. It appears that the other boy was killed before leaving Mr. Ragsdale's place. We followed all day and late at night, without perceptibly gaining upon them.

Although we had a chilling norther this day, with rain in our faces, we made about fifty miles. By starting before day next morning we were at their camp of the night before at seven o'clock, and not more than an hour after they had left it. We now took a brisk trot, overtaking them at ten A. M. The party consisted of seven men and one squaw. They were just crossing the Nueces River near its head-waters, and by making a rapid dash we were within thirty yards of them before they were aware of our presence; but being all well mounted, before we could use our arms they were under full headway for an open cedar brake. We pursued them at the height of our speed, and succeeded in partially bringing them to bay after a chase of about four hundred yards, where we killed one and wounded another, when we took up the race at a more fearful rate than before, over an open space of broken rocks.

We pressed them with all speed for about a mile, when, coming suddenly to a precipitous ravine, they leaped their horses down, and dashing into the dense cedar brake made good their escape. They were mounted on superior American horses, the pick from nearly two hundred, which enabled them to make so good a race. Our own horses were entirely disabled, compelling me to dismount the party and give them horses from those captured. We recovered here one hundred and thirty horses (several of them valuable), and left many on the road killed and disabled.

I am, very respectfully, your obedient servant,

W. B. HAZEN,
*Second Lieutenant Eighth Infantry Commanding.*

To Captain R. P. MACLAY, Eighth U. S. Infantry, Commanding Post.

HEADQUARTERS OF THE ARMY, NEW YORK, Nov. 23, 1860.
*General Orders,* No. 11.

The hereinafter-mentioned combats between the troops and hostile Indians have been brought to the notice of the general-in-chief since the publication of General Orders No. 5 of 1859, showing gallant acts and patient endurance under great and varied hardships. These, however, are but part of the operations constantly going on in the different military departments to afford protection to the border settlers and emigrants against inroads and depredations by hostile Indians; which operations, though highly creditable to the troops, are not narrated when no actual conflict took place.

II. *October* 30, 1859. Second Lieutenant William B. Hazen, Eighth Infantry, with one non-commissioned officer and seven privates of Company F, of that regiment, marched from Fort Inge in pursuit of Indians, who, it was reported, had killed two citizens near Sabinal. He was joined, twenty miles out, by fifteen citizens from Uvalde, and next day by fifteen citizens from Frio. Following the trail till the 3d of November, he came upon the camp of the Indians, eight in number, near the headwaters of the Yanoo, charged upon them, and killed four, and in the pursuit three others were killed or mortally wounded. He captured thirty horses, eight guns (two of these Lancaster rifles of the pattern issued by the Indian Department to Indians of the Northwest), and much other property.

*Wounded :* Lieutenant Hazen severely, the ball passing through the hand and entering his side; Mr. Samuel Everett severely, — gunshot wound in two places; Mr. Pallium slightly, with arrows, in three places ; Mr. Williams slightly, with an arrow. One horse killed and Lieutenant Hazen's wounded. Private Charles Setzar, of Company F, Eighth Infantry, is noticed as always foremost in the fray, and had his horse killed under him. Lieutenant Hazen himself killed an Indian, and reports the entire command as exhibiting determination to chastise these marauders.

Having sent a party to Fort Clarke for assistance, Lieutenant Hazen, in his wounded state, remained on the field four days, when, his supplies being exhausted, he was placed on a horse, and after two days' constant travel reached Fort Inge, where he received medical aid.

The Indians, fully armed with guns, revolvers, and bows, fought with desperation. By command of

Lieutenant-General Scott.

L. Thomas, *Assist. Adjutant-General.*

Headquarters Fort Clarke, Texas, Nov, 5, 1859.

First Lieutenant T. A. Washington, Assist. Adj.-General, Headquarters Department Texas, San Antonio :

Sir, — I have the honor to report that a sergeant and private, with three citizens, arrived at this post last night, reporting an engagement

between a party consisting of a detachment of troops from Fort Inge
under Lieutenant Hazen, and a company of citizens of Uvalde, num-
bering in all forty-two, with a party of Indians, in which the latter
have lost eight killed or wounded. Also that some of Lieutenant
Hazen's party are badly wounded, including Lieutenant Hazen himself.

I am, Sir, very respectfully, your obedient servant,

WM. H. FRENCH,
*Brevet Major U. S. Army, Commanding Post.*

FORT CLARKE, TEXAS, Nov. 5, 1859.
First Lieutenant WASHINGTON, First Infantry :

DEAR SIR, — I regret to learn from the sergeant of Lieutenant
Hazen, that the latter is very severely wounded by a ball through
the hand, which lodged in his right side. Lieutenant Hazen had
killed an Indian previously.

Very truly yours,

WM. H. FRENCH,
*Brevet Major U. S. Army.*

CASTROVILLE, TEXAS, Nov. 14, 1859.

SIR, — I have the honor to report that I inspected Fort Inge on
the 12th instant. It is occupied by Captain Maclay's Company (F),
Eighth Infantry, a captain, second lieutenant, and fifty-three enlisted
men (with an assistant-surgeon, hospital steward, and ordnance-
sergeant ; twelve men are on extra duty, six sick, and one in con-
finement). The Second Lieutenant, Hazen, was severely wounded a
week ago, in the third successful pursuit of Indians, in which he had
exhibited activity, perseverance, and courage.

Most respectfully your obedient servant,

J. E. JOHNSTON,
*Lieutenant-Colonel First Cavalry.*

Assistant Adjutant-General, Headquarters of the Army.

HEADQUARTERS DEPARTMENT OF TEXAS,
SAN ANTONIO, Dec. 12, 1859.
*Special Orders, No.* 111.

Assistant-Surgeon R. L. Brodie, Medical Department, having
arrived in this city with Lieutenant William B. Hazen, Eighth
Infantry, suffering from severe wounds received in an Indian engagement, he is hereby placed on duty here, to date from the 7th instant,
for the purpose of giving his professional attendance to Lieutenant

Hazen, and will remain with that officer until his condition is such as to justify his being left alone.  By order of

Lieutenant-Colonel W. SEAWELL.

T. A. WASHINGTON,
*First Lieutenant First Infantry, Act'g-Assist. Adj.-General.*

Second Lieutenant William B. Hazen of the Eighth Regiment of Infantry, having applied for a certificate on which to ground an application for leave of absence, I do hereby certify that I have carefully examined this officer, and find that a ball has entered the left hand, fracturing the metacarpal bone of the ring finger, injuring severely the entire carpal bones, emerging at the carpo-metacarpal articulation of the thumb, and entering the right side of the chest between the sixth and seventh ribs.  The ball has never been extracted.

And that in consequence thereof he is, in my opinion, unfit for duty.  I further declare my belief that he will not be able to resume his duties in a less period than twelve months.

Dated at Fort Inge, Texas, this 23d day of January, 1860.

R. L. BRODIE,
*Assistant Surgeon U. S. Army.*

I narrowly escaped with my life from these wounds, and yet I feel extremely obliged to the Indian who shot me.  By virtue of my leave of absence I was at the North when my regiment, the Eighth Infantry, was captured in Texas by Van Dorn, at the breaking out of the Rebellion.  The parole given by the officers then with the regiment, — which has always seemed to me proper, — for some reason did not meet the approval of the Government.  They were denied commands, and were thus prevented from entering actively into the war till near its close.

I will venture to add the report of a public meeting held in 1859 by the citizens of San Antonio, Texas, whose action was very gratifying to a young lieutenant, and is still recalled with honest pride.

### Public Meeting.

The adjourned meeting of the citizens was held at the court-house on Thursday evening, which had been previously called to adopt measures expressive of the gratitude of the frontier citizens for the gallant and efficient services which had been rendered by Lieutenant W. B. Hazen in the defence of the lives of the citizens and the protection of their property upon the frontier. Colonel John A. Wilcox was chairman of the meeting, and C. Upson, Esq., secretary.

The chairman of the committee on resolutions submitted his report, which will be read with interest.

. . . . . . . . . .

*Whereas,* Lieutenant W. B. Hazen, of the United States Army, in his services for the protection and defence of our Western frontier from the ravages of hostile Indians; by his uniformly prompt, timely, and determined action in their pursuit; by his deeds of marked daring and bravery in their encounter, of which he bears the unmistakable evidence in a dangerous wound received in his last Indian engagement, which for a time threatened to prove fatal, and has disabled him for life; and by his repeated success in the recovery and restoration to our suffering frontier settlers of their stolen property, has deservedly won the confidence, high esteem, and admiration of the people of Texas, and especially of those upon our extreme frontier and of this community, and alike distinguished himself as a true and gallant officer, winning a high position in the army;

*Resolved,* That the thanks of this community and entire frontier are hereby tendered him.

*Resolved,* That as an evidence of our appreciation of his distinguished services, as a token of our sympathy for his sufferings and wounds, and as an acknowledgment of his noble gallantry, a sword be presented him.

*Resolved,* That Colonel John. A. Wilcox, Hon. Thomas H. Stribling, H. Wechsler, and C. Upson be appointed a committee to raise funds for the purchase of a sword to be presented to Lieutenant W. B. Hazen.

*Resolved,* That a copy of this preamble and resolutions be forwarded to Lieutenant Hazen, and also to the Secretary of War.

JNO. A. WILCOX, *President.*
C. UPSON, *Secretary.*

## FROM THE ARMY REGISTER OF 1884.

### HAZEN, WILLIAM B.

Cadet, Sept. 1, 1851.

Brevet Second Lieutenant Fourth Infantry, July 1, 1855.

Second Lieutenant Eighth Infantry, Sept. 4, 1855.

First Lieutenant Brevet, May 16, 1859, for gallant conduct in two several engagements with Indians in Texas.

First Lieutenant Eighth Infantry, April 1, 1861.

Captain, May 14, 1861.

Captain Seventeenth Infantry, May 14, 1861, — declined.

Colonel Forty-first Ohio Volunteers, Oct. 29, 1861.

Brigadier-General Volunteers, Nov. 29, 1862.

Major Brevet, Sept. 20, 1863, for gallant and meritorious service in the battle of Chickamauga, Georgia.

Lieutenant-Colonel Brevet, Nov. 24, 1863, for gallant and meritorious service in the battle of Chattanooga, Tennessee.

Colonel Brevet, Sept. 1, 1864, for gallant and meritorious service in the capture of Atlanta, Georgia.

Provisionally appointed Major-General Volunteers, Jan. 12, 1865.

Brigadier-General Brevet, March 13, 1865, for gallant and meritorious service in the capture of Fort McAllister, Georgia.

Major-General Brevet, March 13, 1865, for gallant and meritorious service in the field during the war.

Commissioned Major-General Volunteers, April 20, 1865, to rank from Dec. 13, 1864 ; for long and continued service of the highest character, and for special gallantry and service at Fort McAllister.

Mustered out of Volunteer service, Jan. 15, 1866.

Colonel Thirty-eighth Infantry, July 28, 1866.

Transferred to Sixth Infantry as Colonel, March 15, 1869.

Brigadier-General, and Chief Signal Officer, U. S. A., Dec. 15, 1880.

General Hazen was also Military Attaché at Vienna during the war between Russia and Turkey in 1876–1877.

# INDEX.

[1] This officer was severely wounded, captured, taken to Libby, and was chiefly instru-
mental in effecting the remarkable escape of a large number of prisoners by tunnelling
under the walls.